Seeds of Liberation

SEEDS OF LIBERATION

edited by Paul Goodman

George Braziller, New York

"Let us suppose that certain individuals
resolve that they will consistently oppose
to power the force of example; to authority,
exhortation; to insult, friendly reasoning;
to trickery, simple honor. They would be
preparing the future. Who can fail to see the
positively dazzling realism of such behavior?"

ALBERT CAMUS

Preface

1

We need information about the world that is practical, but what we get is the "news" of what has happened. The *Times,* A.P., Reuters, or Tass guess what is important and the broadcasters and magazines follow their lead, but history goes its way regardless. Reporters are *then* hurriedly sent to the spot and the public learns the news. It turns to each blow after it has struck.

Reviewing *Liberation* as it turns into its tenth year, we see that this has not been its pattern. The topics it has treated are still with us and indeed are more in the "news" than when the articles were written and published. Let me give some examples. It did not generally seem in 1956, when the magazine started, that the para-political and sometimes para-legal demonstrations of small groups could be of any historical importance. Especially nonviolence—sitting in front of trucks and filling jails—was strictly for the Hindoos. By 1956 there was a conspicuous rise of delinquency and anomie, but it was not yet fashionable to point out that the economy had a built-in structural defect; few noticed the hard-core poverty. And in the galloping growth of the Gross National Product and the drive to an affluent standard of living, it was simply "utopian" to raise questions about the moral and psychological worth of jobs and middle-class schooling, or about the human use of technology. It was not "realistic" to oppose bomb-testing and fall-out shelters, nor to be alarmed that other powers beside NATO and the USSR would soon brandish atomic weapons. The news of the day did not yet take seriously the fact that the social revolution in the technologically underdeveloped regions of Latin America, Africa, and Asia would not so easily be contained in the policies of either the West or the USSR, but must become a new factor in the world. Finally, in 1956 we were at the beginning of the flood-tide of brilliant "social criticism" that has challenged every part of the American mores, from the I.Q.'s and the advertising to the urbanism and the pesticides; yet for years almost all the criticism was negative; the few critics who doggedly proposed positive alternatives tended sooner or later to write for *Liberation*.

Thus, one could say that the "news" has been catching up to *Liberation*. And the implication might be that the editors of *Liberation* have some acute scientific theory that gives better predictions than the assumptions of the A.P., Reuters, or Tass. But the editors have not told us this theory and, having sat at many of their meetings, I don't think there is any. If anything, they probably allow themselves to be more confused than the average, and they certainly have clashing opinions—though each one respects that the others must mean something or other.

In my opinion, the explanation of their editorial success is simpler. They are concerned. They deal with what they consider to be humanly important, and the factual test of importance is that they themselves get personally engaged in the events. In the long run—if one can stay alive—this must get one into closer touch with the underlying. Thus, Reuters might cover a bomb-test in the Sahara as news (A.P. might not bother at all, it is so far away), but an editor of *Liberation* was with Africans trying to stop the test. And there is another aspect to such engaged editing: it is impossible to overlook injustice, ugliness, or stupidity that is gross and glaring, even though it is not "newsworthy" because it has persisted so long, people take it for granted, and it seems that nothing can or will be done about it. But if one is concerned, the more ingrained the offense the harder must one persist, for nothing is relevant except to get rid of it. This is very different from the *exposés* in the *N.Y. Post* or one-shot conversation-pieces in the *New Yorker*.

2

Perhaps *Liberation* does have a theory. It is the hopelessly indefinite one that human events are caused by and happen to human beings. As Kant pointed out, "What is Man?" is one of the unanswerable questions.

Such a theory has an oddly optimistic side. It means that vague aspiration, sudden indignation, animal perseverance, improbable fortitude, spontaneous invention, and even common sense are sometimes likely to become political factors, although both *realpolitik* and scientific sociology regard them as trivial. On this theory, it does not seem absurd to hope for social justice and love. Not that thoughts or sentiments have much effect, but that, beyond a certain point, reason flouted and feeling insulted do assert themselves, something in human nature is abiding; and since human beings are responsible for what they do and suffer, they might accept the responsibility.

But the theory also has a very dark side. For it means that it is impossible to blink away brutal human facts, no matter what fine explanations are given by statesmen, game theorists, and mathematical economists. For example, if a vast and increasing proportion of the wealth of nations is devoted to nuclear weapons, it is *not* possible to assume that we are not all going to be annihilated, and it is not possible to accept quietly the present world structure of Great Powers, even though it appears impossible to alter it. Somebody is responsible. If the hard core of poverty in fact rigidifies and increases in our present economic structure, it is not possible to be cheered by the Gross National Product, new technical marvels, or *communiqués* from the War on Poverty. And if the political and social style everywhere in the world is increasingly centralized, regimenting, and brainwashing, it is not possible to blink that we are heading toward 1984, even though this is nobody's "intention."

Because of its principle of engagement, *Liberation* is one of the few political groups—in the world—that takes for granted that social-psychology exists and is about something, that social-psychological causes have political effects, just as, as the Marxists hold, the political and economic structure has social-psychological effects. Let me again give an example. In the little *Tract for the Times* that introduced the first issue in 1956, there is a curious listing of the problems that Liberals have neglected: "War, poverty, boredom, authoritarianism, and other evils of modern times." Of these, war and poverty are classical themes of radical politics, but it is highly character- istic that boredom and authoritarianism are mentioned with the same status. Boredom, in 1956, partly referred to the era of Eisenhower—it was a cliché of the Liberal columnists—but to *Liberation* it also meant urban anomie, front politics and public relations, mass-communications, the suburban standard of living. It was unusual at that time to consider these things as political rather than esthetic, but we are learning otherwise. Again, authoritarianism referred somewhat to dictatorships— though Hitler, Mussolini, and Stalin were off the scene—but even more, I think, the editors meant top-down direction in every sphere, whether parties, corporations, labor-unions, fam- ilies, or schools; they meant the reduction of democracy to democracy-by-consent, and the "authoritarian personality" of the sociologists, with its compulsions, prejudices, and need for petty triumphs. These things are still not considered of political importance. We shall see.

To put it in a word, *Liberation* is edited authentically. Its news is not what is official, what is sensational, what will sell, what people are talking about, or what suits a party program, but what the editors know is relevant because they themselves cannot keep out of it, and what they need to find out and re- port in order to win allies.

Let me say at once, however, that this principle itself is problematic. You can certainly become so involved in events that you can't see straight. Consider, by contrast, an amazing situation that we have gotten used to: the police-dog is at- tacking the child and the TV-cameraman is grinding away. This is dismaying, yet in my judgment the professional journal- ist is not *necessarily* in the wrong. The crucial question is an existential one: Is he giving us the "news" or the truth? And a related question, How in fact is the TV-viewer taking it, the moment before the scene changes to the ad for tires that are like tiger's paws? (The bother with "objective" journalism is that the audience too is pretty "objective.")

This problem faces *Liberation* in a very concrete form. The magazine has the defect of its virtue. The editors are intelligent, energetic, craftsmanlike; they are learned and have considerable literary ability. But it is quite impossible to be at strategy meetings in India and Sweden, to be sitting in assorted jails, to be visiting Cuba by a circuitous route, to be on the executive board of umpteen committees, to be organizing a mass march, and to picket the Atomic Energy Commission, and still do the desk-work and correspondence necessary to turn out a consistently excellent magazine. It does not help, either, that the magazine is (inevitably) always in the red. I don't know any solution for this dilemma.

3

Yet all this is mighty big talk for a very small and not especially brilliant magazine, granting that it is influential beyond its circulation, and occasionally first rate. A more accurate description of *Liberation* is that it is the annals of people who, like the editors, put their bodies on the line for justice as they see it and try to live in community in a society that has given up on community. *Liberation* is the house-organ, so to speak, where these people can get firsthand accounts of the Times Square demonstration where the police rode into the crowd, the sailing of a small boat into the nuclear test zone, a walk to Moscow to hand out leaflets, the fortitude of the children of Birmingham, conditions in a Georgia jail, the founding of a small industry among destitute sharecroppers, and education in a Summerhill school. Recently, the magazine is being read—especially in colleges—by people who have become interested in these people and their activities.

Needless to say, these active people do not number in the millions or hundreds of thousands, nor does the readership of *Liberation*. Does this tiny fringe have much significance for the general future of the country and the world? I hope so—for usually these few people make sense; and alas! in crucial moments they sometimes make all the sense there is.

Looked at with a quick frank glance, *Liberation* is a very paradoxical magazine. On the one hand there are the remarkable surveys of world power (to my mind A. J. Muste is the keenest political analyst in America), the epochal manifesto of the Triple Revolution, the best reporting of Cuba that has appeared anywhere, the beautiful study of sexual morals by the English Friends, the thorough science of Gorden Christiansen on fall-out; such things are the contents of a general national magazine of the first order. But on the other hand, there are sentimental accounts of the joy of solidarity, confessional breast-beating, small details of interpersonal conflict and reconciliation—the kind of thing that fills a parish newsletter. (One almost expects a social-notes column telling us where is Jim Peck this month, and where is Judith Malina, and has M.I. made up with B.L. since their quarrel on the Walk?) The idea of *Liberation* is, evidently, that there is no discrepancy between these tones, or at least that they are all of a piece.

As would be expected, the poetry in *Liberation* is the most accurate expression of how it is these days with intensely political and nonviolent humanists. The editors make no pretension to be "literary," they choose the verse entirely by feeling —what strikes them as interesting and meant. Thus, the poetry is a kind of projection of what they themselves mean when freed from the stoical or polemical necessities of political prose.

Unlike other "radical" poetry, the poems are almost entirely devoid of slogans, either affirmative or hostile. There is no party platform.

The content veers to two extremes that come to the same thing. Either there is a desperate affirmation of simple nature, including sexual love and childhood; or there is a total rejection of what man has done, in a tone sardonic or apocalyptic or violent. Sometimes there is a kind of deism, sometimes blasphemy.

But deeper than content is an acute self-awareness of a noteworthy kind, that seems to say, "I *accept* my responsibility, nevertheless I *can't*." The tone of the self-awareness is noteworthy because it is not brooding, introspective, or self-pitying; yet, on the other hand, it is rarely self-condemning or sinful. Thus it is quite different from the usual self-consciousness in modern poetry, which is self-absorbed, self-ironical, self-judging, self-consoling, or embarrassed; but these people are *neither* in the right *nor* guilty.

To be in the right, to be moral, means to be adequate to the situation, to come across; good intentions are not enough;

but the situation is too tough and therefore they are not in the right. Yet they are not guilty because they are not alienated, they do not make provisos or bargains, they do what they can. They are engaged—in an impasse. Creator spirit, come.

Paul Goodman

Contents

III: The Challenge to Community:
Colonialism and Civil Rights

IV: The Center Is Man

V: The New Beginning

I
A Modest Utopia

"If the human race is to survive it will have to change more in its ways of thinking in the next twenty-five years than it has done in the last twenty-five thousand."

KENNETH E. BOULDING
"Post-Civilization"

Editors of Liberation

Tract for the Times*

The decline of independent radicalism and the gradual falling into silence of prophetic and rebellious voices is an ominous feature of the mid-twentieth century. Anxiety and apprehension have invaded the air we breathe. Advances in science and technology, which should have been our greatest triumphs, leave us stunned and uncertain as to whether human life and history have meaning.

Power is everywhere openly or secretly idolized. The threat of atomic or biological war, perhaps even the extinction of mankind, hangs over the earth. Hopes and ideals have become propaganda devices. But those who should furnish vision and direction are silent or echoing old ideas in which they scarcely believe themselves.

This failure of a new radicalism to emerge is an indication, it seems to us, that the stock of fundamental ideas on which the radical thinking of recent times has been predicated is badly in need of thorough reappraisal. Much of its inspiration appears to be used up. Old labels—principally in the Marxist and liberal traditions—simply do not apply any more, and the phrases which fifty years ago were guideposts to significant action have largely become empty patter and jargon.

The changes of recent years—represented by atomic power and by the beginnings of the Second Industrial Revolution and also by the rise of totalitarianism—have filled many thoughtful persons with the strong suspicion that the problems of today must be attacked on a much deeper level than traditional Marxists, Communists and various kinds of Socialists and Anarchists have realized. Proposals and calls to action couched in the old terms fail any longer to inspire much hope

* March, 1956.

or genuine humane enthusiasm, because large numbers of people are aware, or dimly sense, that they do not touch the roots of the trouble.

There is no point, for example, in reshuffling power, because the same old abuses still persist under new masters. The vast energy devoted to reconstructing government is wasted if in a short time the new structure becomes as impervious to fundamental human decency and ethics as the old one. There is no doubt that there are forms of property relationships which are oppressive and destructive of true community, but if these are altered and the average individual finds his life as dull and empty as ever and the enslavement of his hours just as great, little or nothing has been achieved.

It is increasingly evident that nineteenth century modes of thought are largely incapable of dealing with such questions. The changes which are going on in the modern world—which call into doubt many assumptions which almost all nineteenth century revolutionists and reformers took for granted—require also changes in our deepest modes of thought. We require a post-Soviet, post-H-bomb expression of the needs of today and a fresh vision of the world of peace, freedom and brotherhood in which they can be met.

Our Root Traditions

In reexamining our thought—and especially the two great dominant traditions of liberalism and Marxism—we return in part again to root traditions from which we derive our values and standards. There are four of these:

1. There is an ancient Judeo-Christian prophetic tradition which gave men a vision of human dignity and a reign of righteousness, equality and brotherhood on earth. It taught them that building such an order of life was their task, and that a society of justice and fraternity could be built by justice and love and not by any other means.

2. There is an American tradition—far from having been realized, often distorted and all but lost—of a "nation conceived in liberty, and dedicated to the proposition that all men are created equal." It is a tradition

which also emphasizes the dignity of man and asserts that government rests upon consent, and institutions are made for man, not man for institutions. Such names as Jefferson, Paine, Thoreau, Emerson, Debs, Randolph Bourne, the Quaker experiment in Pennsylvania, the Utopian community experiments, the Abolition movement, the Underground Railway, are associated with this tradition.

3. There is the heritage of the libertarian, democratic, anti-war, socialist, anarchist and labor movements in Europe and the United States in the latter half of the nineteenth century and the early years of the twentieth. Multitudes of common people, the impoverished and distressed, believed that through these movements, with the help of modern science and technology, a "class-less and war-less world" had become possible and would in a comparatively short time be achieved.

4. There is a tradition of pacifism or nonviolence which has been exemplified throughout the centuries and in many parts of the world in great teachers and saints—or in such a figure as the Emperor Asoka—who have rejected war as accursed and unworthy of men and have insisted that injustice and violence cannot be overcome by injustice and violence but only by righteousness and peace. In particular, Gandhi stands in this tradition, not as an example to be slavishly imitated, but as a pioneer who in a series of great political and social experiments joined nonviolence and revolutionary collective action.

Critique of Liberalism

In the light of these root traditions we can see that the greatness of liberalism has been its emphasis on humaneness and tolerance, its support of the liberties of the individual and its insistence on the free and inquiring mind and rejection of fanaticism and dogmatism. Its weakness has been its failure to come to grips with war, poverty, boredom, authoritarianism and other great evils of the modern world. These problems it has tended optimistically to leave to "education" and "good will," both of which have so far proved incapable of dealing with them successfully. Liberalism has tried to diagnose our troubles without going to fundamentals—the inequalities and injustices upon which our present social order is based and which no "good will" can wish away.

This failure to raise the embarrassing questions has made liberalism often shallow, hypocritical and dilettantish, all too often lacking in fundamental earnestness. Essentially the liberal accepts the existing order and wants to exploit it and share in it as much as the next man. At the same time he is troubled and wants the good conscience of repudiating its wrongs. Liberalism thus becomes a fashionable pose—for millionaires and generals as well as for intellectuals and editorial writers. It becomes a public ritual lacking roots in private life and behavior, and makes the liberal an easy prey of opportunism and expedience.

As against this liberal attitude a new quality of seriousness and personal honesty is necessary. In this respect what is wanted is not political liberalism but political fundamentalism. We are more interested in concrete situations than in rhetorical blueprints, in individual lives than in "global historical forces" which remain merely abstract. What matters to us is what happens to the individual human being—here and now. We will be just as flexible as the liberal, but we will strive to be more searching, and we will insist on spelling things out in terms of daily consequences, hour to hour, for everyone.

Critique of Marxism

Marxism, like liberalism, has much to teach both positively and negatively. Its fundamental demand for economic justice and its attack on the problem of poverty are permanently valuable. It touches the source of much that is wrong with the world in exposing the property nerve. But many of its attitudes are those of the outmoded bourgeois epoch which it tried to repudiate. Marx was to a much greater degree than he himself realized a spokesman for nineteenth century thought patterns, now hopelessly out of date. His historical determinism, built up by analogy from now out-moded science, is an example. So also is the tendency to sacrifice the present for the future, so that human beings of today are regarded as pawns for bringing about something better in a tomorrow that never comes.

The most serious weaknesses of Marxism, however, are its omissions and its reactionary "realism" in respect to the instruments of revolution. Marx, for all his brilliant analysis of economic power, failed to analyze with equal profundity the questions of military and political power. Hence he underestimated the seriousness of the growth of the State and its emergence as an instrument of war and oppression. In trying to liberate mankind from economic slavery, he failed to see the looming horror of political slavery.

Closely related to this failure is Marx's inability to realize that social betterment cannot be brought about by the same old methods of force and chicanery characterizing the regimes which had to be overthrown precisely because they embodied such evils. It is an illuminating insight of pragmatism that means and ends condition each other reciprocally and that the ends must be built into the means. It is not sound, therefore, to expect to achieve peace through war, justice through violence, freedom through dictatorship, or civil liberties through slave labor camps. Such instruments create the social attitudes and habit patterns which they are ostensibly designed to remove. Dictatorship in any form, as well as spy systems, concentration camps, military conscription, restrictions on travel and censorship of books, papers and political parties must all be decisively rejected. What this means is that a truly radical movement today—if it does not want to fall into the trap which the Russian Communist movement has fallen into—must take these ethical problems much more seriously than many nineteenth century thinkers did, and must commit itself to an essentially democratic and nonviolent strategy.

The Politics of the Future

One of the symptoms of our time is that many people are fed up with "politics"—by which they mean the whole machinery associated with political life. To become significant, politics must discover its ethical foundations and dynamic.

The politics of the future requires a creative synthesis of the individual ethical insights of the great religious leaders and the collective social concern of the great revolutionists.

It follows that we do not conceive the problem of revolution or the building of a better society as one of accumulating power, whether by legislative or other methods, to "capture the State," and then, presumably, to transform society and human beings as well. The national, sovereign, militarized and bureaucratic State and a bureaucratic collectivist economy are themselves evils to be avoided or abolished. Seizure of the war-making and repressive machinery of the State cannot be a step toward transforming society into a free and humanly satisfying pattern. It is the transformation of society by human decision and action that we seek. This is a more complex and human process in which power as ordinarily conceived plays a minor part. Political action in this context is, therefore, broadly conceived. It includes such developments as the Land Gift Movement in India and community and cooperative experiments in many lands. New political alignments in the narrower sense of the term may emerge from basic ethical and social changes, but preoccupation with or dependence upon the machinery of politics, or the violent seizure of power, are evils always to be avoided, and never more so than in the present crisis.

Similarly, we reject the faith in technology, industrialization and centralization *per se,* characteristic of both the contemporary capitalist and Communist regimes. Our emphasis is rather on possibilities for decentralization, on direct participation of all workers or citizens in determining the conditions of life and work, and on the use of technology for human ends, rather than the subjection of man to the demands of technology.

From the synthesis of the ethical and the political emerges a new attitude toward utopianism in social and cultural thinking. Under the impact of Marxism, utopianism became virtually a term of abuse. But this attitude itself was narrow and misjudged the scientific method, not seeing that the essence of science is its openness to new and creative insights and its willingness to test them experimentally. The utopian attitude is one that is permanently needed in human affairs. It represents the growing edge of society and the creative imagination of a culture.

As we recognize more and more the imaginative and speculative element in mathematics and science and as the mechanical determinism of the last century passes away, the outmoded "scientific" aspect of nineteenth century Marxism will begin to disappear, and Marx will then appear in his true light as one of the great visionaries and utopian thinkers of that century. With new conditions, modifications of his utopian thinking are necessary and new utopias will appear, to furnish direction and incentives for action.

The world *can* move toward the abolition of war and toward a society built on responsible freedom, mutuality and peace. Collective effort and struggle to achieve such a society should not be abandoned because the movements of an earlier day have been frustrated or wrecked.

The very presuppositions on which human relationships are based must be revolutionized. This makes it peculiarly difficult to live responsibly as individuals today and to carry on collective efforts for basic changes. In addition, the creation of a movement of dissent and social change in the United States is impeded by a sustained, war-based prosperity, with millions of unionists making a living at war jobs. This makes the task virtually as difficult in the United States as in Russia or other Communist-bloc countries.

The problem of war is one of special gravity for us, as for all our fellow men. It may be argued that for personal ethics there is no distinction between a war in which a few persons are killed at a time and one in which multitudes are wiped out. But from a sociological view, the H-bomb and what it symbolizes—possible extinction of the race itself—present mankind with a new situation. War is no longer an instrument of policy or a means to any rational end. For this reason, if for no other, a central part of any radical movement today is withdrawal of support from the military preparation and activities of *both* the dominant power blocs. Whatever differences may exist between Communist and "free world" regimes, in this decisive respect they are *equal* threats, two sides of the *same* threat to the survival of civilization. The H-bomb is not an instrument of peace in the hands of one and of war in the hands of the other. Nor is it a mere accidental excrescence in either of them but, rather, a logical outgrowth of their basic economic and social orders.

War and war preparation in the hands of any other power or group of powers is not a source of deliverance either. A Third Force based on military power would be reactionary and evil just as the present power blocs are. Any "Third Camp" or "Third Way" grouping of peoples must, therefore, be founded on an essentially nonmilitary, nonviolent base.

There are in Western Europe, Asia, Africa, and Latin America, peoples who live "in between" the two atomically armed power blocs. Of necessity, their prime objective is to keep from being drawn into either bloc and engulfed in the wars for which these Leviathans are arming. Nor can these peoples "in between" escape the peril by seeking to constitute a third atomically armed power bloc. Even if they were permitted by the dominant powers to achieve such military and economic independence as to constitute a decisive "balance," this would only serve to plunge the world into permanent war among *three* totalitarian tyrannies, on George Orwell's model in *1984.*

There are in non-committed areas groups seeking to deal with the problems of economics and politics in a broader way and at a deeper ethical level. They seek to build not another Military Force but a Third Camp or Third Way. They are striving not only to avoid war but to build a socio-economic order and culture different from both Communism and capitalism. Such groups as the Asian Socialist parties, the Gandhian Constructive Workers, and the Bhoodan movement of Vinoba Bhave in India illustrate this trend, as do the nonviolent responses to Colonialism in Africa. The June, 1953, workers' revolts in East Germany were part of a spontaneous movement in this direction.

An important function of *Liberation* will be to provide information about such developments and to draw political and moral implications from them for the United States. It may, in addition, render these movements a genuine service by helping them to clarify their own thinking, on such basic questions as nonviolence in relation both to national policy and to social changes within the nation.

Finally this does not in any degree imply preoccupation with affairs abroad to the neglect of developments in the

United States. Nor does it mean concern with large-scale societal or governmental revolution to the neglect of the "one-man revolution" and of experiments in creative living by individuals, families, and small groups. Such activities are especially important because germinal. What happens in any significant sense in society as a whole is directly related, and to a great degree grows out of, what has already happened in the lives of individuals and small groups.

Liberation will seek to inspire its readers not only to fresh thinking but to *action now*—refusal to run away or to conform, concrete resistance in the communities in which we live to all the ways in which human beings are regimented and corrupted, dehumanized and deprived of their freedom; experimentation in creative living by individuals, families, and groups; day to day support of movements to abolish colonialism and racism or for the freedom of all individuals from domination, whether military, economic, political, or cultural.

Kenneth E. Boulding

Post-Civilization

We are living in what I call the second great change in the state of man. The first is the change from pre-civilized to civilized societies. The first five hundred thousand years or so of man's existence on earth were relatively uneventful. Compared with his present condition, he puttered along in an astonishingly stationary state. There may have been changes in language and culture which are not reflected in the artifacts, but if there were, these changes are lost to us. The evidence of the artifacts, however, is conclusive. Whatever changes they were, they were almost unbelievably slow. About ten thousand years ago, we begin to perceive an acceleration in the rate of change. This becomes very noticeable five thousand years ago with the development of the first civilization. The details of this first great change are probably beyond our recovery. However, we do know that it depended on two phenomena: the development of agriculture and the development of exploitation. Agriculture, that is the domestication of crops and livestock and the planting of crops in fields, gave man a secure surplus of food from the food producer. In a hunting and fishing economy it seems to take the food producer all his time to produce enough food for himself and his family. The moment we have agriculture, with its superior productivity of this form of employment of human resources, the food producer can produce more food than he and his family can eat. In some societies in these happy conditions, the food producer has simply relaxed and indulged himself with leisure. As soon, however, as we get politics, that is exploitation, we begin to get cities and civilization. Civilization, it is clear from the origin of the word, is what happens in cities, and the city is dependent (in its early stages, at any rate) on the existence of a food surplus from the food producer and some organization which can take it away from him. With this food surplus, the political organization feeds kings, priests, armies, architects, and builders, and the city comes into being. Political science in its earliest form is the knowledge of how to take the food surplus away from the food producer without giving him very much in return.

Now I argue that we are in the middle of the second great change in the state of man, which is as drastic and as dramatic, and certainly as large as, if not larger than, the change from pre-civilized to civilized society. This I call the change from civilization to post-civilization. It is a strange irony that just at the moment when civilization has almost completed the conquest of pre-civilized societies, post-civilization has been treading heavily upon its heels. The student of civilization may soon find himself in the unfortunate position of the anthropologist who studies pre-civilized societies. Both are like the student of ice on a hot day—the subject matter melts away almost before he can study it.

These great changes can be thought of as a change of gear in the evolutionary process, resulting in progressive acceleration of the rate of evolutionary change. Even before the appearance of man on the earth, we can detect earlier evolutionary gear-shiftings. The formation of life obviously represented one such transition, the movement from the water to the land another, the development of the vertebrates another, and so on. Man himself represents a very large acceleration of the evolutionary process. Whether he evolved from pre-existing forms or landed from a space ship and was not able to get back to where he came from, is immaterial. Once he had arrived on earth, the process of evolution could go on within the confines of the human nervous system at a greatly accelerated rate. The human mind is an enormous mutation-selection process. Instead of the mutation-selection process being confined, as it were, to the flesh, it can take place within the image, and hence, very rapid changes are possible. Man seems to have been pretty slow to exploit this potentiality, but one suspects that even with primitive man, the rate of change in the biosphere was much larger than it had been before, because of the appearance of what Teilhard de Chardin calls the noosphere, or sphere of knowledge.

Civilization represents a further acceleration of the rate of change, mainly because one of the main products of civilization is history. With the food surplus from agriculture it became possible to feed specialized scribes. With the development of writing, man did not have to depend on the uncertain memories of the aged for his records, and a great process of accumulation of social knowledge began. The past could now communicate, at least in one direction, with the present, and this enormously increased the range and possibility of enlargements of the contents of the human mind.

Out of civilization, however, comes science, which is a superior way of organizing the evolution of knowledge. We trace the first beginnings of science, of course, almost as far back as the beginning of civilization itself. Beginning about 1650, however, we begin to see the organization of science into a community of knowledge, and this leads again to an enormous acceleration of the rate of change. The world of 1650 is more remote to us than the world of ancient Egypt or Samaria would have been to the man of 1650. Already in the United States and Western Europe, in a smaller degree in Russia and in some other parts of the world, we see the beginnings of post-civilized society—a state of man as different from civilization as civilization is from savagery. What we really mean, therefore, by the anemic term "economic development" is the second great transition in the state of man. It is the movement from civilized to post-civilized society. It is nothing short of a major revolution in the human condition, and it does not represent a mere continuance and development of the old patterns of civilization.

As a dramatic illustration of the magnitude of the change, we can contemplate Indonesia. This is a country which has about the same extent, population and per capita income as the Roman Empire at its height. For all I know it is producing a literature and an art at least comparable to that of the Augustan age. It is, therefore, a very good example of a country of high civilization. Because of this fact, it is one of the poorest countries in the world. It is desperately anxious to break out of its present condition. Jakarta is a city about the size of ancient Rome, though perhaps a little less splendid. All this points up the fact that the Roman Empire was a desperately poor and under-developed society. The Roman cities seem to have been always about three weeks away from starvation, and even at its height it is doubtful whether the Roman Empire ever had less than seventy-five to eighty per cent of its population in agriculture.

Civilization, that is, is a state of society in which techniques are so poor that it takes about eighty per cent of the population to feed the hundred per cent. But we do have about twenty per cent of the people who can be spared from food-producing to build Parthenons and cathedrals, to write literature and poetry, and fight wars. By contrast, in the United States today we are rapidly getting to the point where we can produce all our food with only ten per cent of the population and still have large agricultural surpluses. But for the blessings of agricultural policy, we might soon be able to produce all our food with five per cent of the population. It may even be that agriculture is on its way out altogether and that within another generation or so we will produce our food in a totally different way. Perhaps both fields and cows are merely relics of civilization, the vestiges of a vanishing age. This means, however, that even in our society, which is at a very early stage of post-civilization, we can now spare about ninety per cent of the people to produce bathtubs, automobiles, H-bombs and all the other conveniences of life. Western Europe and Japan are coming along behind the United States very fast. The Russians, likewise, are advancing toward post-civilization, although by a very different road. At the moment their ideology is a handicap to them in some places—especially in agriculture, which still occupies forty-five per cent of the people. And, if the Russians ever discover that super-peasants are a good deal more efficient than collective farms, they may cut away some of the ideology that hangs around their neck and move even more rapidly toward post-civilized society.

I'm not at all sure what post-civilization will look like but it will certainly be a world-wide society. Until very recently, each civilized society was a little island in a sea of barbarism which constantly threatened to overwhelm it. Civilization is haunted by the spectre of decline and fall, though it is noteworthy that in spite of the rise and fall of particular civilizations, civilization itself expanded steadily in geographical coverage, from its very beginnings. We must face the fact, however, that post-civilized society will be world-wide, if only because of its ease of communication and transportation. I flew last year from Idlewild to Brussels, and on glimpsing the new Brussels Airport out of the corner of my eye, I thought for a moment that we had come back and landed at Idlewild again.

The characteristic institutions of civilization are, as we have seen, first agriculture, then the city, then war, in the sense of clash of organized armed forces, and finally, inequality, the sharp contrast between the rich and the poor, between the city and the country, between the urbane and the rustic. The state is based very fundamentally on violence and exploitation, and the culture tends to be spiritually monolithic.

In post-civilization all these institutions suffer radical change. Agriculture, as we have seen, diminishes until it is a small proportion of the society; the city, likewise, in the classical sense, disintegrates. Los Angeles is perhaps the first example of the post-civilization, post-urban agglomeration—under no stretch of the imagination could it be called a city. War, likewise, is an institution in process of disintegration. National defense as a social system has quite fundamentally broken down on a world scale. The ICBM and the nuclear warhead have made the nation-state as militarily obsolete as the city-state, for in no country now can the armed forces preserve an area of internal peace by pushing violence to the outskirts. Poverty and inequality, likewise, are tending to disappear, at least on their traditional scale. In civilized societies the king or the emperor could live in a Versailles and the peasant in a hovel. In post-civilized society, it is almost impossible for the rich to consume on a scale which is more, let us say, than ten times that of the poor. There is no sense in having more than ten automobiles!

Another profound change in the passage from civilization to post-civilization is the change in the expectation of life. In civilized society, birth and death rates tend to be about forty per thousand and the expectation of life at birth is twenty-five years. In post-civilized society, the expectation of life at birth rises at least to seventy and perhaps beyond. It may be that we are on the edge of a biological revolution, just as dramatic and far-reaching as the discovery of atomic energy and that we may crack the problem of aging and prolong human life much beyond its present span. Whether or not, however, we go forward to Methuselah, the mere increase of the average age of death to seventy is a startling and far-reaching change. It means, for instance, that in an equilibrium population, the birth and death rate cannot be more than about fourteen per thousand. This unquestionably implies some form of conscious control of births. It means also a much larger proportion of the population in later years.

It is perfectly possible to paint an anti-utopia in which a post-civilized society appears as universally vulgar or dull. On the whole, however, I welcome post-civilization and I have really very little affection for civilization. In most pre-civilized societies the fact that the life of man is for the most part nasty, brutish and short, does not prevent the poets and philosophers from sentimentalizing the noble savage. Similarly, we may expect the same kind of sentimentalizing of the noble Romans and civilized survivals like Winston Churchill. On the whole, though, I will not shed any tears over the grave of civilization any more than I will over pre-civilized society. The credit balance of post-civilization is large. It at least gives us a chance of a modest utopia, in which slavery, poverty, exploitation, gross inequality, war and disease—these prime costs of civilization —will fall to the vanishing point.

What we have at the moment is a chance to make a transition to this modest utopia—a chance which is probably unique in the history of this planet. If we fail, the chance will probably not be repeated in this part of the universe. Whatever experiments may be going on elsewhere, the present moment indeed is unique in the whole four billion years of the history of the planet. In my more pessimistic moments, I think the chance is a slim one, and it may be that man will be written off as an unsuccessful experiment. We must look at the traps which lie along the path of the transition, which might prevent us from making it altogether.

The most urgent trap is, of course, the trap of war. War, as I have suggested, is an institution peculiarly characteristic of civilization. Pre-civilized societies have sporadic feuding and raiding, but they do not generally have permanent organized armed forces, and they do not generally develop conquest and empire; or if they do, they soon pass into a civilized form. An armed force is essentially a mobile city designed to throw things at another mobile or stationary city with presumably evil intent. As far as I know, not more than two or three civilizations have existed without war. The Mayans and the people of Mohenjodaro seem to have lived for fairly long periods without war, but this was an accident of their monopolistic situation and they unquestionably occupied themselves with other kinds of foolishness. If pre-civilized society, however, cannot afford war, post-civilized society can afford far too much of it, and hence will be forced to get rid of the institution because it is simply inappropriate to the technological age. The breakdown in the world social system of national defense really dates from about 1949, when the United States lost its monopoly of nuclear weapons. A system of national defense is only feasible if each nation is stronger at home than its enemies, so that it can preserve a relatively large area of peace within its critical boundaries. Such a system is only possible, however, if the range of the deadly missile is short and if the armed forces of each nation lose power rapidly as they move away from home. The technological developments of the twentieth century have destroyed these foundations of national defense, and have replaced it with another social system altogether, which is "deterrence."

"Deterrence" is a social system with properties very different from that of national defense, which it replaced. Under national defense, for instance, it is possible to use the armed forces; under "deterrence" it is not—that is, if the deterring forces are ever used, the system will have broken down. We live in a society with a positive possibility of irretrievable disaster—a probability which grows every year. Herman Kahn recently said: "All we are doing is buying time, and we are doing nothing with the time that we buy." The armed forces of the world are caught in a technological process which not only destroys their own function, but threatens all of us. Even if a few of us do crawl out of the fallout shelters, it is by no means clear that we can put the world back together again. Even if the human race could survive one nuclear war, it is very doubtful that it could survive a second; and as the purpose of the first nuclear war would be to set up a political system which would produce the second, unless there is a radical change in attitude towards national defense, the prospects of the human race seem to be dim. Fortunately, "there is still time, brother" and evolution can still go on in the minds of men. The critical question is whether it can go on rapidly enough. The abolition of national defense, which is what we must face, is going to be a painful process, as we have come to rely on it to preserve many of the values which we hold dear. If the task can be perceived, however, by a sufficient number of people, there is at least a chance that we may avoid this trap before it is too late.

Even if we avoid the war trap, we may still fall into the population trap. Population control is an unsolved problem even for the developed areas of the world, which have moved the furthest toward post-civilization. An equilibrium of population in a stable post-civilized society may represent a fairly radical interference with ancient human institutions and freedoms. In a stable post-civilized society, as I have suggested, the birth and death rates must be of the order of fourteen per thousand, and the average number of children per family cannot much exceed two. There are many social institutions which might accomplish this end. So far, however, the only really sure-fire method of controlling population is starvation and misery.

In many parts of the world—indeed, for most of the human race for the moment—the impact on certain post-civilized techniques of civilized society has produced a crisis of growth, which may easily be fatal. In the tropics especially, with DDT and a few simple public-health measures, it is easy to reduce the death rate to nine or ten per thousand while the birth rate stays at forty per thousand. This means an annual increase of population of three per cent *per annum*, almost all of it concentrated in the lower age groups. We see dramatic examples of this phenomenon in places like the West Indies, Ceylon, and Formosa; but thanks to the activity of the World Health Organization, it is taking place rapidly all over the tropical world. Perhaps the most important key to the transition to post-civilization is heavy investment in human resources —that is, in education. The conquest of disease and infant mortality, however, before the corresponding adjustment to the birth rate, produces enormous numbers of children in societies which do not have the resources to educate them—especially as those in the middle-age groups, who after all must do all the work of a society, come from the much smaller population of the pre-DDT era.

Even in the developed countries, population control presents a very serious problem. The United States, for instance, at the moment is increasing in population even more rapidly than India. The time when we thought that the mere increase in income would automatically solve the population problem has gone by. In the United States, and certain other societies, in the early stages of post-civilization, the child has become an object of conspicuous domestic consumption. The consumption patterns of the American spending unit seem to follow a certain *"gestalt"* in which household capital accumulates in a certain order, such as the first car, the first child, the washer and dryer, the second child, the deep freeze, the third child, the second car, the fourth child, and so on. The richer we get, the more children we can afford to have and the more children we do have. We now seem to be able to afford an average of something like four children per family, and as, in a post-civilized society, these four children all survive, the population doubles every generation. A hundred years of this and even the United States is going to find itself uncomfortably crowded. It can be argued, indeed, that from the point of view of the amenities of life we are already well beyond the optimum population.

The third trap on the road to post-civilization is the technological trap. Our present technology is fundamentally suicidal. It is based on the extraction of concentrated deposits of fossil fuels and ores, which in the nature of things are exhaustible. Even at present rates of consumption, they will be exhausted in a time span which is not very long measured against human history and which is infinitesimally small on the geological time scale. If the rest of the world advances to American standards of consumption, these resources will disappear almost overnight. On this view economic development is the process of bringing closer the evil day when everything will be gone—all the oil, the coal, the ores—and we will have to go back to primitive agriculture and scratching in the woods.

There are indications, however, that suicidal technology is not absolutely necessary and that a permanent high-level technology is possible. Beginning in the early part of the twentieth century, it is possible to detect an anti-entropic movement in technology. This begins perhaps with the Haber process for the fixation of nitrogen from the air. A development of similar significance is the Dow process for the extraction of magnesium from the sea. Both these processes take the diffuse and concentrate it, instead of taking the concentrated and diffusing it, as do most processes of mining and economic production. These anti-entropic processes foreshadow a technology in which we shall draw all the materials we need from the virtually inexhaustible reservoirs of the sea and the air and draw our energy from controlled fusion—either artificially produced on the earth or from the sun.

This is why I so much resent spending half the world's income on armaments—because the more we do this, the less chance we have of making the transition to a stable, high-level society. The human race is in a precarious position on its planet and it should act accordingly. It has a chance, never to be repeated, of making its great transition, and if it fails, at least one good experiment in intelligence will have gone to waste. I suppose there are similar experiments of this nature going on in other parts of the universe; but I must confess to a hopelessly anthropocentric prejudice in favor of planet earth. It's a nice planet, and I'm in favor of it and I have no desire to see its principal inhabitant blow it up or starve it out.

When we look at the nature of possible remedies for our immediate problems, it seems clear that we are all engulfed in a profound and appallingly dangerous misallocation of our intellectual resources. The misallocation lies in the fact that although all our major problems are in social systems, we persist in regarding them as if they were essentially problems in physical or biological systems. We persist in regarding agricultural problems, for instance, as one of crops, whereas it is clearly fundamentally a problem of farmers. We persist in regarding the flood-control problem as a problem of the river and we even turn it over to army engineers, who treat the river as an enemy. A flood, however, is no problem at all to a river. It is a perfectly normal part of its way of life. The flood, essentially, is a problem of people and of social institutions, of architecture and zoning. Professor Gilbert White, of the University of Chicago, suggests that after spending over four billion dollars on flood control in this country, we are more in danger of major disasters than we were before. What we really mean by flood control is the substitution of a major disaster every fifty or one hundred years for minor inconveniences every five or ten.

In national defense we have fallen into exactly the same trap. We regard this as a problem in physical systems and in hardware, whereas it is essentially a problem in social systems. Here again, we are building into our societies the eventual certainty of total disaster. In face of the fact that war and peace is the major problem of our age, we are putting practically nothing into peace research; even when we do put money into arms control and disarmament research we spend sixty million dollars for Project Vela, which deals wholly with physical systems, and one hundred and fifty thousand on Project Vulcan, which deals with social systems and with unanswerable questions at that. When we look at biological and medical research, and still more, research into population, the disparity is just as striking. We persist in regarding disease as a biological problem, whereas it is fundamentally a bio-social system. Yet the number of sociologists in our medical schools can be counted almost on the fingers of one hand.

Nevertheless, in spite of the dangers, it is a wonderful age to live in, and I would not wish to be born in any other time. The wonderful and precious thing about the present moment is that there is still time—the Bomb hasn't gone off, the population explosion may be caught, the technological problem can, perhaps, be solved. If the human race is to survive, however, it will have to change more in its ways of thinking in the next twenty-five years than it has done in the last twenty-five thousand. There is hope, however, in the fact that we are very far from having exhausted the capacity of this extraordinary organism that we call man. I once calculated the capacity of the human nervous system in terms of the number of different states it might assume, which is a very rough measure. This comes to two to the ten billionth power, assuming that each of our ten billion neurons is capable of only two states. This is a very large number. It would take you ninety years to write it down at the rate of one digit a second. If you want a standard of comparison, the total number of neutrinos, which are the smallest known particles, which could be packed into the known astronomical universe (this is the largest physical number I could think of) could easily be written down in three minutes. I find it hard to believe, therefore, that the capacity of the human organism has been exhausted.

What we have to do now, however, is to develop almost a new form of learning. We have to learn from rapidly changing systems. Ordinarily we learn from stable systems. It is because the world repeats itself that we catch on to the law of repetition. Learning from changing systems is perhaps another step in the acceleration of evolution that we have to take. I have been haunted by a remark which Norman Meier, the psychologist, made in a seminar a few months ago, when he said that a cat who jumps on a hot stove never jumps on a cold one. This seems precisely to describe the state we may be in today. We have jumped on a lot of hot stoves and now perhaps the cold stove is the only place on which to jump. In the rapidly changing system it is desperately easy to learn things which are no longer true. Perhaps the greatest task of applied social science at the moment is to study the conditions under which we learn from rapidly changing systems. If we can answer this question, there may still be hope for the human race.

Albert Camus

Neither Victims nor Executioners

Introduction by Waldo Frank

Camus hated violence; speeding is a form of violence, and he detested speeding. On the fatal day he intended to go to Sens by train and had already bought his ticket. Reluctantly he allowed himself to be persuaded by his friends to go with them by car. Reckoning from the time of their leaving the garage, the driver must have averaged over 80 miles per hour. This meaningless waste of a precious life—for no discernible purpose—is what Camus meant by "the Absurd." Pascal, his spiritual father, had already noted its prevalence in human life and death, and had used the word.

When I first met Camus, shortly after the close of the War, I had a vivid presentiment, which I now recognize as an intuition: This man will not live long. I am certain that I got this message from Camus, himself. He had caught tuberculosis during the bitter, starving days of the Resistance. I thought of this disease as a probable factor in Camus' having no more than a short life. But such a death would not have been "absurd," would have had meaning, as the price Camus paid for his brave underground work against the Nazis. Camus knew that his death would lack such logic. The "absurdity" of what happened brought forward color and passion and pathos to his immediate prose. Camus got over his tuberculosis. His health hardened, and he became world-famous. The Absurd was waiting for him, and I am sure he knew it. His expression of the Absurd as the predicament of modern man was so breathlessly urgent because he already was experiencing it in his own person.

Pascal's great pages memorialize the plight of the intel-

ligent man who can rationalize the human condition only by letting himself be forced back upon the classic Revelation of the Church, which is before and beyond human reason. Camus marks the plight of the more modern man for whom the ancient Revelation is no longer valid—who refuses to fall back on it as contrary to his reason, yet cannot go forward into a new-formed Revelation acceptable to our age of science.

This insoluble dream is the theme of Camus: of the modern who needs to believe and cannot, who needs to know his part in Cosmos and cannot, lacking the strength to replace the part, as his fathers formed it, with terms more valid to our day. Because this plight is common in the West, and because Camus eloquently dramatized it in his plays and stories, he became the voice of the best of an entire generation.

Unlike the neo-orthodox of many creeds (Protestant, Catholic, Jewish), who successfully sink back to an old Order, finding there solace and comfort; and unlike the "beatniks" who simply (too simply) and stupidly give up the search for meaning, Camus confessed his loss and continued his search.

Camus was the writer of prose worthy to be ranked with that of Pascal, his spiritual and more fortunate predecessor. It imaged the man. And for us who knew him personally, the man will always stand forth. An age of incredible violence distilled his hate of violence. An age of cowardly confusions matured his integrity in refusing to give up the search for Knowledge because he had not found it. When I first saw Camus, my thought was of his nobility. This is the final, the definitive term to describe him.

The Century of Fear

[*This first appeared in 1946 in* Combat, *the daily newspaper of the French Resistance, which Camus helped to edit.*]

The 17th century was the century of mathematics, the 18th that of the physical sciences, and the 19th that of biology. Our 20th century is the century of fear. I will be told that fear is not a science. But science must be somewhat involved since its latest theoretical advances have brought it to the point of negating itself while its perfected technology threatens the globe itself with destruction. Moreover, although fear itself cannot be considered a science, it is certainly a technique.

The most striking feature of the world we live in is that most of its inhabitants—with the exception of pietists of various kinds—are cut off from the future. Life has no validity unless it can project itself toward the future, can ripen and progress. Living against a wall is a dog's life. True—and the men of my generation, those who are going into the factories and the colleges, have lived and are living more and more like dogs.

This is not the first time, of course, that men have confronted a future materially closed to them. But hitherto they have been able to transcend the dilemma by words, by protests, by appealing to other values which lent them hope. Today no one speaks any more (except those who repeat themselves) because history seems to be in the grip of blind and deaf forces which will heed neither cries of warning, nor advice, nor entreaties. The years we have just gone through have killed something in us. And that something is simply the old confidence man had in himself, which led him to believe that he could always elicit human reactions from another man if he spoke to him in the language of a common humanity. We have seen men lie, degrade, kill, deport, torture—and each time it was not possible to persuade them not to do these things because they were sure of themselves and because one cannot appeal to an abstraction, i.e., the representative of an ideology.

Mankind's long dialogue has just come to an end. And naturally a man with whom one cannot reason is a man to be feared. The result is that—besides those who have not spoken out because they thought it useless—a vast conspiracy of silence has spread all about us, a conspiracy accepted by those who are frightened and who rationalize their fears in order to hide them from themselves, a conspiracy fostered by those whose interest it is to do so. "You shouldn't talk about the Russian culture purge—it helps reaction." "Don't mention the Anglo-American support of Franco—it encourages communism." Fear is certainly a technique.

What with the general fear of a war now being prepared by all nations and the specific fear of murderous ideologies, who can deny that we live in a state of terror? We live in terror because persuasion is no longer possible; because man has been wholly submerged in History; because he can no longer tap that part of his nature, as real as the historical part, which he recaptures in contemplating the beauty of nature and of human faces; because we live in a world of abstractions, of bureaus and machines, of absolute ideas and of crude messianism. We suffocate among people who think they are absolutely right, whether in their machines or in their ideas. And for all who can live only in an atmosphere of human dialogue and sociability, this silence is the end of the world.

To emerge from this terror, we must be able to reflect and to act accordingly. But an atmosphere of terror hardly encourages reflection. I believe, however, that instead of simply blaming everything on this fear, we should consider it as one of the basic factors in the situation, and try to do something about it. No task is more important. For it involves the fate of a considerable number of Europeans who, fed up with the lies and violence, deceived in their dearest hopes and repelled by the idea of killing their fellow men in order to convince them, likewise repudiate the idea of themselves being convinced that way. And yet such is the alternative that at present confronts so many of us in Europe who are not of any party—or ill at ease in the party we have chosen—who doubt socialism has been realized in Russia or liberalism in America, who grant to each side the right to affirm its truth but refuse it the right to impose it by murder, individual or collective. Among the powerful of today, these are the men without a kingdom. Their viewpoint will not be recognized (and I say "recognized," not "triumph"), nor will they recover their kingdom until they come to know precisely what they want and proclaim it directly and boldly enough to make their words a stimulus to action. And if an atmosphere of fear does not encourage accurate thinking, then they must first of all come to terms with fear.

To come to terms, one must understand what fear means: what it implies and what it rejects. It implies and rejects the same fact: a world where murder is legitimate, and where human life is considered trifling. This is the great political question of our times, and before dealing with other issues, one must take a position on it. Before anything can be done, two questions must be put: "Do you or do you not, directly or indirectly, want to be killed or assaulted? Do you or do you not, directly or indirectly, want to kill or assault?" All who say No to both these questions are automatically committed to a series of consequences which must modify their way of posing the problem. My aim here is to clarify two or three of these consequences.

Saving Our Skins

I once said that, after the experiences of the last two years. I could no longer hold to any truth which might oblige me, directly or indirectly, to demand a man's life. Certain friends whom I respected retorted that I was living in Utopia, that there was no political truth which could not one day reduce us to such an extremity, and that we must therefore either run the risk of this extremity or else simply put up with the world as it is.

They argued the point most forcefully. But I think they were able to put such force into it only because they were unable to really *imagine* other people's death. It is a freak of the times. We make love by telephone, we work not on matter but on machines, and we kill and are killed by proxy. We gain in cleanliness, but lose in understanding.

But the argument has another, indirect meaning: it poses the question of Utopia. People like myself want not a world in which murder no longer exists (we are not so crazy as that!) but rather one in which murder is not legitimate. Here indeed we are Utopian—and contradictory. For we do live, it is true, in a world where murder is legitimate, and we ought to change it if we do not like it. But it appears that we cannot change it without risking murder. Murder thus throws us back on murder, and we will continue to live in terror whether we accept the fact with resignation or wish to abolish it by means which merely replace one terror with another.

It seems to me every one should think this over. For what strikes me, in the midst of polemics, threats and outbursts of violence, is the fundamental good will of every one. From Right to Left, every one, with the exception of a few swindlers, believes that his particular truth is the one to make men happy. And yet the combination of all these good intentions has produced the present infernal world, where men are killed, threatened and deported, where war is prepared, where one cannot speak freely without being insulted or betrayed. Thus if people like ourselves live in a state of contradiction, we are not the only ones, and those who accuse us of Utopianism are possibly themselves also living in a Utopia, a different one but perhaps a more costly one in the end.

Let us, then, admit that our refusal to legitimize murder forces us to reconsider our whole idea of Utopia. This much seems clear: Utopia is whatever is in contradiction with reality. From this standpoint, it would be completely Utopian to wish that men should no longer kill each other. That would be absolute Utopia. But a much sounder Utopia is that which insists that murder be no longer legitimized. Indeed, the Marxian and the capitalist ideologies, both based on the idea of progress, both certain that the application of their principles must inevitably bring about a harmonious society, are Utopian to a much greater degree. Furthermore, they are both at the moment costing us dearly.

We may therefore conclude, practically, that in the next few years the struggle will be not between the forces of Utopia and the forces of reality, but between different Utopias which are attempting to be born into reality. It will be simply a matter of choosing the least costly among them. I am convinced that we can no longer reasonably hope to save everything, but that we can at least propose to save our skins, so that *a* future, if not *the* future, remains a possibility.

Thus (1) to refuse to sanction murder is no more Utopian than the "realistic" ideologies of our day, and (2) the whole point is whether these latter are more or less costly. It may, therefore, be useful to try to define, in Utopian terms, the conditions which are needed to bring about the pacification of men and nations. This line of thought, assuming it is carried on without fear and without pretensions, may help to create the preconditions for clear thinking and a provisional agreement between men who want to be neither victims nor executioners. In what follows, the attempt will be not to work out a complete position, but simply to correct some current misconceptions and to pose the question of Utopia as accurately as possible. The attempt, in short, will be to define the conditions for a political position that is modest—i.e., free of messianism and disencumbered of nostalgia for an earthly paradise.

The Self-Deception of the Socialists

If we agree that we have lived for ten years in a state of terror and still so live, and that this terror is our chief source of anxiety, then we must see what we can oppose to this terror. Which brings up the question of socialism. For terror is legitimized only if we assent to the principle: "the end justifies the means." And this principle in turn may be accepted only if the effectiveness of an action is posed as an absolute end, as in nihilistic ideologies (anything goes, success is the only thing worth talking about), or in those philosophies which make History an absolute end (Hegel, followed by Marx: the end being a classless society, everything is good that leads to it).

Such is the problem confronting French Socialists, for example. They are bothered by scruples. Violence and oppression, of which they had hitherto only a theoretical idea, they have now seen at first hand. And they have had to ask themselves whether, as their philosophy requires, they would consent to use that violence themselves, even as a temporary expedient and for a quite different end. The author of a recent preface to Saint-Just, speaking of men of an earlier age who had similar scruples, wrote contemptuously: "They recoiled in the face of horrors." True enough. And so they deserved to be despised by strong, superior spirits who could live among horrors without flinching. But all the same, they gave a voice to the agonized appeal of commonplace spirits like ourselves, the millions who constitute the raw material of History and who must some day be taken into account, despite all contempt.

A more important task, I think, is to try to understand the state of contradiction and confusion in which our Socialists now exist. We have not thought enough about the moral crisis of French Socialism, as expressed, for example in a recent party congress. It is clear that our Socialists, under the influence of Leon Blum and even more under the pressure of events, have preoccupied themselves much more with moral questions (the end does not justify all means) than in the past. Quite properly, they wanted to base themselves on principles which rise superior to murder. It is also clear that these same Socialists want to preserve Marxian doctrine, some because they think one cannot be revolutionary without being Marxist, others, by fidelity to party tradition, which tells them that one cannot be Socialist without being Marxist. The chief task of the last party congress was to reconcile the desire for a morality superior to murder with the determination to remain faithful to Marxism. But one cannot reconcile what is irreconcilable.

For if it is clear that Marxism is true and there is logic in History, then political realism is legitimate. It is equally clear that if the moral values extolled by the Socialist Party are legitimate, then Marxism is absolutely false since it claims to be absolutely true. From this point of view, the famous "going beyond" Marxism in an idealistic and humanitarian direction is a joke and an idle dream. It is impossible to "go beyond" Marx, for he himself carried his thought to its extreme logical consequences. The Communists have a solid logical basis for using the lies and the violence which the Socialists reject, and the basis is that very dialectic which the Socialists want to preserve. It is therefore hardly surprising that the Socialist congress ended by simply putting forward simultaneously two contradictory positions—a conclusion whose sterility appears in the results of the recent elections.

This way, confusion will never end. A choice was necessary, and the Socialists would not or could not choose.

I have chosen this example not to score off the Socialists but to illustrate the paradoxes among which we live. To score off the Socialists, one would have to be superior to them. This is not yet the case. On the contrary, I think this contradiction is common to all those of whom I speak, those who want a society which we can both enjoy and respect; those who want men to be both free and just, but who hesitate between a freedom in which they know justice is finally betrayed and a justice in which they see freedom suppressed from the first.

Those who know What Is To Be Done or What Is To Be Thought make fun of this intolerable anguish. But I think it would be better, instead of jeering at it, to try to understand and clarify this anguish, see what it means, interpret its quasi-total rejection of a world which provokes it, and trace out the feeble hope that suffuses it.

A hope that is grounded precisely in this contradiction, since it forces—or will force—the Socialists to make a choice. They will either admit that the end justifies the means, in which case murder can be legitimized; or else, they will reject Marxism as an absolute philosophy, confining themselves to its critical aspect, which is often valuable. If they choose the first, their moral crisis will be ended, and their position will be unambiguous. If the second, they will exemplify the way our period marks the end of ideologies, that is, of absolute Utopias which destroy themselves, in History, by the price they ultimately exact. It will then be necessary to choose a more modest and less costly Utopia. At least it is in these terms that the refusal to legitimize murder forces us to pose the problem.

Yes, that is the question we must put, and no one I think, will venture to answer it lightly.

Parody of Revolution

Since August 1944, everybody talks about revolution, and quite sincerely too. But sincerity is not in itself a virtue: some kinds are so confused that they are worse than lies. Not the language of the heart but merely that of clear thinking is what we need today. Ideally, a revolution is a change in political and economic institutions in order to introduce more freedom and justice; practically, it is a complex of historical events, often undesirable ones, which brings about this happy transformation.

Can one say that we use this word today in its classical sense? When people nowadays hear the word, "revolution," they think of a change in property relations (generally collectivization) which may be brought about either by majority legislation or by a minority coup.

This concept obviously lacks meaning in present historical circumstances. For one thing, the violent seizure of power is a romantic idea which the perfection of armaments has made illusory. Since the repressive apparatus of a modern State commands tanks and airplanes, tanks and airplanes are needed to counter it. Both 1789 and 1917 are still historic dates, but are no longer historic examples.

And even assuming this conquest of power were possible, by violence or by law, it would be effective only if France (or Italy or Czechoslovakia) could be put into parentheses and isolated from the rest of the world. For, in the actual historical situation of 1946, a change in our own property system would involve, to give only one example, such consequences to our American credits that our economy would be threatened with ruin. A right-wing coup would be no more successful, because of Russia with her millions of French Communist voters and her position as the dominant continental power. The truth is— excuse me for stating openly what every one knows and no one says—the truth is that we French are not free to make a revolution. Or at least that we can be no longer revolutionary all by ourselves, since there no longer exists any policy, conservative or socialist, which can operate exclusively with a national framework.

Thus we can only speak of world revolution. The revolution will be made on a world scale or it will not be made at all. But what meaning does this expression still retain? There was a time when it was thought that international reform would be brought about by the conjunction or the synchronization of a number of national revolutions—a kind of totting-up of miracles. But today one can conceive only the extension of a revolution that has already succeeded. This is something Stalin has very well understood, and it is the kindest explanation of his policies (the other being to refuse Russia the right to speak in the name of revolution).

This viewpoint boils down to conceiving of Europe and the West as a single nation in which a powerful and well-armed minority is struggling to take power. But if the conservative forces—in this case, the USA—are equally well armed, clearly the idea of revolution is replaced by that of ideological warfare. More precisely, world revolution today involves a very great danger of war. Every future revolution will be a foreign revolution. It will begin with a military occupation—or, what comes to the same thing, the blackmail threat of one. And it will become significant only when the occupying power has conquered the rest of the world.

Inside national boundaries, revolutions have already been costly enough—a cost that has been accepted because of the progress they are assumed to bring. Today, the costs of a world war must be weighed against the progress that may be hoped for from either Russia or America gaining world power. And I think it of first importance that such a balance be struck, and that for once we use a little imagination about what this globe, where already thirty million fresh corpses lie, will be like after a cataclysm which will cost us ten times as many.

Note that this is a truly objective approach, taking account only of reality without bringing in ideological or sentimental considerations. It should give pause to those who talk lightly of revolution. The *present-day* content of this word must be accepted or rejected as a whole. If it be accepted, then one must recognize a conscious responsibility for the coming war. If rejected, then one must either come out for the status quo—which is a mood of absolute Utopia insofar as it assumes the "freezing" of history—or else give a new content to the word "revolution," which means assenting to what might be called relative Utopia. Those who want to change the world must, it seems to me, now choose between the charnel-house threatened by the impossible dream of history suddenly struck motionless, and the acceptance of a relative Utopia which gives some leeway to action and to mankind. Relative Utopia is the only realistic choice; it is our last frail hope of saving our skins.

International Democracy and Dictatorship

We know today that there are no more islands, that frontiers are just lines on a map. We know that in a steadily accelerating world, where the Atlantic is crossed in less than a day and Moscow speaks to Washington in a few minutes, we are forced into fraternity—or complicity. The forties have taught us that an injury done a student in Prague strikes down simultaneously a worker in Clichy, that blood shed on the banks of a

Central European river brings a Texas farmer to spill his own blood in the Ardennes, which he sees for the first time. There is no suffering, no torture anywhere in the world which does not affect our everyday lives.

Many Americans would like to go on living closed off in their own society, which they find good. Many Rusians perhaps would like to carry on their Statist experiment holding aloof from the capitalist world. They cannot do so, nor will they ever again be able to do so. Likewise, no economic problem, however minor it appears, can be solved outside the comity of nations. Europe's bread is in Buenos Aires, Siberian machine-tools are made in Detroit. Today, tragedy is collective.

We know, then, without shadow of a doubt, that the new order we seek cannot be merely national, or even continental; certainly not occidental nor oriental. It must be universal. No longer can we hope for anything from partial solutions or concessions. We are living in a state of compromise, i.e., anguish today and murder tomorrow. And all the while the pace of history and the world is accelerating. The 21 deaf men, the war criminals of tomorrow, who today negotiate the peace, carry on their monotonous conversations placidly seated in an express train which bears them toward the abyss at a thousand miles an hour.

What are the methods by which this world unity may be achieved, this international revolution realized, in which the resources of men, of raw materials, of commercial markets and cultural riches may be better distributed? I see only two, and these two between them define our ultimate alternative.

The world can be united from above, by a single State more powerful than the others. The USSR or the USA could do it. I have nothing to say to the claim that they could rule and remodel the world in the image of their own society. As a Frenchman, and still more as a Mediterranean, I find the idea repellent. But I do not insist on this sentimental argument. My only objection is, as stated in the last section, that this unification could not be accomplished without war—or at least without serious risk of war. I will even grant what I do not believe: that it would not be an atomic war. The fact remains, nevertheless, that the coming war will leave humanity so mutilated and impoverished that the very idea of law and order will become anachronistic. Marx could justify, as he did, the war of 1870 for it was a provincial war fought with Chassepot rifles. In the Marxian perspective, a hundred thousand corpses are nothing if they are the price of the happiness of hundreds of millions of men. But the sure death of millions of men for the hypothetical happiness of the survivors seems too high a price to pay. The dizzy rate at which weapons have evolved, a historical fact ignored by Marx, forces us to raise anew the whole question of means and ends. And in this instance, the means can leave us little doubt about the end. Whatever the desired end, however lofty and necessary, whether happiness or justice or liberty—the means employed to attain it represent so enormous a risk and are so disproportionate to the slender hopes of success, that, in all sober objectivity, we must refuse to run this risk.

This leaves us only the alternative method of achieving a world order: the mutual agreement of all parties. This agreement has a name: international democracy. Of course every one talks about the UN. But what is international democracy? It is a democracy which is international. (The truism will perhaps be excused, since the most self-evident truths are also the ones most frequently distorted.) International—or national—democracy is a form of society in which law has authority over those governed, law being the expression of the common will as expressed in a legislative body. An international legal code is indeed now being prepared. But this code is made and broken by governments, that is, by the executive power. We are thus faced with a regime of international dictatorship. The only way of extricating ourselves is to create a world parliament through elections in which all peoples will participate, which will enact legislation which will exercise authority over national governments. Since we do not have such a parliament, all we can do now is to resist international dictatorship; to resist on a world scale; and to resist by means which are not in contradiction with the end we seek.

The World Speeds Up

As every one knows, political thought today lags more and more behind events. Thus the French fought the 1914 war with 1870 methods, and the 1939 war with 1918 methods. Antiquated thinking is not, however, a French speciality. We need only recall that the future of the world is being shaped by liberal-capitalist principles, developed in the 18th century and by "scientific socialist" principles developed in the 19th. Systems of thought which, in the former case, date from the early years of modern industrialism, and, in the latter, from the age of Darwinism and the Renanian optimism, now propose to master the age of the atomic bomb, of sudden mutations, and of nihilism.

It is true that consciousness is always lagging behind reality: History rushes onward while thought reflects. But this inevitable backwardness becomes more pronounced the faster History speeds up. The world has changed more in the past fifty years than it did in the previous two hundred years. Thus we see nations quarreling over frontiers when every one knows that today frontiers are mere abstractions. Nationalism was, to all appearances, the dominant note at the Conference of the 21.

Today we concentrate our political thinking on the German problem, which is a secondary problem compared to the clash of empires which threatens us. But if tomorrow we resolve the Russo-American conflict, we may see ourselves once more outdistanced. Already the clash of empires is in process of becoming secondary to the clash of civilizations. Everywhere the colonial peoples are asserting themselves. Perhaps in ten years, perhaps in fifty, the dominance of Western civilization itself will be called into question. We might as well recognize this now, and admit these civilizations into the world parliament, so that its code of law may become truly universal, and a universal order be established.

The veto issue in the UN today is a false issue because the conflicting majorities and minorities are false. The USSR will always have the right to reject majority rule so long as it is a majority of ministers and not a majority of peoples, all peoples, represented by their delegates. Once such a majority comes into being, then each nation must obey it or else reject its law—that is, openly proclaim its will to dominate. . . .

To reply once more and finally to the accusation of Utopia: for us, the choice is simple—Utopia or the war now being prepared by antiquated modes of thought . . . Sceptical though we are (and as I am), realism forces us to this Utopian alternative. When our Utopia has become part of history, as with many others of like kind, men will find themselves unable to conceive reality without it. For History is simply man's desperate effort to give body to his most clairvoyant dreams.

A New Social Contract

All contemporary political thinking which refuses to justify lies and murder is led to the following conclusions: (1) domestic policy is in itself a secondary matter; (2) the only problem is the creation of a world order which will bring about those lasting reforms which are the distinguishing mark of a revolution; (3) within any given nation there exist now only administrative problems, to be solved provisionally after a fashion, until a solution is worked out which will be more effective because more general.

For example, the French Constitution can only be evaluated in terms of the support it gives or fails to give to a world order based on justice and the free exchange of ideas. From this viewpoint, we must criticize the indifference of our Constitution to the simplest human liberties. And we must also recognize that the problem of restoring the food supply is ten times more important than such issues as nationalization or election figures. Nationalization will not work in a single country. And although the food supply cannot be assured either within a single country, it is a more pressing problem and calls for expedients, provisional though they may be.

And so this viewpoint gives us a hitherto lacking criterion by which to judge domestic policy. Thirty editorials in *Aube* may range themselves every month against thirty in *Humanité*, but they will not cause us to forget that both newspapers, together with the parties they represent, have acquiesced in the annexation without a referendum of Briga and Tenda, and that they are thus accomplices in the destruction of international democracy. Regardless of their good or bad intentions, Mr. Bidault and Mr. Thorez are both in favor of international dictatorship. From this aspect, whatever other opinion one may have of them, they represesent in our politics not realism but the most disastrous kind of Utopianism.

Yes, we must minimize domestic politics. A crisis which tears the whole world apart must be met on a world scale. A social system for everybody which will somewhat allay each one's misery and fear is today our logical objective. But that calls for action and for sacrifices, that is, for men. And if there are many today who, in their secret hearts, detest violence and killing, there are not many who care to recognize that this forces them to reconsider their actions and thoughts. Those who want to make such an effort, however, will find in such a social system a rational hope and a guide to action.

They will admit that little is to be expected from present-day governments, since these live and act according to a murderous code. Hope remains only in the most difficult task of all: to reconsider everything from the ground up, so as to shape a living society inside a dying society. Men must therefore, as individuals, draw up among themselves, within frontiers and across them, a new social contract which will unite them according to more reasonable principles.

The peace movement I speak of could base itself, inside nations, on work communities and, internationally, on intellectual communities; the former, organized cooperatively, would help as many individuals as possible to solve their material problems, while the latter would try to define the values by which this international community would live, and would also plead its cause on every occasion.

More precisely, the latter's task would be to speak out clearly against the confusions of the Terror and at the same time to define the values by which a peaceful world may live. The first objectives might be the drawing up of an international code of justice whose Article No. 1 would be the abolition of the death penalty, and an exposition of the basic principles of a sociable culture ("civilisation du dialogue"). Such an undertaking would answer the needs of an era which has found no philosophical justification for that thirst for fraternity which today burns in Western man. There is no idea, naturally, of constructing a new ideology, but rather of discovering a style of life.

Let us suppose that certain individuals resolve that they will consistently oppose to power the force of example; to authority, exhortation; to insult, friendly reasoning; to trickery, simple honor. Let us suppose they refuse all the advantages of present-day society and accept only the duties and obligations which bind them to other men. Let us suppose they devote themselves to orienting education, the press and public opinion toward the principles outlined here. Then I say that such men would be acting not as Utopians but as honest realists. They would be preparing the future and at the same time knocking down a few of the walls which imprison us today. If realism be the art of taking into account both the present and the future, of gaining the most while sacrificing the least, then who can fail to see the positively dazzling realism of such behavior?

Whether these men will arise or not I do not know. It is probable that most of them are even now thinking things over, and that is good. But one thing is sure: their efforts will be effective only to the degree they have the courage to give up, for the present, some of their dreams, so as to grasp the more firmly the essential point on which our very lives depend. Once there, it will perhaps turn out to be necessary, before they are done, to raise their voices.

Towards Sociability

Yes, we must raise our voices. Up to this point, I have refrained from appealing to emotion. We are being torn apart by a logic of History which we have elaborated in every detail—a net which threatens to strangle us. It is not emotion which can cut through the web of a logic which has gone to irrational lengths, but only reason which can meet logic on its own ground. But I should not want to leave the impression, in concluding, that any program for the future can get along without our powers of love and indignation. I am well aware that it takes a powerful prime mover to get men into motion and that it is hard to throw one's self into a struggle whose objectives are so modest and where hope has only a rational basis—and hardly even that. But the problem is not how to carry men away; it is essential, on the contrary, that they not be carried away but rather that they be made to understand clearly what they are doing.

To save what can be saved so as to open up some kind of future—that is the prime mover, the passion and the sacrifice that is required. It demands only that we reflect and then decide, clearly, whether humanity's lot must be made still more miserable in order to achieve far-off and shadowy ends, whether we should accept a world bristling with arms where brother kills brother; or whether, on the contrary, we should avoid bloodshed and misery as much as possible so that we give a chance for survival to later generations better equipped than we are.

For my part, I am fairly sure that I have made the choice. And, having chosen, I think that I must speak out, that I must state that I will never again be one of those, whoever they be, who compromise with murder, and that I must take the consequences of such a decision. The thing is done, and that is as far as I can go at present. Before concluding, however, I want to make clear the spirit in which this article is written.

We are asked to love or to hate such and such a country and such and such a people. But some of us feel too strongly our common humanity to make such a choice. Those who really love the Russian people, in gratitude for what they have never ceased to be—that world leaven which Tolstoy and Gorky speak of—do not wish for them success in power-politics, but rather want to spare them, after the ordeals of the past, a new and even more terrible bloodletting. So, too, with the American people, and with the peoples of unhappy Europe. This is the kind of elementary truth we are liable to forget amidst the furious passions of our time.

Yes, it is fear and silence and the spiritual isolation they cause that must be fought today. And it is sociability ("le dialogue") and the universal intercommunication of men that must be defended. Slavery, injustice and lies destroy this intercourse and forbid this sociability; and so we must reject them. But these evils are today the very stuff of History, so that many consider them necessary evils. It is true that we cannot "escape History," since we are in it up to our necks. But one may propose to fight within History to preserve from History that part of man which is not its proper province. That is all I have to say here. The "point" of this article may be summed up as follows:

Modern nations are driven by powerful forces along the roads of power and domination. I will not say that these forces should be furthered or that they should be obstructed. They hardly need our help and, for the moment, they laugh at attempts to hinder them. They will, then, continue. But I will ask only this simple question: what if these forces wind up in a dead end, what if that logic of History on which so many now rely turns out to be a will o' the wisp? What if, despite two or three world wars, despite the sacrifice of several generations and a whole system of values, our grandchildren—supposing they survive—find themselves no closer to a world society? It may well be that the survivors of such an experience will be too weak to understand their own sufferings. Since these forces are working themselves out and since it is inevitable that they continue to do so, there is no reason why some of us should not take on the job of keeping alive through the apocalyptic historical vista that stretches before us, a modest thoughtfulness which, without pretending to solve everything, will constantly be prepared to give some human meaning to everyday life. The essential thing is that people should carefully weigh the price they must pay.

To conclude: all I ask is that, in the midst of a murderous world, we agree to reflect on murder and to make a choice. After that, we can distinguish those who accept the consequences of being murderers themselves or the accomplices of murderers, and those who refuse to do so with all their force and being. Since this terrible dividing line does actually exist, it will be a gain if it be clearly marked. Over the expanse of five continents throughout the coming years an endless struggle is going to be pursued between violence and friendly persuasion, a struggle in which, granted, the former has a thousand times the chances of success than has the latter. But I have always held that, if he who bases his hopes on human nature is a fool, he who gives up in the face of circumstances is a coward. And henceforth, the only honorable course will be to stake everything on a formidable gamble: that words are more powerful than munitions.

(*Translated by Dwight Macdonald*)

II

The Task of Reason: War and Nonviolence

"The task, basically, is not for the United States to liberate peoples from Russia, or for Russia to liberate people from United States imperialism, but for each country to liberate itself, and thus help liberate the other and mankind."

A. J. Muste
"Getting Rid of War"
Liberation, March, 1959

Leslie Dewart

American Leadership and the Future of the West

The most significant fact of international life today is the polarization of the world in a geopolitical field of forces defined by tension between Russia and the United States. We in Canada are particularly aware of this. The clustering of the Western nations around the American pole affects us with singular intensity, since the political reasons therefore are culturally, historically, economically and geographically reinforced. Partly on account of that intensity, but also because unlike the British, whose relished memory of past greatness engenders the wishful thought of patriarchal ascendancy, and unlike the French, whose merely logical realism suggests the unlikely alternative of a third force, Canadians seem fully and for the most part graciously reconciled to the idea that insofar as it may depend upon Western leadership the future of human history rests with the will and the strength of the United States. This is implicit, for instance, in the premises commonly assumed in Canada by those who discuss their concern "whether Canada's prestige abroad is or is not on the wane." We recognize that if we are to have any appreciable influence upon the course of world events it is only insofar as we might impress the United States—and incidentally other countries, of course—with advice and recommendations whose credibility shall rest solely upon whatever reputation we might internationally deserve for sobermindedness, fairness and sound common sense.

Canada, therefore, has legitimate and special reasons to be concerned with the study and assessment of the basic psychodynamics of the United States as leaders of the West: so much of our own future depends upon it. For it is clear that we can best ensure that the United States shall not lead us into the ditch of disaster if we neither blindly entrust ourselves to them, nor let them blindly assume our servile and unconditional acquiescence in their every judgment. But to follow this policy we need thoroughly to understand the American mind. For our own edification, therefore, we should raise the question: what shall we think of the United States as the standard-bearer of the Western culture? Of course, one can hardly expect unanimity as to the nature of the answer. For my part, I have neither simple convictions (nor profound opinions), nor any but tentatively held.

As with individuals, we shall search for clues to the dynamics of the deeper psychic forces of the collective American political personality among the experiential manifestations found in immediate consciousness. There can be no doubt, therefore, as to which American experience we shall have to consider first. The predominant American feeling today and during recent years is a chronic, intense, generalized, inexplicable and frustrating disappointment in the international situation. Americans are unhappy with Russia. They are unhappy or, at least, impatient with neutrals and with allies. The thirst for friends and friendship is unquenchable, in the sense that anything less than agreement with United States policies is perceived as hostile (in the case of an opponent), as outrageous (in the case of a neutral) or, at best, as suspicious (in the case of an ally). The Americans, thus, are least happy of all with themselves, since their experience is the frustration and despair of witnessing that "all the good will in the world" seems inadequate—and, perhaps, irrelevant—to the task of ensuring and preserving international peace.

Unfortunately, this disappointment, this discomfort, is conceptualized falsely and is explained away too quickly and superficially. "We act in good will," Americans tell themselves, "we sincerely want peace, yet we get nowhere with the Russians. The *impasse,* therefore, is in no way our own making. The polarization of the world is wholly the product of Russian international politics. (However, this merely *defines* the perceived situation. Why is the situation experienced as frustrating? Why is the reaction to an apparently wholly undeserved threat not essentially one of dismay, terror and aggressiveness, however much the reaction of discomfort, disappointment, unhappiness and frustration may contain these components?) Since the situation is basically simple, i.e., the guilt is wholly or almost wholly on one side, there must be, in principle, a simple solution to it, whether military or diplomatic, whether capitulation or war. Thus, if we cannot solve it once for all we must in some way be deficient and, therefore to blame. Either we lack the resolve to do what needs to be done, or the ability to determine what needs to be done or, most fundamentally, the will to determine and to do what needs to be done." Hence follow the interminable "great debates" on national purpose, the wrangles on foreign policy and, ultimately, the ascription of frustration and discomfort to "reluctance to take up our role as leaders of the Western world."

It may be significant that the United States does not actually engage in aggression against the perceived "conspiracy" (though the danger is ever present, of course, that the truculence of verbalized aggressive feelings be translated into action). Instead, and for whatever causes—reasonable fear of the awful consequences is part of it, of course—hostility feelings are in large measure introjected, only to reappear on the surface of national consciousness in the amply described syndrome of national *malaise*. But prudence and reasonableness may account for the United States's not lightly entering into thermonuclear conflict. The question remains why a decision that is thought—rightly, of course—to be reasonable and prudent is nevertheless experienced as highly dissatisfying and frustrating. Is it true, after all, that the United States is motivated by some aggressive drive (whose true name is either "capitalism," or "imperialism," or the like simple category) which is superficially overlaid by peacefulness and rationality? I would be the last one to dissimulate the rapacity of the United States, e.g., within Latin America during the last hundred years. But that does not quite explain away the basic American dispositions towards peace and democracy to which Americans often pay much more than lip service. In any event, this is obviously an oversimple hypothesis. The answer is clearly a much more elaborate one.

But first let me remark that this analysis so far coincides in broad outline with David Riesman's in what pertains to the reality and the danger of diplomatic frustration in the American consciousness. But whereas he recommends the "occupational therapy" of channeling the frustration into constructive activities, I am skeptical of the value of this except as a palliative. As I shall remark below, the frustration should be dissipated at the source by transmuting it into the motive power for increased self- and other-consciousness. In any event, the difficulty with the popular self-diagnosis of the American mind is that, as often happens, there is enough truth in it to serve as a potent source of resistance to analysis and insight.

Let us, then, apply ourselves to this proffered diagnosis, to this apparent "reluctance" to discharge the duties of Western leadership. It yields a colorable image because it is true that although only the United States was capable of it, having survived World War II alone among Western nations without major war wounds, it long hesitated to commit itself to a complex system of international relations such as was required for the survival of European civilization even apart from the question whether or not actual military danger threatened it from the East. The Marshall Plan, for instance, was presented to, and perceived by, the American people as a gesture of friendship and charity (or else as a business-like operation of pragmatic altruism) rather than as the stroke of statesmanship and *political* wisdom it really was. The immediate reasons for this hesitation are not far to seek: the United States thought that even in the second half of the twentieth century some form of isolationism might be viable, if no longer behind the moats of two oceans which technology had shrunk to pond size, at least behind the curtain of secrecy afforded by atomic monopoly. But why did the United States, despite expert scientific assurance that atomic monopoly could not be long maintained, nevertheless seize upon it as the last basis of isolationism? (Note, incidentally, a similar inability today to face the fact that it is only a matter of time before membership in the nuclear club is affordable by at least half the nations of the world.) Evidently, only a strong prior attachment to isolationism could make it appear possible under such circumstances: even Wendell Willkie's mild internationalism did not survive except in the vestigial concept of "satellite" nations. But when the hope of atomic isolationism, as vain as it was short-lived, was shattered first by Russia's matching of nuclear fission, then by her thermonuclear lead, and latterly by her prowess in rocketry, the United States lost no time in building up, during Dulles' long tenure, an imposing edifice of international alliances, commitments and roles.

Thus, if the United States nevertheless fails to experience comfort and satisfaction it is certainly not because it can truthfully accuse itself of having shrunk from taking the initiative to do as required, nor because it has lacked the intellectual, diplomatic, economic and physical ability to do whatever its safety required it to do. Indeed, the ambiguity of the diagnosis of "reluctance to assume the role of Western leadership" is made especially clear when we note the relish and zeal with which the American people and the American government discharge their international role. Americans *enjoy* being the leaders of the West and the mightiest world power: as well they might, since they do so, on the whole, within the boundaries of international justice, democracy, and respect for human values. The idea that the United States should return to a secondary position among Western nations is, to Americans, simply inconceivable, and no one has proposed it even in jest: even the contemporary advocates of conscious isolationism base their arguments upon the weakness of the Allies and the ability of the United States to fight alone if need be.

Therefore, we must distinguish. The United States was reluctant to abandon *isolationism* in favor of *collective security*. That in order to obtain the latter it was necessary to lead the alliance was neither distasteful nor is it now relevant, except insofar as it may serve as a handy rationalization of the fact that the best security policy does not somehow produce security feelings. If so, it seems clear that the experience of insecurity is not caused by failure to achieve political security but, on the contrary, precisely by the achievement of political security or, more specifically, by the achievement of the type of political security that under the circumstances reason recommends as the best possible sort. The root of the inner conflict, therefore, according to this analysis, is that the United States can find security today only collectively rather than in isolation. Collective security, therefore, is an ambivalent object. It is desired insofar as it is rationally viewed as the only possible sort at present. It is hateful insofar as it produces an unaccountable feeling of acute discomfort.

But this feeling is unaccountable only if it is not faced up to and broken down by inquiry. It is not inane to suggest that if collective security is distasteful to Americans it is because it is *collective* and not because it is *security;* that is, because it requires them to enter into close international human relations and especially because of the implied consequent loss of independence. The American people dimly and instinctively perceive that collective security, even granted their peculiar position as leaders (indeed, perhaps all the more so because of that position, since their leadership must be exercised democratically and not despotically), requires them to give up a measure of self-determination and sovereignty, just as it requires them to give up a measure of the highly valued ideals of self-reliance and independence. Little wonder, then, if they are inclined to feel that their foreign policy is disappointingly unsuccessful and cause for self-recrimination, even when the Russians, who should know, quite evidently find it disappointingly otherwise. And so, the apparent reluctance to face up to the task and the consequent experience of discomfort are much more than the remnant of Nineteenth Century isolationism. They are manifestations of a new, updated form of isolationism which, in uneasy compromise, permits outward international participation (because it is indispensable for security) while preserving inner isolation (because it is necessary for the continuity and integration of the national personality).

If the United States cannot comfortably occupy the central position among Western countries the reason has to do with its original marginal relation to European culture. Though the proportion between individual and society can be misapplied, it may be useful to remember that the American culture was generated under the sign of parental rejection, and some have

explained as a normal reaction thereto the American idealization of self-sufficiency and self-reliance. The early American society adapted to cultural severance by accepting it *à outrance*,
that is, by investing it with social value. Note, for instance, in
the quotation inscribed on the base of the Statue of Liberty the
ambivalent feelings towards European "refuse" and the evident satisfaction with the ability of the United States to re-
value what Europe has rejected. This is but part of a trend
towards national encapsulation by developing a culture in
which lack of relation to the outside, and its temporal ana-
logue, namely, lack of relation to the past, shall be counted
among the highest values. Hence, for instance, the attraction
of the new and of the home-grown among Americans.

　This is not the place to inquire how this national character
emerged during the first century and a half after the early
settlements nor how it reached maturity during the second
quarter of the Nineteenth Century. The relevant point here is
that the very national character that accounts for the motive
force behind the development of American greatness and
power is fast becoming a liability. For it is becoming the cause
of pain. Pain is, of course, physiologically and psychologically
a danger sign: perhaps it is so culturally as well.

　It is generally recognized that isolationism is a present
impossibility: the American sense of reality is strong enough to
see this. But it would be unrealistic to think that isolationism in
the military order is all that must be transcended: in this consisted Dulles' myopia. National security is no longer a simple
military matter. There was a time when isolated survival being
possible, military defense from outer aggression sufficed for
security, and economic, social and political matters could be
considered "purely internal affairs." Today, however, one cannot wish a plague on both your houses, because modern political epidemics are universal. Or, to vary the metaphor, since
science, population growth, and political consciousness have
shrunk the world to a fraction of its former size, we are now all
together in the same cosmic boat, and either we all survive or
none. More accurately, if national security has become essentially dependent upon international relationships, then *all*
human affairs and, specifically, all economic, social and politi-

cal matters have become essentially collective affairs. But why
should the United States have been sufficiently realistic and
reasonable to give up isolationism, but also sufficiently blind
and inflexible not to give it up completely? The answer is not
simply that cultural habits and social institutions change slowly
and die hard. It is more important to observe that the compromise formation I have described permits outward change to
mask inner immobility. If so, we can now define the basic
etiology created by the disparity between environmental needs
merely outwardly met and the inner dispositions of the American psyche, which may account for the symptoms of discomfort and frustration from which we took our clues originally.
Evidently, it is the characteriological inadequacy to relate to
others and, more specifically, the difficulty in perceiving others
empathically and to facilitate the other's empathic perception
of the United States. Translated into less abstract terms, the
defense mechanism I am trying to describe is the transmuta-
tion of isolationism into ethnocentricity. What is the difference? The isolationist lives alone and likes it, and can get away
with it partly because it is intrinsically possible and partly
because he understands others and therefore is able to avoid
trouble with them, thus enhancing the feasibility of his soli-
tude. The ethnocentric, if he is an isolationist who could no
longer get away with it, lives with others and hates it, and
because he cannot understand others he gets into trouble with
them and thus prejudices the viability of the very society he
needs. In other words, the American problem can be defined
as unbelief in the *total* impossibility of isolationism. I know
that Americans think they have overcome isolationism: in fact,
they do not realize by half how impossible isolationism really
is.

If it is true, as I suggest, that the fundamental American
inadequacy is an inability to *understand* the world, I need
hardly elaborate upon the danger presented by American national and international policies if they are guided by ethnocentric cultural forms. If the United States lacks empathic ability it will find it difficult to realize how transparent its feelings
and intentions can become to others. It is otherwise unintelligi-

ble, for instance, how American legislators will freely express themselves and not only ignore the fact that they will be reported throughout the world, but even object to their being heeded by the world, on the grounds that they do not speak for the executive power: they really believe, apparently, that what they state in chamber or committee room is a purely private matter for exclusive consumption within the borders of the United States. Note, by way of contrast, the perceptiveness of those newspaper editors—American, Japanese and Canadian—in having recently judged that their publication of *Pogo* was not a purely domestic affair. Lack of empathic ability also means that the United States will judge and evaluate others only upon the assumption that others are like themselves. Consequently, the American projection of foreign behavior, both as to allies and as to enemies, is often disastrously mistaken.

Note, for instance, when popular opinion feels that "we have all the good will in the world and we get nowhere, therefore the *impasse* is in no way of our own making," that the mistake in perception due to numbed empathy is twofold. First, note the ambiguity in having "all the good will in the world." It is easy to glide from "we have all the good will required of us" to "we have all the good will that is available." Besides, it is difficult for either of these conditions to be satisfied, and even more uncertain for either to be ascertained. To assume even the first, if not the second, is to run the risk henceforth to reason circularly, if not paranoidally. Second, and more important: the *impasse* in no event can be unilaterally determined. Even with all the good will in the world— indeed, all the more easily with *all* the good will in the world —one's perception of hostile behavior can be distorted precisely because it is truly hostile: it is, after all, much easier to understand one's friends than one's enemies. The point, however, is that to filter our perceptions of the other through the coloring experience of disappointment at the ineffectiveness of our good will is one of the most powerful biases we can permit ourselves: it is exactly what we popularly call bitterness and cynicism.

I trust it is scarcely necessary to remark that no nation is capable of perfect empathy or wholly devoid of ethnocentric-

ity: that is why international misunderstandings even when
unilaterally begun quickly become bilaterally compounded.
But there is a difference other than in degree between American and other ethnocentricities. That of other countries tends
to be shaped by ignorance, provincialism or even backwardness: primitive peoples, of course, are typically ethnocentric.
On occasion it may be due to a deliberately introduced communication bias. But these sorts are not usually built into the
national character and are, therefore, at least in principle, easy
to overcome, since they are not sanctioned by the basic social
values. That is why even the Russians, for all their ignorance
and prejudice about the United States, can understand (e.g.
can predict) American behavior with, on the whole, rather
remarkable accuracy, even when the categories in which they
couch that understanding are contrived and inadequate.

May I remark, while on the subject, that the American
inability to understand Canada specifically is proverbial in this
country. Curiously, however, we reveal our own bias when
we misconceptualize our insight into American behavior in
terms of: "Americans don't know enough about Canada." First,
we seem faintly to imply that there is something *unfair* and
unrequiting in American empathetic deficiency, which is
patent, sulky nonsense. What is required, in any event, is not
knowledge, but understanding. That is why I find it amusing
whenever enterprising professional debunkers and truth-
mongers in Canada open-mindedly set out to prove that the
Canadian complaint is unfounded because *we* know just as
little about the United States. Impartially conducted scientific
surveys may well prove something about our education, our
prejudices, our biases and our attitudes. For all that, we *do*
understand the United States remarkably well. Indeed, under
the circumstances we do so *disturbingly* well, for it may be
that the development of our national character is hampered by
a too vivid background of consciousness of the American way
against which we must fashion our own values, habits and
culture.

Be that as it may, the distinction between knowledge and
understanding is important. It explains, for instance, why lack
of empathy is found not only in the masses but also among the

intellectuals. It is surely not typical, but nevertheless symbolic, that a well-known and justly respected American sociologist recently wrote: "I cannot conceive of myself acting as Castro acted and acts . . . I understand politics through myself—what I would do, what I would feel, what I might conceivably do, what I might conceivably feel. What Lenin did I could not do, nor what Castro. . . ." A country where such a statement by a sociologist, of all people, echoes the national feeling, could not possibly have begun to understand the world revolution of the Twentieth Century even though, living within it, it is experiencing its effects too closely and too well.

Granted the correctness of the foregoing analysis, dare we hope that American leadership shall not fail us in the end? The answer, for my part, is a qualified yes. It depends on whether Americans take advantage of certain character reserves which, as I believe, they possess, and which we must now proceed to isolate.

Consider that paradigm of the American view of the Second World War in Europe, William L. Shirer's *The Rise and Fall of the Third Reich*. Shirer's appreciation is of course, vastly more elaborate and factually competent than that of the ordinary American, but for all its wealth of knowledge and all its documented accuracy it yields a fundamentally untruthful view of Nazi Germany. I trust I need not protest that I do not myself diverge significantly from Shirer's or the average American's own moral conclusion about the evil of Nazism and Hitler's guilt of the crimes of tyranny, murder, torture and genocide: indeed, my judgment is probably harsher than theirs in what concerns Germany's participation in Nazism and complicity with Hitler. But I would maintain that Nazism is historically, culturally and *anthropologically* intelligible, whereas Shirer's recurrent expression is one of disbelief, amazement, and wonder. He is unable to empathize with Nazi Germany. Why? Because Nazi Germany was evil, and he finds it impossible to empathize with evil.

And yet, should one not empathize with evil if one is to understand it as, indeed, one must? Should not he who under-

stands evil, that is, he who is truly aware of the evil of evil, of
its human reality no less than of its enormity, be in the proper
position to evaluate it reasonably rather than to become distracted, fascinated, hypnotized by it? Like Shirer's, the average
American's understanding of the Nazi evil is untruthful because evil scandalizes him. I suggest, on the contrary, that if
one wishes to understand, for instance, what truly happened in
Nazi Germany one's moral judgment thereof, however correct,
is not the relevant category in which to cast one's thought. For
the moral conclusions we may reach, though indispensable for
our own self-government, our own self-understanding and our
own self-respect, are *irrelevant* to our understanding of, our re-
lating to and our respect towards, the other. Though it is true
that human behavior, individual or social, does not lie beyond
good and evil, it is also true that human behavior is not made to
be what it is *because* it is good or evil. On the contrary, it is
because it is what it is that it can be evaluated as good or evil.

Why should Americans be scandalized by evil? Why
should they find it so difficult to empathize with? The ethnocentricity previously described does not of itself account for
this. In fact, let us recall that if any nation has ever been fully,
consciously and purposively ethnocentric none was more so
than Nazi Germany, where ethnocentricity became a political
philosophy. Yet, her ethnocentricity did not appreciably blunt
her empathic capacity: Hitler's political and diplomatic genius
cannot be gainsaid. Nor did it produce any noticeable inner
conflict: even today, after Germany's guilt has been brought
home to her, the only inner conflict, reportedly, is between the
older and the younger generation as they disagree—whether
wholesomely or not is not yet clear—as to their evaluation of
the Nazi past. I suggest that by itself American ethnocentricity
would neither produce national frustration nor be pragmatically inadequate. Trouble arises because of an inopportune
coincidence, as it were, of ethnocentricity and moral sense. For
Americans are much too committed to a humanistic morality
(of obviously not too remote Judaeo-Christian provenance) to
allow their ethnocentricity to generate any sort of master-race
complex. Americans sometimes talk, especially when they face
a hostile interlocutor, as if they thought otherwise. But when it

comes to doing, as everyone knows (fortunately, even the Russians know it), their good nature gets the better of the inner dialectic of their conceptualizations. In other words, just as there can be a non-ethnocentric Machiavellianism, such as the traditional one of the early modern world, and an ethnocentric Machiavellianism, such as Nazi Germany's, there is also a non-Machiavellian ethnocentricity, such as afflicts the United States today. The fact that this ethnocentricity is non-Machiavellian does not make it hazardless. It may, on the other hand, make it superable.

The reason is not far to seek why American ethnocentricity should be non-Machiavellian, that is, why the American inability to *empathize* does not imply the least inability to *sympathize*. It is not unrelated to history. For the American alienation from the Old World had more than one edge: by cutting themselves off from European culture in order to develop independently, the Americans also cut themselves off from the accelerating decay in European political morality. The United States does not have a Non-Conformist origin for nothing. Particularly in what pertains to fidelity to the sense of right and wrong, the United States has preserved all that is best in the faith of the Puritans and the Quakers. It remains as true as it is trite that the ideals of freedom for all, religious toleration, political pluralism and indeed, all the social and political values of the ideals of an ever traduced Christian humanism are deeply imbedded in the fabric of American culture.

It would be cynical, however, to interpret the conflict in question, a sort of struggle between ego needs and super-ego imperatives, in such terms as: "the trouble with us is that we aren't tough-minded enough," as if callousness were the proper corrective for a tender conscience. Nor should one wryly conclude that it is the American people's bad luck that their chance to sin came only when sin could no longer be committed in comfort. Yet there is some truth in both these possible reactions. If Great Britain, for instance, made Machiavellianism pay in the Seventeenth Century, or Germany in the Eighteenth, or France in the Nineteenth, the reason is that theirs flourished at the right time, namely, when it could exist in the vacuum left by the disintegration of medieval Christianity. But as a secular humanist morality (a crypto-resurgence of Christianity, as I maintain) came into being at the end of the Nineteenth Century—Marx had been its Socrates—Machiavellianism gradually became impossible, and Europe has been sufficiently realistic to behave accordingly. Thus, Great Britain has given it up, on the whole, rather graciously; Italy quite unconsciously; France, however, only painfully; and Germany only indecisively and inchoately. In this view, incidentally, Hitler's Machiavellianism was essentially anachronistic. Hitler wanted Europe to revert to the Eighteenth Century pattern of peace, diplomacy, war and politics. He was, therefore, quite out of touch with the reality of the times: therein, of course, his "madness." There is, therefore, a time when one can get away with murder and a time when one cannot. The United States would do well even on pragmatic grounds not to entertain the thought of turning history backwards in time. Nor can it enter into relations with a Europe and a world which no longer exist.

There is also truth in the idea that strength of character must be trained and developed by the United States. But the wrong way to develop the competence, tough-mindedness and "Spartan qualities"—which Kennedy, as David Riesman points out, dangerously and demagogically prescribes—is to presume to improve the inadequacies of ethnocentricity by attempting a Machiavellianism that Americans are too spiritually wise and too morally innocent to try successfully or more strenuously than with half a heart. The failure of Machiavellian policies in Laos, in Cuba and in the Russian stratosphere show that the Americans are much too moral a people successfully to adopt the dispositions of immorality as an acknowledged way of life.

It is, therefore, in that weakness, in their inability to fight fire with fire, as Professor Roger Fisher has so eloquently pointed out, that lies in reserve the great character strength of the United States. There is enough good will—even if it is not all the good will in the world—and enough moral habituation in the American people to inspire a not unreasonable confidence in the Western world that if Americans are given enough time and if they can avoid being tripped up by their own smartness, they will eventually do the right thing, even when the task is as Herculean as transcending the horizons of ethnocentricity.

The Americans, thus, have the spiritual resources required to reverse the naturally entropic course of political events. The tension set up by the opposition between their ethnocentricity and their ethical humanism may well provide the motive to understand themselves and the world. Other than possible lack of time, the great obstacle in the way of achieving this is the temptation to solve the problem easily and definitively. The tension might become so unbearable that the United States might in despair convince itself not only of the feasibility but also of the morality of preventive war. In this respect I must say I am a little concerned with the possibility that my fellow Catholics in the United States, who, as of right, have so much to contribute to the establishment of Christian humanism and to the emergence of an international civilization, might instead play the same rather regrettable role they have played in recent years: so few of them seem to escape religious pragmatism.

Despite official reassurances (and, presumably, present intentions), it is not yet quite clear that the United States has rejected this temptation so decisively that one can discount the possibility of its being seduced by its charms at a later date. Too many agencies are always ready to do the devil's work. I cannot forget, for instance, a certain paranoidal and Goebbelish news program that comes to Americans five evenings weekly over a major radio network whose constant message, year in, year out, is but "total victory" over Communism. They would prefer it peacefully, of course—if possible. Unfortunately, total victory might not only be a morally reprehensible policy, it might also be attainable against opposition only by total war.

The critical time when this key question will be decided is not too far off. For the reasons adduced I am confident that the Americans will reach the only conclusion consistent with both reason and morality. If so, they shall have reached the point at which with increased national self-consciousness the impossibility of nationalism shall be recognized, and with increased realization that humanism implies the unity of the human race, ethnocentricity shall, perhaps, rapidly disappear among them. Thus they shall be in a position to lead the human race towards the first world-wide civilization of mankind as such. It is in that sense and with those qualifications that we in the Western world can say that time is not on Russia's but on ours and on the American side.

A. J. Muste

Politics on the Other Side of Despair*

In the address in which he announced his decision to resume
atmospheric testing, President Kennedy again reminded us, as
we have so often been reminded on the highest and most
respectable authority, that war must be eliminated or it will
eliminate mankind. A series of recent events, not least that
decision itself, have, I submit, provided sobering and dramatic
evidence that the problem of war cannot be solved in the
context of the assumptions and attitudes which govern human
thinking and behavior today on both sides of the Iron Curtain.
It cannot be solved within the existing economic and political
structures, for these structures would undergo vast changes if
war were actually abolished. And it cannot be solved by means
of the instruments now at hand and the procedures which are
being employed to stave off war.

"No American President," Mr. Kennedy asserted, "responsible for the freedom and the safety of so many people, could
in good faith make any other decision." Why not?

In the first place, the military authorities had told him that
military security required resumption of testing. No civilian
head of a modern state (whether Kennedy, Khrushchev, or
any other) can make any other decision when the military tell
him he will be treasonable to the state if he does not add this
new factor to its safety—unless he is prepared to discard the
whole concept of military security and deterrence which he
accepted as the basis of his functioning as chief of state and
head of the armed forces. In that case he can rouse the nation
out of apathy by resigning.

It will be more accurate if instead of speaking of the
"military" we refer to the vast and complicated machine of

* April, 1962.

military technology, the research, experimentation, development, production, incessant "improvement." This machine operates largely by its own laws. It has developed a tremendous dynamism. A head of state who operates with this machine cannot command it or dictate to it. At a critical point it comes up with the answer. He accepts its answer (unless he is ready to discard the machine) and then provides the political and other rationalizations for his, i.e., the technology's, decision.

Secondly, the President pointed out that he had no alternative, not because the Russians were now superior but because if the United States did not resume testing and the Soviet government then staged another series of tests, the Soviets might then be stronger or appear to be stronger, and this was a development the United States could not tolerate. In his column for March 6th, Walter Lippmann pointed out that under the doctrine that "security requires superiority, no test ban treaty is possible. The deadlock is complete. If the Soviet Union accepts the kind of agreement, with elaborate inspection and control, which the U.S. wants, it gives up the possibility of equalling or surpassing the U.S. It accepts permanent nuclear inferiority. If the U.S. accepts the Soviet version of a treaty with inadequate inspection, the Soviets may secretly put on another series of tests and the U.S. is then risking being put into the status of nuclear inferiority." As Lippmann points out, there is nothing negotiable here. The hope of a test ban is, for this period, gone. My only difference with him is that in my opinion there never was any hope of such a ban—unless, of course, testing no longer has *any* military value—and that ever since Hiroshima the United States has in effect demanded superiority and Stalin and his successors have in effect refused to concede it.

A third reason why Kennedy had no alternative was vividly stated by James Reston, head of the Washington bureau of the New York *Times*, in one of his agitated columns commenting on the decision. In one column, he sarcastically suggested that the two K's have a "summit meeting" in a well-guarded cave on Christmas Island so that they could watch a few H-bomb explosions and virtually talk and test at the same hour or minute. In his March 4th column, written in a more sober vein, Reston agrees with Lippmann that "the new U.S. tests are designed to restore the orginal margin of our lead and this, of course, implies a policy of permanent U.S. military superiority, which Khrushchev is not likely to accept if he can avoid it." But in his column for March 7th, Reston defines the dilemma from another angle and declares that "the President had to decide, not on the basis of unquestioned facts but on informed guesses whether to assume the worst of Soviet motives or the best, and in the end he decided that he had to assume the worst. . . . If he had assumed the best about Soviet motives and been wrong, the security of the Republic could have been at stake. But if he assumed the worst at least he was prepared to meet his constitutional responsibility to defend and preserve the nation." Reston would probably acknowledge that Khrushchev similarly holds that it is advisable to assume the worst about American motivations, since if he assumed the best and guessed wrong the security of the Soviet Union would be at stake.

Talk and Test
In a situation which disturbs them profoundly, many citizens take comfort from two things. One is the fact that the President pledges not to go through with the atmospheric tests if before the end of April the Soviet government signs the kind of test-ban agreement that will satisfy us. We have seen that this is exactly what the Soviet government "cannot" do without acquiescing in nuclear inferiority. Moreover, the President is in effect issuing an ultimatum, setting a deadline, and how often the United States government has told the Soviet government that it cannot and will not negotiate under such conditions.

The second source of tempered comfort is that talks about a test ban and disarmament are going to continue. There is, of course, a sense in which it is better for nations to keep on talking than to drop bombs, but it is to our peril that we keep on ignoring the fact that it is behind the smoke-screen of talking that the war preparations go on. If the talking were eliminated and governments not only prepared steadily for war but admitted that this was what they were doing, people would either submit like apathetic slaves in a totalitarian or garrison state or they would revolt. But apathetic slaves who see no future cannot serve the purposes of a modern state. Therefore, "even Communist countries," as the saying goes, have "to arm to parley." The question which is now more sharply posed than ever for those who have grave doubts about the validity of deterrence or have in fact rejected it as the basis of national policy, who are aware of the danger of accidental war and which is posed, of course, for all pacifists and believers in nonviolence is this: What hope is there if we proceed with the same methods that have essentially been used since 1910, let us say; what reason do we have to believe that the result will be any different than it has been hitherto?

I have watched the process of combined war-making and peace-making, or peace-talking and war preparation, of power-struggles, arms races, the development of military technology, and on the other hand of diplomacy, Leagues of Nations, pacts renouncing war, and so on, for half a century. World War I did come, although Norman Angell had proved that it couldn't happen since it would not pay economically. World War II also came, despite the immense revulsion against war which followed the first World War. There was no such visceral revulsion against war after 1945. There was no time before the Cold War set in. Perhaps modern men are not capable any more of such natural revulsion against large-scale, highly organized violence. In any event, military technology has taken a leap greater than all previous advances in civilized history put together. With the splitting of the atom, it has taken off into space, so to speak. It is not stopping, not even slowing down. There is more to come: control of climate, missile bases on the moon (according to General Putt), armed satellites. The means and forces we have applied all these decades have not stopped this development. What smallest reason is there to believe that these means and forces will stop the development now that it has attained an unprecedented dynamism and is so much farther down the slippery slide than ever before?

It is impossible in the space at our disposal to deal even sketchily with the various devices to which non-pacifists and pacifists resort in the desire to be practical and realistic, to evade the drastic choice, the revolutionary act. I can only list some elements in the response which it seems to me should be made to the situation.

1. We should stop being good-natured, easy-going optimists. We have to face and do all we can to get our fellows to face the stark reality of our situation. World War I *did* happen, so did World War II. And *we are doomed,* World War III will come, unless this generation by the grace of God finds new methods, rallies new forces, to prevent it.

2. We must abandon our fascination with, our worship of the word, of talk, of negotiations, which do not correspond to the realities, which are contradicted by the facts. When the arms race is speeded up while governments talk—even the United Nations talks—about stopping it, or slowing it down, we have to see steadfastly that the arms race is real, the bombs, the germ warfare arsenals are real. The rest is unreal, illusion, salve on a cancer.

3. We have to address ourselves resolutely to finding a fresh approach, calling forth new forces for peace. One factor in this process is to stop thinking that the basic fact in modern life is the *conflict pattern*—conflict of states, systems, ideologies, and to see that the handle by which to take hold of the situation is the *pattern of entrapment.* Kennedy and Khrushchev, the United States and the Soviet Union, the West and the East, are trapped by the runaway military technology which they no longer control, trapped by all the attitudes and habits of thinking which may have been applicable in the pre-nuclear age but are not any more.

There is no space to elaborate the point but it should be noted nevertheless that one of the most serious obstacles to rational thinking and policy in the United States is the notion that Communism is a cancer in a society far away, from which the West, even the world, is completely separated. The fact is that Communism, in so far as it is a malady, is a product of Western civilization. The malady afflicts the body of which we are all a part. If the Communists tried to develop a new breed of Communist or Soviet man, it is now clear that they did not succeed, and we do not constitute a peculiar breed either. Underneath surface appearances, societies of East and West and mankind as a whole confront the same problems.

The danger now is not that the Soviet Union will perpetrate a Pearl Harbor on the United States or *vice versa*. The danger is that a global Pearl Harbor, a gruesome nuclear or CBR surprise attack will overtake mankind. The task, basically, is not for the United States to liberate peoples from Russia, or for Russia to liberate peoples from United States imperialism, but for each country to liberate itself and thus help liberate the other and mankind. This has nothing to do with being "soft on Communism," which bothers many Americans, or being "soft on imperialism," which bothers the Stalinists and the Chinese so grievously. And it forbids the assumption that we have a peace bloc (us and our allies) and a war bloc (the enemy, of course). This also is an aspect of Cold War thinking, and diverts attention from the doom which hangs over them all, us all!

They Won't Buy Unilateralism

4. Another aspect of the needed fresh approach is the recognition that if indeed deterrence is no longer to be relied on, then the break with war preparation in this period of history has to be unconditional and the way to disarmament is the unilateralist way. A nation cannot be both in the arms race and not in it, any more than a woman can be partly pregnant and partly not. In a period when "negotiation," what a critic of Sir Stephen King-Hall called "positive *international* action" takes place in the context of an arms race and the other elements we have noted, King-Hall is right in calling for "positive *national* action," the unilateral break which might once again make genuine negotiation, i.e., honest confrontation, possible.

I do not for a moment suggest that this is a simple matter. There is great need at this juncture of material which spells out what steps would and could be taken by a nation which made the basic decision to pull out of the arms race. But that decision—to stay in or get out—is the one which every power faces now and *in fact answers one way or the other*. Thus when people talk about unilateral "initiative" today, the crucial question is whether this means initiatives which are first steps in *executing* a decision to disarm unilaterally or steps which evade or postpone that decision.

In the discussion about unilateralism we are now at a very interesting point. Almost invariably the clinching argument of those who will discuss but not accept unilateralism is: "The American people won't buy it"—often the implied reasoning is: "So what if it is the prudent and the right course to take?" What are we expected to do with this argument? Are the American people more likely to buy the remedy if we stop offering it? Has what they have been willing to buy brought security? Can any one not a believer in deterrence seriously reflect on what at the moment the American people *are* willing to buy and then assert that this is enough to avert doom?

The other side of the contemporary coin is that unilateralism is being discussed with increasing frequency. I have recently been told, in fact, by a very reliable informant that the RAND Corporation people privately say that unilateral disarmament is the one viable, intellectually respectable alternative to present policy. The same informant asserts that the White House even is open to suggestions for "unilateral initiatives." This sort of thing is inevitable now. For each step in the arms race and the developing political situation makes it clearer what the drastic choice is: Disarm or Perish—i.e., break with war unconditionally or perish. The price of survival is *not* superiority in arms but scuttling arms, somehow getting rid of the incubus. This is the one very substantial hopeful aspect of our time. The reality, the stubborn, ineradicable fact, is and will be that mankind, each people, must make this choice. This will become steadily clearer. The *fact* cannot be argued or wished away. It is on the side of the unilateralist. No one can confidently prophesy whether a nation or the decisive elements in it will recognize the fact *in time* and act upon that recognition, but it is certain that survival cannot be had at a lesser price.

The Problem of Morality and Faith

5. There is one other aspect of a sound approach which must be mentioned. A group of brilliant English Roman Catholic social scientists and teachers of philosophy have recently issued a book, *Nuclear Weapons and Christian Conscience,* in which they advocate unilateralism, not on pacifist grounds of objection to the use of force by the state, but on the basis of the traditional Roman Catholic doctrine of the nature of the state and the "just war." The book deserves careful reading by all students of contemporary problems, no matter what their views, among other reasons because the editor, Walter Stein, of the University of Leeds, in his own chapters presents such a tough criticism of the unilateralist position itself. This is partly because, as might be expected from a Roman Catholic intellectual, he takes very seriously the possibility of Communist subjugation or infiltration. Thus he characterizes the position of "nuclear deterrence" as an absurdity. "Prudence itself cannot tolerate a posture so inadequate even in purely military terms, so impotent in the ideological plane, and so recklessly intemperate in its accepted risks." But he then asserts that unilateral disarmament is also absurd for "unilateral disarmament could hardly fail to result in a Communist domination." (At this point he is attempting to state the case "on purely expediential grounds, assuming no new psychological and spiritual factors enter into the equation." My impression is that he understates the case that can be made for unilateralism on prudential grounds but I refrain from elaborating on that point here because unilateralists do need to face unflinchingly the possible risks involved in their position.)

Stein concludes, therefore, that "each case establishes the absurdity of the other; so that neither can establish the expediency of its own." Accordingly, "in the end it is not by argument or counter-argument that the question will be decided." Not merely a "thought-barrier" needs to be broken through but "barriers of the spirit." Quoting a poet whom he does not identify, "Where does one go from a world of insanity? / Somewhere on the other side of despair."

Pointing out that man's ability to calculate the results of his actions in relation to social and political issues is in fact very limited, Stein looks to moral commitment and decision and to religious faith (not necessarily conceived in terms of ecclesiastical dogma) as the element which resolves the fearful dilemma of expediency and creates new possibilities also in the political field. Here we are faced today by the general denigration of moral considerations, a sort of "radio-active decay of all values," and by an attitude which Christian theologians have unfortunately done much to develop, a theory that in effect gives one sphere to power (politics) and another to morality and faith. There results, as Stein points out, "the assumption that morality is not enough, that the morally right course must be shown to coincide (very fortunately) with a balance of foreseeable advantages—or morality is in fact altogether discounted, the better to establish the 'realism' of this sort of thinking."

Pacifists and others who have abandoned reliance on deterrence are also in very many instances the captives of this way of thinking. They shy away from a "merely moral" appeal. They want above all to be "realistic" and make "practical" proposals. But, in the first place, what is to be done in a situation such as already described, where each position conclusively "establishes the absurdity of the other"? More importantly, it is not possible to arrive by way of a calculus of expediencies at a moral standard, at a "value" to live by and if need be die for. It is by way of a moral commitment, of setting a limit beyond which one will not perpetrate atrocities and deface the human image, or the image of God in man, that new possibilities emerge in politics. In Buber's familiar phrase "the plow-share of the normative principle," which in the final analysis is love, must be driven "into the hard soil of political reality." I suggest that so far from being apologetic about the appeal to morality, we should largely concentrate on it. Certainly we have no right to say that the American people are incapable of moral revulsion against the idea of mass murder of another people when we will not even try to bring the issue before them. Instead we begin with the despairing and insulting assumption that nothing will turn their stomachs. It seems to me that there is a grave challenge here to those Christian theologians who in growing numbers declare in private papers or journals and books with limited circulation that the nation may never *use* the weapons of mass destruction but who do not draw the conclusion that this is academic verbiage and not a moral deliverance unless the production of these weapons is stopped *now* and unless the government and the masses are incessantly told by Christian teachers that the use and hence the production of these weapons is forbidden by the Law and the Gospel.

Finally, all of us—pacifists, Christians, humanitarians, social scientists—who no longer have faith in deterrence, are habitually remiss in that we ourselves lack faith in God or man, in the potency of love, in the alternative of nonviolence. To cite one instance, there is the case of the deeply troubled Christian theologian who hopes that if the bomb is dropped— i.e., if we drop it—it will fall on him, since "the moral situation will be intolerable." Yet he and many others are unable to call men to faith in breaking with war preparation and embarking on a venture in "massive reconciliation" and nonviolence. They dare not sound forth the promise that "the Gates of Hell shall not prevail" if the Church will stop blessing or condoning "massacre of the innocents in defense of the things of God." But these theologians of little faith have their counterparts in other circles, including those who profess belief in nonviolent revolution.

This takes place in a time when the American people desperately need a vision and faith, as all the nervous discussions about the "goals of American society" testify. They are told—President Kennedy did so at a Democratic fund-raising dinner soon after his tragic announcement of the resumption of nuclear tests—that they must look forward to at least two or three decades of arms rivalry, Cold War and the rest. No people can survive, much less flourish, in such an atmosphere devoid of hope and challenge. There must be something— something else to live *for*, not merely just live *with*. The politics which they are now offered can only be characterized as a politics of despair. They need a politics "on the other side of despair," a politics based on the conviction that another kind of society must and can be built. But only faith can engender faith. How shall the American people believe unless we believe much more firmly and joyously than we do in the alternative of nonviolence?

It is quite true that we can only dimly discern what the new society will be like. This has always been true in revolutionary periods. The future did not correspond to the blueprints if men ventured to make blueprints. This is as it should be because like Abraham and other men of faith, we do not want to stay in or go back to the City—which is all we are, alas, familiar with and which is doomed. This is the one temptation we must not succumb to. It is better to go out, not knowing whither we go, precisely because the city of peace and fraternity which we seek has yet to be built and must not be like what we now know and can readily describe.

Bertrand Russell

Three Statements*

Call from Brixton Prison

To all, in whatever country, who are still capable of sane thinking or human feeling:

Friends,

Along with valued colleagues I am to be silenced for a time —perhaps for ever, for who can tell how soon the great massacre will take place?

The populations of East and West, misled by stubborn governments in search of prestige and by corrupt official experts bent on retaining their posts, tamely acquiesce in policies which are almost certain to end in nuclear war.

There are supposed to be two sides, each professing to stand for a great cause. This is a delusion—Kennedy and Khrushchev, Adenauer and de Gaulle, Macmillan and Gaitskell are pursuing a common aim: the ending of human life.

You, your families, your friends and your countries are to be exterminated by the common decision of a few brutal but powerful men. To please these men, all the private affections, all the public hopes, all that has been achieved in art, and knowledge and thought and all that might be achieved hereafter is to be wiped out forever.

Our ruined lifeless planet will continue for countless ages to circle aimlessly round the sun unredeemed by the joys and loves, the occasional wisdom and the power to create beauty which have given value to human life.

It is for seeking to prevent this that we are in prison.

* October, 1961.

Statement in Court

If the court permits, I should like to make a short statement as to the reasons for my present course. This is my personal statement, but I hope that those who are accused of the same so-called crime will be in sympathy with what I have to say.

It was only step by step and with great reluctance that we were driven to nonviolent civil disobedience.

Ever since the bomb was dropped on Hiroshima on August 6th, 1945, I have been profoundly troubled by the danger of nuclear warfare. I began my attempts to warn people by entirely orthodox methods. I expressed my fears in a speech in the House of Lords three months after the bombs were dropped on Japan. I called together scientists of the highest eminence from all parts of the world and am now chairman of their periodic meetings. They issue wise and reasoned reports concerning nuclear warfare, its probable disastrous results, and ways of preventing its occurence. No newspaper notices these reports and they have no effect either on governments or on public opinion. The popular Press minimizes and ridicules the efforts of those working against nuclear warfare, and television, with rare exceptions, is closed to us. In recent months, one television company, and only one, offered me two minutes for general platitudes, but when I said I should wish to speak on Berlin the offer was withdrawn.

It has seemed to some of us that, in a country supposed to be a democracy, the public should know the probable consequences of present Great-Power policies in East and West. Patriotism and humanity alike urged us to seek some way of saving our country and the world. No one can desire the slaughter of our families, our friends, our compatriots, and a majority of the human race, in a contest in which there will be only vanquished and no victors. We feel it a profound and inescapable duty to make the facts known and thereby save at least a thousand million human lives. We cannot escape this duty by submitting to orders which, we are convinced, would not be issued if the likelihood and the horror of nuclear war were more generally understood.

The general ignorance is illustrated by a recent advertisement of a new factory to be established in Penzance which, it says, is "away from the bomb area" and "in the safest area in the country." Everyone who has studied the effect of H-bombs knows that there will be no place in Britain which will be a "safe area," and that, in a nuclear war, Cornishmen will perish along with Londoners. In our opinion, it is those who prevent such facts from being generally known who are the true criminals.

Nonviolent civil disobedience was forced upon us by the fact that it was more fully reported than other methods of making the facts known, and that caused people to ask what had induced us to adopt such a course of action. We who are here accused are prepared to suffer imprisonment because we believe that this is the most effective way of working for the salvation of our country and the world. If you condemn us you will be helping our cause, and therefore humanity.

While life remains to us, we will not cease to do what lies in our power to avert the greatest calamity that has ever threatened mankind.

Appeal for an International Resistance Movement

At any moment of any day the slightest miscalculation can bring nuclear war. Rockets are poised at a few minutes' notice. H-bombers are continually in the air, radar is totally unreliable. Radioactivity kills and maims our children. War is always imminent.

To use the vast scheme of mass murder, which is being prepared, nominally for our protection, but in fact for universal extermination, is a horror and an abomination. We call upon people everywhere to rise against this monstrous tyranny.

We call upon scientists to refuse work on nuclear weapons. We call upon workers to 'black' [boycott] all work connected with them and to use their industrial strength in the struggle for life. We will not tolerate the incineration of human beings because governments are occupied with idiotic matters of prestige.

Stephen King-Hall

Armies Are Now Obsolete

It seems wholly wrong to assume without any investigation that what may broadly be called military power is the *only* way in which defence can be made effective.

Nor should we be impressed or unduly influenced by the fact that from the earliest known times to the present day, physical force and weapons from the spear to the atom bomb have been the outward and visible signs of defence.

Victors' Position

Today it is generally recognized that a victorious war cannot be expected to pay a cash dividend. On the contrary, the plain facts emerging from two world wars is that after a short period of material suffering the vanquished emerge in a stronger economic position than that of the victors. The victors find themselves in the absurd position, for reasons which appear to be directly in their own interests, of having to finance the recovery of the vanquished and the more complete the physical losses of the enemy the more up-to-date is the new economy which rises from the ashes of defeat. (The late David Lloyd George told us that he had come to the conclusion that it was a great mistake to win a total military victory.)

An interesting and recent example on a small scale of this phenomenon is to be seen in the experience of the Kikuyu tribe in Kenya. The other tribes are saying with a deal of reason: "Look at the money and effort which are being expended on social services, rehabilitation, etc., for the Kikuyu. Is it necessary to stage a Mau Mau rebellion in order to receive all these good things?"

An honest answer would be: "Not necessarily, but it might be helpful."

There is another relatively new factor in history which must be taken into account.

We seem to have reached a stage in military evolution in which resistance, both passive and active, of a civilian population which refuses to acknowledge defeat even though its professional forces have been defeated or because it had no conventional forces to be defeated is a new factor in war.

Gandhi's passive resistance campaign in India, the German passive resistance which defeated the French in the Ruhr in the 1920's; the Sinn Fein nationally supported terrorist campaign; the Israel victory over the British mandatory administration; the Algerian struggle; the EOKA movement in Cyprus; the resistance movements against the Nazis, all belong to the new development.

It seems to be of significance that all these "civilian" resistances were part of ideological struggles and illustrated the truth of the saying that one can do most things with bayonnets except sit on them.

Tentative conclusions are as follows:

1. We aim to defend an *idea*.

2. There are some grounds for believing that an *idea* can prevail even when the opponents of the idea are physically superior and able to occupy the territory of those defending the *idea*.

3. In the modern world a military victory cannot produce an economic dividend. Still less can there be any profit in a military victory obtained by nuclear weapons.

Defense by Extermination

As mentioned above it is generally taken for granted that the basis of defence against aggression must be military force. We have however reached an unprecedented state of affairs in the evolution of destructive force through the invention of nuclear weapons.

They possess two characteristics which are novel.

The first is that their destructive capacity is so enormous that there is no practical physical means of defence against these weapons. This fact has been self-evident so far as the UK is concerned for several years but is now officially accepted.

The second novel characteristic of these weapons is that each time one of them is tested there is an addition to the pollution of the earth's surface and atmosphere.

Although the whole subject of fallout and the strontium risk is a matter of scientific controversy there is agreement that if tests were carried out over a long period on a large scale the human race would probably exterminate itself in preparing to defend itself.

The peculiar character of the nuclear weapon has given a very real meaning to the hallowed principle that all nations maintain defence forces for protection against aggression. In the pre-nuclear age it was always said that the purpose of armed forces was to prevent war and there was some truth in the statement, but the use of the word "deterrent" and the idea it expresses is a product of the nuclear age. It is insufficiently appreciated that our defence strategy is now based on the belief or hope that an *idea* will be effective and the *idea* can be summarized as follows:

"Nuclear war would be mutual suicide. It is not rational to be suicidal. You—the aggressor—can destroy us but your own destruction will be practically coincidental."

The facts lead to the conclusion that the time-honored theory that defence against physical aggression *must* take the form of physical means has worn very thin and needs to be regarded with much suspicion.

Moreover, experience has shown that aggression by the Communist States can also be political and since 1945 this form of aggression has been the most dangerous and insidious. Para. 27 of the White Paper on Defence writes about British responsibilities under the Bagdad Pact to *prevent Communist encroachment and infiltration* and goes on in the same paragraph to refer to *bomber squadrons based in Cyprus capable of delivering nuclear weapons*. The value of nuclear bombardments as a means of preventing (say) a Communist *coup d'état* in Persia is not clear to this writer.

Total Destruction

There is a theoretical or philosophic reason for doubting whether military force is any longer assuredly the best way to counter military aggression of a nuclear type. It is an established principle that to every form of attack there must exist a means of defence. We have now reached a stage in the development of the attack which enables total destruction to be achieved and as it is physically impossible to put the whole of a modern social system 100 feet underground and turn the United Kingdom into a nation of troglodytes it might seem at first glance that the principle has broken down.

But it seems to have been forgotten that the principle does not say that the answer to an attack must be of *the same order of things as the attack*.

If the answer to a nuclear attack creating total destruction is merely to enlarge the area of destruction, nothing of value has been achieved.

If, however, having reached the *ne plus ultra* of physical attack we are imaginative enough to realise that we have not simultaneously reached the frontiers of human thought we should have no difficulty in moving forward beyond the physical into the psychological.

The Drift to Disaster

The object of the new strategy of defence is to change the minds of the men in the Kremlin.

To those that will at once raise the cry that this is asking the impossible the reply must be:

1. They are human beings who have for one reason or another changed their minds on several occasions since 1945.

2. Through the policy of the nuclear deterrent we hope —and some people believe—we are already operating on their minds and influencing their thoughts. If we are not the deterrent idea has failed.

If our strategy should be to change the minds of the men in the Kremlin how is this to be achieved technically? There seem to us to be two broad lines of approach: the direct and the indirect.

The direct approach consists in doing things which might make an immediate impact on the minds of the rulers; the indirect approach is composed of policies designed to influence the minds of the masses in the Communist-controlled countries.

At this moment we are disposed to think that as part of our psychological campaign for defence there are strong arguments for considering whether the UK should not announce unilaterally that it will *not* carry out any further tests and that the forthcoming test will be abandoned.

Something dramatic and easily understood by mankind needs to be done to break the deadlock and arrest the drift of disaster.

Do the chiefs of staff really believe that an announcement of this nature would leave the UK more defenceless against nuclear attack than it is at present?

Having taken this step we should use it as the starting point for a tremendous and world-wide educational campaign explaining the horrors of nuclear war, the dangers of tests, etc., and say: "Now you can see why Her Majesty's Government has taken a lead and perhaps risks in this matter."

I picture a sum of £100,000,000 being spent on this propaganda which ought to be an all-party effort. I refuse absolutely to admit that given imagination, energy and funds the great educational campaign should not penetrate beyond the iron curtain.

In this connection and beginning with the satellite States a really great effort (£50,000,000) should be made to increase contacts with the masses in those countries. Every effort should be made to organise exchange visits between young people on a very large scale. We should put as much effort and money for this kind of thing as we do into a nuclear-bomb test.

Conventional Forces

No doubt these ideas will be very startling to many people but we beg and entreat them to remember that we are faced today with the old problem of defence in a completely novel setting.

It is almost as novel as if we woke up some day to find that this world of ours was liable to aggression from another planet. Our present problem is of this novel nature.

The *Manchester Guardian* wrote on April 15 that "Dependence on the ultimate deterrent is inevitable." It went on to say that the alternative was "conventional forces on a massive scale" or "a fully pacifist policy." A point worth thinking about is that *if* we succeed in producing some form of standstill in development of nuclear weapons and do *not* succeed in making progress with disarmament in conventional weapons are we likely to be able to persuade the people of the West to stand the racket of "conventional forces on a massive scale"? We doubt it.

What about a fully pacifist policy?

The truth is that this possibility has never been thoroughly examined from a strictly political-stratetical angle. The "pacifist" policy has usually been defended from a moral point of view.

I am thinking of a policy which it would be more accurate to call "defence by passive resistance."

I am not saying it would work. I am saying that no one has thoroughly studied its possibilities in the light of the novel and unprecedented defence problem which now faces the UK, Western Europe, and to a lesser extent the USA.

In order to find out some more about this I have reached the conclusion that a Royal Commission should be established with the task of expressing an opinion upon the problem of whether our way of life could be defended by passive resistance and if so what the plan should be. If a Royal Commission is not considered to be the best instrument, then a special committee of the Imperial Defence College should be put on to the job.

We have said quite bluntly in the White Paper that we cannot afford our present expenditure on defence. We have made heavy cuts in our conventional forces and transferred our faith to nuclear weapons with all the imponderables and unknowns which go with them.

I remarked to a well-known MP: "Suppose Great Britain only had three air-borne divisions, a few tactical aircraft and a very small navy—what would happen apart from the obvious and immense gain to our economy?"

He replied: "My first reflection is that our influence in the world would at once decline"—he paused and added—"at least I suppose it would."

Is this certain? Gandhi's influence rose with the rise of passive resistance; so did that of the African bus boycotters.

Has it or can it be proved that a United Kingdom with an intelligent and sophisticated population educated to regard a national plan of passive resistance as the defence policy of the country would lose influence? I think there is a case for a very thorough investigation of this matter.

Mulford Sibley

What About Unilateral Disarmament?

The position for which I argue is an eccentric one and an unpopular one. But it is a position which in my judgment is one of the more "realistic" attitudes to take in the present state of the world.

Briefly and bluntly put, this statement defends the proposition that if a general universal disarmament agreement cannot be reached in the immediate future, it would be desirable and highly "realistic" to adopt a policy of unilateral disarmament. While it is not claimed that unilateral disarmament is a panacea in any sense—it must be viewed in a wider context which will include, of course, greater use of machinery like that of the United Nations, vast expansion of international economic development, and the adoption by the United States of Gandhi-like organization for nonviolent resistance—it is argued that unilateral disarmament is wise and might conceivably initiate revolutionary changes essential for a true world order.

The considerations which led to this conclusion may be outlined as follows:

Insanity of Defense

It is widely accepted now by many, if not most, of the major leaders of the world that another great war, if it should unhappily "break out," would result in mutual suicide. Thus General Douglas MacArthur has been quoted as saying:

> *War is no longer rationally a means of settling international problems. Its destructiveness has become so great that* there can be no winner. *Both sides lose. It is almost a form of mutual suicide.*

Commenting on the Korean War, the general remarked:

This experience again emphasizes the utter futility of modern war—its complete failure as an arbiter of international dissensions. A nation has been gutted, and we stand today just where we stood before it all started. Nothing has been settled. War is outmoded. Its threat must be abolished if the world is to go on.

President Eisenhower has been quoted along the same lines; and only recently Marshal Bulganin made a very similar statement.

Many of those who have studied the possibilities of long-range missiles seem to suggest that it is fantastic to expect any real protection against their horrors. One reason both the American and the British people are so apathetic about civil defense is probably because they realize, perhaps subconsciously, that the whole idea is a farce—that "civil defense" cannot "defend," or, if conceivably it could be made to do so, it would cost so much that even a wealthy nation would become bankrupt. All the agitation involving the alleged superiority of the Soviet Union in certain types of weapons, implying a fear that the United States may not be "keeping up," illustrates anew the futility of an arms race for the promotion of "security" (however that rather ambiguous term may be defined).

We live in a world, in short, where the waging of war would be so destructive that in sheerly utilitarian terms it would not "pay," whatever the probable circumstances; a world, moreover, in which the mere preparation for such a war promotes national insecurity and even constitutes a serious hazard to human life (as in the atomic and hydrogen bomb tests). Every time the United States builds a new jet, I feel more insecure; every time the Soviet Union constructs a new guided missile, I find my security lessened.

The "Necessity" of Mutual Suicide

Why, then, do we continue to arm against one another? It is partly, I suggest, because we will not or cannot face up to the implications of our very admissions about the nature of war and preparation for war. On the one hand it is admitted widely (and obviously I share the view) that losses from any conceivable war with modern weapons would be far greater than any imaginable gains; on the other hand, we still seem to be saying that, *despite* this admission, we are still willing to go to war under certain circumstances, knowing full well that no victor can emerge. This is not rational, and we should frankly admit that it is not.

Either MacArthur, Eisenhower, Bulganin, myself, and many others are dead wrong in their estimates about the destructiveness of a future war, in which case they should be corrected by someone, or they are right, in which event we should think in terms of a vastly changed policy. I happen to think they are right. If this is true, our policies—which are still based on the notion that war may somehow be "necessary" (despite the fact that it will lead to mutual suicide)—ought to be altered in a revolutionary way.

Threats—Empty or Suicidal

Those policies assume that, in the absence of international agreement on armaments, we must still prepare nationally for what is admitted to be probable suicide. Sometimes such policies are defended by saying that, of course, their intention is to "threaten" others in order to keep the peace—as if a threat means anything unless we are *prepared* to wage a war in case of presumed "necessity." Threats without probable action cease to be threats and so-called realists ought to recognize this. Building national armaments today, in short, is building for probable suicidal war, which can in no sense "defend" this country. National armaments, under modern circumstances, and if the objective be "national defense" (whether physical, economic, or political), are inappropriate, ineffective means for the alleged objective. They are, in other words, unrealistic, "utopian" means. At the very least, they are useless, and at their worst (as in hydrogen bomb testing) are a positive menace to both contemporary and future life. Unilateral disarmament, if this analysis be correct, is not some "idealistic" and "impractical" notion; rather it is an exemplification of good sense.

If I should take a poodle to assist me in hunting, I should

be termed crazy, and rightly so—the rational act would be to discard the poodle and get a hunting dog. Charles Lamb, in a famous essay, rightly ridiculed those who burned down their houses in order to get roast pig. So it is with the vain attempt to get "national defense" and "security" through armaments. All the paraphernalia of the national war machine—espionage, counterespionage, National Security Council, hydrogen bombs, guided missiles, and so on—constitute the poodle dog, or, if you will, the burning of the house. And actually, burning down one's house can produce roast pig, albeit at an unbearable price; while armaments cannot give us "security" or "peace" *even* at an unbearable price. At international conferences it seems generally to be assumed that any surrender of armed might would be highly dangerous—hence all the talk of "fool-proof" guarantees, international inspection, and so on. But if the analysis of this statement be supported, a nation is not giving up anything really valuable when it surrenders armed might—rather is it giving up something valueless, something, moreover, which is probably a positive detriment in the quest for "defense" and "security."

Objections to Unilateral Disarmament

This is not as outrageous a view as it may seem to be. In his suggestive study *Power*—which examines the ramifications of power relations in human society—the well-known British philosopher Bertrand Russell says (p. 152): "The actual harm which a nation would suffer from unilateral disarmament is very much less than most people suppose." We have in this statement, of course, gone much beyond the negative of Russell's observation and have suggested positive considerations which would seem to point in the direction of unilateral disarmament.

I am aware, I think, of most of the objections to such a policy and shall attempt to deal with them in conclusion:

a) It is often alleged that the United States actually disarmed after World War I and World War II and that the disarmament did not work to promote peace or security. Of course, the answer is that the United States did not

"disarm." Its level of armaments was always much higher
than in pre-war years. It is true that it may have reduced
its armaments more rapidly than the Soviet Union after
World War II, but this was far, far from a policy of disarmament carried out within a context of positive alternatives such as we suggest below.

b) The context of unilateral disarmament is all-important if we are to criticize the policy intelligently. In a
narrow sense, unilateral disarmament means the voluntary
destruction of all our war-making potential and an invitation to the rest of the world to send inspectors to check on
our claims. But this narrow meaning of disarmament must
be seen in the context of other proposals which are and
must be organically connected with unilateral disarmament. Simultaneously, we would immediately turn over
to an international agency all the resources we had
hitherto been using in preparation for war. We would do
this each year for an indefinite period. The international
agency would use the resources to develop underdeveloped areas, construct and maintain international libraries,
establish and support international universities, and so
on. The cost of one destroyer would build 80 schools; the
price of one bombing plane would build some 400 $15,000
houses.

c) Objectors to unilateral disarmament often fail to
realize how this revolutionary act would in itself probably
change the political atmosphere of the world—and for the
better. Even the Soviet Union's current modest reduction
in armaments has shaken world opinion. What would
not unilateral disarmament by the United States do, if
carried out in the context outlined above? We cannot, of
course, predict exactly because we have never tried anything remotely resembling it. But it is safe to suggest that
the whole international climate would undergo drastic revision. It is probable that other heavily armed powers
would follow the lead of this country and we would have
a competition in disarmament, rather than competition in
armaments: it might be a repetition of the competitive
actions of French nobles in giving up their privileges at
the beginning of the French Revolution.

d) But, it may be objected, you have not ensured peace by this act and "aggression" may and probably will still occur. The answer to this objection is two-fold:

(1) No action, however complicated and ingenious, can ever make "peace" certain; but I submit that an act of this kind, in its appeal to human rationality, imagination, and sympathy, would go further in the direction of building the atmosphere conducive to peace than our present insanity, which, if we are honest with ourselves, we will admit must result in war.

(2) No act of unilateral disarmament, even in the context suggested above, should be initiated without a clear realization that an ineffective and dangerous means of "national defense" is being surrendered as good riddance in favor of a more "realistic" method. In addition to the positive and constructive acts mentioned above, that more "realistic" method would include some American adaptation of the Gandhi technique of nonviolent resistance. Organized potentiality for nonviolent resistance should, in other words, accompany unilateral disarmament. If we were to devote only 5% of our present so-called defense budget to training for possible nonviolent resistance (which might never be needed), we would, in my judgment, have a far more effective and far less dangerous defense against possible aggression (even assuming that the Soviet Union remained heavily armed, which is highly improbable) than our present unrealistic and "utopian" methods provide.

It is a commonplace to say that we live in a revolutionary age. This statement has been a plea that we seriously consider revolutionary means to cope realistically with one of the crucial problems of that age. These revolutionary means would imply that we no longer have any faith in war and preparation for war and that what would begin ostensibly as a revolution in technique would prove to be basically a revolution in attitude and outlook.

Gordon S. Christiansen

Fatal Illusion*

I am opposed to the currently advocated Civil Defense shelter program for two major reasons. The first of these is because it is ineffective and will not accomplish what is claimed for it. The shelter program will not provide a full and abundant life underground; it will not provide the basis for the recreation of a community life and culture after the attack; it will not defend our liberties and our way of life; it will not prevent a nuclear war. All of these have been claimed as attributes of the shelter program which are supposed to justify our sacrifices to CD. In my opinion, which is based on a careful study of the effects of nuclear weapons and the probable conditions of a nuclear war, none of these claims will in fact be realized.

My second reason for opposing the Civilian Shelter program is that I believe that it will actively contribute to the likelihood of war. From the point of view of our own military capabilities, the widespread belief by the people of the United States that they are in fact protected against a retaliatory strike provides the last remaining requirement for our ability to *start* a nuclear war by adding to our weapons and policy actions the element of *credibility* to our "first strike" capability. From the point of view of the uncommitted nations of the world, the spectacle of the free and proud people of the United States spending thirty billion dollars in order to dig themselves underground while the majority of the world's people remain inadequately clothed and fed and with inadequate shelter against the *natural* elements (and I don't mean radioactive elements), this spectacle can only have the effect of driving the sympathies of that majority further away from us. And finally, this act of total mobilization, in which our whole population

* March, 1962.

takes the stance of obvious anticipation of a nuclear war, could only be interpreted by the people and governments who are antagonistic to us as an extremely provocative act at this time of great tension.

Because adoption of the shelter program would have this effect of increasing the likelihood of war, I would oppose it even if I thought it might have some useful defensive aspects. But in this article I will center my argument around the question of effectiveness.

The history of Civil Defense planning during the ten or so years of the existence of CD agencies has been a baffling series of changes and confusions. For years the problem was largely ignored. Then we were told: *First*, build blast shelters. *Second*, any type of shelter is useless; the thing to do is to evacuate our cities. *Third*, build or improvise fallout shelters. *Fourth*, No! Don't build a shelter; evacuation is again the way to salvation.

Throughout the late summer and autumn CD seemed set on the plan to have each family build its own simple shelter in the basement or backyard. The public relations promotion of this plan was done in the grandest and most powerful way possible, invoking endorsement by our most prestigious molders of public opinion. *Time* magazine, *Life*, *Fortune*, and almost all of our local and national newspapers made it clear that the creation of a concrete cubicle in the cellar is a patriotic requirement of plain citizenship. President Kennedy gave his imprimatur to *Life's* fatuous compilation of misinformation, and asserted that family shelters would prevent war. Dr. Edward Teller, the "father of the H-bomb," told us that a shelter in every basement and fire doors on the New York subways would save ninety per cent of the population. Dr. Willard Libby, our Nobel Laureate ex-Commissioner of the A.E.C., told us that a thirty-dollar structure of sandbags and railroad ties is the answer to any nuclear war. And the ultimate endorsement of financial backing was handsomely offered by Congress when it tripled the Eisenhower budget for Civil Defense promotion to a total of three hundred million dollars.

During the last two months we have again been subjected to the newest sudden twist in CD plans and advice—and it is still too early to see just which way it is going. On the last day of November, President Kennedy disclaimed entirely the individual family shelter program and came out hard for large group and community shelters. Teller had made the shift much earlier; an interview in the September 25th *U.S. News and World Report*, within a week after his AP syndicated series of articles was published, quoted his rejection of family shelters as inadequate and his commitment to large group shelters. Libby's denial was more direct; a few days after *his* syndicated series of articles was published, his poor-man's shelter was destroyed by a Los Angeles forest fire.

The confusion and uncertainty of CD plans have been maintained and extended. On December 1st, the day after the President spoke, Mr. Pitman, Assistant Secretary of Defense for Civil Defense, told *his* press conference that he still favored family shelters. Then, as the new year began, the goverment made available twenty-five million copies of the famous pamphlet which had been heralded for half a year as the final and complete instructions on how to survive a nuclear war. This booklet was first promised last August and has been worked over exhaustively by many experts, including a group of editors from Time, Inc., and a number of high government officials. It seems reasonable to assume that this is, if not the *last* word on CD, at least the most recent.

This little yellow booklet falls far short of its pre-publication promise as the clear and forthright manual of survival. It is the same old equivocal, evasive, platitudinous mixture of re-assurance and exhortation. One of the CD officials who wrote it was quite frank in his statement in the New York *Times* of December 31st:

> Somebody would say, "that phrase will scare such-and-such a group" and so that part would get cut. Then something else would be objectionable, and that would get cut. What we finally came up with was something pretty bland, but pretty candid too, as far as it went.

The trouble is that it didn't go very far; and even as far as it went the blandness far exceeds the candor.

I review this history of the wild and apparently senseless erratic shifts in CD policy and the constant equivocation and uncertainty, not in scorn or criticism of CD officials, but rather as a statement of the facts of modern technological development in warfare and weaponry. These facts are that with each passing week, each month, each year, new developments are being encountered that change entirely the basis of defense plans. Each of the shifts in CD planning was made in response to new awareness of the nature and magnitude of the destruction of nuclear war—but each was far behind the actual state of weapons development. Blast shelters were abandoned some time *after* general awareness of the massive and widespread blast destruction of hydrogen bombs. Plans for evacuation of cities were dropped, partially because of the ultimate realization of the impossibility within warning times that could be expected, but also because of the late dawning awareness of the extent and intensity of fallout radiation (an awareness delayed over a year, incidentally, by A.E.C. suppression of information). It was finally realized that people might evacuate a blast target, only to find themselves in a lethally destructive radiation field with no protection at all. The shift to group and community shelters is under way because it is now apparent that the basement and backyard shelters offer *no* protection against the inevitable fires, are far less than sufficient defense against fallout, and are woefully inadequate as a base for post-attack recovery.

Now, just when the Russians are developing 50-and 100-megaton bombs, Civil Defense has published the new booklet in which the worst conditions considered are those associated with the explosion of a *single* 5-megaton weapon. This description of weapons effects is one example of the blandness of the booklet, which is admitted by one of its authors. The description is candid as far as it goes; it just fails to mention many of the more unpleasant facts. The pamphlet is quite candid about many other questions; examples are: its complete dismissal of the possibility of evacuating cities; an admission that shelter protection against blast, heat and fire effects is impracticable; and a statement of strong preference for group shelters rather than individual family shelters. But then, having taken this position, the booklet spends seven pages describing a series of rudimentary family shelters and only two pages on group shelters. It offers almost no facts about either type, and description of the group shelters is non-existent, except for two minimal drawings which emphasize such non-shelter use of these caverns as "Juke box hangouts for gregarious teenagers." The family shelters are described in more detail; it is stated that they would have a protection factor against fallout radiation of about 100; it is also claimed that each can be built for a hundred and fifty dollars or less. This may be possible, since the most elegant one has a headroom of less than five feet. The hundred-and-fifty-dollar model is an eight-foot section of corrugated pipe, four feet in diameter, in which a family of four are expected to stay for at least two weeks. This space will be occupied by the four people plus their two weeks' supply of food and water (56 gallons is recommended), plus their bedding, tools, first-aid kit, radio, books of CD instructions, and their accumulated garbage and human wastes. It is possible that a family might be able to survive such exigencies for a few days; but it is highly unlikely that they could stand it for the two weeks that the CD pamphlet says is necessary; and it is certain that they could not survive these conditions for the time required by a more realistic estimate of the probable level of attack.

A technical evaluation of the effectiveness of civilian shelters as protection against modern war would logically begin with a consideration of the weapons capabilities of probable antagonists, both in numbers and types of weapons available and in effects of individual weapons.

The technology of weapons development is by all odds the most rapidly expanding field of applied science—and it covers practically every facet of science. These facts are understandable in view of the massive commitment of money, resources and manpower to this activity. A few factual tidbits help to describe the level of this commitment:

—Half of all the money spent on research in the United States is Federal money provided by the military departments for weapons research.
—President Nathan Pusey of Harvard stated in his annual report last year that to his knowledge two major Eastern

private universities get more than four-fifths of their operating budgets from Federal research-funds.
—Massachusetts Institute of Technology ranks 48th
among prime defense contractors—well below General
Dynamics, Lockheed and Boeing, but still among the top
fifty, a remarkable record for an institution whose product
is research, not ships, planes and missiles.

Oscar Morgenstern, the theoretician of deterrence and an
expert on arms control, described this situation in a chapter of
his book called *The Fascination of War:*

> *The most important things in science at present are done
> only if they are related to war. War preparations are
> necessary in order to justify the deepest human desire for
> knowledge.*

Some of the current and prospective results of this deepest
human desire for knowledge are indeed fascinating. We have
been assured by our defense scientists that truly effective
"doomsday machines," those ultimate deterrents that are supposed to stabilize international relations by the threat of total
destruction of the earth, are not yet entirely feasible. But those
same defense experts also see to it that any conceivable
scheme, however frightful or fantastic, is thoroughly and impartially studied for feasibility. These possibilities include such
things as the physical breaking up of the earth; the modification
of climate; and blanketing the earth with a devastating level of
radiation. In the realm of current potentialities are schemes for
burning-over huge land areas. A 100-megaton bomb detonated
at a height of a few miles would set fire to every combustible
thing in an area as large as a medium-sized state. Another
possible use of such "monster" weapons, currently being studied, is the devastation of coastal areas by tidal waves produced
in deep underwater detonations.
A significant part of existing arsenals of mass-destruction
weapons is chemical and biological warfare poisons. Our Army
Chemical Corps is now engaged in a very large development
and production program in chemical-biological warfare, which
is justified on the basis of intelligence reports that the Russians

are developing and making these monstrous devices for mass killing. The only prudent conclusion is that the Soviet Union has a supply of these agents and would use them along with their other weapons if a major war started.

But the most spectacular and the most important part of our arsenal, and also that of the Russians, is the nuclear bombs and warheads, and on these several reliable estimates of numbers have been made. About a year ago Dr. Ralph Lapp, a consultant to the A.E.C., estimated that we had on hand at the end of 1960 over three hundred and fifty tons of weapons-grade fissionable materials. He also made a projective estimate that we would have by 1966 at least a thousand tons. These seem like trifling amounts; but when they are expressed in explosive terms, they take on fantastic proportions. If the three hundred and fifty tons of uranium and plutonium were all used in the extremely inefficient form of the old, Hiroshima-type, atomic bombs, they would make fifty thousand weapons, each with an explosive power of about twenty thousand tons of TNT. If the same material were all used in high-yield weapons such as the 20-megaton hydrogen bombs, we could have an explosive equivalent of over a million megatons of TNT—about four hundred tons of TNT explosive for every human being on earth. This is what we had on hand last year; our procurement plans for the next five years will *triple* this amount.

Fortunately for the human race, all this weapons-grade fissionable material undoubtedly will not (and probably could not) be used in maximum-yield weapons. A quite different but equally reliable minimum estimate of actual weapons in being has placed our supply at something over sixty thousand megatons TNT equivalent and the Russians at forty to fifty thousand megatons. But before we become too optimistic we should compute our *pro-rata* share in this big bang. We could provide explosions (and the other attendant unpleasantnesses) equivalent to three hundred tons of TNT for every person in the Soviet Union; they have about two hundred and fifty tons for each of us. And again, it is worth remembering that we have the capability—and the plans and intentions (and we must presume the Russians do too)—of increasing these amounts by a factor of 3 by 1966.

There has been a vast amount of discussion in the past few months about the effects of nuclear weapons. Most of this discussion has taken two forms. One is a general expression of deep concern over the long-range damage caused by world-wide fallout from the recent Russian tests. There is no doubt that serious damage is being done right now, and will continue to be done for many months and years to come. But in a consideration of the extreme conditions of a general nuclear attack, this world-wide fallout would be an inconsequential contribution to the horror of the situation.

The other aspect of the recent discussion has been the consideration of the close-in effects around the burst of a single large weapon. These depend on such factors as the diameter and depth of the crater dug by the awesome blast; the area of total blast destruction, which might extend out a few miles; and the area of total killing by the intense instantaneous radiation from the detonation, which would cover about the same area. Beyond these are widening circles of less intense blast damage. And still further out are the less localized effects of the fire storm and the field of radiation from the so-called "local" fallout pattern.

If a person is primarily interested in his personal chances of survival, determined by conditions in his own neighborhood, he can make a reasonable estimate by transferring these circles of destruction to a map of his own area. But there are always the questions of which of the many sources of data on what sized weapon should be used, and on what hypothetical target. The new CD pamphlet offers a highly optimistic statement of the close-in effects for a 5-megaton detonation; *Newsweek* of October 30th, 1961 does the same for a 50-megaton; *Consumer Reports* of January 1962 has a detailed comparison of these effects of 100-megaton and 3-megaton bombs.

But such diagrams of devastation deal only with the least of the problems of survival. There is always the chance that one's own community will be spared; the bombs may all fall somewhere else. Furthermore, even the most dedicated Civil Defense planners, including the authors of the new CD booklet, concede that there is no hope of protecting people against these close-in direct effects. And beyond these considerations, the question of the possibility of general survival is much greater than individual survival or even the continued viability of a single community. The value of any plan of national defense must be judged primarily on its ability to defend the national entity. Does it not only save the lives of most of the people, but does it preserve those values which characterize a people as a nation? Does it preserve the community structure? Does it maintain freedom? Does it provide for a continuity of a way of life? Does it save those irreplaceable creations of our culture without which we could not recover?

Most of these survival factors depend on community organization at levels higher than a single city or even a single state. The minimum viable fragment of the United States would probably be some regional section, such as the Northeastern Seaboard area. It would seem that a sensible approach to disaster planning would be to postulate some reasonable level of attack on the whole United States; then to determine the conditions to be expected in the selected area; and finally to judge the effectiveness of a proposed defense system against the conditions determined. I would like to make such a comparison for the area bounded by Washington, D. C., and Portsmouth, New Hampshire, and running about a hundred miles inland, under the conditions of the hypothetical attack postulated in the Holifield Congressional Subcommittee report. I use this hypothetical attack because it is the best known, because it has been the basis of several lengthy studies, and because it is the basis of much of current CD planning. I choose the 400-by-100-mile Northeastern Coastal area because it is the heartland of the nation, containing a major fraction of the population and even bigger fractions of all those activities which make up the essence of our national culture and being, and because this rich concentration of national resources is most likely to be hit heavily in any serious nuclear attack.

This hypothetical attack and the conditions associated with it are described in the Holifield Report.[1] This book contains a good deal of Congressional-type talk in its 966 pages,

[1] *Biological and Environmental Effects of Nuclear War.* Hearings before the Special Subcommittee on Radiation of the Joint Committee on Atomic Energy, Congress of the United States, 86th Congress, first session, June 22-26, 1959.

but scattered among the long dry stretches is much highly useful and pertinent information. The attack which this report studies consisted of 263 weapons ranging in size from 1 to 10 megatons and totalling 1446 megatons, scattered over 224 strategic and population targets throughout the United States. Of these, 56 weapons with a total explosive force of 295 megatons were placed in the rough rectangle 100 by 400 miles from Washington to Portsmouth. Within this 40,000-square-mile area there is *no place* which is more than fifty, and very few which are further than twenty-five, miles from a bomb detonation. The whole area would be covered by a single huge fire or possibly by overlapping firestorms. The prime targets, which would be totally and immediately destroyed by the blast effects, include virtually *all* centers of population, government, industry, commerce, transportation, and communication, and most organized community activity. And the whole area would be covered by a devastating intensity of fallout radiation.

The radioactive products which are contained in the fallout particles from thermonuclear detonations arise mostly from the fission reactions; a smaller but unspecified (in unclassified literature) fraction of the residual radioactivity is induced by the burst of neutrons from the fusion part of the detonation. Most publicly available calculations of fallout intensity ignore the induced radioactivity and are based solely on estimates of the fraction of the energy of the explosion which came from fission reactions. Estimates of the fraction of fission energy in small-megaton bombs vary between a low of fifty and a high of ninety per cent. The Holifield Report of 1959 used fifty per cent; a more reasonable and still highly conservative estimate is two-thirds fission.[2] It should also be added that the expression "kilotons of fission products" is commonly used to describe fallout concentrations. This term does not refer to actual weights of particles but rather to the radioactive materials arising from a fission explosion equivalent in power to that many tons of TNT.

[2] Ralph Lapp uses this figure in an essay called "Nuclear War" in the book *Fallout* (John M. Fowler, editor; Basic Books, Inc., New York, 1960). In the same book (p. 18) Fowler states that the weapon of the United States' "Castle-Bravo" test was ninety per cent fission.

A conservative calculation of the fallout intensity in the Northeastern Seaboard area from the 295 megatons of weapons placed there in the Holifield Report's hypothetical attack would begin then with about two hundred megatons of fission products. Of these, eighty per cent would fall out locally[8]; the remainder would pass into the stratosphere and contribute to world-wide fallout. Thus, there would be 160 megatons (160,-000 kilotons) of fission products scattered over the 40,000-square-mile area. The average distribution would be 4 kilotons per square mile.

Page 126 of the Holifield Report is a table of intensities of radiation at various times after detonation corresponding to 1 kiloton of fission products per square mile. The data in this table were determined by the Naval Radiological Defense Laboratory and were presented to the Holifield Subcommittee as the most modern and reliable estimates available. The table indicates that the initial level of radiation (end of the first hour after detonation) is 3629 roentgens per hour for 1 kiloton of fission products per square mile. With 4 kilotons per square mile we would have about 14,500 roentgens per hour as the initial *average* level of radiation throughout the whole Northeastern Seaboard area.

In translating this radiation level into survival chances, a good deal of clarification can be established right in the beginning by recognizing two major points: 1) radiation is injurious, and 2) protection is possible. Radiation from *any* source, medical treatment, direct radiation from nuclear explosion, or the residual radiation from fallout products, is injurious even in relatively small doses and is severely damaging or lethal in large doses. There is some uncertainty as to the dose levels which will cause various biological effects, but there is no doubt that a whole body radiation dose of around 200 roentgens would cause some radiation sickness; 500 roentgens would cause very serious radiation sickness and would be lethal in about fifty per cent of the cases; 1000 roentgens would be lethal to all subjects. In mitigation, it must be added that for small doses spread over a long time, the sickening and killing levels might be as much as three times as great as these.

[8] Holifield Report, p. 44.

On the other hand, it is probably true that genetic damage by radiation is strictly cumulative.

Protection against these effects is possible by the apparently simple expedient of placing enough *mass* between oneself and the source of radiation—and keeping it there long enough. Basement and backyard fallout shelters have a protection factor of about a hundred; that is, a person inside one of these shelters would receive only about one per cent of the radiation he would in the open. The ninety-three-million-dollar program for locating shelters in existing buildings is searching for space with an average protection factor of 20 or greater. Deep, self-contained group or community shelters have a protection factor of around a thousand—which is sufficient to avoid death or serious injury from radiation. And if even greater protection is needed it is only mildly more difficult, though a great deal more expensive, to provide protection factors as high as ten thousand by digging a few feet deeper and making a generally more elegant construction.

But the obvious difficulty, and the point at which the Civilian Shelter plan fails miserably, is the need to maintain the protection high enough and long enough to survive the intensely radioactive period which would follow a nuclear attack.

A person in the open, exposed to the radiation levels we have estimated for the Northeastern Seaboard area, would be killed by radiation in less than five minutes; in an ordinary basement he would die in about an hour. With a protection factor of 20, as in the shelter spaces being located, marked and stocked in existing buildings, the cumulative dose to a person inside would be just over 1000 roentgens in the first six hours— enough to guarantee 100% fatalities. Inside a good family-type shelter with a protection factor of 100, the radiation dose integrated over two months would be about 450 roentgens, enough to kill half the occupants and totally incapacitate any who were not killed. In a deep, self-contained community shelter, buried under four feet of earth and with no contamination or leakage, the dose to a person remaining inside constantly for two months would be only one tenth this, or 45 roentgens (assuming a protection factor of 1000). And in a year of con-

stant occupancy it would only increase to about 50 roentgens—
a trivial dose.

But the difficulty is to maintain protection long enough.
One cannot remain forever inside a shelter, even a very good
one. If a person stayed in this excellent deep shelter constantly
for the first two weeks and then started a schedule of one hour
a week outside, he would almost certainly not suffer serious
radiation damage. Assuming that he entirely avoided hot spots
on his excursions outside, in six months time he would only get
about 50 roentgens in addition to the 50 roentgens which he
was unable to avoid even inside his shelter. A total dose of 100
roentgens spread over half a year is not serious. But if he tried
to increase the time outside to as much as an hour a day, he
would certainly be badly injured and would be in danger of
dying from radiation sickness. His total dose of radiation for
the six months would be about 400 roentgens—a little less than
the fifty per cent lethal-dose level.

And even after six months the radiation field outside
would be intense enough to prevent human occupancy. According to the data on page 126 of the Holifield Report, the
level would be about 0.35 roentgens per hour, which adds up
to a dose of over eight roentgens per day. If a person tried to
leave the shelter permanently after six months, he would almost certainly become very sick from radiation injury and
would be in grave danger of dying.

It is hardly necessary to spell out the equation of surviva-
bility under these conditions. If a person stays underground in
an *excellent* shelter he can avoid death or serious injury from
radiation—but he will probably die of starvation or disease (if
not boredom). If he attempts to leave the shelter, even for
brief and infrequent foraging excursions, he will probably be
killed or seriously injured by radiation.

But we have so far said nothing about the bleak and
unpromising conditions he would face when he did come out
—if he could. Almost all living creatures—except those which
are notably more resistant to radiation, such as insects—would
have been killed. The whole landscape would have been
burned over by the mass conflagrations and firestorms, an inevitable result of the clusters of nuclear bursts postulated in

the Holifield Report. The huge fireball from these nuclear explosions reaches temperatures in the hundreds of millions of
degrees and the searing heat which radiates down over vast
areas causes temperatures on the ground to rise to a thousand
degrees. This heat sets fire to all combustible things in the
open, trash, trees, grass, frame buildings, gasoline; the huge
fires near the center cause a tremendous updraft, sweeping the
air and the fire from outlying areas in toward the center at
hurricane velocities. The fire would rage unchecked, limited
only by the consumption of everything combustible, including
most of the oxygen. Shelters, however elegant, would become
fiery traps in which those saved from radiation would be consumed by suffocation and heat.

This is *not* a hypothetical description; it actually happened in several cities during World War II as a result of
conventional firebomb raids. In 1943, the city of Hamburg lost
seventy thousand people in one night—people who had taken
shelter in the massive blast-protection bunkers; the temperatures in the streets reached fourteen thousand degrees; most of
the survivors were those who took to the rivers and canals
before the fire got going well—an alternative not available to
shelter occupants in an area of radioactive fallout.

Finally, it should be emphasized that all of these conclusions of post-nuclear-attack conditions are based on a hypothetical attack (postulated by the Congressional Committee
most directly concerned with CD preparations) that assumes
only 1446 megatons spread over the whole United States. This,
compared with the conservatively and reliably estimated Russian weapon capability of forty to fifty *thousand* megatons,
amounts to about three or three and a half per cent of the
nuclear weapons that *might* be used against us. A much more
realistic hypothetical attack, and one that should *certainly* be
planned for by any serious and earnest disaster defense program, would be ten or twenty times as great—and this would
mean that all the effects discussed would be greater by the
same factor of ten or twenty.

It is probably not necessary to add to these horrors a
consideration of the possible inclusion of chemical and biological warfare agents among the elements of the weapons-mix for

a hypothetical attack. And certainly the Civil Defense planners have scrupulously avoided doing so. But the possibility has been raised repeatedly since the early 1950s by the Army Chemical Corps and has been discussed in detail by such un-biased experts as Dr. York, Assistant Secretary of Defense for Research and Engineering under the Eisenhower administra-tion, Dr. Winter of the RAND Corporation, and the American Chemical Society's Committee on Civil Defense. In the inter-ests of completeness it must be pointed out first, that these experts "conclude that the threat from chemical and biological weapons is just as great as is the threat from nuclear weapons." Second, a population huddled in closely packed underground cubicles, physically and psychologically weakened, makes an ideal targeting arrangement for the use of these weapons of mass destruction. And third, the incubation period of many of the biological warfare agents matches exactly the magical two-week time period which is generally asserted (although quite unrealistically) to be the necessary time of occupancy of fallout shelters. In any case, this is the time at which shelter occupants *must* come out to forage, whether or not the radiation is toler-able, because this is when food and water will run out.

One could even suggest that a responsible CD program, which will take years to implement, should also concern itself with the probable weapons of the future. But it is apparent that the Civil Defense Agency faces an impossible problem even in dealing with the existing threats. Any program that has a chance of being significantly effective is impossible of attain-ment; anything that we can afford or that does not completely destroy our cultural and community structure is only margin-ally effective.

From these considerations I conclude, as I believe any reasonable and thoughtful person would, that Civilian Shelters and the advice contained in CD's little yellow booklet are *not* the answer to the threat of nuclear war. I cannot accept the prospect of the American people being led like bewitched and haunted creatures from one defensive scheme to another, each more humiliating and destructive of human values than the one before, attempting to defend a way of life by abandoning it, concerned only to prolong our lives a few miserable weeks while sacrificing all the values which might make life worth living. Bare survival *may*, just possibly, exist underground; but the facts of life are that *living* takes place in the open, above ground.

Let us continue, while we still can, to live and act like human beings; let us devote our energies and resources to preventing these hypothetical disasters rather than to planning how to save ourselves in actual ones.

Kay Boyle

The Triumph of Principles

I think it should be cause for great rejoicing that there were a number of American writers among the hundreds of people who refused to take shelter in City Hall Park on the 3rd of May of this year [1960]. It is always good when the students of a country can rely on their writers not only to speak, but to act for them. For too many years I have felt that the writers of France—first André Malraux and then Albert Camus—spoke and acted for the students of America, and, in a sense, for the students of the world, and this is clearly not as things should be. I want to believe that the demonstrations in City Hall Park, in which so many college and high school students took part, and the demonstrations on the campuses of New York colleges, fervent and passive as they were, are a signal of the awakening of the young people of our country to the responsibility that is theirs.

No writers were arrested on the 3rd of May, and this was certainly intentional, for writers are potentially explosive material. Thomas Mann once said that if the writers of Germany through their vision and their expression of that vision had made richer and more impelling promises than those Hitler made, it would have been Hitler, and not the writers of Germany, who would have been forced into exile. It is *always* the intellectuals, however we may shrink from the chilling sound of that word, and, above all, it is *always* the writers who must bear the full weight of moral responsibility. Frenchmen will tell you that the decision to speak out is the vocation and life-long peril by which the intellectual must live. I remember the days in Paris when we who were writers, or painters, or composers, wrote pamphlets and distributed them in the streets and cafés. I remember when we signed manifestos and read them aloud on street-corners, following without any humility whatsoever in the tradition of Pascal, Voltaire, Chateaubriand, Victor Hugo, Zola, so that the world would know exactly where we stood, for we considered ourselves a portion of the contemporary conscience, and we had no pity on the compromiser or the poor in spirit of our time. But now the pamphlet and the manifesto are practically non-existent in American letters, although here in America they flourished with great vitality in pre-revolutionary times. American intellectuals, indeed, prepared and oriented our revolution: the only revolution in history, one French critic has pointed out, which did not destroy the intellectuals who had prepared it, but which carried them to power. "By tradition," this French critic said, "the European intellectual has a special character—a vocation beyond the limits of his own profession of writing or science or teaching. He believes himself called to a more universal responsibility than are other men, and that is to keep watch on the world, and to call the plays as he sees them, at whatever risk to himself. The dangers of his position are as real as poverty, exile, prison or death; and—unlike the soldier or the priest—he has no organized body to defend him."

No organized body defended the twenty-seven women and men who stood before a New York Youth Term magistrate in criminal court on the afternoon of May 3rd. But they themselves, in a very humble way, were defenders of humanity. Earlier that day, these twenty-seven women and men had remained in a park, with nearly a thousand others, and refused to take shelter during a civil defense drill. That was their crime. They had carried placards explaining their action, and they had sung as they walked in the square. One of the songs was "We Shall Not Be Moved," and another was "The Battle Hymn of the Republic," and another "I Ain't Goin' To Study War No More." One of the placards said quite simply: "Let's Stop this Nonsense." Another bore the words of George Kennan, a man of whom America should be particularly proud, which said, in part: "Let us divest ourselves of this weapon altogether; let us stake our safety on God's grace and our own good consciences and on that measure of common sense and humanity which even our adversaries possess; but then let us at least walk like men, with our heads up, so long as we are permitted to walk at all." It is a good day when the writers speak out loudly and clearly. Read Stuart Chase's book *Live and Let Live* for a program of American action. Listen to him saying: "It is no longer a question of defending one's home by defending one's nation. Now, it is only by defending all mankind that one can save his country." And listen to Adlai Stevenson crying out: "We need ways of motivating our young people to be creative individuals, to be daring and different. We must make America a center of intellectual vitality!" Because of voices like these, young people moved by high principle and deep moral conviction to protest know that they do not protest alone.

A Multitude of Ghosts

The twenty-seven who were arraigned in criminal court on May 3rd stood there as representatives of all of us who believe in the totally impractical value of drills and shelters against nuclear attack; and who believe that the insistence upon such drills is the cruelest kind of deception; for it is a deception which scales down to quiet human acceptance the ghastly finality of nuclear warfare.

When the New York magistrate said to those twenty-seven defendants that in America we have always expressed our opinions by means of the ballot box, and not by public demonstration, not by defiance of the law, the laughter in the courtroom was the laughter of many generations of Americans, for surely nothing more historically inaccurate could have been said. Perhaps the magistrate realized this when he flared into anger and offered the defendants Cuba, Korea, or Turkey, as alternative undemocratic homelands. But it was too late then for him to take back his words. For a multitude of ghosts— ragged ghosts, for the most part, but completely American ghosts—made their way down the aisle of the courtroom. They moved through the groups of college and high-school students who sat on the floor in that august building, doing their homework as they waited for sentence to be pronounced on their fellow-demonstrators, and thus, in like measure, on themselves.

John Brown's Soul

John Brown was in the crowd of them that moved toward the bar, and he spoke first, saying slowly and distinctly in the courtroom: "We should never allow ourselves to be tempted by any consideration to acknowledge laws and institutions to exist if our conscience and reason condemn them." Facing the magistrate who had just offered other countries to the defendants, John Brown said: "A minority convinced of its rights, based on moral principles will, under a republican government, sooner or later become the majority." And then Henry Thoreau, in his old grey trousers and his battered straw hat, spoke out from among the ghosts, saying: "The character inherent in the American people has done all that has been accomplished here. It would have done somewhat more if the government had not sometimes got in its way." That day in the New York criminal court, Thoreau addressed all of us, directly, unequivocally, saying: "Under a government which imprisons unjustly, the true place for a just man is also in prison." Because the magistrate had not perceived these other Americans standing before him, and because the guards had not heard these other voices speaking, Thoreau was able to go on saying that a government and its laws are merely a mode which the people have chosen to execute their will, and that when the laws fail to implement the people's will, then those laws, and that government, are inexpedient.

The ghost of a man called Emerson also stood at the bar, and he said: "It demands something godlike in him who has cast off the common motives of humanity and has ventured to trust himself as taskmaster. High be his heart, faithful his will, clear his sight, that he may in good earnest be doctrine, society, law, to himself . . . for nothing can bring peace to man or country but the triumph of principles!" In that group of fearless and indestructible ghosts were a number of men who had read our Constitution within hours after it was drafted, and who had immediately cried out in protest: "Where is there any provision made in this document to prevent the government from interfering with the right of citizens to meet together peaceably? Where are the safeguards of our right to say what

we think in public and to print our considered opinions in
newspapers?" Patrick Henry was in that group, and because he
and these men spoke out, we know that the Bill of Rights was
forthwith drafted in order to assure those safeguards.

But the spirit of the Bill of Rights was not in a place of
authority in the New York criminal court on May 3rd. Nor did
it animate those who passed judgment on the fifty-three students of Brooklyn College who were temporarily suspended
for their orderly protest against the civilian defense drill. It
had been forgotten, as well, by those who subjected the Hunter
College and City College students to "college discipline" because of their refusal to take part in the sinister farce of seeking shelter from nuclear attack. "The Bill of Rights is our abiding testament of faith in democracy," Chester Bowles reminds
us in his recent book, *New Principles for a New Age,* "but the
Bill of Rights might not be voted today because too few of us
understand the need to protect the freedoms of those with
whom we disagree."

If the authorities in the courts, and the authorities in the
colleges and high schools, failed to recognize the deeply happy
meaning of the passive demonstrations of May 3rd, there are
others who place this protest of high-minded, non-conforming
American citizens in true context in our history. To these others,
Stuart Chase's words point out a direction for Americans to
follow, a direction which implies a new concept even of law.
"The nuclear age," Chase writes, "calls for a whole new system
of values, habits, and beliefs, and calls for them AT ONCE!"

Lanzo del Vasto

The Fifth Alternative: Nonviolence

[*The following is the transcript of an address given by Lanza del Vasto at a conference held in Brussels on February 9, 1962:*]

First of all, what is nonviolence? We shall answer quite simply that it is the solution of conflicts. Thus the existence of conflict is assumed, and we avoid an all too common blunder, namely, the idea that nonviolence consists in doing nothing. That is not nonviolence, it is simply—nothing.

I said that nonviolence is the solution of conflicts. *The* solution, for there is no other. The other methods that are supposed to be successful in settling disputes are in reality no solutions at all.

When faced with a conflict, we can choose from four possible courses of action: First, to remain neutral and do nothing at all, especially if we are not directly attacked; we always have enough courage to bear the injuries done to our neighbors. The second possibility is to return blow for blow and, hopefully, two blows for one. The third is to take to our heels. The fourth is to surrender, throw up our hands, and beg for mercy. Do you see any other way out?

There is a fifth alternative: it is the way of nonviolence. This way excludes equally the other four. It rules out neutrality, strife, flight or retreat, and capitulation as well. What then are we to do, if we do not want to remain neutral or fight or run away or give up? Well, we have only to read the manual. We have only to thumb through the manual and look up the instructions it contains. This manual can be found everywhere. It is the little book that is called the Gospel. And what do we find there, regarding legitimate defense, punishment of the wicked, and other respectable reasons for exterminating our fellows?

> *If a man strikes thee on thy right cheek, turn the other cheek also to him; if he is ready to go to law with thee over thy coat, let him have it and thy cloak with it; if he compels thee to attend him on a mile's journey, go two miles with him of thy own accord.*

Since you are all Christians, I assume that you all do these things, and that you never do otherwise. But why? Not because you are depraved and enjoy receiving two blows rather than one. It is simply that rather than beg for mercy or draw in our claws or slaughter our adversary, we are ready to go out and meet more suffering, more danger. We will act just the opposite from the man who runs away.

The adversary will not shake us off so easily. For as I said, the nonviolent man desires the solution of conflict, which means that he wants to obtain the same thing that ordinary men are trying to obtain when they resort to force. Now force is certainly needed. Nothing can be obtained without force. What force then are we going to set in motion? How are we going to control it? Or better, how can we enable it to proceed and take effect? What impels us to take this unusual approach? It is so unusual that whenever we adopt it or speak of it we meet with astonishment; the enemy expected everything but this. And the conflicts that occur concern more than blows on the cheek and stolen coats.

Varieties of Conflict

We are concerned with the resolution of all conflicts, whether public or private: conflicts with ourselves, with our neighbors, with the city, and between cities. We must find the solution to all these conflicts. There is no plane on which nonviolence cannot be applied much more effectively than those solutions which the world deems acceptable and praiseworthy but which may well cause it to perish.

Why do I act this way? Why am I nonviolent? Because I keep in mind a single truth: that my adversary is a human being. But what kind of discovery is that, you will ask; it is

perfectly obvious, everyone knows it. True, but for the com-
batant it is the contrary that is obvious. Any man taking part in
a fracas is powerfully tempted to regard the man facing him as
a monster, a ferocious beast, Evil incarnate. The evil can be
overcome only by suppressing that monster, that social class,
party, race, or nation. It is up to me never to forget that this is
simply not true: what is true is that my enemy is a man like
me, that the spirit of justice exists in him as it does in me, and
that the evil exists in me as it does in him. To assign all the evil
to the other side is the purest nonsense. The dividing line
between good and evil passes, not between the other and me,
but right down the middle of my forehead, between my left
side and my right. We must therefore state as a principle that
justice exists in our enemy as it does in ourselves.

Now, justice is a simple matter; simple as two and two
make four. Two and two make four for everybody. And justice
remains the same for the just and the unjust, for white, red,
yellow, and black people, for believers and unbelievers. Observe the compelling force of this kind of proposition: whether
or not two and two make four in no way depends on my
intelligence or stupidity, on whether I am in a good or bad
mood. So I suggest that you defend a "just" cause only when
its justice is as patent as the fact that two and two make four.
And if justice exists in all men, who is the unjust? My enemy—
that cold, calculating monster, that odious brute? My enemy
"is a man, a man who is deceiving himself," nothing more.
From now on your duty with respect to the enemy is indicated.
When someone says something that is untrue, you immediately
correct him. "No, sir, you are mistaken; it is not like that at all."
Thus you have an obligation to undeceive the enemy. Now, no
one deceives himself deliberately; there is always some obscu-
rity that has prevented him from seeing where the truth lies.
And his confidence in the validity of his erroneous idea renders
him aggressive, because a man has to believe that he is in the
right before he will fight.

The strong man who crushes a weak one will always argue
that he has done the right thing, that it was for the good of
humanity, that he killed him in order to teach him how to live!
And the same holds true for all of us. Whether it is a case of
two fishwives having it out with brooms or two nations doing

the same thing by means of diplomacy, everybody presents his case and no one listens to it. Hence the concept of just war, doubly just, since it is just on both sides. And the more its justice is demonstrated in the eyes of the contending parties, the more crimes and atrocities this justification will blanket. Because the sinews of war are not money, the sinews of war are the mania to be in the right and the horrible blindness and pride of those peoples who take it upon themselves to redress wrongs, and this is true of both sides at the same time. Once the problem has been posed in this way, only the right of the stronger prevails.

But is there not a force for justice? I spoke of the compelling force of "two and two make four." Once a man is compelled to admit to himself that he is in the wrong, he will not continue the struggle. But, you will reply, some people will never be wrong. This is the case with all the violent, who will always be in the right until they are killed. Nonviolence accomplishes miracles: the vilest brute stands gaping, muttering to himself: "What? Things cannot go on like this . . ." and pauses.

Does nonviolence consist in always saying yes, in being amiable, smiling, agreeable, serene, self-controlled? No, for these qualities can just as well mark the hypocrite, the coward, or the well-bred worldling. A man can certainly get angry without ceasing to be nonviolent. The nonviolent man is the one who aims at the conscience of his adversary; that is the touchstone that enables us to recognize him. Does a man insist on settling disputes in his own way, in spite of everything? Then he is not nonviolent. Does he want to induce the enemy, by aiming at his conscience, to settle the dispute for himself? In that case, he is nonviolent. Admittedly, the nonviolent man most often responds with absolute calm to the frenzy of the enemy: "Pardon me, sir. Do not leave. You have forgotten something. You have forgotten that I have two cheeks. So come back!"

Aggressive Nonviolence

But the enemy is not always in a rage. It sometimes happens that the enemy is calmly resting in his injustice, sure of his power and not particularly inclined to make use of it. This may be the very moment when we ought to get angry, knot the cords, and drive the money-changers from the temple. After all, what harm were the money-changers doing? Everyone was contented, everything was going along well. . . . But it was precisely the general contentment that constituted the scandal.

Do not imagine that nonviolence is always defensive; it is sometimes aggressive. The nonviolent man who lives in Brussels may well take a train or a plane to Algeria, to India, or to other places where terrible things are happening. He can enter the thick of the fighting, assail the tyrants and bear the message of peace at his own risk (for it is likely enough that both sides will let him have it). But the desired solution consists in two things: conversion and reconciliation. These are the normal results of nonviolent combat, which ought not leave anyone the loser. Violent combat always leaves at least one loser, and sometimes two. If there is only one loser, the other antagonist will lose next time, because the chain of legitimate acts of violence is not snapped by the end of the fighting.

Just as Jesus Christ did not have for his enemies thieves, murderers, or prostitutes, the nonviolent do not have to worry about thieves, murderers, or prostitutes. Nonviolent resisters meet such people in dank holes where they have been thrown together and manage to get along with them quite well. Jesus Christ did not strike down the sinners. No, he pardoned them, saying: "Go, my friend, and sin no more, lest something worse befall you." For sins and failings are not interesting, they are nothingness. They do not concern us.

Violent Justice

What does concern us is the ferocity of the respectable people who have hit upon a perfect outlet in the form of "Justice." What concerns us is the concatenation of legitimate acts of violence. We must reassess something that is at the very foundation of our society: Violent Justice. Take a man who has killed another: what do we do with him? We cut his head off. How many dead does that make? Does one plus one equal zero? "The punishment washes away the crime." "The guilty serves his time." Not at all; the crime is intensified and aggravated, and this without the excuse that murderers have, of ignorance, passion, or what have you. Judges, policemen, and soldiers do not have these excuses; they are on the contrary well indoctrinated, well schooled in this sanguinary foolishness.

Beyond the concatenations of violent justice there is the unchaining of legitimate violence. The just war. Who wage wars? Murderers? Evil men? Bandits? By no means. It is the good churchgoers like yourselves, loving fathers and dutiful sons. These worthy folk can commit in the course of one day more crimes than all the malefactors in the world have in a century. Who are the people working on the Bomb? Scoundrels? Monsters? Killers? No, honorable scientists who are doing their job. We are dying, because they are doing their job!

Excuse me if I am partial to crime that is called crime! The linked acts of legitimate violence and the unleashing of violent justice have brought the world to the very edge of the abyss, and that is exactly where we stand. These things have been at the same time criminal and cloaked with the sanctions of morality and legality, they have been obvious yet well concealed. Which is why nonviolence demands that we cry out: "Look at what you are doing, I say, look at what you are doing, and at least wake up before you die to the fact that things cannot go on this way." Actually, at present, it is no longer a question of some scattered victims; all of us are in the line of fire. It is precisely in this historical moment that the national and international political power of nonviolence is revealed.

It is owing to the epic of Gandhi that this word *nonviolence* entered our language. Whenever Gandhi was asked if he was the inventor of nonviolence, he would reply: "Nonviolence is as old as the hills." Indeed we come across it in the Gospels, and five centuries earlier Buddha had said: "Evil is not checked by evil, but by good." And he added: "Such is the ancient law." When we respectable folk hear a particularly atrocious crime described, how do we react? "What a monster! I hope they catch him quickly and give him a dose of his own medicine. Hanging is too good for him; it's over too quickly." When we say this, we are forging a link in the chain that will end in annihilation. This simple judgment initiates the sequence of crimes that are called, not crimes, but patriotic glory, liberation, etc.

What does nonviolence say? "What an unfortunate man! How can we set to work and produce some good that will be equal to all that evil, so that the evil can be truly compensated for and wiped out, so that life can arise from death, so that we can enter into the liberty of life and not into an infernal cycle?"

There is a task for you! For it is a matter of reversing all our accustomed ways of doing things and looking at things. Such a reversal is actually a rectification, for we have managed to construct a world that is inside out. We could say that Babel made a tower mounting up to heaven, but the people of Babel were suspended with their heads down and their bodies in the air; they seemed to be building but they were really digging. They used baked bricks and asphalt for cement, now we go on with explosions. It was then a question of reaching heaven. We are already at the moon. A splendid achievement! The moon is the celestial hell! The more we build, the more we destroy. The primary thread, the atom, has been split; we have only to press the button and everything will unravel like a stocking. And it is not the wicked who have brought us to this pass but respectable scientists, decent citizens—and moreover it has all been done for the good of humanity. And many good people are naive enough to believe this.

Nonviolence Begins at Home

Before proceeding, let us observe that it is useless to try to put the world in order if we have not put our own house in order, or our own house if we have not put ourselves in order. We all know great humanitarian pacifists who are continually quarreling with their wives and with every representative of humanity whom they encounter. We have to begin by practicing on ourselves the labor of conversion that will make us genuinely nonviolent. If nonviolence is an external device, a technique, a tactic, it is ignoble. In order to have the right to practice nonviolence, we must be nonviolent ourselves, at least to a degree, and the first work must be done on ourselves.

We cannot wish to make our children cannon fodder. We

want them to grow into men, free men, who will live and not merely function. We do not want prisoners, nor well-fed, well-paid slaves who can be bribed into doing anything and who look no further than the ends of their noses. Nonviolence will teach us to heighten our attention and to question ourselves as to where each one of our actions will take us.

I promised to speak of nonviolence in contemporary life. It was necessary to approach our subject in this way; we are coming to it now. I trust that you are all familiar with the epic struggle of Gandhi and know how he liberated India from a magnificently armed enemy, which retreated, in spite of all its guns and gold. If it retreated, it was because it was forced to, and thus nonviolence *is* a force. Has the time not come to apply this force to National Defense instead of continuing to reason as if we were still in Mac-Mahon's time? The next conflagration will mean total destruction. Under pretext of defending our goods we will annihilate everything that we have, and ourselves to boot. We must not imitate those imbeciles who say: "Just the same, you can't turn back progress." Progress is a fine thing, provided we know what we are progressing towards. If it is towards the abyss, what is the use of it?

It does not follow that we must not defend ourselves; it is just that evil means of defending ourselves are henceforth ruled out, unless we want to commit suicide. It is therefore time to study the right way of defending ourselves against a possible assailant. Let us study the methods Gandhi used in India. Perhaps, by dint of study and practice, we shall find ways to avoid the conflict, or limit it, or salvage something from the ruins. If a train is launched on the rails at top speed with no brakes, it will overturn. Nonviolence means applying the brakes and refusing to let ourselves be carried along at top speed to the abyss.

The Threefold Revolution

In India, Gandhi solved three problems: territorial liberation, restoration of dignity to the untouchables, and cessation of the war with Pakistan. Let us not imagine that these are remote problems. They are identical with ours: defense of freedom, social justice, and an end to the war. Resistance to tyranny, and to all forms of abuse, must continue. Every abuse is an embryo from which, sooner or later, the most serious acts of violence will emerge. In man's willingness to rebel against injustice lies his nobility.

How can a nonviolent revolution be carried out? How can we act upon the words: "If a man strikes thee on thy right cheek, turn the other cheek also towards him"? Which means: "Impel your enemy to do twice the evil he intended." Because, if he has done wrong, he is well aware of the punishment he can expect. He expects to get what he deserves. Instead, you make him double, triple, or quadruple his offense. Now every evil-doer has a point beyond which he will not go, where he says: "No! This I cannot do!" We must therefore induce the enemy to go on piling up wrongs until something inside him tips the scales and obliges him to stop. If you are dealing with a government, it suffices to attack it because of an unjust law or a violation of its own laws that it hopes to get away with. This is where we seek the nonviolent point of attack and corner the government with its own unjust law, force it to disgorge the malice of its unjust law. How do we do this? By freely exposing ourselves to its blows, as many as possible, and as quickly as possible. But sometimes a single blow will suffice.

The system of defense of the law is grounded in the cowardice of the individual citizen, who has little liking for fines and still less for jail or blows. Questioned by the police, he covers himself with apologies, and if he thinks he is going to be collared, he takes flight. But what can the law do to people who insist that penalties be applied to them for infractions of the law that do not impinge on morality? This is known as *Civil Disobedience*. To obtain a trial can be one motive. The trial is a free soapbox offered by the government to the nonviolent resister, in which he can tell the public everything that the government does not want them to hear and reach the consciences of judges, policemen, armies and public opinion.

Peaceful Warriors

Pitched battles of nonviolence took place in India. People advanced with their arms at their sides, their hands open but not raised, and they kept on coming until they were pressing

against the cordons of armed police, when the order was
given: "Fire!" or "Strike!" The enemy fired or struck and the
ones who were hit fell. Then two more would step up, unarmed and with their hands open. Madness? Collective suicide? But experience demonstrates that this method involves
much less loss of life than the slightest armed skirmish. If a
thousand lives are lost, it is over, and you have won. The
police will not fire any more, even when they are threatened
by their superiors. They are no longer functioning; now they
understand.

No doubt, you will say, but India is far off and the Indians
are such gentle people. Wrong on both counts. Indians are not
gentle, and we are not incapable of nonviolence. If you know
anything about the history of India, you know that it is, like all
histories, replete with horrors. For no man is born nonviolent,
any more than he is born charitable. We become charitable by
conversion, by domination of our natures and modification of
our natural feelings. All of us are violent and cowardly by
nature, and the more cowardly we are the more violent; it is
this combination of violence and cowardice that makes up the
brute strength of every army. To practice nonviolence is to
rise above violence and fear and their linkages. Gandhi said:
"Be courteous, truthful, and fearless."

Let us recall the long and glorious tradition of nonviolence in the West. We could find examples in the most
remote stretches of antiquity, but we shall begin with the civil
disobedience and noncooperation practised by the early Christians, and the method of the martyrs. For it was a method, one
that the pagans of their time and ours have had difficulty in
grasping. When did the martyr make his nonviolent stand? At
the moment when the magistrate commanded him to burn
incense before the idol?

What is an idol? A piece of wood. And what is incense? A
puff of smoke. As a realistic modern, when I am constrained by
force, I tell myself: "All I have to do is burn a little smoke
before a block of wood and they will let me alone. I shall go to
the catacombs and pray. . . . If they cut off all the best heads,
what will become of the movement? Whereas, with the help of

some carefully planned schemes, the show of force at the right moment . . ."

But without calculating, the early Christian refused, and even broke a piece off the statue to show that he was not in the least alarmed and that nonviolence is not as mild as people think. When one perished, twenty or a hundred were aroused by his example. And the Roman Empire was conquered and overthrown, and the barbarian invaders were conquered in their turn.

To witness for justice unto death, that is enough; and not to kill anyone, because if you have killed anyone you are unjust and all your work for justice has been meaningless.

What a revolution it would be to base our entire social doctrine on this simple foundation: "Thou shalt not kill"! Which also means: "Thou shalt not prepare to kill; thou shalt suppress every institution and every system that condones murder; thou shalt seek for an alternative, and thou shalt find one. For an alternative must be found, but it can never be found unless it is sought for."

The Present Age

Let us pass on to modern times. How many violent revolutions have we not witnessed in the past hundred years, and with what dubious results! Certainly it is an act of justice to get rid of a tyrant. To attain this end, we choose leaders who are cleverer and stronger than the tyrant, and if we are lucky and succeed—well then, we have a tyrant of our own choosing. It was not the end that was wrong; the mischief entered with our choice of the means.

If you have a just end, make use of just means and allow the injustices to accumulate on the other side. Returning the adversary's blows does not stop him, but provokes him. It takes two to fight; two must have agreed to fight. But if you will not agree, you must not be the accomplice of the violent. Do not imitate your enemy. If you believe that he is doing wrong, then you must not act as he does. When someone calls on you to put out a fire, you come with buckets of water, not with torches.

During the reign of the czars, Poland, which was groaning

under the Russian boot, petitioned the Emperor for a parliament. It happened that a great poet and patriot was being
buried, and the entire city of Warsaw followed his casket. The
police were made uneasy by the seemingly endless queue of
mourners. The procession was ordered to halt, but it kept on;
the police then charged and a number of people were killed or
injured. The procession re-formed. That was all that happened.
And Poland obtained its parliament. Later on, lacking leadership and organization, the country slipped back into its accustomed violence and its armed revolt was crushed by the Russians, who had been waiting for precisely this opportunity.

South America is not particularly noted for its revolutionary nonviolence. In 1931, the dictator in Chile was a general.
When a child was killed under his régime, a whole city filed
behind the tiny coffin. The next day the dictator departed. He
was an intelligent dictator. In 1956, Colombia was ruled by
what was generally regarded as the best-armed dictatorship in
the hemisphere. The students began to distribute little slips of
paper on which the word *libertad* was printed. Large posters
soon appeared on the walls announcing that those who continued to distribute *los papelitos* would be subject to the death
penalty. That same night, the whole city descended into the
streets and distributed the papers. The police clubbed the
demonstrators indiscriminately and arrested as many as they
could. But the next morning this dictator had departed, for he
too was an intelligent dictator. Who would have believed there
were so many?

The Aldermaston marches in England originated when a
single man made the trip carrying a placard that read: "No to
Atomic Death." Last year, tens of thousands massed at Trafal-
gar Square; their theme was: "Disarm first without waiting for
others to follow. We do not want this kind of 'defense.'" Each
year has seen thousands of new participants. Men like Bertrand Russell, who in his eighties had the courage to sit down
on the sidewalk and insist on being arrested. Up until then, he
had tried to publicize his warnings and the press had steadfastly ignored them. Now we are able to say that we have just
as much right as murderers do to be honored by the attention
of the mass-circulation press.

Resistance in France

Even before the English demonstrations, eighty of us in France entered the atomic plant and refused to leave until we were dragged out. At that time, France did not have the Bomb, the government was pretending that it didn't want it, and the engineers and scientists were solemnly swearing that never . . .

Action Civique Non-Violente is trying to make the law disgorge its malice. Our first target was five concentration camps where Algerian suspects were being detained. Our thirty volunteers went to these camps and asked to speak to the director. They said to him: "We know that in these camps are suspects, most of them French, and against whom no judgment has been rendered. Now we too, sir, are most of us French, and no charge has been made against us. We therefore fulfill the necessary conditions and we are asking you to agree to lock us up in your camp along with them." Well, far from locking us up, they loaded us into trucks, drove us out into the country and scattered us in the fields. There was nothing for it but to return on foot and begin all over.

We encountered one camp director who was entirely friendly. To our request, he answered: "Gladly, gentlemen, but to lock you up I must have an order from the Ministry. Go to them and ask for such an order." So we went to see the Minister. The receptionist asked us if we were expected. "Expected? Certainly. He has been expecting us for the past month." The Minister did not come to greet us on the landing. Other representatives of the Republic had preceded us.

The government began by playing the game of nonviolence with us. It issued orders that the nonviolent resisters were not to be touched. It is quite remarkable that if anyone else had done a quarter of what we did, he would have been locked up and would still be behind bars. When it came to us, the whole sport consisted in sending us back.

But the swollen, haughty beast that is known as Power ends by falling into the trap. The government hurled itself on its prey as the fish hurls itself on the worm, without noticing that it conceals a hook. . . . We finally obtained the trial we

were looking for, and prison as well. It is true that this demonstration centered around a different aspect of the Algerian
war: it concerned the *malaise* of the youth of France in regard
to military service in Algeria.

For those who refuse war, a poor course is to take flight[1]
or to go over to the enemy, even if they believe that the enemy
has the better cause. If the enemy were nonviolent, this would
be a different matter, for then, both cause and means employed being good, we would go to his aid without hesitation.
We had launched appeals addressed to the young: "Resist the
Algerian War, make your intentions clear, go to prison." Now
you cannot urge other people to go to prison without being
prepared to go along with them. Which we did.

We had proposed to the government that we go to Algeria
and work for the welfare of its people by forming a civil service there. Since the government would not let us perform this
service in Algeria, we were doing it in France on behalf of the
Algerians.

Forbidden Games

Thus, for example, Paul Dupont, who rejects military service,
is working in our shop, having duly notified his colonel. The
police arrive and ask for Paul Dupont.

"Just a moment, gentlemen, we shall find him for you."

A few minutes later, ten men appear, all chained to one
another. The police regard them with astonishment.

"But which one of you is really Paul Dupont?"

"We are all Paul Dupont," they answer.

The police turn to us. "Tell us which one is really Paul
Dupont."

"We can say nothing. Ask them."

"Your papers?"

Since none of the ten have any papers, they are all arrested.

"And until you have admitted who you really are, you will
all remain in prison."

[1] The speaker later explained that he was not making a blanket condemnation of those who do desert; he was simply emphasizing that
flight, which does not eliminate the grounds of dispute, is not a solution.

During the next several weeks, inquiries are pursued, the men's identities are established by the authorities, and only Paul Dupont is kept in jail. The nine who have been released then start the game over again, with a new objector. And this goes on up to the trial.

It is a trial whose like has not been seen since the days of Gandhi. The public prosecutor eulogizes the lofty motives of the accused and their courage in affirming what they believe to be true, even though their actions cannot be permitted under the laws in force; he hopes that the tribunal will find a way to reconcile the demands of the law with those of conscience, that some day humanity will have discovered its true vocation and that the courts will no longer have to concern themselves with matters of this kind.

I hope I will be excused for talking about ourselves; I began with large truths and I am ending with sundry events. But in these matters the most humble act of witness, provided it is both pure and clear, is worth more than the most brilliant theories.

(*Translated by Martin J. Corbin*)

Bradford Lyttle

On Nonviolent Obstruction*

During the summer, a group of pacifists and pacifist sympathizers demonstrated against the Atlas intercontinental ballistics missile base site being constructed near Cheyenne, Wyoming. Five demonstrators were imprisoned for trespassing during demonstrations conducted at missile launching site A, the first site under construction. One of these people, Kenneth Calkins, was struck by a truck while sitting in the gateway to the site. Before being sentenced to jail, he was hospitalized for ten days.

The Cheyenne demonstrations have raised important theoretical questions concerning the use of nonviolent resistance. They have given rise to a new distinction, that of a difference between *civil disobedience*, the violation of a law in course of a nonviolent demonstration, and *nonviolent obstruction*, the nonviolent physical obstruction of actions one believes to be morally wrong. The distinction arose partly because of the peculiar physical location of the missile site at which the demonstrations took place. Site A is an enclave. The land for the site is owned by the government, and construction companies working on the site have been granted access to it by the private parties owning the surrounding territory. People wishing to demonstrate at the site therefore were compelled to pass over private land at the risk of violating a trespassing law (civil disobedience). Trucks enter the government property through gates in the surrounding fence. Some demonstrators nonviolently obstructed the passage of trucks and other equipment by standing, sitting or lying in the gateway or on the road leading to it. Such obstruction was termed nonviolent obstruction.

* November, 1958.

There was agreement among participants in the project that civil disobedience was justified and within the moral right of the demonstrators. Civil disobedience involved no obstruction and usually trespassing occurred because a demonstrator wished to exercise the democratic right of distributing leaflets or talking to construction workers.

However, differences of opinion arose regarding the use of nonviolent obstruction.

The use of this technique was criticized on several main grounds. One is that obstructing the passage of equipment and harassing the construction workers, even by nonviolent methods, involves infringing upon their rights to do what they see to be their right and duty. The demonstrators believe that it is morally wrong to build missile sites. The construction workers believe that it is right—missiles are needed for national defense. Those who argue against nonviolent obstruction say that under these circumstances demonstrators have the right to appeal verbally to the workers but no right to harass or obstruct them.

Other arguments raised against nonviolent obstruction were that the technique can be misinterpreted easily by the public, tends to support an unfavorable image of the demonstrators, and tends to create public hostility. The public, it is argued, sees the technique as obstruction only and misses the moral reasons behind it.

Let us look at these arguments more carefully:

Infringement upon the rights of the workers. Here is a possible hypothetical situation:

If you see a man beating a woman or child with a club, has he the moral right to continue unobstructed? Do you have no moral right nonviolently to prevent his action?

Clearly, to me, the most responsible behavior would be to use every nonviolent means at your disposal to stop the beating, even if this meant interposing your body between the attacker and his victim, and taking the blows on yourself.

This is much the situation at the missile base. The truck and equipment drivers are constructing a ghastly weapon that can cremate alive millions of innocent human beings. They may believe that they are morally right in building the base;

they may need the wages they earn to support their families. Nevertheless, I can see a moral imperative for *obstructing* their work by every moral, nonviolent means available. Do not the lives of ten million men, women and children threatened by the base make nonviolent obstruction a responsible policy?

The true principle seems to me to be this: that everyone has the moral right to try and frustrate what he regards as evil by means which are not bad in themselves.

Violation of the democratic process. Those who use this argument have forgotten, or never read, Thoreau's essay "On Civil Disobedience." An act of a majority should never *bind* a minority. The democratic process is a valuable political technique and tradition but if the will of the majority is to do evil, it becomes the moral duty of the minority who sees what is right to oppose that will. I respect the democratic process whether or not it is in its proper place in relation to conscience and moral law. But respect for the *process* does not entail giving priority to its *results* rather than priority to conscience. In Cheyenne, a result of this process is the construction of a missile base which can cremate alive millions of innocent people.

Generation of hostility. An increase in immediate public hostility should not bring panicky abandonment of a tremendously powerful educational tool.

Many pacifist leaders felt that the great hostility and misunderstanding produced in Cheyenne by the use of nonviolent obstruction was hurting the pacifist movement and should not be used. I wonder if these leaders, who wish to discard an educational technique because it produces hostility, remember, or have read, George Fox's *Journal,* or *At the Feet of the Mahatma* by Rajendra Prasad. Fox and his fellow "ministers of truth" barely survived the beatings they endured in their proselytizing. Hundreds of Indians were shot by the British in the Amritsar, Jallianwalla Bagh massacre.

Gandhi never suspended civil disobedience or discarded an educational technique because it produced hostility. He stopped only when hostility or violence crept into the action of his followers. Gandhi judged the nonviolence of his educational techniques before he employed them. He did not use a technique, then judge its nonviolence by the effect it produced.

I believe that the hostility at Cheyenne was produced by the exceptional power of the educational technique of nonviolent obstruction. At this point it seems to me valuable to explore the possible sources of this power.

Nonviolent obstruction dramatizes the importance of the issue. Most missile site construction workers probably see little more than a weekly pay check in their work. It is doubtful that they fully understand the arguments used by opponents to the base. You can dismiss a man who hands you a leaflet without taking him seriously. It is very difficult to dismiss him if he sits down before your truck. He is either crazy or motivated by something very important to him.

Nonviolent obstruction makes real to the construction workers the issues symbolized by the missile base. A construction worker and the public may regard a missile base as a new source of income for the locality, a glamorous toy (Air Force propaganda talks of "Missile Slinging Cheyenne"). Actually, a missile can cremate alive three million people and pulverize the largest city. The realities of death are excluded from an American city, but a nonviolent resister sitting in front of a truck raises these realities to public consciousness. The truck driver finds himself faced with the choice of running over the man and killing him or stopping and dragging him out of the way. The idea of murder is not normally associated with the missile base for him. Now it is. He sees a man sitting in the dust before his truck who is silently saying to him, "Kill me before you build this missile base; kill me before you help kill a million innocent people." Nonviolent obstruction raises the moral issue of murder, the reality of death.

To a Christian or theist, nonviolent obstruction can be interpreted as an act of atonement. In this interpretation, the changes in the minds of construction workers that would lead them to give up work on the base would be wrought by God. The resister prays: "Lord, I offer to you my life that this hideous weapon of death may not be built. I will risk death so that these construction workers and the American people in general may be redeemed from their wicked design."

Misinterpretation of the technique. Pacifists have long

been articulate with tongue, typewriter, and mimeograph. It isn't misinterpretation from which their cause suffers most; it is from not being listened to. Before nonviolent obstruction was used at Cheyenne, the project was ignored. All the releases and leaflets made little dent on public apathy. Nonviolent obstruction shattered the apathy, local and national. Many of the people of Cheyenne may have been made hostile; they were also made *aware*.

Elements of the situation are similar to those which caused the British general strike of 1929 to fail. Fenner Brockway, in his brilliant history *Inside the Left,* says that the strike failed because Britain's labor leaders did not really believe in their slogans of socialist revolution and became fearful when the immense nonviolent power of their strike brought national political power within their grasp. It would sadden me greatly to think that leaders of the pacifist movement were equally uncertain of their professed intentions, equally timid in the use of their nonviolent weapons.

One sponsor of the *Golden Rule* told me that participants in nonviolent action projects were confident that the odds heavily favored their escape without injury. I consider participation under such persuasion unrealistic and unwise. At Cheyenne, my constant admonition to demonstrators was, "If you sit in front of trucks you face death." Before Ken Calkins' injury no one seemed to agree with me.

Much of the weakness of the peace movement is due to anemia caused by too much middle-class prudence, too little imagination and resolute action. We must think and act on the assumption that we can bring about a nonviolent revolution against the tradition of military power.

Juanita Nelson

A Matter of Freedom

In March 1959, I hunted through the Sears-Roebuck sales cata-
logue for something to throw around my nakedness when I
emerged from the bath or lounged around the house, an eco-
nomical garment to double as a beach robe. I finally ordered
J934: white terrycloth, full back, worn with or without a belt,
three-quarter length sleeves, shipping weight 1 lb. 12 oz. Over
the left breast was a green, yellow, red and blue emblem, a
garish enough flower for a rebel coat of arms.

I give the preceding account in all its triviality because
three months later, on June 1, the versatile robe became
something more than either Sears or I had intended; it became
a provocative "kimona" around which revolved considerable
consternation on the part of certain public officials and a great
deal of reassessment on my part.

The first link between the robe and my intellectual processes was my declination to pay income taxes because most of
the money goes for H-bombs and other combustibles capable
of setting off conflagrations which cannot be extinguished by
the average hook-and-ladder company. I balk at the notion of
contributing so directly to making atomic hash of others and
perhaps of my own wonderful self. The final bond was forged
by the early hours kept by those who execute the orders of the
United States government. They, apparently, do not require as
much sleep as I do. Perhaps if I had business as important to
attend to—bringing in the Body—I would not need so much
sleep either, or I would forego it for the important job I had
to perform. Justice, I suppose, never slumbers, and she must
demand the same insomnia of her bondmen. But I, not being
affiliated in any way with justice or the Department of Justice
was sleeping soundly and in my accustomed nudity when the

doorbell rang at 6:30 a. m. I slipped into the bargain bathrobe
and stumbled to the door.

Two somber men stood there. As if they were in some way
hooked to the hinges, they flipped open their identification
wallets as soon as the door began to swing open. I did not
bother to examine their credentials, accepting their word that
they were U. S. marshals. I invited them in. They were all
brusqueness and business as they sat on the edge of the sofa to
which I waved them.

"We have an order for your arrest," said one, and thrust
toward me a blue-covered legal-looking document.

I was startled. For eleven years, my husband, Wally, and I
had neither paid withholding taxes nor filed any forms, fully
aware that we were operating on a brink-of-imprisonment
policy. Wally managed to find work that did not come under
withholding tax provisions. I was, therefore, able to claim him
as my dependent and could earn up to about twenty-five dollars on any one job with no tax withheld. I usually held a
couple of such jobs and so earned a taxable income. Then,
several years ago, the revenuers tardily checked on two part-
time jobs I had held simultaneously from 1952 to 1955 and
began billing me for a sum which finally mounted to $959.83,
including penalties for interest and fraud. And in March I had
been served with a summons to appear at the Internal Revenue office in Philadelphia with my records. Our procedure all
along had been not to cooperate with the collection of information, and we felt we would probably not cooperate with an
arrest. Protest through individual income-tax refusal appears to
most folks about as effective as scooping out the Pacific Ocean
with a spoon; it seemed even more hopeless to dump each
spoonful of water into a tunnel which led back to the ocean. I
had refused even to accept the summons and had heard no
more from that quarter. In spite of Wally's warnings that "you
never can tell what those guys will do," I think that way down
I had come to disbelieve that I could ever be considered
enough of a threat or an affront to the government to stir up
anything more than this kind of bureaucratic feinting. But
even with the best intentions in the world of going to jail, I

would have been startled to be awakened at 6:30 a. m. to be told that I was under arrest.

When the marshals offered me the order I said, "I am not interested in that," keeping my hands tightly clasped in my lap. I tried, in words which sounded hackneyed to my ears, to explain my position briefly.

"*We* are not interested in *that*," they said. "You can tell it to the judge."

"I would be glad to tell it to the judge," I said, "if he will come to see me. But I do not wish to go to jail to tell him these things. I am not paying taxes because the overwhelming percentage of the budget goes for war purposes. I do not wish to participate in any phase of the collection of such taxes. I do not even want to act as if I think that anyone, including the government, has a right to punish me for an act which I consider honorable. I cannot come with you."

There was less fuss than I had thought there might be. Clearly, these men had studied my dossier and were undoubtedly informed of my friendship with Maurice McCrackin, tax-refusing minister, who had just completed a six months sentence for the same offense. Mac had not been at all clerical— they'd had to carry him into court each time. And Wally they knew about, too—his 33 months in prison after walking out of Civilian Public Service camp during World War II, the 108-day fast (with force-feeding by tube) which had preceded his release.

At any rate, they seemed not inclined to philosophize. After a few appeals to my common sense, the sterner of the two marshals said mildly, "Well, if you won't come with us we'll have to carry you in." He left to summon a red car.

I realized that I was actually going to jail. And, at that point, I became acutely conscious of the robe. Should I quietly excuse myself, get dressed, then return to take up my recalcitrant position? It would have been simpler, of course, if they had left and made their entrance again, with me fully aware that they meant business. Debating the question, I went to the bathroom, brushed my teeth, ran a comb through my hair. These simple acts of grooming brought me back to reality sufficiently to realize that I might be spirited away. Wally was off on a sales trip, and I had no way of reaching him. I put the cap back on the toothpaste and went to the telephone, which is on a wall between the dining room and the kitchen, a considerable distance down a long, high-ceilinged hallway from the living room where I'd left the deputy. I was still on the phone when I heard the click of the door announcing reinforcements. There was a tentative, "Mrs. Nelson," as though there was some fear I might be in too delicate a position to be barged in on. As I raced to get information to a friend, the deputies and two policemen converged on me. Other policemen trooped in. I remember saying as I hung up, "I'm surrounded."

Seven law enforcement officers had stalked in. I sat on the stool beneath the telephone, my back literally to the wall, the seven hemming me about in a semicircle. All of them appeared over six feet tall, and all of them were annoyed.

"Look," said one, "you're gonna go anyway. You might as well come peaceful."

There they stood, ready and able to take me at any moment. But no move was made. The reason was obvious.

"Why don't you put your clothes on, Mrs. Nelson?" This was a soft spoken plea from the more benign deputy. "You're not hurting anybody but yourself." His pained expression belied the assertion.

One policeman snorted when I attempted to say that they needn't take me at all.

The benign deputy made a last try. "Do you believe in God, Mrs. Nelson?" Irrationally, stalling for time, I asked, "Are you asking me as an individual or as an official?"

The marshal answered as if the question were not at all out of the ordinary, at least no more than the whole situation.

"I'm asking you as an individual."

"No," I said.

Taken aback, he did not go on to explain the connection he had evidently been going to establish between God and dressing for arrest.

When the affairs of men have reached a stalemate, there seems always some man of action to come forward. There was such a one among the seven. He was not a member of a debating society. These questions had nothing to do with him.

I cannot describe his physical appearance, for he was not a face or a personality; he was a no-nonsense voice and a pair of strong arms.

"Listen, we don't have to beg her to do anything. We'll just take her the way she is, if that's the way she wants it." He snapped a pair of handcuffs around my wrists and, with another pair of brawny arms, half carried, half dragged me down the hall, the other five trooping after. In the street, the no-nonsense transporter delighted in maneuvering me into a position to expose the nakedness under the robe. One of the unencumbered tried desperately to arrange my limbs so that the robe would fall circumspectly and unrevealingly about my ankles. On my part there was a fleeting anxiety about the exhibition, but I was too engrossed in anticipating next steps to worry overmuch, especially as, at that early hour, there were few around to gawk. I thought fleetingly of Corbett Bishop, World War II C. O. who practiced such consistent noncooperation that he suffered a roach to go down with the mush he was being tube fed. I did not shift from the spot where I was dumped on the floor of the paddy wagon as we drove down Market Street to the Federal Court Building.

When the doors opened, I continued to sit. My thoughts were like buckshot, so scattered they didn't hit anything or, when they did, made little dent. The robe was a huge question mark placed starkly after some vexing problems.

Why am I going to jail? Why am I going to jail in a bathrobe? What does it matter in the scheme of things whether or not you put on your clothes? Are you not making at best, a futile gesture, at worst, flinging yourself against something which does not exist? Is freedom more important than justice? Of what does freedom of the human spirit consist, that quality on which I place so much stress? How important is the exercise of that freedom if it conflicts or seems to conflict with the maintenance of the dignity of other individuals or of institutions? Was it enough, in any case, to have made the gesture of refusing to pay for weapons of destruction? What was the purpose of extending that gesture to such complete noncooperation with legally constituted authority? Was it only a gesture? How much is one demeaning himself when he kowtows either to authority or to custom, in short, to myths? When one does not yield is he simply being rigid, humorless, arrogant, or is he defending that innermost place, the last sanctuary of selfness?

And all these questions turned around a basic question: Who am I? If I could know who I was, at least who I conceived myself to be, then I would be able to approach those other questions.

The same two stalwarts yanked me from the van, hardly giving me time to alight under my own power had I wished to do so. They divined my attitude correctly. I was becoming increasingly rigid as the situation became more ridiculous and I less certain of myself. They carried me by the elbows down a long corridor and up a flight of stairs to an elevator. One patiently endured while the other impatiently endured. I really did relate to the two men at one point. I realized how heavy an almost inert body can be as I saw the perspiration run down their faces. But did they have any conception of how difficult it was for me to be carried? They let me slide to the floor in the elevator, from where, fortunately, it was only a few steps to the cell. They sat me on the bench and left, vastly relieved to have finished their part in the business.

I did not know the time. I did not know precisely what charges had been lodged against me. I did not know when I was to be tried. I had the beginnings of a nagging headache. I had been plopped onto a wooden bench which ran along two sides of the tiny barred cell. There was a toilet and a washstand with a drinking fountain attachment. This was the first time I had been in such a cage, having been confined in ordinary rooms in previous jail experiences. A narrow corridor ran between the cell row and the outside wall. I contemplated dappled bits of sunlight scurrying through the venetian blinds covering the window opposite the cell. I could not see anyone, but I heard the murmur of voices around one end of the hall where, I supposed, were the administrative offices.

I was just soaking things in. I was feeling more sensitive about the robe, not being quite able to determine its role in the affair. I did come to one conclusion. Until I made up my mind about what I was doing and why, I would continue in the most extreme position. I would not do anything, only suffer what was done to me. Almost as if I had divined what was coming, I resolved not to leave the cell under my own power for any reason whatsoever except to go home. I remembered almost excrutiatingly an experience in the Cincinnati County jail on a charge of disorderly conduct for trying to gain admission to an amusement park which barred Negroes. I did not eat during the nine days. I would not wear the prison uniform. But, thinking I was exercising what degree of freedom I had, I wandered about the floor at will and bounced downstairs to see visitors. But there was always the agony of afterwards. I could not endure being dragged upstairs each time, and returning voluntarily was degrading.

So, when the deputy interrupted my reverie to announce visitors, whom I could see in the waiting room, I told him I would leave only to be released. He shrugged his shoulders and left. Well, I thought, they're not going to get themselves into a stew about this.

In a few minutes I heard a hearty, "Well, good morning." Two fellow pacifists, one of them also a tax refuser, had been permitted to come to me, since I would not go to them. I asked them what was uppermost in my mind, what they'd do about getting properly dressed. They said that this was something I would have to settle for myself. I sensed that they thought it the better part of wisdom and modesty for me to be dressed for my appearance in court. They were more concerned about the public relations aspect of getting across the witness than I was. They were also genuinely concerned, I knew, about making their actions truly nonviolent, cognizant of the other person's feelings, attitudes and readiness. I was shaken enough to concede that I would like to have my clothes at hand, in case I decided I would feel more at ease in them. The older visitor, a dignified man with white hair, agreed to go for the clothes in a taxicab.

They left, and on their heels came another visitor. She had been told that in permitting her to come up, the officials were treating me with more courtesy than I was according them. It was her assessment that the chief deputy was hopeful that someone would be able to hammer some sense into me, and was willing to make concessions in that hope. But he had mis-judged the reliance he might place in her—she was not as critical as the men. She did not know what she would do, but she thought she might wish to have the strength and the audacity to carry through in the vein in which I had started.

And she said, "You know, you look like a female Gandhi in that robe. You look, well, dignified."

That was my first encouragement. Everyone else had tended to make me feel like a fool of the first water, had confirmed fears I already had on that score. My respect and admiration for Gandhi, though not uncritical, was deep. And if I in any way resembled him in appearance I was prepared to try to emulate a more becoming state of mind. I reminded myself, too, that I had on considerably more than the loincloth in which Gandhi was able to greet kings and statesmen with ease. I need not be unduly perturbed about wearing a robe into the presence of an His Honor.

I had, I think, been immobilized partly by a sense of my own failures as a human being. Here was I, still struggling with the meaning of my own life and standing, it seemed some-times, on dead center. How, then, did I have the effrontery to question a whole way of life that had been evolved slowly and painfully through the ages by the accumulated wisdom of mankind? How could I presume to have so much of the truth that I would defy constituted authority? What made me so certain of myself in this regard? I was not certain. But it seemed to me that if I should see only one thing clearly, it was not necessary to see all things clearly in order to act on that one thing.

One pinpoint of clarity was that it was time for man to grow out of the short pants of barbarism, of settling things by violence, and at least to get into the knee breeches of honestly seeking and trying ways more fitted to his state as a human. To take life, especially in cold-blooded, organized fashion, seems to me to be the province of no man and of no government. In the end, no government can do it—it is only men who fire guns, drop atom bombs, pierce with bayonets. If an entity called gov-ernment could slay another such entity, no great harm would be done and maybe even good would come of it—at least the destruction of files of papers. My repudiation of violence is not based on any conventionally or conveniently religious motivation. I cannot say that it is against God's will, since I do not know that there is a god, nor would I be able in any case to assume that I was conversant with his will. But I do not consider, either, that men are gods, that they should determine when another man should die. I do not consider that I am capable of such judgments, either of my own volition or at the command of others. Such behavior in others I abhor, but may not be able to affect. I *can* control my own behavior. And I do not think that my participation in stupid or immoral acts can add to my stature as an individual—I think, rather, that it might detract, take me even further afield from the discovery of myself.

It may be that most people think it necessary, if wicked and perhaps self-defeating, to build atom bombs to drop on such races of devils as inhabit Hiroshimas. We must save our skins, protect our way of life. Let me first excise the horns from my own head, since it was made, I think, for something besides butting. Besides, I cannot accept any package labeled "way of life," only those particular values which seem to me worth protecting, and I must protect them in a way which seems fitting to those values.

Suppose, though, that most citizens eagerly pay their money into the government's war chest before the tax deadline, and some sacrificially give more than their share. I have decided that this is not the best depository for the fruits of my labor. But believing as I do, I must, it seems, comply in order to uphold the system of law and to act in concert with my fellows. Holding that law can be an aid but never a substitute for individual integrity, responsibility, and perception, I want immediately to know: In concert for what? If it seems that the purpose of the united action is to create misery, cannot, in fact, have any other effect, then I must decline my part in the performance. In order for men to live together, it seems efficient for them to work out bodies of regulations. But efficiency can in no way supplant morality. Is the height of man's being obedience to the common will? I think it a higher purpose to live in a creatively oriented relationship than to adopt a slavish

attitude toward rules and regulations. I think it the worst part
of folly to be so enamored of acting in unison that I am herded
into acting inhumanly.

If those with opposing beliefs hold them so strongly, they
have at least the same choice of throwing their whole weight
into bringing about that state of affairs which they espouse—
not by bringing me to heel, but by giving all they have to their
own visions. I cannot think that the measure of one's belief is
the extent to which he tries to coerce others into believing it or
acting upon it, but the extent to which he is willing to sacrifice
for it himself. If, for instance, I am, because of my well-intentioned but mistaken notions, depriving the Department of Defense of ten dollars per year for making a guided missile, why
does not someone convinced of the necessity of the weapon
come forward and voluntarily make up that ten dollars? Is it
not mere pettiness to insist that I would stand to be "protected" by this sacrifice? (I would also stand to be annihilated
by it.) The money spent trying to make me comply could be
squandered, instead, on the purposes for which my tax money
would be used.

But, no, this non-compliance constitutes an affront which
cannot be ignored. It is no doubt the fear that even one insig-
nificant defiance will produce a rent in the whole fabric, and
that the cloth may some day be beyond repair. Perhaps we do
not need the garment at all and should throw it into the rag
bag before it is completely in tatters. If the idea I champion is
worthless, not many will be impressed to follow suit and my
intransigence can be regretted, deplored and suffered. If, on
the other hand, only the law keeps most people from acting
with me, then this must be the worst kind of despotism—it
must be the minority who are keeping the majority in line with
the whip of the law. Or perhaps everyone is being kept in line
with the whip, and no one dares look the thing in the face for
what it is.

Most people who take any notice of my position are appalled by my lawbreaking and not at all about the reasons for
my not paying taxes. Instead of trying to make me justify my
civil disobedience, why do they not question themselves and
the government about a course of action which makes billions

available for weapons, but cannot provide decent housing and education for a large segment of the population? Actually, many people seem envious that I have for so long been able to "get away with it," with not paying taxes. I wonder what would happen if the income tax laws were repealed tomorrow. Let everyone be sent a statement of what his fair share would be, to be paid on a voluntary basis. How many of the people who bark at me, "Do you think you should use the highways if you won't pay taxes?" would send in their assessments?

Anyway, because I believe that it is more important to do what is right than what is lawful or expedient, I have declined to pay the tax. All right, then, having determined this course of action for yourself, should you not be willing to accept punishment for your defiance? Why should I? I have stated that 1) I believe this particular measure to be so intolerable that I cannot abide by it; 2) I believe that I have every right, nay, every responsibility, to act according to my best judgment, not waiting for one hundred and fifty million others to concur. This one act may not lead inevitably to a good end, but I do not see that it can lead to a bad one. Why should I expect or accept punishment for exercising my best judgment? I was not a whit more contrite when the marshals came to arrest me than when I first declined to pay the tax. Would I go peaceably in order to show my compatriots that I do not utterly despise them and their institutions? If I must go to jail in order to demonstrate my respect, then they will have to believe as they believe; if I should go to jail willingly for that, I should undoubtedly end up despising myself at least. And how can one have respect for others without self-respect?

I think that what I was saying with my robe was that I was doing what I thought right. I was convinced enough to feel that it would be good if others were moved to do likewise. But I some time ago gave up the notion that it was my province to reform the world. But I think that if I have helped to start a fire, the first thing I must do is stop adding fuel to it. I could not very well help going to jail when seven strong men were determined I should go, but I did not wish them to think for a moment that I was on their side. You will do what you think you should, what you have been ordered to do, but I

shall not help you do it, no, not even to the extent of getting
dressed so that you may feel more comfortable in your mission.
If a law is bad or unjust, is not every phase of its enforcement
simply an extension of the law, and to be as greatly resisted?

I wanted passionately, perhaps grimly, to be myself.
Somewhere that self existed, independent of, though cognizant
of, all other selves, a being and a striving to be in inevitable
loneliness. I wanted to strip to the skeleton and clothe it with
my own humanity, my own meaning. Some parts of that self
could be satisfied only in the context of other selves, but that
participation would have to be voluntary, whether bound to
other selves in marriage, social club, or government. There is
no collective conscience. I think it is too bad that anyone
should suppose that holding me within their bounds, forcing
me to do what they think is good, is within their prerogatives.
It is no palliative that they do it impersonally, without having
thought through anything, but only because actions have become automatic through codification. I saw a movie about a
woman who was put to death by the state in a gas chamber.
Not the man who dissolved the crystals, nor the man who
pulled the switch, nor the woman who sat guard to keep the
prisoner from killing herself, nor the priest who heard her last
confession, nor the governor who might have commuted the
sentence, not one was anxious to have any part in that degrading performance. And yet each swallowed his revulsion like
vomit and, when he could not be saved by some decree,
played out his part.

It is, as far as I can see, an unpleasant fact that we cannot
avoid decision-making. We are not absolved by following the
dictates of a mentor or of a majority. For we then have made
the decision to do that—have concluded because of belief or of
fear or of apathy that this is the thing which we should do or
cannot avoid doing. And we then share in the consequences of
any such action. Are we doing more than trying to hide our
nakedness with a fig leaf when we take the view expressed by
a friend who belonged to a fundamental religious sect? At the
time he wore the uniform of the United States Marines. "I'm
not helping to murder," he said. "I'm carrying out the orders of
my government, and the sin is not mine." I could never tell

whether there was a bitter smile playing around his lips or if he was quite earnest. It is a rationalization commonly held and defended. It is a comforting presumption, but it still appears to me that, while the seat of government is in Washington, the seat of conscience is in me. It cannot be voted out of office by one or a million others.

I had not answered all the questions when I was wheeled into the courtroom in an office chair mounted on casters. I had not even asked all the questions.

But I had asked and answered enough to be able to leave behind me the brown paper bag holding my clothes. The commissioner received me in my robe. A friend who was in the courtroom noted that I was "brave but halting." Even so, it was necessary for me to suppress a smile or two. The consequences for me might be grave, but it *was* a comical situation.

The commissioner cited the law which empowered him to imprison me for a year and fine me a thousand dollars, or both. But he did not wish, he said, to be the first to commit a person to jail for flouting the law. He gave me until the following Friday, this was Tuesday, to comply with the court order.

At 2 p. m. Friday I was at the ironing board, rather nostalgic that this might be the last time I would perform that humble task for some time. In baggy blue jeans, I was disreputably but more respectably dressed than I had been three days before. But they did not come for me. Some weeks later I learned from a news release that charges had been dropped, since it could not be proven that I owed anything. (I was not, as a matter of fact, arrested for not paying the tax, but for contempt arising from refusal to show records.) Still, in my Christmas mail there was a bill from the Internal Revenue Service for $950.01.

If this was the prelude to another abduction, I can only hope that those attached to the court will have achieved that degree of nonchalance which I think I have attained regarding proper court attire. Or that they will at least first send out their intelligence agents to scout for more favorable circumstances for taking me into custody.

Albert S. Bigelow

Why I Am Sailing into the Pacific Bomb Test Area*

My friend Bill Huntington and I are planning to sail a small vessel westward into the Pacific H-bomb test area. By April we expect to reach nuclear testing grounds at Eniwetok. We will remain there as long as the tests of H-bombs continue. With us will be two other volunteers.

Why? Because it is the way I can say to my government, to the British government, and to the Kremlin: "Stop! Stop this madness before it is too late. For God's sake, turn back!"

How have I come to this conviction? Why do I feel under compulsion, under moral orders, as it were, to do this?

The answer to such questions, at least in part, has to do with my experience as a Naval officer during World War II. The day after Pearl Harbor was attacked, I was at the Navy recruiting offices. I had had a lot of experience in navigating vessels. Life in the Navy would be a glamorous change from the dull mechanism of daily civilian living. My experience assured me of success. All this adventure ahead and the prospect of becoming a hero into the bargain.

I suppose, too, that I had an enormous latent desire to conform, to go along with the rest of my fellows. I was swayed by the age-old psychology of meeting force with force. It did not really occur to me to resist the drag of the institution of war, the pattern of organized violence, which had existed for so many centuries. This psychology prevailed even though I had already reflected on the fantastic wastefulness of war—the German *Bismarck* hunting the British *Hood* and sending it to the bottom of the sea, and the British Navy hunting the *Bismarck* and scuttling it.

* February, 1958.

I volunteered, but instead of being sent to sea, I was assigned to 90 Church Street in New York and worked in project "plot," establishing the whereabouts of all combat ships in the Atlantic. In a couple of months I escaped from this assignment and was transferred to the Naval Training Station at Northwestern University.

I had not been at Northwestern very long when I sensed that because of my past experience I would be made an instructor there and still not get to sea. So I deliberately flunked an examination in navigation and before long was assigned to a submarine chaser in the Atlantic.

The Turkey Shoot

From March to October of 1943 I was in command of a submarine chaser in the Solomon Islands, during the fighting. It was during this period that more than 100 Japanese planes were shot down in one day. This was called "the Turkey Shoot." The insensitivity which decent men must develop in such situations is appalling. I remember that the corpse of a Japanese airman who had been shot down was floating bolt upright in one of the coves, a position resulting from the structure of the Japanese life belts, which were different from our Mae Wests. Each day as we passed the cove we saw this figure, his face growing blacker under the terrific sun. We laughingly called him Smiling Jack. As a matter of fact, I think I gave him that name myself and felt rather proud of my wit.

Later in World War II, I was Captain of the destroyer escort *Dale W. Peterson*—DE 337—and I was on her bridge as we came into Pearl Harbor from San Francisco when the first news arrived of the explosion of an atomic bomb over Hiroshima. Although I had no way of understanding what an atom bomb was I was absolutely awestruck, as I suppose all men were for a moment. Intuitively it was then that I realized for the first time that morally war is impossible.

I don't suppose I had the same absolute realization with my whole being, so to speak, of the immorality and "impossibility" of nuclear war until the morning of August 7, 1957. On that day, I sat with a score of friends, before dawn, in the Nevada desert just outside the entrance to the Camp Mercury testing grounds. The day before, eleven of us, in protest against the summer-long tests, had tried to enter the restricted area. We had been arrested as we stepped one after another over the boundary line, and had been carried off to a ghost town which stands at the entrance to Death Valley. There we had been given a speedy trial under the charge of trespassing under the Nevada laws. Sentencing had been suspended for a year, and later in the afternoon we had returned to Camp Mercury to continue the Prayer and Conscience Vigil along with others who had remained there during our civil disobedience action.

In the early morning of August 7 an experimental bomb was exploded. We sat with our backs to the explosion site. But when the flash came I felt again the utterly impossible horror of this whole business, the same complete realization that nuclear war must go, that I had felt twelve years before on the bridge of U. S. S. *Dale W. Peterson*, off Pearl Harbor.

I think also that deep down somewhere in me, and in all men at all times, there is a realization that the pattern of violence meeting violence makes no sense, and that war violates something central in the human heart—"that of God," as we Quakers sometimes say. For example, when each of us at the trial the afternoon before had told why we were committing civil disobedience against nuclear tests, our attorney, Francis Heisler, said: "There isn't one of us in this court room who doesn't wish that he had walked into the testing grounds with these people this morning." Everybody, including the police and court officers, nodded assent.

Society of Friends

However, I am ahead of my story. At the close of the War, in spite of what I had felt on the bridge of that destroyer, I did not break away from my old life. For a time I was Housing Commissioner of Massachusetts. Like many other people who had been through the War, I was seeking some sort of unified life-philosophy or religion. I did a good deal of religious "window-shopping." I became impressed by the fact that in one way or another the saints, the wise men, those who seem to me truly experienced, all pointed in one direction—toward nonviolence, truth, love, toward a way and a goal that could not be reconciled with war. For quite a while, to use a phrase of Alan Watts', I "sucked the finger instead of going where it pointed." But finally I realized that I did have to move in that direction, and in 1952 I resigned my commission in the Naval Reserve. It was promptly and courteously accepted. I felt a bit proud of doing it a month before I would have come into a pension. Such little things we pride ourselves on!

I came into contact with the Quakers, the Society of Friends. My wife, Sylvia, had already joined the Society in 1948. As late as 1955 I was still fighting off joining the Society, which seemed to me to involve a great, awesome commitment. I suppose I was like the man in one of Shaw's plays who wanted to be a Christian—but not yet.

The Hiroshima Maidens

Then came the experience of having in our home for some months two of the Hiroshima maidens who had been injured and disfigured in the bombing of August 6, 1945. Norman Cousins and other wonderful people brought them to this country for plastic surgery. There were two things about these girls that hit me very hard and forced me to see that I had no choice but to make the commitment to live, as best I could, a life of nonviolence and reconciliation. One was the fact that when they were bombed in 1945, the two girls in our home were nine and thirteen years old. What earthly thing could they have done to give some semblance of what we call justice to the ordeal inflicted upon them and hundreds like them? What possible good could come out of human action—war—which bore such fruits? Is it not utter blasphemy to think that there is anything moral or Christian about such behavior?

The other thing that struck me was that these young women found it difficult to believe that *we*, who were not members of their families, could love *them*. But *they* loved *us;* they harbored no resentment against us or other Americans. How are you going to respond to that kind of attitude? The newly-elected president of the National Council of Churches, Edwin T. Dahlberg, said in his inaugural talk that instead of "massive retaliation" the business of Christians is to practice

"massive reconciliation." Well, these Hiroshima girls practiced "massive reconciliation" on us, on me, who had laughed
derisively at "Smiling Jack." What response can one make to
this other than to give oneself utterly to destroying the evil,
war, that dealt so shamefully with them and try to live in the
spirit of sensitivity and reconciliation which they displayed?

As I have said, I think there is that in all men that abhors
and rejects war and knows that force and violence can bring
no good thing to pass. Yet men are bound by old patterns of
feeling, thought and action. The organs of public opinion are
almost completely shut against us. It seems practically impossible, moreover, for the ordinary person by ordinary means to
speak to, and affect the action of, his government. I have had a
recent experience of this which has strengthened my conviction that it is only by such acts as sailing a boat to Eniwetok
and thus "speaking" to the government right in the testing area
that we can expect to be heard.

Tell It to the Policeman

I was asked by the New England office of the American
Friends Service Committee to take to the White House 17,411
signatures to a petition to cancel the Pacific tests. Ten thousand signatures had previously been sent in. I realize that even
a President in good health cannot see personally everyone who
has a message for him. Yet the right of petition exists—in
theory—and is held to be a key factor in democratic process.
And the President presumably has assistants to see to it that all
serious petitions are somehow brought to his attention. For
matters of this kind, there is Maxwell Rabb, secretary to the
Cabinet.

Twenty-seven thousand is quite a few people to have
signed a somewhat unusual petition. The A. F. S. C. is widely
known and recognized as a highly useful agency. I am known
to Maxwell Rabb with whom I worked in Republican politics
in Massachusetts. I was a precinct captain for Eisenhower in
the 1952 primaries. Yet a couple of days' work on the part of
the staff of the Friends Committee on National Legislation
failed to secure even an assurance that some time on Tuesday,
December 31, the day I would be in Washington, Max Rabb

would see me to receive the petitions. On that day I made five calls and talked with his secretary. Each time I was assured that she would call me back within ten minutes. Each time the return call failed to come and I tried again. The last time, early in the afternoon, I held on to the telephone for ten minutes, only to be told finally that the office was about to close for the day.

Each time I telephoned, including the last, I was told I could, of course, leave the petitions with the policeman at the gate. This I refused to do. It seems terrible to me that Americans can no longer speak to or be seen by their government. Has it become their master, not their servant? Can it not listen to their humble and reasonable pleas? This experience may in one sense be a small matter but I am sure it is symptomatic—among other things—of a sort of fear on the part of officials to listen to what in their hearts they feel is right but on which they cannot act without breaking with old patterns of thought. At any rate, the experience has strengthened in me the conviction that we must, at whatever cost, find ways to make our witness and protest heard.

I Am Going Because . . .

I am going because, as Shakespeare said, "Action is eloquence." Without some such direct action, ordinary citizens lack the power any longer to be seen or heard by their government.

I am going because it is time to *do something* about peace, not just *talk* about peace.

I am going because, like all men, in my heart I know that *all* nuclear explosions are monstrous, evil, unworthy of human beings.

I am going because war is no longer a feudal jousting match; it is an unthinkable catastrophe for all men.

I am going because it is now the little children, and, most of all, the as yet unborn who are the front line troops. It is my duty to stand between them and this horrible danger.

I am going because it is cowardly and degrading for me to stand by any longer, to consent, and thus to collaborate in atrocities.

I am going because I cannot say that the end justifies the means. A Quaker, William Penn, said, "A good end cannot sanctify evil means; nor must we ever do evil that good may come of it." A Communist, Milovan Djilas, says, "As soon as means which would ensure an end are shown to be evil, the end will show itself as unrealizable."

I am going because, as Gandhi said, "God sits in the man opposite me; therefore to injure him is to injure God himself."

I am going to witness to the deep inward truth we all know, "Force can subdue, but love gains."

I am going because however mistaken, unrighteous, and unrepentant governments may seem, I still believe all men are really good at heart, and that my act will speak to them.

I am going in the hope of helping change the hearts and minds of men in government. If necessary I am willing to give my life to help change a policy of fear, force and destruction to one of trust, kindness, and help.

I am going in order to say, "Quit this waste, this arms race. Turn instead to a disarmament race. Stop competing for evil, compete for good."

I am going because I have to—if I am to call myself a human being.

When you see something horrible happening, your instinct is to do something about it. You can freeze in fearful apathy or you can even talk yourself into saying that it isn't horrible. I can't do that. I have to act. This is too horrible. We know it. Let's all act.

Jules Rabin and *Karl Meyer*

San Francisco to Moscow Walk

1. HOW WE WENT

Jules Rabin

The great adventure is over. Our Walk, which commenced in San Francisco's Union Square on December 1st, 1960, concluded in Moscow's Red Square on the afternoon of October 3rd, 1961. At 2 o'clock we filed up the short slope beside the Historical Museum. Ahead of us lay the great plaza, with the jumbled, bejeweled cake of St. Basil's Cathedral occupying the front horizon, and the tall, heavy wall of the Kremlin to our right. The Walkers were granted two hours in Red Square to conduct our final demonstration. After performing the courtesies of the press we arranged ourselves in a quiet line facing St. Basil's, and stood in silent vigil. It took some minutes for us to establish our separateness from the crowd that pressed around us, and more minutes for the activities of photographers and reporters to subside. But eventually the sense of the vigil established itself.

England has had her Aldermastons, with tens of thousands marching the few score miles to London. It is perhaps fitting that America's young and faltering peace movement should have signified her concern with a gesture of continental breadth. Ten thousand kilometers, six thousand-odd miles, the Walk carried almost through four seasons.

And the Walk in Russia, what was that really like?

Russia was climactic. To Americans of this century, Russia must always be of especial fascination, because it is proclaimed the forbidden land, the dangerous land . . . because Russia is

the *they* of our lives. So we walked in Russia, especially during the first days, like children in a land of wonder. On our first
evening in Russia, we met an overflow audience in Brest. The
stage was draped in red and gold, the colors of Soviet glory.
On either side of the stage were portraits of Lenin, Marx and
Engels. On the streets we had seen statues and busts of Lenin
and Stalin, gleaming in silver paint, and posters, always in red,
exhorting and proclaiming. That is what Russia is like on first
encounter: the forbidden symbols have become vernacular elements of the civic landscape.

Russia was important to us because of this fascination,
and it was important for the more serious reason that in Russia
we recognized the other great voice in the dialogue of power
which makes the world tremble today. Here was the central
drama of the Walk, that some of us from the United States
should carry to the Soviet Union the same message that we
had spoken and acted on in our own country, sometimes at the
price of imprisonment. We had demonstrated against military
installations wherever we encountered them, in little Belgium
as well as at the Pentagon, in England and both Germanys and
Poland. But Russia was especially important to us because it is
her power, alone, that matches the power of the United States,
and uniquely provokes it. To have the ear of both these great
nations, that was the heart's desire of our Walk. To demonstrate in one's own country is not too great a feat, but this
opportunity to say *No* to the official *Yes* of Soviet military
policy, on Soviet soil, was to us both rare and impressive.

Moscow was the terminus of our Walk, and it was a precious goal insofar as it meant the completion of our long labor,
and the achievement of what we had months before set out to
do. We have the impression that our Soviet hosts would have
liked us to regard our entry into Moscow as an arrival at a
Mecca consecrated to Peace. For as earnestly as we of the Walk
expressed our concern for an immediate and total solution to
the armaments race, the Soviets insisted that their concern
matches ours, and outdistances it. They have endured a war
which touched America only lightly; they have established
professional committees for the defense of peace, and have
long had laws which make it a criminal offense to foment war.

A member of the Soviet Peace Committee, who greeted us warmly on the day following our arrival, suggested that we might have felt like the ten thousand of Xenophon as we entered the great space of the Red Square. He thought we might have wanted to cry out "Thalassa, Thalassa," as the Greeks had done when they saw the Black Sea after their long flight before the Persians, and understood that rest and the assurance of safety lay close at hand.

It is tempting to respond in an accommodating way to the kind words of a well-intentioned host. The Soviets, our last hosts along the way, wished to be generous towards us, to take us under their wing, to persuade us. I believe they would have been content to receive from us a simple accord with their call for *Mir* and *Druzhba* (peace and friendship) . . . after which we might all have dozed off in the warm, pleasant tea of that unassailable sentiment. The Russians have sloganized the term *peace* and the idea of peace—much as the West has sloganized the idea of freedom—till it seems their very own invention and property. Why would we not accept Moscow as the peace-lover's Mecca, when we had heard countless times in our journey across the land the most earnest (and *believable*) protestations that the Russians desire peace above almost all else, and that they shudder to think of enduring again what they suffered between 1941 and 1945? But like harsh-minded fools we were bound to reiterate our unilateralist stand and disturb the calm of our hosts. Our position is one of refusal to assess degrees of blame in the crescendo of armaments preparations which is making the world tremble. Rather, it locates the possibility for disaster in a readiness from any quarter to respond to menace with menace, to offense with offense.

The idiocy of it. Here were two parties, ourselves and the Russians, who would turn almost boastful in declaring the depths of their concern for peace. We were the honored guests of the land, the Walkers who had done this strange thing of coming so great a distance to convey our desire and our plan for peace. Across from us stood the Russians, a people who had suffered more, in absolute numbers, than any other participants in the great war. They begged us to believe that they craved peace, that they are a peace-loving people . . . as

though they feared that there are other peoples elsewhere who
are perhaps peace-hating, who crave war for its own bloody
sake.

We faced the Russians on numerous platforms (seventeen
arranged meetings, perhaps sixty informal wayside meetings),
and from either side could be found not much more than token
words of regard for the full reach of the other's peace program.
To the Russians we seemed like unintentional subversives. We
proposed that they undertake unilateral disarmament, and that
in the spirit of individual responsibility, each Soviet citizen
who regarded war as intrinsically evil should on his own initiative abstain from all phases of military activity, including
civilian labor in armaments industry. We made it as clear as
we could that we were not a band of foxy delegates from the
West who aimed to soften the Soviet's defenses for the eventual new assault by a neo-Nazi Germany—which the Soviets
fear more than the hell-fires of hydrogen warfare itself. We
exposed the battle ribbons and battle wounds which are peculiar to pacifist activists of today: prison sentences, physical violence, and calumny, endured in our own lands in the course of
our proposal of the same unilateralist position that we brought
to the Soviet Union. But what stayed uppermost in their minds
was the impression of a strange band from the West proposing
seriously that they should disarm, immediately and irrespective
of what their world neighbors might do.

To us, the Soviets seemed like the creators of their own
undoing. While protesting their deep love of peace, they
would reiterate with a violent passion their determination to
remain militarily strong as long as the West retained any
power for military assault. In the course of our several weeks in
the Soviet Union, the atonality of the official—and popular
—position on the questions of peace and armaments became
familiar to our ears. The Soviets are determined to maintain
their position of military strength—in *defense*, as they habitually allege, of the peace and of their territorial integrity—as
long as their appeal for complete and general disarmament,
multilaterally implemented, goes unheeded.

As persons affected by the Gandhian and Christian traditions of nonviolence, we Peace Walkers found this disharmony

of the Soviet position harsh to our ears. How can one simul-taneously protest that one loves peace, and avow implacable hatred and annihilation of a prospective enemy?

As persons who had endured the incredible sufferings of an unmitigated Nazi invasion and occupation, our Soviet inter-locutors found our appeals for unilateral disarmament childish —we were laughed at by great audiences—and downright offensive. These audiences would shout indignantly when the full implications of our program were declared. And the fact that we were appealing in the same terms to both East and West, and that we were condemning both East and West in the same terms, seemed often not to register.

This is the depressing idiocy I speak of, that we and the Russians seem often to have talked *past* each other. Each party to our discussions would perform a careful minuet within his own sphere of logic, always in support of his own dream of a just and sound peace. But the two spheres of logic would rarely intersect, and the rival claims of programs, of resistance with armed violence and of resistance without armed violence, would be left unadjusted. And because each party regarded the other as representing a threat to his own dream of the establishment of peace, we addressed each other sometimes as antagonists, rather than as collaborators in this precious work.

To be thus at odds with our audiences was of course no new thing to us. In the West, in the United States, we had encountered identical positions, except that the implacable demon was named World Communism, instead of International Capitalism.

I write these notes the day after my return to New York. I have in hand an article of A. J. Muste's, and there is a benefit to me in obtaining his perspective. I don't refer to the perspective of his years and experience, but the perspective of one who has observed the Walk closely, but has not been on it. For the last six months I have gone with the Walk daily. It has been a way of life, and so absorbing and demanding a way of life that I can comment on it only from within.

The question returns to my mind over and over again: What was it really like?

The reality of the Walk is manifold. There is the reality Muste speaks of, which from the outermost perspective seems to be the Walk's great achievement: we have perhaps, through this Walk, made a small difference in the fearsome dialogue that goes on between the United States and the Soviet Union. If we are serious men and if we are correct in our judgment that an apocalypse confronts the world, this small difference we have made is a gladdening thing. Here have we thirty-odd people gone out into the world like Quixotes, carrying our banners in the boggy woods of Russia, in the deserts of America's Southwest, and in some great cities between. Here are we, thirty people without any direct connection with the standard sources of power in today's world, and we have been able to make a difference. How much of a difference, we cannot judge. Muste's article gives a generous estimate of our achievement. If he is one-tenth correct, we are glad. In a world in which it is common to say, What can an ordinary person *do*?—thirty ordinary persons have made a difference on an issue that could determine the lives and deaths of countless of us.

But the other realities of the Walk are closer to my mind. We aimed to be world-shakers and peace-makers: this was the ostensible reason most of us joined the Walk. *The* reason. But a strange way of life lived for six months or ten months entails multiple motivations. No person, I believe, functioned on the Walk solely as Peace Walker. We had many other moments besides those of peace work. When we entered Poland after the heavy difficulties of our stay in East Germany, we behaved for several days like kids, cavorting along the way in response to the lighter, more generous spirit our Polish hosts showed us. During the tired, tense days of our forced march in Russia, when we had to accomplish a five-weeks journey in eighteen days, a strange totemic humor developed among us. We divided into two rival parties, the Giant Ants and the Leaky Buzzards, who dwelled in a strange empire of the imagination that resembled the comic-book empires of the real world.

We sometimes squabbled among ourselves, in a way unbecoming to people professing the Gandhian philosophy. We were time and again exacerbated by the physical hardships of the Walk, the emotional hardships of little privacy, and the spiritual hardship of lack of repose. We knew no Sundays, and were confused about the other days of the week. I heard Lyn Marsh ask once, "Is this Saturday?" and receive the answer, "No, it's Tuesday." The occasional layover our schedule would allow in a large city would find us, on the day the Walk resumed, welcoming the open road like people starting on a holiday.

But after six months on the Walk I am tired of certain things. I am tired of walking, and I am tired of pure politics.

It was a deliberate pleasure to watch a familiar landscape sweep past the train window as I rode the Moscow to London Express west to England, a few days ago. Distances that I had labored over on foot were now accomplished effortlessly, magically, as we sat reading and drinking tea. Every hour spent on board the train counted for two days' journey on foot.

And the curious, tight logic of politics—some of us are glad to have passed temporarily out of that, and no longer to have the responsibility of conveying the Walk's message to curious strangers.

I remember the first night aboard the Moscow-London train. Six of us had established ourselves cosily in two adjoining compartments, and were sipping tea served from the car's samovar. One of the car attendants brought in two young Soviet soldiers who had heard of our Walk and were curious about the details; they were incredulous, in fact, concerning the physical accomplishment of the Walk, the distance covered. I remember the special concern I used to feel in East Germany and Poland, when encountering Soviet soldiers. I sought every opportunity to speak with them, or at least to deliver them the Walk's leaflet. The fact of the great dialogue in today's world is one that I have borne constantly in mind; and this special opportunity to speak to the East in the same manner that we have spoken to the West has seemed to be of incalculable value.

But that first night on board the train I was weary and the rest of us were weary. We would rather not have spoken to the curious soldiers. The romance and import of that kind of contact were dissipated in a weariness of sensibility, which must inevitably overtake people who endure so long a trance of action such as this Walk was. Our message was threatening to become a line, and we would rather be silent for a time than repeat things in a hackneyed way.

And again, what was it really like? It is tempting to speak of a grand action in terms that suggest waving banners and all the other panoply of public occasions. (We were a public occasion —I remember dozing off on the green in a small Polish town, at the end of lunch, and waking up to find myself surrounded, like Gulliver, by a dense circle of children, all contemplating me silently.) There is a traditional language of celebration for public occasions of this scope, but it is apt to be embarrassing, inept, beside the point. I remember a strange fellow who attached himself to the Walk for several days in eastern Belgium. He wore a wide, greasy raincoat and a wide-brimmed hat pulled low on his forehead. He coursed along beside us, shouting at people as we went, "Applaud them, applaud them! Here are the Marchers for Peace come all the way from San Francisco on foot." This was one face of the Walk, and it is worth describing.

We might say: this Walk distributed so and so many hundreds of thousands of leaflets, and addressed so and so many tens of thousands of persons, East and West. We were handed bouquets of flowers in many places, and were stopped on our way, as often as half a dozen times in one day, by civic officials who wanted to convey their community's regard for us. We were sometimes like hardened theatrical troupers lending only our physical presence to these occasions: cherishing them, perhaps, because the interruption gave us a few minutes rest, besides the ten minutes we allotted ourselves after each hour's walking. We acted like hardened troupers to the cameramen who attached themselves to our Walk along the way, no longer looking around when the cine-camera buzzed, no longer startled when a photo-flash bulb popped.

Mayors, burgomeisters, chairmen, we did not always heed your every word when you came out to greet us, but you will understand this if you count the number of towns we passed through, the number of formal speeches of welcome and con-

cern that were addressed to us, sometimes after each meal of
the day, sometimes before a meal, when we were aching with
fatigue, cranky with hunger, wet to our chilled skins. Spring in
America this year was cold and wet, and the first part of our
European summer was unprecedentedly gray and chill. A
climate for toothache.

What the March was really like. We were all of us spiritually imperfect persons; no *Bodhisattvas*, no Mahatmas. That
could be to the good. Our infirmity signifies that we are of *this*
existence, the same crabbed existence which exasperates the
relationship between the United States and the Soviet Union.
There were times in America when some of us watched the
Walk with a special concern, because we asked ourselves, if
not we, then who else? If we could not create among ourselves
that mood of cherishing trustfulness, of expectation and concern—we pacifists, we who professed Gandhism—if we become paltry among ourselves, what could we fairly expect of
the world, of men who boasted a responsible worldliness, and
identified that with reality?

I remember, back in the United States, our encounter with
a Puerto Rican migrant worker who was attracted to our group
because we seemed decent and friendly and generous. It
seemed to some of us fitting to invite this fellow to share our
meal of the evening, and our lodgings for the night. We were
to be the guests of a Quaker farmer, and the question arose
among us: Could we, as guests of this man, impose on him the
presence of a person we could not vouch for? One of our
people, whose chief possession was a golden beard, said that
the Puerto Rican's smile was all the validation he needed to
remain among us. He cited the story of Jean Valjean in *Les
Misérables,* and said that our Quaker host should be educated
to the relative values of silver candlesticks and a man's smile.
And Sue Barksdale, in these matters always unyielding in her
gentle, Christian way, said that it was hypocritical for us to ask
the Russians, ultimately, to trust their neighbors in a gesture of
unilateral disarmament if we preacher-types could not trust
the stranger who came among us.

The Puerto Rican shared our hospitality that night and remained with us for some days. But our attitude of trust was not

always so exemplary. And if I ask again, what was it really like among us, were we able among ourselves to practice the concern and confidence that one might reasonably stipulate as ingredients of the program of unilateralism and nonviolent resistance, could I give an encouraging answer? If a cosmic sport had assembled us together, to determine if we could, in microcosm, establish the harmony among ourselves that we were seeking for the squabblers in the concourse of nations, what prospects for founding a trustworthy peace does the experiment offer?

The answer is a sad one, in part. We were human, all too human; with the implications which that phrase offers of every pettiness, and of possibilities for reconciliation.

Our accomplishment is a more estimable one if we regard it on more prosaic political grounds. We did reach many people, many tens of thousands in direct encounter. And because our caravan somehow piqued the world's fancy, we reached some tens of millions through the conventional news media. No one knows how to estimate the value of this sort of impact: two and a quarter minutes on TV, a scanty, slanted article in a newspaper, which reports austerely the fact of our arrival in such and such a place, or racily, how many pairs of sneakers such and such a Walker has worn out. But some may feel the appeal of even this small notice won by the passage of our Walk. The world heard of us, the world glimpsed some of our slogans and saw us carry them into strange places.

And again, what was it really like? In America we ate peanut butter and oatmeal, and not always enough of that. I remember in Ohio having had beans and cabbage for supper, and the same for breakfast. And I remember once in the Soviet Union being offered a plate of *hors d'oeuvres* by a vegetarian neighbor. I had finished my own portion, and said I was glad to have more sturgeon, but didn't care for any more caviar. Not just the statement, but the fact that it was made without self-consciousness, is what I remark. We were treated as honored guests in many places in the Soviet Union, and the three dollars a day per person which we paid to our hosts, the Peace Committee, were multiplied several times over, I suppose, providing food and lodgings of a class that we were unaccustomed to. Russia, traditionally and splendidly hospitable, is proud of her present wealth, and perhaps just a little showy in its display. In America we had slept free of charge on church floors, and fed ourselves on a budget of fifty cents a day.

The encumbrance of coping with elaborate meals in Russia and Poland detracted from time that we would have preferred to spend meeting people along our way. We had had, in Belgium and West Germany, long successions of days in which we had to make do with cold, knotty foods: bread, cheese, and sausage. The hot meals we consumed across Poland and Russia were in themselves welcome; we would have regretted their passing. And we could not in sense and decency complain of the attentions of barbers and shoe-repairmen, who would wait into the night to serve our needs. But, like people of other places who regret the loss of a simpler life, the while holding tight to the comforts of a more elaborate condition, we could in the final reckoning have wished the Soviets were less generous towards us. And there was repeatedly this anomaly, of ourselves having uttered strong words about the Soviet armaments policy, which would bring cries of protest from the audience; and then sitting down to a formal and elaborate meal with persons who on the platform had been our antagonists and now were our hosts. We Walkers were most of us provincial folk in relation to the demands of professional diplomacy, and did not always take comfortably to this game of dining amicably with persons with whom we had just exchanged strong words.

And that is what extended peace walks are made of. Fatigue, and sparse or heavy foods, strained tempers, awesome challenges, misapprehensions. There are too the gilded moments, of mutual persuasion and understanding. If I have said little about these moments, it is because the Russian experience is freshest in my mind, and there was small evidence of ideological penetration in Russia. But we did make this first *necessary* move in that direction; we have started a new path of dialogue. And perhaps people of sounder faith and more reasonable temper can carry us further on the way to reconciliation. It is necessary.

2. STILL VIRGIN SOIL

Karl Meyer

[*Following is the text of a talk given at Community Church in New York City at a packed meeting to welcome the Walkers on their return from Moscow:*]

Before I begin I want to say hello to an old man in the audience; and believe me, I am not doing it for his sake; I am doing it for your sakes, because I want to have a decent excuse for telling you something about his life. I am speaking of Max Sandin of Cleveland. He is in his seventies. He was born in Russia, and may Russia send us thousands more like him. He came to America in his youth. During World War I, he was sentenced to be shot for refusing to wear the uniform or to fight in the War. His sentence was commuted, but he spent several years in Leavenworth prison under the terrible conditions that prevailed there during the War. He hasn't ever given up his work for peace. He keeps right on going. He doesn't believe in paying taxes for war, and he doesn't pay them, and that is something unusual. Recently the government took away his Social Security to pay the taxes he hadn't paid. He went down to Washington to make a protest, and they tried to shut him up in a mental institution. He is here tonight, and we are honored by his being here.

Now let me say what I think I have to say about this Walk from San Francisco to Moscow:

"*Tovarish, Sovietski Soyuse, Sovietski Narod, Sovietski Pravietyelstva*—Comrades, the Soviet Union, the Soviet People, the Soviet Government, desires peace; it needs peace; it demands peace. *Myr, Myr, Myr*—Peace, Peace, Peace. The Soviet Union, the Soviet People the Soviet Government, needs peace so urgently that it is ready to resort to nuclear weapons, if necessary, to defend the peace against fascist aggression. And we can lick the man who says it isn't so."

Friends, I hope you won't find this amusing, because I believe it is an accurate paraphrase of the words I heard in the Soviet Union—again, and again, and again. Words that I heard without a sound of dissent, except that one voice, which was not a sound, but rather a secret note passed to Bradford Lyttle at the Moscow University meeting, while the words I have just paraphrased were ringing through the hall—a secret note which read in full:

> *My dear friends, do not believe absolutely this dirty official and his common demagogic phrases. Go your path, we are with you.*

When I remember these words—the shouted words and the silent words—it makes me angry to hear people in our peace movement gloating and saying, "for years we have been told to go tell it to the Russians, and now we can say we have gone and we have 'told it to the Russians.'"

I am not going to lie to you.

I hope that you will not say that I have been to the Soviet Union.

I hope that you will not say that you have been there.

I hope you will not say that our ideas have been presented there.

The fact is that we have not touched the Soviet Union. We flicked in and out of the Soviet Union so fast that we hardly knew we were there. Our hosts had us so tied up in knots we had to roll along the ground from Brest to Moscow.

Hear a parable of the sower and the seed: A sower went out to sow, and as he sowed, some of the seed fell by the roadside, and the birds of the air devoured it as soon as it fell. Other seed fell on shallow, rocky ground and it sprang up quickly but it had no roots, and when the drought came it withered and died. And finally other seed fell on good ground, and when it had taken root it grew and yielded fruit a hundredfold.

Now hear an explanation of this parable: The seed that fell by the roadside and was devoured by birds is those eighty

thousand leaflets we distributed and those talks to villagers
along the roadside. We sowed the wind and we reaped the
wind. The seed that fell among briars is those public meetings you heard about where the party liners sprang to their
feet and strangled our message with a barrage of words almost
before we had finished speaking. The seed that fell on shallow
rocky soil is that meeting at the Moscow University, where the
students heard our message so eagerly and yet had not the
courage to speak out a word of dissent from official policy,
even when we were there, but had to pass up their dissent in
secret notes. How will they grow when the water leaves them?
As for the seed that fell on good ground, I do not know that it
was ever sown. We haven't touched the Soviet Union with our
ideas. Perhaps not much more than Richard Nixon touched it
in his famous kitchen debate. The Soviet Union is still virgin
soil. Before you can sow the good soil, you have to plow the
ground. And I mean plow the ground. And once having set
your hand to the plow you must not turn back.

I have told you that we haven't touched the Soviet
Union yet. And how could we hope to touch them when we
haven't touched ourselves yet. How could we hope to reach
them with our message, when we haven't even reached our
own souls through the fat layers of our American existence.

If we want to reach them, we have to go and reach them.

If we want to speak with them, we have to go and speak
with them.

And if we want to live in peace with them, we have to go
and live in peace with them, personally disarmed, in labor and
in poverty, again, and again, and again!

Dave Dellinger

Growing Pains in the Peace Movement

"I just hope you provoke me, because I'd love to smash your face in." These words, snarled at a young girl by a policeman as he held his club against her bust and pushed her, give an idea of the reaction of the police to the anti-nuclear-testing demonstration held in Times Square on March 3rd [1962]. "Why . . . why, you don't even know me," stammered the bewildered girl, revealing an unfamiliarity with the real function of the police that is common to many pacifists.

The actions of the police were shocking, but they were not untypical of police behavior when faced with an aroused and determined crowd. What was untypical was not the mood of the police but the mood of a considerable number of the demonstrators. The police, not being responsible for the decision to resume nuclear testing, were not the objects of the demonstrators' indignation, but they must have sensed that the attitude of these people was different from that of most war objectors they have been called upon to supervise, or even arrest, in recent years. The mood was not one of self-expression through symbolic protest but of collective horror at the resumption of testing, and, on the part of some at least, a consequent determination to do whatever is necessary to change the course of events. Compared with the slaughter of the innocents through fallout and the imminent destruction of the world through war, any inconveniences that might result from failure to observe the ordinary ground rules for avoiding traffic jams or minimizing the impact of political protest seemed inconsequential.

Even during World War II and the Korean War, there was little feeling among pacifists that "*this* war must be stopped and we will do everything within our power to stop it." Not that any of them wanted either war to continue, but the dominant psychology was one of personal non-participation in a catastrophe which had been sanctioned by the democratic process and, in any event, was beyond their power to shorten or stop. Since the advent of the nuclear bomb, with its peacetime fallout and its potential of wartime "humanicide," there has been a delayed but growing reaction which has brought a new emphasis on historical effectiveness. This new emphasis does not necessarily reflect a more optimistic attitude but rather a greater sense of historical urgency based on the feeling that the world must abandon the arms race or perish. The decisions, first by the Soviet Union and then by the United States, to resume testing have intensified this feeling. I am not speaking of the political opportunism which has also been growing in recent years, mostly among some of the more ambitious peace leaders, and which, under the name of political effectiveness, eats away at the moral basis of rugged integrity and nonconforming love without which, oddly enough, there can be no real historical effectiveness. As a matter of fact, both approaches were reflected in this demonstration, and their unstable mixture diminished its impact.

Because most pacifists lead "respectable" and privileged lives, and because the anti-war movement has not yet succeeded in presenting a serious challenge either to the military or the economic *status quo* (in fact shows no active interest in challenging the latter), most of us have not had to suffer the indignities which are customarily practiced on those who either lack our connections or represent a serious threat to the established order. What has always been commonplace for the poor, for convicts, and for Negroes, Puerto Ricans, Mexicans, and others when they asserted their human rights, came as a shock to many pacifists who had been spared such experiences in the past. In the thirties, when unemployment and poverty impelled people to insistent action, much as Strontium 90 and the danger of catastrophic war are beginning to move people now, the police were not noted for their delicacy in handling strikes, marches of the unemployed, and political demonstrations. As the peace movement proceeds further into its new phase of historical concern, the dead-earnestness of our struggle will communicate itself to the authorities and, among other things, bring the risk of a correspondingly intensified response. We will all have to choose, more clearly than at present, between being liberals who limit expression of our idealism to activities and goals which minimize personal risk (lobby for peace, pray for peace, support the peace efforts of the administration against the war-now advocates) and being radicals who concentrate on historical exigency rather than on personal safety. This is a prospect from which we all instinctively shrink —and the human capacity for evasion of social responsibility is universally powerful—but there is no sense in pretending that the outlook is more comforting than it is.

There is of course a fundamental difference between positive nonviolence and the methods used by the unemployed and the labor movement in the depression—even on those occasions when they refrained from overt violence. Since large-scale, indignant, and turbulent *nonviolent* action is almost without precedent in the United States, it is not surprising that the police responded to the Times Square demonstration in the manner in which they have habitually responded to militant demonstrations in the past. When they learn that even our most disobedient crowds are not going to throw stones, press lighted cigarettes against their horses' flanks, or otherwise attack them, they may learn to distinguish between a militant, extra-legal demonstration conducted in the spirit of nonviolence and the demonstrations they have been conditioned to expect. But we must go far beyond this by combining open and forthright refusal to obey their arbitrary or demonstration-deadening orders with an active good will which will express toward them the love for our enemies which characterizes the nonviolence to which we aspire. Since the very concept of *satyagraha* is foreign to our culture, we will not communicate it by words or by acts of appeasement (these symbolize only weakness, passivity, historical irrelevance) but are most apt to break through to them, *to ourselves,* and to society at large by intensifying both the conflict and the love. Some of us learned in prison during World War II that intensifying the conflict, in response to prison injustice, forced us either to intensify or abandon the love. In a culture which puts a premium on rationalized conformity it is easy to *think* we love our enemy as long as we do not defy him. But this is not the kind of love that suffers long and is kind—and that introduces a revolutionary element into human relations.

No one knows how far this spirit can go in overcoming, or at least neutralizing, hostility and the traditional violence of police, but it is important not to fall into the trap of thinking that whenever the police resort to brutality the failure is ours. (Actually, of course, each of us tends to attribute the failure to our associates.) Gandhi remonstrated with his followers when *they* resorted to violence, and called off some of his campaigns on this account, but he did not condemn them when they fell victim to the violence of the British—as happened on countless occasions. Since the Times Square demonstration, there has been a rash of memoranda and statements, from both liberals and radicals, assuming that somehow it was the fault of one group or another of pacifists that the demonstrators were brutally set upon by the police. Both groups attribute the violence to the fact that the police did not expect the sit-down, but the liberals place the onus on those who sat down and the radicals place it on the liberal leadership for having refused to face up to the fact that a sit-down was apt to occur. I do not remember half so many memos analyzing the reasons for the greater ineffectiveness of some previous demonstrations that did not provoke police brutality but failed to challenge either police or public because of the mild sentiments expressed or because the leaders complied with some arbitrary order of the police which nullified the purpose of the demonstration. In fact, no one, so far as I know, has bothered to get out a memo on the fiasco of the hastily called protest against police brutality which took place in New York four days after the Times Square demonstration and which calmly acquiesced in a police request not to march as planned to Times Square, the scene of the crime they were supposed to be protesting. Of course there is a sense in which we fail as long as we are unable to persuade the President to replace the armed forces with nonviolent volunteers (at the risk of impeachment), the generals and soldiers to resign, our neighbors to withdraw from war work, *and* the police to eschew the violence which is their ultimate weapon in defense of the established order. But we are so far from having the moral power or historical effectiveness to accomplish *any* of these "miracles" that it seems strange to single out our failure to transform the police as the occasion for special *mea culpas,* for attacks on our associates, and for a panicky withdrawal from the area of vital conflict which we have just begun to enter. We want to act in such a way as to show the transforming power of love, but we will not accomplish this by taming the militants in our ranks or by advocating a less revolutionary program than is needed.

There is an element in our ranks, however, that wears the mantle of militancy and does need to be tamed. As the plight of mankind becomes more desperate and the peace forces move haltingly toward ever more radical prescriptions and dramatic action, some disruptingly compulsive characters are beginning to join us in the fray. I am thinking of persons who (irrespective of whether or not they wear beards or violate the bourgeois dress code—relatively superficial matters) are so wounded in their inner selves by the mounting stupidity of the Cold War or by other baneful aspects of our culture, that they have become seriously unbalanced emotionally and bring to their peace activities powerful personal drives that conflict with the spirit of nonviolence. Better to be driven temporarily off balance by society than to be peacefully adjusted within it, and I hope that none of us would rather see these people spending their time happily making munitions or serving in the police force than participating in demonstrations and thereby adding to the complexities of pacifist logistics. But we cannot understand the difficulties of the Times Square demonstration and of future activities unless we recognize the problems presented by these people and the mutually parasitic relationship that has grown up between them and some of the more authoritarian elements in the peace leadership. Before the Times Square demonstration, one of the leaders is reported to have stated that it was their job to decide how "five coordinators can impose their will on five thousand demonstrators." I have heard such things said many times in the past, and the justification has always been that this is the only way to prevent an irresponsible and unstable minority from creating chaos. On the other hand, the "unstable minority" feeds on such statements and the actions which proceed from them, not only to justify its own erratic tendencies but to make a factitious appeal to new or militant participants to act unilaterally and without adequate sensitivity to the over-all situation and the attitudes of other participants. If there was an element of tragedy in the Times Square demonstration, it stemmed from the mutual distrust of these opposing minorities and the fact that the great bulk of the participants were caught in the middle. Not only did this distrust lead to some bad mistakes in advance planning and coordination but it led to a confused and divided response when Richard Bell fainted and was manhandled by the police. A mixed bag of participants rushed to join him—some who apparently did not even realize that he had fainted or was being manhandled but who were itching for a chance to practice the "bureaucratically forbidden" sit-down, and others who were reacting creatively to the emergency by coming nonviolently to his defense. I was not present at the demonstration (having recently got out of the hospital after an operation), but reports indicate that some of the leaders, distrustful of the sit-downers and caught in their own rigidity, tried to force an unnatural continuation of the silence (which had been up till then very effective), and the strict conformity to law, under vastly different circumstances than they had been designed for. If one of our cohorts were being killed, would responsible nonviolence require us to stand by in prearranged silence and passivity rather than interpose our bodies between him and his assailant? Ten days after the demonstration one of the leaders, in the midst of a long and otherwise excellent statement, could first acknowledge that "those who did sit down were responding in the way they thought best to the beating the police had started to give Dick Bell, the young man who had fainted in the street and who was lying helpless," and then go on to "deplore the lack of discipline on the part of that handful of the crowd which sat down." There are many occasions when we want to plan actions which do not call for civil disobedience, but we should not surrender, or expect others to surrender, the right to *defensive* civil disobedience.

I have gone into so much detail not because I think it is easy to respond creatively to the rapidly changing circumstances in a militant nonviolent action but, on the contrary, because I see no other way to indicate how complex the problems are and because there is a real danger that the peace leadership will feel that demonstrations must be tightly controlled from the top down in order to avoid worse problems in the future. This would tend to prevent what I think is the only real solution—the gradual maturing, through experience, of more and more persons in imaginative nonviolence. We must remember that as yet we have had to face only a small part of the opposition that will develop in the future if we continue to take nonviolence beyond the narrow confines of symbolic protest to action that will have a real impact on history. The English demonstrators whom Bertrand Russell speaks of tried to "immobilize" the American Air Base at Wethersfield, England. Nonviolent resistance will not replace military defense until it shows itself capable of immobilizing invading armies and domestic "defense forces." To attempt to do this will require a mass of resolute and inventive individuals who, while sensitive to over-all strategy, are not dependent on orders either from the police or from their own professional leaders, some of whom inevitably suffer from the occupational disease of wanting to pre-determine the exact course of events.

III

The Challenge to Community: Colonialism and Civil Rights

"One local Negro leader told me, 'You might as well say that we never heard of Gandhi or nonviolence. But we are determined to get our freedom. And in the course of struggling for it, we came upon nonviolence, like gold in the ground.'"

DAVE DELLINGER
"The Negroes of Birmingham"
Liberation, Summer, 1963

Nelson Mandela

Why I Am Ready to Die

[*On June 12, 1964, Nelson Mandela and seven other members of the African National Congress were sentenced to life imprisonment for acts of sabotage and offenses under the Suppression of Communism Act. Protest may be directed to Prime Minister Verwoerd, Praetoria, South Africa. The following is Nelson Mandela's opening statement to the Court. Following this is a comment on South Africa by Paul Goodman.*]

I am the first accused. I hold a Bachelor's Degree in Arts and practiced as an attorney in Johannesburg for a number of years. I am a convicted prisoner serving five years for leaving the country without a permit and for inciting people to go on strike at the end of May 1961.

At the outset, I want to say that the suggestion made by the State in its opening that the struggle in South Africa is under the influence of foreigners or Communists is wholly incorrect. I have done whatever I did, both as an individual and as a leader of my people, because of my experience in South Africa and my own proudly felt African background.

In my youth in the Transkei I listened to the elders of my tribe telling stories of the old days. Among the tales they related to me were those of wars fought by our ancestors in defense of the fatherland. The names of Dingane and Bambata, Hintsa and Makana, Squngthi and Dalasile, Moshoeshoe and Sekhukhuni, were praised as the glory of the entire African nation. I hoped then that life might offer me the opportunity to serve my people and make my own humble contribution to their freedom struggle. This is what has motivated me in all that I have done.

Some of the things so far told to the court are true and
some are untrue. I do not, however, deny that I planned sabotage. I did not plan it in a spirit of recklessness, nor because I
have any love of violence. I planned it as a result of a calm and
sober assessment of the political situation that had arisen after
many years of tyranny, exploitation and oppression of my
people by the whites.

I admit immediately that I was one of the persons who
helped to form *Umkonto We Sizwe* [The Spear of the Nation
—the main sabotage movement in South Africa], and that I
played a prominent rôle in its affairs until I was arrested in
August 1962.

I, and the others who started the organization, did so for
two reasons. Firstly, we believed that as a result of Government
policy, violence by the African people had become inevitable,
and that unless responsible leadership was given to canalize
and control the feelings of our people, there would be out-
breaks of terrorism which would produce an intensity of bitterness and hostility between the various races of this country
which is not produced even by war. Secondly, we felt that
without violence there would be no way open to the African
people to succeed in their struggle against the principle of
white supremacy.

But the violence we chose to adopt was not terrorism. We
who formed Umkonto were all members of the African National Congress, and had behind us the A.N.C. tradition of
nonviolence and negotiation as a means of solving political
disputes.

Our problem was not whether to fight but how to continue the fight. We of the A.N.C. had always stood for a non-
racial democracy, and we shrank from any action which might
drive the races farther apart than they already were. But the
hard facts were that 50 years of nonviolence had brought the
African people nothing but more and more repressive legislation, and fewer and fewer rights.

It may not be easy for this court to understand, but it is a
fact that for a long time the people had been talking of violence—of the day when they would fight the white man and
win back their country, and we, the leaders of the A.N.C., had

nevertheless always prevailed upon them to avoid violence and to pursue peaceful methods. When some of us discussed this in May and June of 1961, it could not be denied that our policy to achieve a non-racial State by nonviolence had achieved nothing, and that our followers were beginning to lose confidence in this policy and were developing disturbing ideas of terrorism.

It must not be forgotten that by this time violence had, in fact, become a feature of the South African political scene. How many more Sharpevilles would there be in the history of our country? And how many more Sharpevilles could the country stand without violence and terror becoming the order of the day?

At the beginning of June 1961, after a long and anxious assessment of the South African situation, I, and some colleagues, came to the conclusion that as violence in this country was inevitable, it would be unrealistic and wrong for African leaders to continue preaching peace and nonviolence at a time when the Government met our peaceful demands with force.

Umkonto was formed in November 1961. Umkonto was to perform sabotage, and strict instructions were given to its members right from the start that on no account were they to injure or kill people in planning or carrying out operations.

The fight which held out the best prospects for us and the least risk of life to both sides was guerrilla warfare. [Mandela here described how in 1962 he went to seek support in Africa and Britain.]

I started to make a study of the art of war and revolution and, whilst abroad, underwent a course in military training. If there was to be guerrilla warfare, I wanted to be able to stand and fight with my people and to share the hazards of war with them. I approached this question as every African Nationalist should do. I was completely objective. The court will see that I attempted to examine all types of authority on the subject— from the East and from the West, going back to the classic work of Clausewitz, and covering such a variety as Mao Tse-tung and Che Guevara on the one hand, and the writings on the Anglo-Boer War on the other.

Another of the allegations made by the State is that the

aims and objects of the A.N.C. and the Communist Party are the same. The allegation is false. The ideological creed of the A.N.C. is, and always has been, the creed of African nationalism. It is not the concept of African nationalism expressed in the cry, "Drive the white man into the sea." The African nationalism for which the A.N.C. stands is the concept of freedom and fulfilment for the African people in their own land. It is true that there has often been close cooperation between the A.N.C. and the Communist Party. But cooperation is merely proof of a common goal—in this case the removal of white supremacy—and is not proof of a complete community of interests.

It is perhaps difficult for white South Africans, with an ingrained prejudice against Communism, to understand why experienced African politicians so readily accept Communists as their friends. But to us the reason is obvious. Theoretical differences amongst those fighting against oppression is a luxury we cannot afford at this stage. What is more, for many decades Communists were the only political group in South Africa who were prepared to treat Africans as human beings and their equals, who were prepared to eat with us, talk with us, live with us and work with us. They were the only political group which was prepared to work with the Africans for the attainment of political rights and a stake in society. Because of this, there are many Africans who, today, tend to equate freedom with Communism.

It is not only in internal politics that we count Communists as amongst those who support our cause. Although there is a universal condemnation of *apartheid,* the Communist bloc speaks out against it with a louder voice than most of the white world.

I turn now to my own position. I have denied that I am a Communist, and I think that in the circumstances I am obliged to state exactly what my political beliefs are.

I have always regarded myself, in the first place, as an African patriot. After all, I was born in Umtata 46 years ago. My guardian was my cousin, who was the acting paramount chief of Tembuland, and I am related both to the present paramount chief of Tembuland, Sabata Dalinyebo, and to Kaizer Matanzima, the Chief Minister of the Transkei.

It is true, as I have already stated, that I have been influenced by Marxist thought. But this is also true of many of the leaders of the new independent States. Such widely different persons as Gandhi, Nehru, Nkrumah and Nasser all acknowledge this fact. We all accept the need for some form of Socialism to enable our people to catch up with the advanced countries of this world and to overcome their legacy of extreme poverty. But this does not mean we are Marxists. Indeed, for my own part, I believe that it is open to debate whether the Communist Party has any specific rôle to play at this particular stage of our political struggle. The basic task at the present moment is the removal of race discrimination and the attainment of democratic rights on the basis of the Freedom Charter. In so far as that party furthers this task, I welcome its assistance. I realize that it is one of the means by which people of all races can be drawn into our struggle.

From my reading of Marxist literature and from conversations with Marxists, I have gained the impression that Communists regard the parliamentary system of the West as undemocratic and reactionary. But, on the contrary, I am an admirer of such a system. The Magna Carta, the Petition of Rights and the Bill of Rights are documents which are held in veneration by democrats throughout the world. I have great respect for British political institutions, and for the country's system of justice. I regard the British Parliament as the most democratic institution in the world, and the independence and impartiality of its judiciary never fail to arouse my admiration.

I have been influenced in my thinking by both West and East. All this has led me to feel that I should tie myself to no particular system of society other than of Socialism. I must leave myself free to borrow the best from the West and from the East.

Basically, we fight against two features which are the hallmarks of African life in South Africa and which are entrenched by legislation which we seek to have repealed. These features are poverty and lack of human dignity. South Africa is the richest country in Africa, and could be one of the richest countries in the world. But it is a land of extremes and remarkable contrasts. The whites enjoy what may well be the highest standard of living in the world, whilst Africans live in poverty and misery. The lack of human dignity experienced by Africans is the direct result of the policy of white supremacy. White supremacy implies black inferiority. Legislation designed to preserve white supremacy entrenches this notion.

Africans want to be paid a living wage. Africans want to perform work which they are capable of doing, and not work which the Government declares them to be capable of. Africans want to be allowed to live where they obtain work, and not to be endorsed out of an area because they were not born there. Africans want to be allowed to own land in places where they work, and not to be obliged to live in rented houses which they can never call their own. Africans want to be part of the general population, and not confined to living in their own ghettos.

Above all, we want equal political rights, because without them our disabilities will be permanent. I know this sounds revolutionary to the whites in this country, because the majority of voters will be Africans. This makes the white man fear democracy. But this fear cannot be allowed to stand in the way of the only solution which will guarantee racial harmony and freedom for all. It is not true that the enfranchisement of all will result in racial domination. Political division, based on color, is entirely artificial and, when it disappears, so will the domination of one color group by another.

This then is what the A.N.C. is fighting. Their struggle is a truly national one. It is a struggle of the African people, inspired by their own suffering and their own experience. It is a struggle for the right to live.

During my lifetime I have dedicated myself to this struggle of the African people. I have fought against white domination, and I have fought against black domination. I have cherished the ideal of a democratic and free society in which all persons live together in harmony and with equal opportunities. It is an ideal which I hope to live for and to see realized. But if needs be, my Lord, it is an ideal for which I am prepared to die.

Paul Goodman

A Tour of South Africa

The New York *Times* of June 4 [1961] contained one of its frequent special advertising supplements devoted to the industry and tourism of a nation of the world. This one was "sponsored and the material prepared by South African and American business interests as a guide to South Africa." Because of the racial policy of the Union of South Africa, there is a melancholy interest in describing this document.

Its principle is explained in the foreword statement, "Workshop of a Continent," in the following paragraphs:

> *Dr. Ernest Dichter, president of the Institute of Motivational Research, makes the point that even the average American tourist in Johannesburg looks at fact-filled pamphlets publicizing the country and says to himself mentally: "I know you're trying to pull the wool over my eyes. You're trying to tell me that things in this country aren't too bad—well, who are you kidding? I know what goes on here." He has rejected the facts rather than change his mind.*
>
> *Dr. Dichter suggests that information on South Africa should read something like this: "So you've heard that in this country we have* apartheid, *a police state, slave labor, etc., well, we'd like to tell you a few other things."*

Dr. Dichter has explained to me at length that science, including his psychological science, is purely neutral and objective and can be applied to a good or a bad cause. I presume that he was amply rewarded for his advice to this bad cause.

Let us turn to this fact-filled pamphlet. It contains 35 photographs showing human beings; four of these show Negroes. The actual white population of South Africa is less than 20%.

One photo showing a Negro is the cover. It is a busy scene
of traders on the floor of the Johannesburg Stock Exchange; on
the balcony is a young Negro marker alertly waiting to chalk
the figures.

The other three figures are part of a two-page spread of 22
photos called "Take a Tour of South Africa." There are whites
fishing, working in a mine, surf-riding, bus-drivers conversing,
shopping, father-and-daughter, a comic behind, a pin-up girl,
merchant mariners drinking, dining. The photos of Negroes
are: cute five-year-olds singing; two youths playing "penny
whistles"; and a merry fat mammy balancing a valise on her
head and perched on the handle-bars of a bicycle pushed by a
spooky-eyed coon.

It is appalling that this kind of stereotyped garbage can
still be printed, and paid for by Americans (and passed by Dr.
Dichter?). In this magazine no Negro is shown working. The
whites must work terribly hard, in that Workshop of a Continent, to support a colored population more than four times
their own.

On page seven, in parallel columns, with photographs, are
statements by C. R. Swart, the South African Minister of Justice, and John F. Kennedy. Mr. Swart's statement starts by
pointing out the similarity of the pioneer settlement of South
Africa and the United States. (On another page is a drawing
of a covered wagon being attacked by savages.) He ends with
the remark that "South Africa and the United States have
mutual interests in defense strategy and are cooperating exten-
sively in space research. Slowly people are beginning to realize
that the Republic of South Africa is not a stretch of steaming
jungle, but rather a modern Western nation, vital and highly
civilized, differing from the Republic of the United States
basically only in size."

Cheek by jowl with this, the face of President Kennedy
tells us:

> [Africa] is a land of immense importance to the world
> and to the United States. Some may look at it from the
> viewpoint of the vital natural resources and strategic ma-
> terials. Some may be interested in military bases or new

allies against Communism. Some may feel a responsibility in Africa because the West thrust itself upon the area and cannot be indifferent to the consequences. Some may have a real concern for Africa and her people. But whatever one's point of view, one fact cannot be denied—the future of Africa will seriously affect, for better or worse, the future of the United States.

The colossal moral stupidity with which the President of the United States here regards ordinary human concern as one possible "viewpoint" among several—which one may or may not have—must not pass unnoticed. And in this context! This is the fellow who dares to urge our young people into a Peace Corps for service.

Most of the products advertised are industrial. The only ones that seem subject to boycott by ordinary consumers are travel and South African Rock Lobster Tails.

Julius K. Nyerere

Communitarian Socialism

Sociologists may someday find it interesting to try to find out why our societies in Africa did not produce any millionaires—for we certainly had enough wealth to create a few. I think they will discover that it was because the organization of traditional African society—its distribution of the wealth it produced—was such that there was hardly any room for parasitism. They may also say, of course, that as a result of this Africa could not produce a leisured class of landowners, and that therefore there was nobody to produce the works of art or science which capitalist societies can boast. But works of art and the achievements of science are products of the intellect—which, like land, is one of God's gifts to man. And I cannot believe that God is so careless as to have made the use of one of his gifts depend on the *mis*use of another!

Defenders of capitalism claim that the millionaire's wealth is the just reward for his ability or enterprise. But this claim is not borne out by the facts. The wealth of the millionaire depends as little on the enterprise or abilities of the millionaire himself as the power of a feudal monarch depended on his own efforts, enterprise or brain. Both are users, exploiters, of the abilities and enterprise of other people. Even when you have an exceptionally intelligent and hard-working millionaire, the difference between his intelligence, his enterprise, his hard work, and those of other members of society, cannot possibly be proportionate to the difference between their "rewards." There must be something wrong in a society where one man, however hard-working or clever he may be, can acquire as great a "reward" as a thousand of his fellows can acquire among them.

Apart from the anti-social effects of the accumulation of

personal wealth, the very desire to accumulate it must be interpreted as a vote of "no confidence" in the social system. For when a society is so organized that it cares about its individuals, then, provided he is willing to work, no individual within that society should worry about what will happen to him tomorrow if he does not hoard wealth today. Society itself should look after him, or his widow, or his orphans. This is exactly what traditional African society succeeded in doing. Both the "rich" and the "poor" individual were completely secure in African society. Natural catastrophe brought famine, but it brought famine to everybody—"poor" or "rich." Nobody starved, either for food or for human dignity, because he lacked personal wealth; he could depend on the wealth possessed by the community of which he was a member. That was socialism. That is socialism. There can be no such thing as acquisitive socialism, for that would be a contradiction in terms. Socialism is essentially distributive. Its concern is to see that those who sow reap a fair share of what they have sown.

The production of wealth, whether by primitive or modern methods, requires three things. First, land. God has given us the land, and it is from the land that we get the raw materials which we reshape to meet our needs. Secondly, tools. We have found by simple experience that tools do help. So we make the hoe, the axe, or the modern factory or tractor, to help us produce wealth—the goods we need. And, thirdly, human exertion—or labor. We don't need to read Karl Marx or Adam Smith to find out that neither the land nor the hoe actually produces wealth. And we don't need to take degrees in economics to know that neither the worker nor the landlord produces land. Land is God's gift to man—it is always there. But we do know, still without degrees in economics, that the axe and the plough were produced by the laborer.

In traditional African society *everybody* was a worker. There was no other way of earning a living for the community. Even the elder, who appeared to be enjoying himself without doing any work and for whom everybody else appeared to be working, had, in fact, worked hard all his younger days. The wealth he now appeared to possess was not *his,* personally; it was only "his" as the elder of the group which had produced it.

He was its guardian. The wealth itself gave him neither power nor prestige. The respect paid to him by the young was his because he was older than they, and had served his community longer; and the "poor" elder enjoyed as much respect in our society as the "rich" elder.

When I say that in traditional African society everybody was a worker, I do not use the word "worker" simply as opposed to "employer" but also as opposed to "loiterer" or "idler." One of the most socialistic achievements of our society was the sense of security it gave to its members, and the universal hospitality on which they could rely. But it is too often forgotten nowadays, that the basis of this great socialistic achievement was this: that it was taken for granted that every member of society—barring only the children and the infirm—contributed his fair share of effort towards the production of its wealth. Not only was the capitalist, or the landed exploiter, unknown to traditional African society, but we did not have that other form of modern parasite—the loiterer, or idler, who accepts the hospitality of society as his "right" but gives nothing in return.

Those of us who talk about the African Way of Life, and, quite rightly, take a pride in maintaining the tradition of hospitality which is so great a part of it, might do well to remember the Swahili saying: "Treat your guest as a guest for two days; on the third day give him a hoe!" In actual fact, the guest was likely to ask for the hoe even before his host had to give him one—for he knew what was expected of him, and would have been ashamed to remain idle any longer. There is no such thing as socialism without work. A society which fails to give its individuals the means to work or, having given them the means to work, prevents them from getting a fair share of the products of their own sweat and toil, needs putting right. Similarly, an individual who can work—and is provided by society with the means to work—but does not do so, is equally wrong. He has no right to expect anything from society because he contributes nothing *to* society.

The other use of the word "worker," in its specialized sense of "employee" as opposed to "employer," reflects a capitalist attitude of mind which was introduced into Africa with the coming of colonialism and is totally foreign to our own way of thinking. In the old days the African had never aspired to the possession of personal wealth for the purpose of dominating any of his fellows. He had never had laborers or "factory hands" to do his work for him. But then came the foreign capitalists. They were wealthy. They were powerful. And the African naturally started wanting to be wealthy too. Unfortunately there are some of us who have already learnt to covet wealth—and who would like to use the methods which the capitalist uses in acquiring it. That is to say, some of us would like to use, or exploit, our brothers for the purpose of building up our own personal power and prestige. This is completely foreign to us, and it is incompatible with the socialist society we want to build here.

Our first step, therefore, must be to re-educate ourselves; to regain our former attitude of mind. In our traditional African society we were individuals within a community. We took care of the community, and the community took care of us. We neither needed nor wished to exploit our fellow men. And in rejecting the capitalist attitude of mind which colonialism brought into Africa, we must reject also the capitalist methods which go with it. One of these is the individual ownership of land. To us in Africa, land was always recognized as belonging to the community. Each individual within our society had a right to the use of land, because otherwise he could not earn his living and one cannot have the right to life without also having the right to some means of maintaining life. But the African's right to land was simply the right to *use* it; he had no other right to it, nor did it occur to him to try to claim one.

The foreigner introduced a completely different concept— the concept of land as a marketable commodity. According to this system, a person could claim a piece of land as his own private property *whether he intended to use it or not*. I could take a few square miles of land, call them "mine," and then go off to the moon. All I had to do to gain a living from "my" land was to charge a rent to the people who wanted to use it. If this piece of land was in an urban area I had no need to develop it at all; I could leave it to the fools who were prepared to develop all the other pieces of land surrounding "my" piece, and in doing so automatically to raise the market value of mine. Then I could come down from the moon and demand that these fools pay me through their noses for the high value of "my" land—a value which they themselves had created for me while I was enjoying myself on the moon! Landlords, in a society which recognizes individual ownership of land, can be —and they usually are—in the same class as the loiterers I was talking about: the class of parasites.

The African Tradition

The Tanganyikan African National Union government must go back to the traditional African custom of land holding. That is to say, a member of society will be entitled to a piece of land *on condition that he uses it.* Unconditional, or "freehold," ownership of land (which leads to speculation and parasitism) must be abolished. We must regain our former attitude of mind—our traditional African socialism—and apply it to the new societies we are building today. T.A.N.U. has pledged itself to make socialism the basis of its policy in every field. The people of Tanganyika have given us their mandate to carry out that policy, by electing a T.A.N.U. government to lead them. So the government can be relied upon to introduce only legislation which is in harmony with socialist principles.

Just as the elder, in our former society, was respected for his age and his service to the community, so, in our modern society, this respect for age and service will be preserved. And in the same way as the "rich" elder's apparent wealth was really only held by him in trust for his people, so, today, the apparent extra wealth which certain positions of leadership may bring to the individuals who fill them, can be theirs only insofar as it is a necessary aid to the carrying out of their duties. It is a "tool" entrusted to them for the benefit of the people they serve. It is not "theirs" personally; and they may not use any part of it as a means of accumulating more for their own benefit, nor as an "insurance" against the day when they no longer hold the same positions. That would be to betray the people who entrusted it to them. If they serve the community while they can, the community must look after them when they are no longer able to do so.

In tribal society, the individuals or the families within a tribe were "rich" or "poor" according to whether the whole tribe was rich or poor. If the tribe prospered, all the members of the tribe shared in its prosperity. Tanganyika, today, is a poor country. The standard of living of the masses of our people is shamefully low. But if every man and woman in the country takes up the challenge and works to the limit of his or her ability for the good of the whole society, Tanganyika will prosper, and that prosperity will be shared by all her people. But it must be *shared*. The true socialist may not exploit his fellows. So that if the members of any group within our society are going to argue that, because they happen to be contributing more to the national income than some other groups, they must therefore take for themselves a greater share of the profits of their own industry than they actually need; and if they insist on this in spite of the fact that it would mean reducing their group's contribution to the general income and thus slowing down the rate at which the whole community can benefit, then that group is exploiting (or trying to exploit) its fellow human beings. It is displaying a capitalist attitude of mind.

Creeping Capitalism

There are bound to be certain groups which, by virtue of the "market value" of their particular industry's products, *will* contribute more to the nation's income than others. But the others may actually be producing goods or services which are of equal, or greater, *intrinsic* value although they do not happen to command such a high *artificial* value. For example, the food produced by the peasant farmer is of greater social value than the diamonds mined at Mwadui. But the mineworkers of Mwadui could claim, quite correctly, that their labor was yielding greater financial profits to the community than that of the farmers. If, however, they went on to demand that they should therefore be given most of that extra profit for themselves, and that no share of it should be spent on helping the farmers, they would be potential capitalists!

As with groups, so with individuals. There are certain skills, certain qualifications, which command a higher rate of salary for their possessors than others. But, here again, the true socialist will demand only that return for his skilled work which he knows to be a fair one in proportion to the wealth or poverty of the whole society to which he belongs. He will not, unless he is a would-be capitalist, attempt to blackmail the community by demanding a salary equal to that paid to his counterpart in some far wealthier society.

European socialism was born of the agrarian revolution and the industrial revolution which followed it. The former created the "landed" and the "landless" classes in society; the latter produced the modern capitalist and the industrial proletariat. These two revolutions planted the seeds of conflict within society, and not only was European socialism born of that conflict, but its apostles sanctified the conflict itself into a philosophy. Civil war was no longer looked upon as something evil, or something unfortunate, but as something good and necessary. As prayer is to Christianity or to Islam, so civil war ("class war") is to the European version of socialism—a means inseparable from the end. Each becomes the basis of a whole way of life. The European socialist cannot think of his socialism without its father—capitalism.

Brought up in tribal socialism, I must say I find this contradiction quite intolerable. It gives capitalism a philosophical status which it neither claims nor deserves. For it virtually says "Without capitalism, and the conflict which capitalism creates within society, there can be no socialism." African socialism, on the other hand, did not have the "benefit" of the agrarian revolution or the industrial revolution. It did not start from the existence of conflicting "classes" in society. Indeed I doubt if the equivalent for the word "class" exists in any indigenous African language; for language describes the ideas of those who speak it, and the idea of "class" or "caste" was non-existent in African society.

"Ujamaa"

The foundation, and the objective, of African socialism is the extended family. The true African socialist does not look on one class of men as his brethren and another as his natural enemies. He does not form an alliance with the "brethren" for the extermination of the "non-brethren." He rather regards *all* men as his brethren—as members of his ever extending family. *Ujamaa,* then, or "familyhood," describes our socialism. It is opposed to capitalism, which seeks to build a happy society on the basis of the exploitation of man by man; and it is equally opposed to doctrinaire socialism, which seeks to build its happy society on a philosophy of inevitable conflict between man and man.

We in Africa have no more need of being "converted" to socialism than we have of being "taught" democracy. Both are rooted in our own past—in the traditional society which produced us. Modern African socialism can draw from its traditional heritage the recognition of "society" as an extension of the basic family unit. But it can no longer confine the idea of the social family within the limits of the tribe, nor, indeed, of the nation. For no true African socialist can look at a line drawn on a map and say "The people on this side of that line are my brothers, but those who happen to live on the other side of it can have no claim on me." Every individual on this continent is his brother.

It was in the struggle to break the grip of colonialism that we learned the need for unity. We came to recognize that the same socialist attitude of mind which, in the tribal days, gave to every individual the security that comes of belonging to a widely extended family, must be preserved within the still wider society of the nation. But we should not stop there. Our recognition of the family to which we all belong must be extended yet further—beyond the tribe, the community, the nation, or even the continent—to embrace the whole society of mankind.

A. J. Muste

Tiger at the Gates

The warlike reaction of the Indian government and people to the border crisis in the autumn of 1962, like the forcible take-over of Goa a year or so earlier, was a considerable shock to many in the world. The image of India had been related in people's minds to nonviolence and Gandhi. That image has now been marred. The reaction has been partly, of course, one of gloating that India is no better than we are; but para-doxically, as so often happens in human life, there has also been sorrow over the sudden death of a hope that a saving element had somehow been introduced into history.

The Chinese military movements in the Ladakh area and far-ther east in NEFA (North East Frontier Authority), in Octo-ber-November 1962, were a complete surprise to Indians generally, and also, it is my impression, to members of the gov-ernment. The element of shock was greater because tradition-ally the Himalayas had been regarded as a bastion assuring the sub-continent of much the same kind of security that the oceans provided for the United States in the era before the aer-oplane. Suddenly, the incursion of the Chinese into the ter-ritory south of the mountains put an end to this isolation. For a time, it looked as though the Chinese could have kept on moving south into the plains indefinitely. In any case, as Vinoba Bhave put it, "Science has levelled the mountain barrier and these two great peoples, who between them constitute a third of the earth's population, are now next-door neighbors."

The element of shock for the Indians was greatly com-pounded by the fact that the Nehru government had appar-ently pursued a policy of friendship and good will toward China. War between them was simply not thought about. The effect of the Chinese attack may therefore be compared to that of Pearl Harbor on the United States, only more so, since on the eve of the latter it was known that war between Japan and the United States was imminent.

The immediate effect was an electrifying one and caused almost as much surprise as the Chinese attack itself. Indian nationalism was, of course, a reality as against British domination, but once India was freed, there were many divisive tendencies in this huge land. There was also the traumatic factor of the partition which constituted Pakistan, a Moslem state, part of it in the northeast and part in the northwest section of the sub-continent. To many, even now, it is Pakistan rather than Communist China which is the chief enemy. However, a wave of nationalism swept over India after the Chinese attack and it is clear that a degree of national unity, a feeling of "nationhood" well beyond that which previously existed has been one of its chief products. The patriotic upsurge has been marked by all the manifestations with which we are, alas, so familiar: flag-waving, heaping praise on the bravery of "our soldiers" in retreat, reporting enemy atrocities, demonstrations, popular donations to the Defense Fund, stepping up recruiting, and so on *ad infinitum*.

It should, no doubt, be pointed out that such a reaction is not surprising among a people who not many years ago achieved their independence after a long and in many ways glorious struggle. Furthermore, as some Indians have pointed out, it is a long time since Indians have been involved in war —except as soldiers in British armies—and they have had little, if any, direct experience of its effects.

To all who think in conventional terms about the development of nations, national "interests," and defense of the nation and its way of life, this upsurge of national feeling has been gratifying. Preceding the present development, there existed in the West apprehension that India's association with nonviolence, whether in ancient tradition or in relation to Gandhi, implied a lack of the manlier virtues on the part of its people and of toughness on the part of its government. Now it is felt that Indians have awakened from their dream and prove to be just as manly and militant as the rest of mankind!

It is difficult, even for one who has followed Indian affairs

fairly closely for a long time and has had the opportunity
recently of spending several weeks there, to judge political
trends. This is especially true when the Chinese have unilaterally instituted an armistice and withdrawn from a large part of
the territory they occupied during the advance. It seems to me
that Nehru and those in the Cabinet and among the intelli-
gentsia who support him, on the whole still exercise a restraining influence, in favor of negotiation and maintenance of a
measure of civil liberties. Along with all the talk and action
about stepping up military preparations and driving out the
foe forever from the soil of Mother India, there is still a strong
current of idealism, of professions of desire for peace, of "non-
alignment." I do not think that this talk is for the most part
hypocritical, certainly not consciously so. But the importance
of these idealistic comments is, in my view, exaggerated by
Gandhians and by defenders of Nehru, and this leads to considerable confusion.

For example, Nehru's "non-alignment" policy is still
thought of as a Gandhian approach to international relations.
In a limited sense, this is true, and one can understand that
this consideration should be a part of the motivation of persons
who spent most of their active life under Gandhi's massive
influence. But in terms of political reality, the non-alignment
policy simply represented from one angle the "national interest" of a relatively weak and newly independent nation bor-
dered by two powerful and expansionist nations, the Soviet
Union and Communist China. From another angle, it represented the natural impulse of this newly independent nation to
stand aloof from the policies of the West, which represented
the colonialism by which it had been exploited and oppressed.
It was very like George Washington's "no-entangling-alliances"
policy for the infant United States. Americans long tended to
regard this as a virtuous rather than merely expedient policy,
keeping us clean of the wars, corruptions and monarchies of
the Old World. There was, that is to say, nothing uniquely
wicked about the tendency to idealize the non-alignment policy (with a certain anti-West bias) and use it for moralistic
purposes, but it was not realistic to do so, and it aroused some
understandable resentment in the West. Jayaprakash Narayan

is among the few leading Indians who have openly criticized
Nehru's tendency to be much more critical of American nuclear testing than of Russia, of British action in Suez than of
Russian in Hungary. Faithfulness to a policy of non-interven-
tion in the affairs of another poeple, not to mention Gandhian
nonviolence, would certainly have dictated some strong criticism on the part of Nehru of the take-over in Tibet. Yet India
even abstained, in the United Nations, on the question of violation of human rights in Tibet.

There was a definite tendency on the part of both Nehru
and Krishna Menon to use a double standard in judging the
behavior of nations. It is not at all unusual to encounter such
moral aberrations among politicians and statesmen, but it is
not to be condoned in one case more than another. Some
would argue that an even more grievous error was committed
by Nehru and Menon in misjudging Chinese intentions and
leaving the country politically and militarily unprepared for
what happened. No political leader should be guilty of the
calculation that a régime which seized the Tibetan highlands
in the presumed interest of its security in a world transformed
by the latest developments in both military and non-military
technology, would let matters rest there. China was bound, for
example, to want a better connection between Sinkiang and
Tibet, which is what it was doing when it—secretly, it is
alleged—built the road in Ladakh which it now wants to secure. The Chinese régime moreover knew (as Indian leaders
should have known) that science had levelled the Himalayan
barrier. It "had" to be concerned about what was going on in
places like Nepal and Assam. I doubt if anyone would deny
that India was trying to bind these peoples closer to the Indian
state.

India, in doing this, was operating in territory that traditionally belonged to it, if only in that it lay south of the mountain barrier. It is also a fact that the Indian state has at the
moment no expansionist designs. Nevertheless, in a world
which operates on the basis of power and "balance" of power,
and in which the Chinese People's Republic is faced with the
presence of American power in Japan, in Taiwan, in the Pacific, in some of the Southeast Asian countries, and even in

Pakistan, Mao Tse-tung and Chou En-lai were bound to be concerned about what was happening south of the Himalayan border. Even if its relations with India had been entirely friendly in the past, it was only behaving as a proper power state in assuming they might not remain so and in seeking to extend its defense area where it had the power to do so.

Thus the Indian government and people have no business to be as "surprised" as they are—or perhaps, in the case of some, make out to be—at the Chinese military operations. I am inclined to agree with the Indian viewpoint that these operations were "aggressive." It certainly cannot be denied that Chinese forces moved ahead and kept doing so for some time. This required considerable previous preparation. It is equally clear that the Indian troops were not moving ahead *in force* and were not prepared for the scale of operations which occurred. Chinese, like Russian, expansionism is not a phenomenon which arose with Communism, any more than Western expansionism was an anti-Communist phenomenon. (Some actually regarded it as Christian!) The so-called border dispute has certainly been going on for some years and no one denies that India took some steps to "strengthen its position." Naturally it claimed that these measures were purely defensive, as governments always do in such situations. By the same token, they never seem purely defensive to the other government involved. How is it to know when the "defense" will become strong enough to move ahead and secure a more advanced and stronger "defensive position?" And is it not the responsibility of the second government to its peoples to take no chances in a situation of this kind but rather to undertake "defensive-offense" itself? I have not read in detail the documents about the McMahon Line, the negotiations and the military maneuvers of the respective armies. Bertrand Russell and others have concluded that the Chinese were actually reacting to an Indian "aggression" at the time hostilities broke out in October, 1962. I still doubt that. On the part of most who reach this conclusion, I sense a tendency to an idealization of Chinese behavior. It seems to me, moreover, that the military facts are against them. In addition to what I have already said on that point, the Menon policy was certainly that of concentrating Indian forces on the Pakistan border rather than in the north.

When independence was imminent, the present leaders of the government chose the course of forming a state after the conventional pattern and equipping it from the start with a relatively large military establishment. Those who sit in on the game of nationalism and power will not escape the pressures of their fellow-players nor be exempted from the consequences of the struggles which are the essence of the game. The so-called border dispute is not a technical or legal one as to where a line somebody drew years ago runs or a new line should run. If it were, it would never have arisen or would have been resolved long ago. It is a dispute about power, about national sovereignty, about "honor," about "our sacred soil." It may be in one sense a struggle between ways of life, between contrasting or conflicting moral and spiritual values and as such of vast, even supreme importance. But then, of course, the crucial question arises as to how moral and spiritual values are in fact defended and vindicated? And if the "defense" is by essentially identical military means in each case, what is then the difference between the "values" in the end? No state is ever as "innocent" as many Indians seem to think India is at this moment. There are no "innocents" and no "devils" in such a situation, but only unfortunates caught in the same trap.

India's "independence" now depends on the world situation, on other powers, who will not first of all be primarily concerned about India's welfare and who will expect India to pay a price for their support. Its "non-alignment" is subject to the exigencies of power relationships in the world and its dream of leading an independent force of non-aligned nations has been brushed aside by the tide of events. A group of "neutral" nations—the Colombo group—now steps forward to mediate between India and China!

When India approached the day of independence, Gandhi proposed to the Congress Party, which had been the organizational instrument of the struggle for freedom, that it should not take power, form a government along essentially conventional lines and function as a political party in office—and naturally wanting to stay in office. He proposed that it instead become an organization of "Servants" who would work at the social base to heal communal strife, develop "basic education" suited to the Indian people and their condition, remove caste distinctions, build economic equality and village economy. The Congress Party leadership, headed by such men as Nehru and Patel, did not accept Gandhi's proposal. In a sense all that has followed in Indian political life stems from that decision. One result is the division which now exists between the governing elements in India and such groups as the *Sarva Seva Sangh* and *Shanti Sena.*

The latter have been attempting to carry on, in the main, the program which Gandhi wished the Congress Party to undertake. During the past decade or so this has been under the leadership of Vinoba Bhave. Prominent in the program has been *Bhoodan* (landlords and land owners generally urged to turn over land to those who have none or not enough). Lately this has been broadened and deepened into *Gramdan* (the village organizing itself on a cooperative basis as a family, with land and industrial facilities belonging to the village). Ideally this would build up into a sort of federation of village republics with state and central government agencies counselling the republics rather than controlling them. Until the crisis arose, the attitude of the government was, so far as I know, uniformly a benevolent one toward *Bhoodan* and *Gramdan.* The government itself took over parts of the development program, and I gather that younger and more militant Gandhians regard this as a misfortune: "People again look to the government to do things for them."

In face of the crisis, there is a strong tendency to relate the Gandhian "service" program to the national defense effort. This does not mean that there is no recognition at all of a contradiction between nonviolence and the building up of armed forces. There is, however, no clear effort to separate the two. On the one hand, it is assumed that government cannot behave nonviolently, "the people are not ready." With this is associated a guilt feeling on the part of Gandhians that they have not done more to make the people ready for a nonviolent response and that they themselves are not able to field a *Shanti Sena* which might make a showing against an invader. On the

other hand is the feeling that unless and until there is a *nonviolent social base*, war cannot be eliminated anyway. By the
same token, if nonviolent forces are built at the base, even as a
part of the defense effort for the time being, these forces will
eventually gain the upper hand and either compel government
to alter its policy or change the nature of the state and of
government.

It seems to me a delusion to suppose that the nation as a
whole can enter upon a program of military build-up, with all
this involves for the national economy and for the psychology
of the people, and not sweep over the comparatively meager
forces of nonviolence. What happens in the village or school
where the Gandhian "servant" or *Shanti Sainik* is at work when
the government rabble-rousers and recruiting agents come
along? If the impression is given that everybody is working for
"defense," the same kind of defense, it is surely the recruiting
agent who will prevail. If, to put it the other way round, the
young men of a village republic have been trained not only for
nonviolent defense of the village but to be nonviolent in spirit,
to live with their neighbors as one family, how can they at the
same time accept training in shooting, bayoneting and drop-
ping bombs on Chinese invaders? What happens if they see
the contradiction and refuse to fight? What does it say about
the training in nonviolence which they have allegedly received
if they do not see the contradiction—any more than multitudes
of Christian youth in the West see no contradiction between
military service and what they have been taught in the Gospels?

It seems to me that only a moderate amount of reflection
is necessary to drive home the conclusion that opposition to
(thorough-going non-cooperation with) war and the building
of a nonviolent social base are inseparable. A violent society
will wage war, it is true. It is equally true that a society which
wages war will not develop a nonviolent social order.

Vinoba himself several years ago pointed out the dilemma
in which reliance on military force would involve India. "If we
decide for violence," he said, "we shall have to take either
Russia or America as our *guru*. . . . It would take us at least
fifty years to get any strength from them" (become equal in

strength, the context indicates). "Is that what we want—that in the name of freedom we should become either a slave or a threat to the peace of the world?"

As for the people not being ready for nonviolence, how do we know, if they have no leadership and if the question is not even put up to them?

Granted that it is morally better to resist evil than not to resist or not to protect the helpless because of apathy or cowardice. But recklessness is not courage. Waging peace, practicing nonviolence (or "nonviolent assistance" in one of Vinoba's happy phrases) also requires courage, and admittedly of a higher order. If men can be *quickly* trained to fight in an emergency, what could not be accomplished if leaders undertook to provide the same resources and the same inspiration for training in nonviolent action!

Vinoba called attention to the psychology of military rivalry: "Russia says America has dangerous ideas so she has to increase her armaments. America says exactly the same thing about Russia. . . . The image in the mirror is your own image; the sword in its hand is your own sword. And when we grasp our own sword in fear of what we see, the image in the mirror does the same. What we see in front of us is nothing but a reflection of ourselves. If India could find courage to reduce her army to the minimum, it would demonstrate to the world her moral strength." But he adds: *"We are cowards and cowards have no imagination."*

Vinoba was extremely clear on the point that "the Lord has so shaped the destiny of India that she must either commit herself wholeheartedly to the path of nonviolence or find herself enslaved to those who are adepts of violence." Again, "I must tell you plainly that if we as a nation accept the idea that well-meaning people may use violence in order to put their ideas into practice, India will be broken into fragments, and will lose all her strength. Violence may appear to solve one problem but another will appear in its place."

Dave Dellinger

Cuba: Seven Thousand Miles from Home*

Introduction

I went to Cuba legally, with a valid American passport and
State Department permission, granted me as a journalist on
specific assignment from a regularly publishing non-Commu-
nist periodical. The shortest way was by Mexico City, the only
city in the Western Hemisphere from which there are passen-
ger flights to Cuba. Cubana Airlines is allowed to make two
flights a week. They must get in and out of Mexico City on the
same day, and they are not permitted to use airplanes pur-
chased from the Soviet Union, but only those bought some
years ago from Britain, heavy planes which are less practical
than the Soviet ships for the special requirements of this flight.
The combination of intense heat and low-pressure atmosphere
frequently found in Mexico City makes it unsafe for them to
take off on a hot day. (My flight was delayed eight hours by
this factor, causing us to arrive in Havana long after midnight.)

Because I had been warned that it is extremely difficult to
get permission from the Mexican Government to reenter Mexico from Cuba, I began applying for a reentry permit at the
Mexican Consulate in New York, but was told that I must
apply in Mexico City. In Mexico City I wasted a day going to
three different offices but in the end was told that nothing
could be done until I filed application at the Mexican Consulate in Havana. In Havana I wasted two more days going back
and forth, along with two other stranded journalists, among
the Mexican Consulate, the Mexican Embassy, and the Swiss
Embassy (which represents Americans in Cuba). The Swiss
were extremely courteous but explained that they could not do

* June, 1964.

much to help us. In the end we were given a message from the Mexican Ambassador that the United States State Department had instructed the Mexican Government not to issue reentry permits for Americans who go to Cuba. We were told that our only hope was to call the United States Embassy in Mexico City and ask them to instruct the Mexican Government to send word to the Mexican Consulate in Havana to issue the permits. One of the other journalists made the call while I was keeping a previous appointment. The repeated words of the American Embassy were: "There is nothing we can do to help you. We cannot interfere in the internal affairs of the Mexican government."

If I had been willing to wait indefinitely in Havana and wage a costly campaign of cables and phone calls to Washington—thereby frustrating one of the purposes of my trip, which was to visit the interior of Cuba, and probably at the same time overstaying the period for which the State Department had validated my passport—I might have gotten a visa in the end. I don't know. Instead, I accepted the offer of the Cuban Government to pay the cost of transportation to New York by way of Czechoslovakia, a distance of over ten thousand miles and costing $662, economy fare. (Added to the distance from New York to Havana, by way of Mexico City, this made a round trip of approximately fourteen thousand miles; hence the title, "Cuba: Seven Thousand Miles from Home.") When I flew to Prague the plane was loaded with Latin Americans (visitors from Chile, Argentina, Brazil, *etc.*) who also had been forced to take the long route home—from Havana to Gander, Newfoundland (where no one is allowed to leave), to Prague—and back to Paris and the "free world."

The good side to all this was that I got a chance to spend eight days in Czechoslovakia and compare its ethos and practices with what I had observed in Cuba. I know a lot less about Czechoslovakia than I do about Cuba, but I did have a number of good contacts there, and even without them I think the contrast would have been shocking. There is no question in my mind that the revolutionary euphoria that still exists in Cuba is totally absent from Czechoslovakia, and for that matter never existed there, even at the beginning of its "revolution," which after all came in with the assistance of the Soviet Army. The close two-way identification between the people and the government which is so evident in Cuba does not exist in Czechoslovakia. Without entering into a discussion, at this point, of the successes or failures of Czechoslovakian socialism, it is clear that the Czechs have a higher standard of material living and far less freedom than the Cubans. There is no longer the kind of terror that there was in the early fifties, and a process of intellectual ferment and liberalization is clearly under way. But the best people I talked with, both "men-in-the-street" and Marxist intellectuals, were thoroughly disillusioned with the rigid and bureaucratic authoritarianism which doggedly resists the forces of enlightenment.

Part I

There are people who believe in the Cuban Revolution on faith, because it is socialist, much as they (or their predecessors) believed in the Soviet Union all through the days of Stalinist terror and hypocrisy. And of course there are others who believe just as dogmatically that the Cuban people cannot possibly be free or happy because they do not have a parliamentary system of government, a two-party system, and presidential elections.

It seems more fruitful to examine the Cuban Revolution pragmatically. To what extent is it succeeding in overcoming the poverty, humiliation, and servitude which were the lot of most Cubans during sixty years of highly profitable United States domination? Is it encouraging the intellectual, religious, and political liberty of the people, or is it "merely" (as well-to-do Americans sometimes put it) improving their economic lot at the expense of their political freedom (freedom, by the way, which the people did not possess before the Revolution, when the United States was well satisfied with Cuba)? Now that Cuba has become a Marxist-Leninist country and a member of the Soviet bloc, is it being run or controlled by the Soviet Union? Does it appear to be succumbing to the centralized authoritarianism and stifling bureaucratism which continue to

plague the European socialist countries, even as they are being
forced to yield ground slowly and erratically to the post-Stalin
forces of liberalization and relaxation? (I am writing these
words after eight days in Czechoslovakia.) Does the system
work in Cuba or is it a chaos of disorganization, inefficiency,
and shortages? The answer to these questions is more important than the name given to the system or the forms and for-
mulas under which it operates.

As I begin to deal with these questions, I am haunted by
the words of a journalist who visited Cuba late in 1962. The
day he returned to the United States he said to me: "I don't
know how I shall ever write about what I saw. The truth about
Cuba is so different than the American people think that if I
write the facts no one will believe them." Faced with a similar
problem after spending twenty-three days in Cuba from April
29th through May 21st, I find that I simply cannot adopt the
role of a propagandist; that is, I cannot tone down the facts in
order to make them believable—or palatable—to skeptical
Americans. The history of man's attempts to abolish exploitation, selfish privilege, overweening political and military power
—all too often only to see them reappear under different
names, in different forms, or with different excuses—is too
disheartening to allow me to pretend, in the interests of political or journalistic expediency, that the Cuban Revolution is
any less triumphant than it is. For if the accomplishments of
the last five years are anywhere near as impressive as I found
them to be (despite the existence of unresolved problems and
some danger signals), they transcend the pros and cons of
politics on either side of the Cold War and carry a whole new
message of desperately needed hope.

Perhaps most Americans are incapable of receiving this
message, not just because of the propaganda of the press, the
government, and the C.I.A.-sponsored exiles, but because of
the lack of comparable experience in American life from which
to extrapolate. The only thing I know in the United States that
comes close to the everyday spirit of liberated Cuba is the
surge of faith and hope and love that often occurs in a Negro
mass rally or action for integration in the South—or that took
place at the March on Washington. On the other hand, the

unfulfilled and bitter mood that more frequently characterizes, or at least runs through, Northern rallies and demonstrations —and recently has begun to appear in the South as well—is completely foreign to the Cuban ethos. "We never dreamed that we would own a house like this or that life could be as wonderful as it is now," one family said to me in a *Granja de los Pueblos* (Peoples' Farm) in Matanzas—and this is the mood I found all over the island, in the fishing cooperatives, the factories, the new schools and housing projects, and even, surprisingly enough, among those who still live in wretched *bohíos* (huts) or in the remaining slums of Havana, Santiago, and other cities. Those who still lack decent housing show other signs of enjoying a rising standard of living and of being caught up in the general enthusiasm. The first time I stopped to photograph some sordid dwellings, I was amazed to see the new and attractive clothes everyone was wearing, from aged grandparents to small children. This turned out to be commonplace. "Come take a picture of my ugly house," one attractively dressed woman said, lightheartedly. Far from expressing bitterness or despair (as one would expect from similar words in the United States), she seemed to be saying that her house was an anomaly left over from days that are fast disappearing.

The poorest people receive so many unprecedented benefits that they take in their stride whatever hardships or poverty remain (and by comparison with the material standard of living in the United States there are many). They have been taught to read and write. (Nearly one fourth of the Cubans were illiterate in 1958.) Their children are getting a free education, and there are allowances for food and spending-money for secondary school and university students. For the first time in their lives there is regular work at an eight-hour-a-day job (often including time spent at classes in the factory, in subjects ranging from elementary Spanish or arithmetic to science and technology), money in their pockets, and a month's paid vacation, which can be enjoyed at the beach or in the mountains, at one of the new tourist centers or in one of the formerly exclusive resorts that have been thrown open to the public at greatly reduced rates. On my first visit three and a half years ago, all of the new housing was being put up by the government, in the form of projects for slum dwellers or units for the newly formed agricultural cooperatives. This type of building is being continued throughout the island (contrary to rumors that I heard not only in the United States but even among critics in Havana). But in addition, there is now a tremendous amount of new housing being put up by independent farmers and workers as a result of improved conditions of employment and the expanded domestic market for the farmers' products.

In Oriente alone, I saw hundreds of new houses in various stages of construction—anything from a pile of bricks in a yard to a neat new house of brick, cinder block or cement, that had recently replaced a primitive *bohio*. The only discontent I found was not among those whose lot is still hard, by United States standards, but among members of the middle-class who complained of shortages, the inferior quality of consumer goods formerly imported from the United States but now made in new Cuban factories or imported from Socialist countries, and the fact that "under Communism there is no chance to make big money." One college student, whose parents are in Miami, kept complaining to me that "The Revolution is no good." When I pressed him to explain in detail so that I could report his complaints on my return to the United States, he took hold of my shirt and said: "Is that an American shirt? It is much better than this one which was made in Cuba. Before the Revolution there were many more nice things in the stores." Although it was not hard to find opponents of the regime (especially in bars, hotels, and the more expensive restaurants), I was never able to find any whose objections were more searching than this. The most rigorous questions about the Revolution were raised by members and supporters of the government.

A Return Visit

As a pacifist and personalist (anarchist, if you prefer), I was not predisposed to like the Cuban Revolution, either on my first trip in November 1960, when I spent three and a half weeks on the island, or this time. My first trip turned out so utterly different than I had expected that I realized it was impossible to predict what I would find on the second one. But

I must confess that after being subjected to more than three years of false reports, invented facts, and devastating analyses by ex-Cubans and other experts who have not even seen Cuba during several years of swiftly moving developments, I half expected to be as disappointed and disillusioned this time as I had been inspired and exhilarated in 1960. Only after I had been back in Cuba for some time did I realize how much the constant propaganda had sapped my morale and clouded my vision. It had done so even though I was aware all along that most of it was propaganda and although I had maintained more contact with Cuba than is possible for most Americans, through letters, study of available literature, and discussions with journalists who had visited Cuba and Cuban representatives at the United Nations.

Not even in Havana, the hangout of foreign correspondents, Communists-in-exile and the so-called middle bureacracy, is one apt to understand the real depth of the Revolution. For the Revolution is a very tangible phenomenon that tends to elude intellectual analysis and sophisticated political discussion. Furthermore, the greatest changes are taking place outside Havana, where the greatest poverty, disease and illiteracy existed. Only by travelling the length and breadth of the island (as I did by automobile) can one begin to savor the amazing success of the Revolution in providing houses, schools, hospitals, food, clothing, socially useful work, dignity, freedom, and an atmosphere of social solidarity and brotherly love.

I do not want to give the impression that the Revolution has passed Havana by. In addition to everything else, prostitution, the gambling casinos, venality, gangsters, beggars, and the high-priced pampering of American tourists and local parasites have disappeared—and now flourish in other American outposts instead (such as San Juan, or at least so I am told by reliable people who have visited Puerto Rico recently). By contrast, Havana is flooded by *beccarios* or scholarship students (over a hundred thousand secondary school students alone, mostly from poor families outside Havana, are now living in the abandoned homes of the bourgeoisie) and vacationing *obreros* and *campesinos* (workers and peasants) who

never had the money to travel before but are now enjoying the
hotels, beaches, and clubs formerly reserved for wealthy white
people. And when on May 1st Fidel told the people of Havana
that the first increases in food supply would go not to Havana
but to the countryside, beginning with the poorest province,
Oriente, because the need was greater there, a great roar of
approval went up from the crowd—a sign both that the people
of Havana are not exactly starving (as some Americans believe) and that they have developed during the Revolution a
wonderful new spirit of humanism that has long since disappeared from American cities. Can anyone imagine any American politician daring to tell the people of any city that new
government contracts (for example) would go to another section of the country first because other people needed them
more? Would anyone dare predict a spontaneous ovation from
the crowd if he did? Yet this is the kind of unrehearsed response that breaks through in countless unforseen ways every
day in Cuba, in individual conversations or in a crowd, among
friends or strangers, and that tells more about what is actually
happening than any of the learned analyses by people who
have not been there.

As Herbert Matthews of the New York *Times* wrote, after
visiting Cuba from October 24th to November 3rd, 1963:

> It is axiomatic in journalism that it is not possible to
> know what is happening anywhere unless you go there.
> . . . The freedom for Americans to know and to travel has
> been curtailed, so far as Cuba is concerned. For teachers
> and students this is frightening. As scholars they are not
> allowed by the United States Government to go to Cuba
> to study one of the most important political and social
> phenomena of modern times. As a result none of our lead-
> ing Latin Americanists know what is happening in Cuba;
> they cannot teach with authority on the subject of Cuba;
> they cannot even read the many books and articles on the
> Cuban Revolution now being published with the ability
> to judge whether they are right or wrong, good or bad.
> . . . One of my overwhelming impressions of the trip is
> how little I really knew the situation in Cuba, although I

*had done my best to read everything I could get hold of
and talk to everybody who had visited Cuba.*

Later Matthews adds:

*Cuba has been transformed. This should be obvious, al-
though it seems impossible for Cuban exiles and most
Americans to realize. Not only the Cuba of 1958 but the
Cuba that the exiles left has ceased to exist. (Emphasis
added.)*

Incidentally, it would be a mistake to think that the American public was able to read Matthews' analysis in the New
York *Times,* of which he is a senior editor. Perhaps the following sentence, in which he explains his long absence from Cuba
(more than three years) also explains why the *Times* did not
print any dispatches from him when he finally did go:

*The intensely hostile climate of opinion in the United
States, some of which is directed towards me and the New
York Times, and the difficulties placed in the way of all
visitors by the United States and Mexican Governments,
made an earlier trip seem unwise.*

Matthews' report cleared up many widely disseminated inaccuracies about Cuba, inaccuracies on the basis of which
the United States continues to take illegal and aggressive actions which definitely worsen the international situation and
involve at least some risk of setting off a chain reaction that
could lead to World War. But it was not published in the
Times or any other newspaper or mass circulation periodical.
Instead, it appeared in the *Hispanic American Report,* a schol-
arly journal which is published by the Institute of Hispanic
American and Luso-Brazilian Studies of Stanford University,
with a circulation of 2200.

A Guest of ICAP

When I arrived at the airport in Havana, a representative
of the Cuban Institute for Friendship with the People (ICAP)
greeted me and offered me the use of a car with a driver and a
guide-translator. Even before I had a chance to inform ICAP

that I distrusted guided tours and did not want to get swallowed up in one, my guide said to me: "If you have any place you want me to take you or any appointments you would like me to try to make, I am at your disposal, but if you prefer at any time to be on your own all day or any part of the day, we understand that. We are here to help you, not to restrict you. Naturally you are free to go anywhere you want and speak to anyone about anything. I only tell you this because we know that Americans have been told a lot of strange things about Cuba."

It turned out to be an ideal arrangement. I did wander on my own or make my own contacts and appointments more than half the time, talking to people for hours in complete privacy; but through ICAP I was enabled to travel with a minimum of effort to out-of-the-way places and see a wide range of people whom I might otherwise have missed. As we drove through Cuba, when I saw anything that looked interesting, sometimes because it was out of the mainstream of the Revolution, such as a Seventh Day Adventist Seminary, a local headquarters of the Jehovah's Witnesses, a Baptist bookstore and publishing house, a town that looked poorer than most, I simply asked the driver to stop while I investigated. Always the guide would say: "Do you want me to come with you or do you prefer to go on your own?" If I went alone, as I did most of the time, he would arrange to meet me at whatever time I suggested or wait patiently by the side of the road for anything from five minutes to an hour or more. [I will report in Part II on my interviews with the Seventh Day Adventists (with my guide present) and the Jehovah's Witnesses and Baptists (without him).]

Almost as amazing as this total freedom (in the Cuban context it soon ceased to be amazing), was the courtesy and patience of my guide and my driver. Like most of the Cubans, they were so proud of the Revolution, so confident that an honest man could not fail to be impressed by it, that they kept saying: "All we want you to do is to see as much as possible and talk to as many people as you can so that you can report objectively to the American people." When I complained at one point that I had not been able to find any intelligent or disinterested opponents of the regime, my guide suggested an area in Havana where I might be more successful in finding some who were at least intelligent. He did not think I would find any without a special axe to grind. "I will take you there, and leave you," he said, "just in case anyone might not speak as freely in my presence, or if you prefer you can go alone by bus."

Dozens, perhaps hundreds of times, I struck up conversations in bars, coffeehouses, parks, and on streetcorners, often pointing out at an appropriate juncture that "I am not a Communist but an American journalist who has come to try to find out the truth about Cuba." I raised all sorts of provocative, even insolent, questions: "How much money do you earn? How much did you earn before? Do you have more freedom now or did you have more before? Why is it necessary to have volunteer brigades to help with the sugarcane harvest? Are they really volunteer or are you put under pressure to join? By your boss? by the Party? the Union? Has Cuba won her freedom from the United States only to lose it to the Soviet Union? Why is it necessary to guard so many stores and public places? Who are they afraid of? I know that Fidel denounced political sectarianism in 1962 [when the Cuban leaders revealed an old-line Communist attempt to take over ORI (the new political organization which has since been replaced by P.U.R.S.)], but if this type of thing happened once how do you know that it won't happen again? Is there any evidence that it is happening right now? Do you have any say at all in the government? Why is there not freedom of press and speech and political opposition?" (The usual answer to this was that I had no idea how much freedom there actually was, but I will defer discussion of this subject for Part II.

No one ever seemed afraid to speak freely—though on two occasions I met critics who, after pouring out their complaints practically from the moment they met me, in such loud voices that it would have been hard for other people *not* to have heard them, made a show of dramatically lowering their voices and saying: "It's not safe to talk in Cuba."

By day and by night—often after midnight—I wandered and snooped, in residential and commercial areas, warehouse and factory districts, slums and wealthy neighborhoods, even around the docks of Santiago. I was never asked to produce any identification or justification for being there. One Soviet technician got a little annoyed once and wanted to know who the hell I was, when I asked him if it was true that there was a lot less freedom in the Soviet Union than in Cuba. But this is the only occasion I can remember when anyone balked at any of my questions.

The Forms of Democracy

In looking at the Cuban Revolution, whose forms are so different from those which most Americans are accustomed to associate with democracy and freedom, it is important to remember that operational forms which are liberating at one stage of a people's development often outlive their usefulness and, if not replaced by new forms, can become in their turn instruments of coercion and repression. Something of this kind has happened in the United States, where the forms that once provided democracy and freedom have not evolved to keep pace with the changes in population, technology, industrial organization and financial control. As a result they have gradually lost their original content and become the forms of a constrictive pseudo-democracy and pseudo-freedom instead. Cuba's experience with U.S.-style Batista democracy was especially disillusioning. Be that as it may, it is both arrogant and provincial for residents of the United States to insist that the liberation of Cuba and other Latin American countries can only take place—or for that matter can take place at all—if they adopt the same forms of economic and political organization that were liberating for the 18th Century American colonists under vastly different technological, social and political conditions. As Herbert Marcuse has written, in *One Dimensional Man*,

> *The higher culture of the West—whose moral, aesthetic, and intellectual values industrial society still professes— was a pretechnological culture in a functional as well as a chronological sense. Its validity was derived from the experience of a world which no longer exists and cannot be recaptured.*

Ironically, the "Popular Assemblies" that take place regularly (usually once a week) in the Cuban factories, *granjas,* cooperatives, schools, and housing projects fulfill a grassroots democratic function similar to that formerly provided in the United States by the New England town meeting. In conjunction with other institutions that are gradually evolving (but whose eventual character cannot be predicted with certainty—see discussion of P.U.R.S., in Part II) they constitute a far more effective and dynamic form of "democracy" or popular participation in decision-making than has existed in the United States for some time.

But conveniently overlooking these assemblies (if indeed they know about them, so little interest do most of the critics show in what is actually happening in Cuba), the American critics continue to insist that there will be no democracy in Cuba until something similar to our Presidential and Congressional sweepstakes takes place. The Negro in Mississippi can't vote. The Negro in New York can vote but (token exceptions aside) his vote can't get him a house in a "white" neighborhood, an education, job, or salary equivalent to those of a white person with comparable abilities. That eliminates twenty million Americans (almost three times the population of Cuba) from real democracy. Most of the rest of us can live in whatever neighborhood we can afford and, in some states, can even rejoice in our right to vote for a socialist or other minority candidate, who, of course, has no chance of election since he inevitably lacks the financial-industrial and mass-media backing necessary to make him a valid candidate. Finally, in foreign policy, results of United States-style "democracy" impinge upon the Cubans in the form of economic blockade, attempted invasion, guerilla attacks, and pressure on other countries of the "Free World" not to trade with Cuba.

As I watched Cubans stand in line waiting in the hot sun for buses which are in short supply because the State Department will not allow Americans to sell Cuba either buses or replacement parts for the pre-revolutionary buses still on hand, I wondered what kind of a twisted mind it is that thinks it will win friends and influence people by denying them the chance even to buy necessities of life. Meanwhile buses are arriving from Poland, Czechoslovakia, Hungary and Russia—

and of course from England, despite the anguished protests
of the United States—and I wonder if Dean Rusk and President Johnson think that this contrast between American and
socialist attitudes will turn the Cubans toward "democratic"
capitalism.

Is it any wonder that the Cubans, who feel free for the
first time in their lives and have seen their freedom growing
through five years of revolution, are not in the least responsive
to calls from American liberals and democratic socialists to
model their institutions after those prevalent in the United
States? No wonder they prefer to work out their own indigenous forms of political and economic organization in accord
with their own evolving experience. But this is the one item of
democracy, the one aspect of the American heritage which
neither the United States government nor most of the liberals
and social democrats are willing for the Cubans to have: the
right to carry out their own revolution in their own way.

May Day in Havana

My trip to Cuba at this time was occasioned by an invitation
from the Cuban government to attend the May Day celebrations in Havana. Notification was late and since I had been
denied an American passport in 1962 (and going to Cuba
required special State Department validation as well), I was
skeptical of the possibility of getting approval in time to get
there by May 1st, if indeed I could get permission at all. Accordingly, when I asked the Cuban *chargé d'affaires* in New
York if the invitation would still hold if I found I could not get
to Cuba until after May Day, he replied that he would have to
check with his government in Havana, since the purpose of the
invitations was to enable visitors to see the impressive outpour-
ing of people and demonstration of solidarity on May Day.
This struck me as a little corny. Patriotic observances and mass
gatherings usually bore me, with their routine and irrelevant
invocations of past glories. Or if they turn out to be emotional,
they frighten me with their hate-filled orations and appeals to
an irrational mystique.

Besides Fourth of July celebrations, I can remember some
pretty ugly gatherings in the United States and England that

were called in the name of the International Solidarity of the Proletariat. Still, I thought I should try to make it for the First, if at all possible, since the tone of what happened then would provide an early clue to what had happened to the Revolution. If it had become as much a matter of stereotyped slogans and hysterical conformism as I tended to suspect, I might as well get a preview at once. Besides, it seemed to me that such a celebration was bound to be largely military, and as a pacifist I thought I had better face up to that problem from the very beginning of my trip.

My application for a validated passport (which presented special problems because of my principled objection to taking the usual oaths of allegiance and that I am not a member of the Communist Party—heaven forfend) was handled promptly and with extreme courtesy by the State Department.[1] I received the necessary documents in about a week and when May Day arrived found myself sitting in the reviewing stands, close enough to the speakers' platform to have heard Fidel Castro without the loudspeakers.

The first minor surprise was that the ceremonies began exactly on time (quite different from the last time I heard Fidel speak in Havana) with the firing of a twenty-one gun salute and the release of an equal number of doves of peace. This was the closet thing to militarism that was to take place during the next two and a half to three hours. Only near the end of the parade was there a very brief display of what I gathered were anti-aircraft rockets and, later, the appearance of the first group of draftees under Cuba's new conscription law, marching hand in hand with their mothers. There might have been something else military that I missed, but if so it was completely dwarfed by the jubilant workers, male and female—most of them with the faces of the obviously honest and long-suffering poor, and many carrying their youngsters or leading them by the hand—and the eager scholarship students

---

[1] Sadly enough, A. J. Muste, who had also been invited, was denied validation. Apart from the fact that he already had a passport, he is a far too widely respected, even venerated person for me to have guessed that the State Department would run the risk of looking as foolish as it did in turning him down.

and other young people, whose joy and pride showed more in their exuberant smiles and gestures than in any highly trained or coordinated manner of walking.

The motif of the parade was the celebration of the first five years of the Revolution: the Year of Independence, the Year of Agricultural Reform, the Year of Education, the Year of Organization, and the Year of Economy. There was no mistaking that this was a day of heartfelt thanksgiving for the fruits of the Revolution, the kind of communal thanksgiving that never takes place any more in the United States, though we have a day set officially aside for that purpose. And it was a day of determination as well, determination, as Fidel expressed it, on the one hand to press ahead to new accomplishments and, on the other hand, never to surrender to the imperialists no matter how great the military odds in their favor might be. This is part of what he said:

> *On a day like this, we can see how far we have advanced. . . . Does this mean that we are satisfied? No. That we have already accomplished enough? No. Quite the contrary. What we have already accomplished will help us to reach higher achievements . . . Perhaps we will never feel proud, perhaps we will never be satisfied and the people will always have newer and newer aspirations, newer and newer things to be done. Fortunately life gives us this incentive, the incentive of having many things ahead to accomplish, many things to achieve. And if on one occasion our incentive was to end illiteracy, later it was to have every worker reach the sixth grade, and after that it will be to have every citizen complete secondary education. And as often as we achieve a goal, new goals will appear. We can say that we have not wasted time. Some people accused the Revolution of moving too fast. We were in a hurry because we had lost more than fifty years . . . and therefore each year has to be multiplied. Every single year of the Revolution must represent several years of progress.*

And, when he spoke on the nature and extent of the Cubans' determination never to surrender, he was interrupted many times by shouts and applause:

The imperialists are buying themselves the worst problem of their lives. I am not speaking of international problems. I don't want anyone to think that if we speak out clearly, that if we speak out with dignity, we are doing so because we have a feeling of impunity, that we are doing it at the expense of other peoples, at the expense of the friendship and solidarity of the Soviet Union. No, when we speak in this way we speak for Cuba, and we speak in the name of Cuba. We do not speak thinking in terms of intercontinental missiles, because if we spoke in this way backed by rockets, what meaning would our words have? How serious would our statements be? . . .

When it comes to defending our sovereignty and our dignity we do not measure the strength of the enemy or our own strength. The only thing that we consider is that we have the duty to defend that right and that we know how to fulfill that duty and that we are ready to fulfill that duty. Because this is our right and our dignity. There is no doubt that the imperialists have more planes and more guns than we have, but they do not have more right and more reason, and they would never have more courage.

Courage is not an animal concept, not a biological concept; courage is a moral concept, a spiritual concept. Peoples with more courage than others really do not exist; or men with more courage than others. Courage as a moral and spiritual concept is born from reason, from the force that inspires it—from justice, law, from the legitimate aspirations of the peoples—and therefore those who attack us would never have even a shadow of our courage to fight against us.

We are not thinking only of frontal engagements. If they attack us we will fight frontal engagements with the appropriate weapons, but at the same time we would prepare ourselves for a long struggle, a struggle that would never end for our enemy. We know our people, the moral and revolutionary force which inspires them, and we know that our nation can be invaded, can be occupied, but it will never be defeated. Never!

. . . Let's imagine that the imperialists invade us. That, by the strength of numbers and at a very high price they succeeded in occupying our territory. Would the struggle end there? No. Just a stage of it, and a second stage would begin in the cities, in the countryside, and everywhere. . . . A long drawnout struggle would begin in which they would have to face a real people. . . .

If the imperialists should invade this country, you would have to realize that the majority of the leaders of today would die in the struggle. But the people will remain, and the party would remain. There would be no need to ask for names or for men. Each one of us would do his duty in the way demanded of him and do it well. . . . That's why we say that we are an invincible people and we say this thinking only of our own strength. That's why our people deserve the utmost respect and that's why even our bitterest enemies will have to respect us. . . .

The rights that our people have won and defended are not rights that were inherited, they are not privileges granted to us, they are rights that were won in struggles, rights that were won fighting. We did not win our rights in a lottery nor in a game of chance. They are the result of history, the result of the whole life of a nation. And we will know how to defend the rights that we have won.

We want a prosperous, peaceful, and happy future; we want it from the bottom of our hearts; we want to see the results of our work and of our efforts; we deeply desire it. But if they force us to fight and force us to make the most inconceivable sacrifices, it will not be our fault. And we must never grieve over things that are not our fault.

If life offers us triumphs and successes, may the triumphs and successes that we win come with dignity and with honor. If life offers us sacrifice and struggle, may the sacrifice and struggle be welcome, because that is what life offers us, with dignity and honor.

That is why we may all go back to our homes calm, serene, happy, facing the future with courage and serenity, with joy and optimism, conscious of our strength, of the strength of our principles, of the prestige of our cause. . . .

Our Revolution has many things, many experiences interesting and useful to all people. But above all our nation has something wonderful. . . . Our country has these people and these people are the most admirable thing the Revolution has.

When Fidel said that "the majority of the leaders of today would die in the struggle," this was not rhetoric. Fidel himself nearly lost his life in a tank, helping repel the invaders at Playa Largo (Bay of Pigs) in 1961—and again last fall in rescue operations at the height of Hurricane Flora. Are such acts of personal involvement romantic? Irresponsible? They probably are, by ordinary standards. But on the other hand, perhaps only the stimulus and contagion of this kind of leadership could have led to the rebirth of a whole country which is so manifest in Cuba, to the emergence of a nation of leaders, so that for all their distinction and value, Fidel and the other veterans are less and less indispensible with each succeeding year of the Revolution.

In the early struggles of other revolutions, the leaders have been willing, at one point or another, to sacrifice the lives of their political opponents to ensure the triumph of their own ideas (or the advancement of their own power position). In Cuba, though opponents have been executed openly for specific acts of murder, torture, or sabotage (and I deplore this fact; as I told my Cuban friends it would have been more in keeping with the Revolution's humanism to have sent them to rehabilitation centers), so far as I have been able to find out no one has been bumped off, Stalinist fashion, for political deviation. In fact the whole idea is foreign to the Revolution's character and I mention it at all only because of the terrible history of the Communist International in this respect and the widely held misconceptions about Cuba in the United States. In point of fact, it is their own lives that the leaders are prepared to lay on the line.

It was against a background of this kind of personal commitment that Fidel posed his famous question to Senator Barry Goldwater a few months ago, when Goldwater urged that the Marines be sent in to turn the water back on for the

Guantánamo Naval Base. Fidel asked Goldwater if he was prepared to lead the first wave of attack personally. No doubt many Americans thought of this as a cheap political rejoinder, and resented the suggestion that the life of one of our Senators should be risked in an engagement with a minor enemy. But to the Cubans Fidel's question dramatized the difference between the integrity of their leaders and the irresponsible antics of American politicians, who are more ready to risk other people's lives than their own. Indeed, after spending some time in the heady atmosphere of Cuba, one wonders how long the Congress, the State Department, and the rest of the Executive would continue to push on with their war in Vietnam if President Johnson, Dean Rusk, and a random assortment of Senators and Representatives were expected to take their turn, Cuban style, fighting in the jungles and rice paddies. The Cubans are wiser than we are. No man should advocate a war he is not prepared to risk being the first to die in.

There is another contrast which was not lost on the Cubans. Most of the politicians whom the United States supports in Latin America keep big bank accounts in Switzerland and the United States—and an escape route ready in case of emergency. But every Cuban knows that Fidel and the other leaders operate from an entirely different set of principles and that the welfare of the people and the leaders is inseparable —in case of counterrevolutionary attack and, by the same token, in everyday affairs.

Finally, it is instructive to contrast Fidel's integrity with the cynical maneuverings of an administration which sends mercenaries to their almost certain death in coastal landings (several took place while I was there) which have no chance of succeeding and apparently are not even intended to succeed. Far from being a major part of United States policy—or even an admitted part of official policy at all—these suicide operations represent a minor ploy in the political "game" the administration is playing. Their purpose appears to be three-fold: 1) to fortify Washington's attempts to impose its policy on its Latin American satellites and NATO junior partners; 2) to strengthen the administration's position in the internecine wars of domestic politics; and 3) to serve as a warning to the restless and impatient people of Latin America that the United States will fight every inch of the way against any attempts they might make, Cuban fashion, to secure land, food, and freedom.

The attacks are a means of raising the ante in the poker game of power politics the United States is currently engaged in with its allies. Most of the other Western countries are increasingly reluctant to sacrifice trade and other benefits of good (or at least civilized) relations with Cuba. But so long as the United States can preserve a state of international tension and uncertainty, they find it harder to resist American pressure to continue the economic and political isolation of Cuba from the Western World. Thus, by needlessly sacrificing human lives, the administration deprives its Republican opposition of the opportunity to make a major campaign issue out of charges that the Democrats have gone soft on Cuba—or that its program is a failure. Meanwhile, of course, with its other hand it gathers in the liberals, through Senator Fulbright's speech and its rejection of the most fanciful proposals of the Right (such as to bomb Havana or launch a full-scale invasion). The program of the Right is so completely beyond the pale of sanity and human decency that no one should be cowed by it into thinking that the Kennedy-Johnson administration is either moral or liberal.

In his May Day speech, Fidel commented on the unprincipled and undemocratic pressure the United States exerts on its allies. He began by reading a cable by United Press International from Washington, dated April 30th. Its tenor is indicated by the following excerpts:

> *British sources had previously expressed the opinion that the question of British-Cuban trade would not be raised during the visit of Butler to Washington. However, Butler received the first indication that the problem would arise in his interview with Dean Rusk. Rusk told him that President Johnson was very displeased ["That man is going to develop a liver complaint." (Interjection by Fidel)] at the news that Great Britain would sell not only more buses to Cuba, but also locomotives and cranes.*

It is understood that Rusk asked Butler why, if this trade was so small, Great Britain persisted in continuing it, and so risking the worsening of relations with the Johnson administration. . . .

The President told Butler that he was very displeased at the fact that Great Britain is still violating a policy that the United States understood was proper, and in the interests of the West.

Then Fidel made some typical comments:

Now you see the logic of the United States. They never raise the question of principles. . . . They say: "If the trade is so small, why are you selling to them?" They are not capable of understanding that the question of freedom of trade is a principle that is not measured by the amount bought and sold. . . .

This cable is very revealing. It reveals the peculiarity of the imperialists. Look at what they say: "Great Britain is violating U.S. policy." To them U.S. policy is a universal law and any country that does not accept this policy is committing a crime, a violation of this policy. . . .

This cable shows how the United States treats its allies. They really treat them as true satellites, with the utmost insolence and contempt. . . . Great Britain is at present in a pre-electoral period and all these questions in connection with the freedom of trade are questions which the British politicians are interested in defending, because those who elect the British government are the British people, and what interests the British people are British interests.

. . . So the U.S. Government through this pressure is putting its friends in Britain, who are on the eve of an election, on the spot and is backing the British government against the wall. If the British government doesn't yield to U.S. pressure, then President Johnson and Dean Rusk will be displeased, and if it yields to the pressure of Johnson and Rusk, and doesn't sell locomotives to Cuba and gives up the possibility of selling to Cuba, then the British voters will be displeased.

Several times during the parade and later during Fidel's speech, I left the stands and went down to the street to look at the people more closely, in order to observe their facial expressions and gestures. It was as if the Negroes of Mississippi and Harlem (and the inhabitants of all the other slums, ghettoes, and Appalacias) were holding a great festival to celebrate five years of freedom and happiness. To understand the mood of this laughing, singing, exuberant crowd of eight hundred thousand people (more than a tenth the population of Cuba), you would have to imagine that the Negroes had done far more than to break out of their ghettoes and desegregate the schools, restaurants, parks and employment agencies. You would have to imagine that in the process of doing this, Negroes and their white allies had developed a spirit of brotherhood which made it impossible for them to be satisfied with integrating into the existing commercial culture and engaging in its selfish competition for personal profit and prestige. You would have to imagine that those who clung to capitalism as their ideal had emigrated and the rest of the population was engaged in the infinitely more exciting business of working out a whole new society in accord with their deepest yearnings for brotherhood. You would have to imagine (for instance) that rents had been abolished in the poorest sections of Harlem and that overcrowding, rats, and the *de facto* segregation of schools had been eliminated by building free housing in the suburbs, with the people who had lived in the worst conditions getting priority. You would have to imagine that huge estates like Ruleville (Senator Eastland's Mississippi plantation) had been turned into people's farms, with new houses, schools, hospitals and workshops, and with democratic assemblies in which all the people participate and elect their own representatives to other political bodies. You would have to imagine, sad to say, that Senator Eastland had objected to these "violations of (his) democracy and freedom," had refused to accept compensation for that part of his estate that had been expropriated, and had moved to Madrid (or Durban, South Africa), along with a number of disgruntled police chiefs, White Citizens Council leaders, bankers, and industrialists—and that after their departure, the mansions and remaining land that

224]   DAVE DELLINGER

they abandoned had been converted into schools, hospitals, tourist centers, social and recreational clubs (open to the public for a nominal fee), and even rehabilitation and retraining centers for ex-prostitutes. (In the United States I suppose these would include rehabilitation centers for alcoholics and the mentally ill.)

Even sadder still, to understand the mood of Cuba on May Day (and to a great extent every day), you would have to imagine that the people had found it necessary to repulse five years of guerilla warfare, sabotage, raids, and attempted invasion by the expatriates—and that the Eastlands and Wallaces had been supported by a few members of the Negro bourgeoisie (who had wanted freedom for their people but thought the movement went too far) and by sincere liberals and social democrats who were alienated when the new government abolished private ownership of large factories, corporation farms, department stores, and apartment houses.

Of course if our imagined Second American Revolution (for that is what it would be) followed the Cuban precedent, it would allow private owners to maintain ownership of three buildings: their place of residence, a second house for vacations and similar uses, and a place of business (in general if it did not employ more than five persons). What is more, the Cuban government guarantees former landlords and owners of businesses or farms a monthly income for life equal to their former income, up to a maximum of $600 a month (which in Cuba is roughly double the monthly earnings of a skilled worker, and goes much further than it would in the United States).

Is all this too much to imagine? Are these developments outside the possibilities of the American dream? If they are, then those who are desperately defaming or trying to overthrow the Cuban Revolution can relax. For they need not fear that the Cuban example will awaken the American people from their torpor. And certainly they will never succeed in reconverting the Cuban people to capitalism.

The Revolution in Cuba is basically irreversible. Even if Cuba should suffer military defeat and American occupation, the people would never forget the glorious years they have had, the discovery they have made that human nature does not have to be selfish and cruel, and brotherhood an empty slogan frustrated by the economic and political realities of the system. But the real question remains. Who will take up the Cuban example and fashion a new life of brotherly relationships indigenous to their own culture and responsive to their own needs?

In Czechoslovakia, an intelligent and humane Marxist told me that for him and many of his countrymen the Cuban Revolution is the most exciting development of the last twenty-five or thirty years. "It may transform the whole Socialist world, which has long since gone stale. For all its genuine idealism, socialism has been bogged down for years in a stultifying bureaucracy. And although the Socialist countries have thrown off the worst aspects of Stalinist terror and Russian control, real freedom is still more of a hope than a reality. The stimulus of Cuba may speed up our liberation by years."

As I listened to this man speak, I wondered how many Americans are equally open to the message of Cuba. Are we too frightened by the words "Communist" and "Marxist-Leninist" to study the Cuban Revolution dispassionately, and perhaps introduce some of its concepts into the mainstream of American political discussion? Are we convinced that the backward-looking refugees and the State Department know, and are able to tell us the truth about what is actually happening in Cuba, so that there is no need to upset the travel ban? Are we so satisfied, basically, with the American Way of Life, its affluence, its "free press," "democracy," and "Free World" alliances that we feel we don't need to find out for ourselves about the experiment the Cubans are engaged in?

Part II

I have been back from Cuba about a month. Almost every day the American papers print new evidence that Cuba is "a prison surrounded by water." Kid Gavilan, former boxer, is reported to be serving a five-year sentence for preaching as a Jehovah's Witness in a suburb of Havana. (New York *Times,* June 24th.)

Fidel Castro's sister Juanita escapes to Mexico and reports "with tears in her eyes" that Fidel has "abandoned the ideals of the Cuban Revolution" and "turned Cuba over to the Soviet Union and Communism." (New York *Times,* June 30th.) I read with horror that "Castro twice ordered his sister investigated by secret police, exile sources said—once for her suspected link with a black market operator and again for her work as a government head." (New York *Post.*) The *New York Times Magazine* prints a picture with the following caption: "DEFIANCE—'If they impose war on us we will fight,' says this billboard on the Havana waterfront. *The U. S. is a handy scapegoat.*" (June 21st, emphasis added.) John Chamberlain writes on the editorial page of the New York *Journal American:* "Castro has claimed recently that his agricultural shortcomings are due to 'inexperienced young administrators.' The fact is that the Cuban peasants won't work for the government. Castro's economic czar, 'Che' Guevara, said on April 2o: 'We must look carefully to find where the cane-cutters have gone to.'" Chamberlain goes on to state that in order to get into a university, "you have to be a member of the Communist Party, or an enrolled Young Communist, or a certified 'integrated' student (meaning that you are pro-Castro). Says Fidel's Minister of Education, Armando Hart: 'The courses are first, second, and third, intended to impress on the student an understanding of Marxist-Leninism.'"

I give a talk on Cuba at a pacifist conference and state that I would like at this time to postpone questions of political analysis and interpretation and simply set the record straight on certain *facts,* as I experienced them personally. I tell of the complete freedom I had to go everywhere and talk with anyone; I report that I wandered all over the island at practically every hour of the day and night and was never so much as looked at cross-eyed, let alone stopped, questioned, or asked to produce any identification. I tell of the overwhelming enthusiasm of the Cuban people for the Revolution, and describe how they tell spontaneously of their complete freedom and their improved economic position. When I finish, a pacifist leader says to me privately: "You are making a terrible mistake. Your opposition to American militarism should not lead you to praise totalitarianism."

Is it possible that I have been "taken in"? Did I miss "police terrorism" and "religious persecution" (New York *Post*, June 30th), the "Communist dictatorship that succeeded Batista's tyranny" and which "many veterans of the July 26th movement . . . could not stomach" (New York *Post* editorial, July 1st)? I think that I learned a long time ago that glossing over unpleasant truths is no real service to anyone or anything, that failure to look at the worst in those people or causes that we love (or may want to love) is only to damage both them and ourselves. If we want the Cuban Revolution to avoid the pitfalls that led to Stalinism in Russia, the least we can do is to be more perceptive of the true state of affairs in Cuba than a whole generation of foreign observers were in the Soviet Union. As a respected Czechoslovakian friend said to me: "I have thought sadly of how Romain Rolland and Henri Barbusse, basically honest and humanitarian intellectuals whom we trusted, betrayed us at a crucial time by denying the existence of Stalinist terror in the Thirties. None of us, in our own lesser roles, must repeat their mistake. Even if the truth seems for the moment to support those who are attacking socialism for the wrong reasons, we must be fearless in expressing it. How much better it would have been if Rolland and Barbusse had admitted the terrible truths of the trials and purges and concentration camps, and then had gone on from there to defend the need for socialism."

Let us look at the newspaper reports I have referred to and compare them with my own findings in Cuba.

Religious Freedom

The story of Kid Gavilan's arrest is in an Associated Press dispatch from Miami. It states: "Exiles said today that he was arrested three months ago while preaching in Marianao, a suburb of Havana . . . [as] an active Jehovah's Witness. Francisco Valle, head of the Teacher's Anti-Communist Front, an anti-Castro organization, quoted Cuban underground sources as having said Gavilan was serving a five-year term in Havana's La Cabaña prison on charges of conspiracy." (New

York *Times,* June 24th.) This would place the date of Gavilan's arrest on March 23rd, or thereabouts. I was in Cuba from April 29th through May 21st. Here is what I found out about relations between the Jehovah's Witnesses and the government.

When I was grilling a young enthusiast for the Revolution, in Havana, on the supposed lack of freedom in Cuba, he cited the Jehovah's Witnesses as an example of the fact that people have the freedom to go beyond normal religious observance and "even attack everything the Revolution stands for, in the name of their religion." "We know," he said, "that the Jehovah's Witnesses are filled with former supporters of Batista who use their supposed religion as a cover-up for counter-revolutionary activities. But because we believe in complete religious freedom we do not interfere with them. But of course if they are caught in the act of committing sabotage, that will be different." A second friend who was present said: "If I had my way, they'd all be in jail, because I think they are a front, but Fidel says that we must not persecute such people."

A few days later, I was in Santa Clara, in Las Villas province, and was raising my usual points about the importance of political and religious freedom, to a Cuban worker. Among the instances he mentioned to show that I had been misinformed about the actual state of affairs in Cuba was that of the Jehovah's Witnesses. "Every Friday and Saturday night," he said, "and often on other days as well, you will see them in the main square, passing out their stupid leaflets and trying to convert people." "Do they have any trouble?" I asked. "Not any more," he replied. "A few years ago some of the young people got excited and roughed them up a couple of times, but the police put a stop to that. Since the defeat of sectarianism in 1962, the Revolution discourages such narrowness toward ignorant people."

After this conversation, I mentioned to various friends in Santa Clara that I would like to take a picture of a J.W. passing out leaflets. Later that same evening, one of them came chasing after me, as I was on my way to a bookstore, to tell me that two Witnesses were handing out literature on the main square. We hurried back, but all I saw was a woman in a long white gown, across the park and about a block away. By the time I got through the heavy shopping crowd to where she had been, I could not find her. But about ten days later, while driving through the town of Jaguey Grande, in the province of Matanzas, I noticed a storefront with a prominent sign: "*Testigos de Jehovah.*" I sent my car ahead and knocked on the door. I met an attractive young couple and an older man, the father of one of them. They lived in the apartment behind the meeting hall and supervised the center. We talked together for about three quarters of an hour. They told me unequivocally that they had not been persecuted by the government, and that they preach the Gospel from house to house all over Cuba. "In some towns," the woman said, "local officials have given us a little trouble, because some of them do not realize that the government wants us to have complete freedom. Besides, everything is decentralized in Cuba and they do things differently in different places. Also," she added, "some people are confused about our ideas and are hostile. But we are used to persecution, you know; a lot of our people have been in prison." "Oh," I said, sensing a news break. "Where? How many? What for?" "Not in Cuba," she replied. "Mostly in the United States and Germany, but in quite a few other countries as well."

Their only complaint concerning their treatment by the government was that they have difficulty getting as many copies as they want of *The Watchtower* and *Awake*, Jehovah's Witness publications which are sent to them from the United States. "We think," said the man, "that our government does not like us to get them. But some always get through," and he showed me a stack of them. The Witnesses told me that they have no trouble getting out their own Cuban materials and gave me the address of their headquarters and printing plant in Havana. When I mentioned that I had visited a Seventh Day Adventist seminary, the three Jehovah's bristled and suddenly displayed a hostility they had not manifested toward the government. On the one hand, the narrow but sincere religious zeal of these three people made it appear unlikely that a group of Batista-ites would get very far in attempts to infiltrate the Jehovah's Witnesses for political purposes, at least in Jaguey

Grande. The readiness of my two Havana friends to say that
the J.W.'s are filled with ex-Batista-ites was an unhealthy sign.
Circulation of such rumors can arouse dangerous prejudices
and lead to gross injustice in time of stress (such as a period of
heavy C.I.A. sabotage or actual invasion). On the other hand,
I find it hard to imagine that Kid Gavilan or anyone else has
been sent to jail for five years—or any length of time—for
preaching as a J.W. Certainly the J.W.'s in Cuba were not
aware of any such arrest, about seven weeks after it was supposed to have taken place. More likely, if he is in jail it is for
some other act which the exiles in Miami prefer not to mention, since they can arouse more anti-Castro sentiment by
charging "religious persecution."

Seventh Day Adventists

My visit with the Seventh Day Adventists also came about
through chance. One day, as I was leaving the beautiful new
Central University of Las Villas, near Santa Clara, I noticed an
impressive mansion at the end of a long aisle of trees. I asked
the professor whom I was with if it was part of the University.
"Oh no," he said. "That is a Seventh Day Adventist school."

We drove in, discovered that there were several
other buildings, including a farm, and that the whole com-
prises a seminary for training ministers and providng advanced religious instruction of laymen, as well. We talked in-
formally with a number of students, who were lounging on the
lawn after lunch, and had a fairly lengthy conference with the
director, a Dr. Vincent Rodriguez, who received his Master's
degree in history at the University of Nebraska in 1956. The
seminary has a hundred and sixty students and is supported by
contributions from the six thousand Seventh Day Adventists
who are scattered through Cuba and belong to eighty
churches. Most Seventh Day Adventists are conscientious objectors to military training and service, and they have been
given complete exemption under the new conscription law.
There are no requirements, as there are in the United States,
for alternative service. The church's primary schools were shut
down in 1961, along with all other private grade schools, but it
has complete freedom to conduct its own schools for religious

instruction at all levels. Everyone I talked to made it clear that there is no religious persecution of any kind. Besides regular services and other activities for their members, they hold frequent evangelical campaigns to win converts. Far from showing any apprehension at my questions, Dr. Rodriguez seemed rather pleased to be interviewed, and remarked twice that I was the first "newspaper man" who had come to see him since the Revolution. I indicated that I had spent three years in prison as a conscientious objector, in the United States, and was interested to find out how a Peace Church was faring in Revolutionary Cuba.

Dr. Rodriguez pointed out that he values the new government because of all the work it is doing to improve the lot of the poor, after years of neglect. When he told me this, I mentioned Fidel's statement that is often quoted or publicly displayed in Cuba: "To betray the poor is to betray Christ." He nodded appreciatively, and continued: "Most of the people who come into our church are from the middle class down. That may explain their receptivity to the Revolution. In any event, there has been absolutely no interference by the government, and very few if any of our people have left Cuba. I know for certain that no pastor or leading member of our church has left on account of the Revolution."

He told me that many of their members have been elected Exemplary Workers in the factories. He pointed out that this is quite an accomplishment since their religion forbids them to work on Saturday and most Cuban factories work Saturday mornings. In view of charges that only enrolled or certified Communists and narrow Marxist-Leninists are tolerated in the revolutionary process, it is interesting to think of Seventh Day Adventists, members of an old-fashioned and rather fundamentalist sect, being honored in this fashion at assemblies of their fellow workers. Being elected an Exemplary Worker is the first step toward becoming a member of the United Party of the Socialist Revolution (P.U.R.S.), which is currently being organized, and the election of some Seventh Day Adventists indicates the broad and tolerant spirit that I observed in most sections of Cuban society, especially at the important grass-roots. This supports my observation, as I talked with members

of P.U.R.S. all over the island, that they are an extremely
varied and non-sectarian group whose main unifying characteristic is their personal dedication to bettering the economic
and spiritual lot of the Cuban people. On the other hand when
I asked Dr. Rodriguez if any Seventh Day Adventists had
become party members, he said that he did not know for sure
but rather doubted it since they could not bear arms and
membership in the people's militia is generally considered to
be one of the duties of party members.

In addition to Jehovah's Witnesses and Seventh Day
Adventists, I questioned at length officials or active laymen in
several other religious groups. With one perhaps minor exception, all were forceful in stating that there has been absolutely
no interference with religious freedom. A Catholic deacon in
Camaguey told me, at the end of a crowded Sunday afternoon
mass, that there never had been any religious persecution. "At
first there were some disagreements between the clergy and
the government, but they were all political. Once the Spanish
clergy were sent back to Spain, the problems ceased." A leader
in the Evangelical Church of Cuba quickly denied the existence of any interference with religion and said: "The Revolution is helping the poor, and Jesus said: 'Inasmuch as you do
something for the poor, you do something for me.' " [An interesting free translation of the Scripture.] "Rich people who had
businesses and made a lot of money off the poor were against
the Revolution, but most Cubans were poor and they like it.
Even some of the rich people like it."

The one complaint about religious freedom that I heard
came from a woman who manages a Baptist bookstore in Havana. She said that the Baptists are not allowed to hold church
services in the public park. Like the others, she told of a wide
range of religious activities that are being carried on without
interference and praised the government for having helped
them get supplies for their conference and Bible-training center in the country during a period of food shortages. The book
store had a large selection of tracts, pamphlets, and books,
including Spanish translations of books by John McKay (of
Princeton Seminary) and of *Christ and Communism* by E.
Stanley Jones (published in Havana in 1961). Many of these

items were printed in an adjoining plant owned by the Baptists and leased to a friendly printer. "That's not working too well right now," the lady sighed, "because there is a shortage of paper and after the old man died, the sons discovered they could make more money printing jobs that come in off the street. So we have some of our books printed by the Presbyterians, who also have their own plant and have not rented it out." She told me that the Baptists emphasize complete separation of religion and politics—"So we never discuss the Revolution in church; that's politics. But the Presbyterians are very friendly to the government and one of the leading Presbyterian ministers, Rev. Paul Fernandez Cebalos, writes a column every day for *El Mundo* [one of the Havana newspapers]." I had been told previously that a Quaker pastor who is enthusiastic about the Revolution is a director of *Prensa Latina* (a news bureau) in Havana and in charge of its section on religious news.

I am sure that some of the people who hate the economic levelling of the Revolution identify this policy with Communism, identify Communism with atheism, and atheism with religious persecution. But it is inexcusable for anyone who knows conditions in present-day Cuba to speak of religious persecution as one of the characteristics of governmental policy or public practice. When Fidel's sister and other exiles speak of religious persecution, they are really telling us that either they do not know the facts or they are willing to bring in any emotion-laden charge, however false, in order to turn us against the régime. Their charges help whip up anti-Castro sentiment in the United States, but simply isolate them even further from the Cuban people.

Fidel's Sister

One fascinating aspect of the handling of news of Juanita Castro's defection is that first we read that "her voice broke as she read a long statement. She said the break was a 'hard decision.'" (New York *Times*.) We are horrified to learn that Castro twice ordered the secret police to investigate his own sister. (New York *Post*.) This seems to support her charges of "police terrorism [in which] sons inform on their parents

[and] the military intelligence knocks on doors at all hours."
But then we read in later dispatches (after we have accepted
the newspaper image of her as an idealistic heroine?) that:

> Juana Castro Ruz (*sic*), oldest sister of Cuban Premier
> Fidel Castro, has been working as an undercover agent
> for counterrevolutionary forces and the Western intel-
> ligence community inside Cuba for almost four years,
> she disclosed. . . . "I helped buy and hide arms for coun-
> terrevolutionary groups. . . . I helped by maintaining
> my contacts in government circles and receiving data
> which I passed on to counterrevolutionary intelligence."
>   . . . the nerve center for her counter intelligence activi-
> ties was a boarding house she owned in Havana. It
> served . . . as her hub for maintaining wide contacts, in-
> cluding government and military officials, underground
> counterrevolutionaries, and even some Western diplo-
> mats. (New York *World Telegram*.)

This is a sad story at best. But who is revealed as a "terrorist"
and betrayer of his people, the sister who supplied weapons
for murder, arson, and sabotage or the brother who had some
suspicion that this might be taking place and investigated? Is it
any wonder that some of her friends and accomplices dreaded
a knock at their doors, or that some of them may have ended
up in prison? Can their arrests really be attributed to "police
terrorism and religious persecution"? How seriously can we
take the lofty moral tone of the New York *Post*, which was in
possession of the facts and yet printed the following editorial?

> Juanita Castro's account of her break with her brother
> is a moving document whose impact on Latin America
> is likely to be very great.
>   What about the impact upon Fidel Castro himself?
>   He has been able to shrug off the many veterans of the
> July 26 Movement who broke with him because they
> could not stomach the Communist dictatorship that suc-
> ceeded Batista's tyranny.
>   Will he now equally easily brush aside his sister's tear-
> ful charge that "he has betrayed the Cuban Revolution
> that many of us lived and died for"?

Perhaps. Ideological fanaticism is a corrosive acid to which not even the closest ties of family and friendship are immune.

But though Castro may be able to close his mind and heart, the world will not.

The sister's moving and tearful testimony reveals that she aided and abetted the murder of innocents and tried to deliver her country over to a foreign power, the very power whose military occupation and subsequent economic domination left a sixty-year heritage of poverty, disease and illiteracy. As to the heartless brother who is presumed to have brushed aside her charge that he betrayed the kind of revolution that she and the exiles had in mind, Herbert Matthews, writing after his visit last November, says: "Fidel spoke proudly, when we saw him, of the fact that not a single surviving figure from the days of the attack on the Moncada barracks and the beginning of the Sierra Maestre adventure has defected. . . . Almost all, including the women, are serving the government in some post or other." (*Hispanic American Report,* Institute of Hispanic American and Luso-Brazilian Studies.) The *Post* is wrong about the meaning Juanita's break will have to the people of Latin America, at least to its impoverished millions. They will have their own interpretation of facts which the *Post* printed: "Juanita, one of four daughters and three sons born to a rich sugar plantation owner, lived with her mother in the luxurious Miramar section of Havana until last August when Mrs. Castro died." Their sympathies will not be with the wealthy sister who responded negatively to the Revolution's policies of political independence and economic sharing, and conspired with the United States to turn her people back to the domination of the United Fruit Company, the Chase Manhattan and National City Banks. If anything, they will take this family separation as further evidence that the Revolution has steadfastly refused to betray the Cuban poor, even though this refusal has provoked the enmity of the United States and most well-to-do Cubans. They will agree with Fidel when he says: "If I had been one of those governors who made millionaires of their relatives, I would not have suffered from this problem."

In Cuba I was told repeatedly that no one is arrested for speaking or writing against the régime. Juanita and other exiles speak of seventy-five thousand political prisoners. Apart from whatever tendency there may be on either side to exaggerate, the statements may not be completely irreconcilable. To the exiles, a man who is put in prison because he blew up a house and killed a child is a political prisoner. To the Cubans he is a murderer. If (in the spirit of the United States blockade and probably with materials supplied by the C.I.A.) a counterrevolutionary burns down a sugar mill to prove that communism won't work. I would call him a politically motivated arsonist— though in some cases he may simply be a mercenary adventurer. The Cubans do not consider it police terrorism or political persecution to try to apprehend and incarcerate him. To those refugees who are fighting to restore capitalism to Cuba, a man who risks his life to commit such acts is a hero of the Free World's fight for democracy. We can hardly blame the Cubans if they have a less charitable view. In any case, his arrest— even his execution, shortsighted and deplorable as it is—does not prove that Cuba is totalitarian, in the accepted sense of the word.

I have had a number of personal experiences, beginning shortly after my visit in 1960, of seeking out exiles in the United States to find out what information they had about political persecution in Cuba. If things were as bad as charged, I was prepared to add my small voice to publicizing and criticizing them. In some cases I was given the names of people in prison, but questioning always brought out that they had committed *acts* of violence. If one believes that expropriation of huge farms, businesses, and apartment houses (even with compensation) constitutes tyranny and that such tyranny must be overthrown by violence, then one is displaying commendable personal commitment and courage by trying to overthrow the Cuban government violently. But somewhere along the line the reasoning has become circular. The Cuban government's attempts to defend itself against those who are trying to overthrow it has become evidence of the need to overthrow it. People who share the economic and social goals of the Revolution are being bamboozled into opposing it, as a result of the confusion created by the travel ban, the press distortions, and the cries of the exiles that the arrest of their counterrevolutionary comrades is totalitarian.

The ease with which a visitor to Cuba can find openly outspoken critics of the régime substantiates the Cubans' claim that opponents are not in danger of being arrested for attacking the government—unless they attack it with guns or similar weapons. I found that people did not hesitate to speak freely against Fidel, Communism, and the government. One critic told me, in a crowded hotel lobby in Camaguey, after ten minutes acquaintance, that he preferred Batista to Castro. An article by Richard Eder in the New York *Times* for July 10th suggests that he is having the same experience. He writes:

> *Santiago, like the rest of Cuba, is divided between those who believe passionately in Fidel Castro and those who are sure, or fear, that he has betrayed them. But in this persistently small-town city . . . it is like a fight within a family*—more open, less fearful *and perhaps ultimately more dangerous. . . .* [Emphasis added.]
>
> *José Llanusa, a towering, stout man, strode toward the Cespedes Park on a Sunday evening. . . . "I want to show you one of our leading worms (opponents)," said Mr. Llanusa. . . . "He's a doctor. He was from a poor family, very intelligent, but he married a rich girl and so he's against us."*
>
> *Mr. Llanusa spoke with satisfaction. It pleases Cuba's leaders when they can explain somebody's opposition by his money.*
>
> *. . . Mr. Llanusa went up to a tall young man in a white shirt who was with a friend. The two exchanged greetings, their words drowned out by the music. They stood for a moment with smiles on their faces and blew cigar smoke at each other across the abyss that divides Cuba.*

It appears to me that Eder has written with a calculated attempt not to offend his anti-Castro audience. (I have no idea what his own views are.) Among other things he gives the impression of a much more even division between supporters and opponents of the Revolution than I found. In my experience, an overwhelming percentage of the people "believe passionately in" the Revolution. But if one stops to think about it, the article provides indirect, and therefore convincing, evidence that the opponents of the régime are not in hiding or in jail, but free to confront its supporters in a public park.

This does not mean that there are no innocent people in prison in Cuba today. In the first place, in a campaign of violence there are innocent victims, such as the woman and child who were shot in a counterrevolutionary coastal attack on a sugar mill, a few miles from a fishing village I was visiting at the time. And in a campaign against counterrevolutionary violence there are undoubtedly and regrettably some innocent victims as well. Inevitably some people who have limited themselves to verbal or written opposition find themselves unjustly suspected of complicity in the acts of violence and terrorism. Secondly, there is no surer way to make people suspicious of their outspoken neighbors, and to create an atmosphere in which those who do not believe in free speech can argue that it is expendable, than to do what the United States and the exiles are doing: continue to land saboteurs and weapons in order to bomb, burn, and blast in the night. There are persons in Cuba who are intolerant of *all* criticism and would like to make Cuba more like the State Department says it is. I found fewer such people than I meet in the United States, but every externally imposed crisis tends to strengthen their hand.

The one time that I know of when a considerable number of innocent people were arrested in Cuba was during the Bay of Pigs invasion in 1961—an invasion which followed a period in which department stores, water mains, power stations, airstrips, and sugar fields were burned or blown up by saboteurs. Even a holiday crowd at a parade was sprayed by bullets from counterrevolutionaries. This was also the period when a group of old-line Communists, under the leadership of Aníbal Escalante, were emboldened to try to capture the governmental apparatus and did succeed in dominating public policy in a number of cities and towns. But the Cubans insist that the last of the arrested persons was tried, and the innocent ones released, within three months. They also make a point that after these arrests most of the sabotage stopped. And in March,

1962, Escalante and his cohorts were publicly denounced by Fidel, and removed from office by vote of the National Directorate—but not arrested or "liquidated," as has happened to political rivals in some other Revolutions. By all indications, the Revolution reasserted its basic humanism and has not departed from it since.

Danger Signals

Despite the inaccuracy of the exiles' charges and the general atmosphere of freedom that exists in Cuba, there are several danger signs that should not be overlooked, particularly in view of the persistent pressures created by United States' blockade, attempts to isolate Cuba from the rest of the hemisphere, and counterrevolutionary sabotage. I shall discuss these under three headings: intolerance, conscription, and freedom of the press.

Intolerance. The amount of tolerance most Cubans display toward North Americans and Cuban dissenters is truly remarkable. I think that it can only be explained by the fact that they find their daily lives so satisfying and free that they do not have psychological needs (as many Americans do) to take out frustrations on people who disagree with them. Fidel said something of the kind in an interview with Richard Eder:

> As for the Cubans, he [Castro] suggested that they might have a less impassioned view of the United States than the Americans do of Cuba.
> "Our people do not hate you. Hatred accumulates when people feel frustrated, hopeless. People here are indignant when there is an attack—but indignation is very different from hatred." (New York Times, July 6th.)

Perhaps the Revolution's continued accomplishments will keep this spirit alive. But here and there I saw signs of the kind of narrowness which people under attack are always tempted to succumb to. I have already referred to the prejudice against Jehovah's Witnesses. Similarly, my guide was indignant at the thought that the Seventh Day Adventists were conscientious objectors, who would not fight (militarily) to defend the Revolution. He indicated that he would give short shrift to such people. Fidel himself drew cheers, on May Day, and a chant of *"Paredon"* (to the execution wall) when he said that the next invaders will not be exchanged for food and medicine, as the Bay of Pigs prisoners were. I was appalled by some of the replies I got to persistent questions about the execution of Marcos Rodriguez, an informer whose trial for having turned three fellow students over to Batista was a controversial event in March. (The students were tortured and killed by Batista in 1958.)Three different people said to me: "Besides, he was a homosexual," as if that should end the matter. When I asked if the Revolution would have been endangered by sending him to a rehabilitation center, or even into exile, I drew the incredulous reply: 'What, an informer?" (I should point out that others were more sympathetic to such an idea.)

Raul Castro charged, while I was in Cuba, that a number of officials in the Ministry of Internal Commerce were C.I.A. agents, who had been sabotaging distribution of food and consumer goods. We all know that the C.I.A. *does* bribe people to cause chaos and confusion, but such revelations should not be accompanied, as they were, by suggestions that repeated mistakes were a sign of treachery. It would have been far better to emphasize that mistakes are human and to caution against drawing McCarthy-like conclusions from them.

These may seem like small complaints, but one of the Revolution's glories is its broad and humane spirit. Once that is perverted, everything is in danger. Although the examples I have given include disturbing statements by both Fidel and Raul Castro, and instances of prejudice in a few rank-and-file revolutionists, the overwhelming impression one gets is that a libertarian spirit dominates both the top leadership and the majority of ordinary Cubans. Similarly, I visited seven or eight P.U.R.S. headquarters in different parts of the island and found the same refreshing emphasis on positive accomplishments and goals rather than on conformity to political dogma. Similar attitudes prevailed among factory managers I talked with and directors of schools, cooperatives and other grassroots organizations. Everyone takes it for granted that the Revolution is continually experimenting and must learn as it goes along. An indispensable part of this process is full and frank discussion of a diversity of ideas and analyses, including frank exposure of mistakes.

The narrower, more dangerous attitude crops up more frequently in certain sections of the middle bureaucracy, particularly in Havana, where the old political rivalries persist beneath the surface. Although the Revolution has brought to the fore many young leaders who have flowered in the prevailing libertarian atmosphere, inevitably there is some carry-over of trained professionals and politically sophisticated partisans from the old days. There are a number of cases in which these people have temporarily violated the policy of political freedom, only to be overruled by the National Direction or Fidel. In at least one case, a quantity of leaflets put out by a minority political group was confiscated, but the group appealed to Fidel and was allowed to resume publication and dissemination of its literature. Early this year, Blas Roca, the lone former member of the Popular Socialist (Communist) Party in the six-man executive committee of the government, launched an attack on the practice of showing *avant-garde* films from capitalist countries. After considerable public controversy, Roca gave up the attack and the films continued to be shown. (Perhaps the only film-producing country not represented in Cuban theatres is the United States, which expresses its devotion to freedom by not allowing the work of its producers to cross its government-imposed blockade.)

Freedom of the Press. After I had been in Cuba about two weeks, a Cuban journalist asked me my impressions of various aspects of Cuban life. "And what do you think about our press?" he asked. "Have you found that we have a free press in Cuba?" It was clear from his tone of voice and the context of his question that he personally was convinced that there is complete freedom of the press and that any open-minded investigator would have to come to the same conclusion. Unfortunately, I find the question of what constitutes a free press far more complicated than my friend did.

As we talked, he pointed out that he had been a journalist before the Revolution and that he and his colleagues had been forced to color the news in order to hold their jobs. He spoke not only of the direct censorship under Batista, but of pressures from private owners whose viewpoint inevitably reflected the fact that newspapers could only be owned by people of great wealth or compromising financial connections. "Now," he said with obvious pride, "I write the truth as I see it and no one changes what I write in order to make it conform to the prejudices of advertisers or wealthy publishers." Naturally, I asked him if he or anyone else doctored it to conform to the views of P.U.R.S. or the government. His answer was an unequivocal no, as was the answer of everyone I questioned. Whenever I raised the question of how much freedom there is to criticize and dissent, I was shown or referred to numerous magazine articles, newspaper columns, and letters to the editors which criticized bureaucracy and inefficiency in one department or other of the government.

The editor of *Vanguardia*, a daily newspaper in Santa Clara, told me that the counterrevolutionaries tried to take advantage of the "letters to the editor" column to spread malicious rumors and confusion. "Now", he said, "we assign someone to investigate the complaint in order to see if there is any basis in fact, so that we will not spread wild charges." But he said that they never suppress publication of responsible criticism. He read to me, from that day's paper, a complaint that in some sections of the city, milk deliveries were made so late that people had already left for work or school, with the result that the milk often spoiled before the people got a chance to take it in. The paper backed the complaint, but also referred to difficulties presented by the shortage of delivery trucks.

I agreed that the existence of freedom to make this kind of criticism was encouraging, but asked about criticisms with more far-reaching political implications. For example, thirty per cent of Cuban agriculture is still in private hands. Most, but not all, farms over a hundred and fifty acres are nationalized. Undoubtedly, some people feel that a larger percentage of agriculture should be taken over by the people's farms in order to allow more efficient planning and coordination, while others feel that private agriculture should be continued, so long as it does not involve exploitation of workers by absentee owners. Is there freedom to discuss and argue such questions? The answer (which I easily verified later) was that there is a great deal of public discussion and controversy about such matters. Most of it takes place in the political magazines, such as *Cuba Socialista,* rather than in the newspapers, which are considered dispensers of news. But from time to time the columnists or reviewers in the newspapers get into protracted conflicts about ideological matters. I have already referred to the controversy which arose when Blas Roca attacked the policy of showing "non-socialist" films. This was carried on in *Hoy, Revolución,* and other newspapers, as well as in magazines. One of the disputants, Alfredo Guevara, director of the Cuban Institute of the Art and Film Industry, wrote the following:

> *Only . . . by grasping or trying to grasp life as a whole, is it possible for man to find the strength to realize himself, to improve his being and to strive that the same phenomenon should take place in the society in which he lives. . . . Whatever makes him better informed and increases his depth, whatever makes him more earnest and coherent in his judgments, and whatever ensures a more complex and qualified critical attitude, makes man to be a true man.*
>
> *Only live thought, anti-routine, anti-dogmatic, always innovating and creative, respectful of its own nature, is capable not only of giving birth to true works of art but also of ensuring the level of production and its development. Without intellectual daring there is not, nor can there be, an efficient technology.. A new form of censorship could never be the source of that climate of freedom in which thought finds its true dimension, and science and art their full development.*

The condition of live and anti-dogmatic thought that Guevara describes did not exist in the newspapers during a period of several months late in 1961 and early in 1962. As a result of many pressures—the widespread sabotage, the Bay of Pigs invasion, some initial confusion over what it meant to become a Marxist-Leninist country, and a determined drive by a group

of old-line Communists to entrench themselves and their attitudes—the newspapers took on a frighteningly monolithic
quality of strident and narrow patriotism. Today they are
much more interesting, less hysterical, and more varied in tone,
content and point of view.

Fidel Castro continually emphasizes the importance of
honest criticism. On the 26th of July, 1962, he said:

> *The criticisms we wish to make we should voice in our
> places of work, in the unions, in the mass organizations.
> . . . Criticisms should be made not only in the places we
> have just mentioned but also in the revolutionary news-
> papers, and no administrator should get angry because he
> is criticized; he has the right to defend himself, to explain.*

In addition, it is significant that bookstores—and even P.U.R.S.
libraries—carry a wide range of *both* Soviet and Chinese publications, which contain each country's charges and counter-
charges against the other. From what I can ascertain, Cuba is
the only "Communist" country in the world which permits full
presentation of both sides of the bitter Sino-Soviet conflict by
the disputants themselves. (This throws a little light on facile
charges that Cuba is controlled by Moscow.)

There is no doubt that Cubans, including most Cuban
intellectuals, are satisfied that there is adequate airing of all
important questions and ample opportunity for expressions of
dissent. On the other hand, there are honest social democrats,
among the exiles, who are equally convinced that there is *not*
freedom of the press in Cuba. What is the explanation? Can
the differences in viewpoint be explained exclusively in terms
of the well known ignorance or unreliability of most of the
exiles? I think not. Once again, the apparent contradiction
stems from a difference in definitions and philosophy.

The catch is that by and large all printed and organized
dissent takes place within the context of general support of the
Revolution. (As I have pointed out this is not true of verbal
dissent or religious tracts.) Fidel said, in the speech quoted
above:

> *All the things that are wrong we should discuss. . . . But
> criticism expressed by revolutionaries is one thing,*

criticism voiced by our enemies another, and that we will not tolerate. (Emphasis added.) *Counterrevolutionaries criticize in order to destroy, revolutionaries to help overcome difficulties. . . . Revolutionaries criticize to help; counterrevolutionaries to demoralize, to spread pessimism.*

The basic question narrows itself down, then, to whether one believes that counterrevolutionaries should be allowed to advocate such policies as giving the oil companies back to Texaco, Shell, and the international oil cartel, and the people's farms to United Fruit Company (along, perhaps, with the hundred thousand individually owned farms that were given free to former squatters and sharecroppers under the first Agrarian Reform Law). The Cubans maintain that freedom to argue for a reimposition of servitude and exploitation is a specious freedom that has nothing to do with genuine freedom of the press. When I argued (somewhat weakly, I am afraid) for "total" freedom, including freedom to advocate reactionary and immoral programs, one newspaper man asked me if I thought that his paper should provide space for those who believe that Negroes should be denied access to beaches and a variety of other public accommodations (as they were when the United States dominated Cuba). "We have too many real questions to discuss," he said, "without allowing C.I.A. agents and would-be exploiters to bring up points of view that have no place in a decent society and are introduced only to confuse and divide people."

I think that the question of total freedom is a legitimate issue to be raised by those who wish to measure Revolutionary Cuba by the standards of perfection. But if they are seriously concerned with freedom, they should raise it in the context of the situation in which the Cuban people find themselves. It hardly provides a legitimate touchstone by which to proclaim that Cuba lacks a "free press," and therefore is totalitarian.

On the one hand, the Cubans are engaged in a desperate struggle against the determination of the wealthiest, most powerful country in the world to reimpose a reactionary régime. This is a fight for survival against a "clear and present danger." We can imagine how much freedom of the press would be granted to Communists, in the United States, if they were blowing up water mains, department stores, and warehouses, as the counterrevolutionaries have done in Cuba. I question the right of anyone who has not known hunger, disease, unemployment, poverty, illiteracy, and torture to turn against the Cuban Revolution because it does not provide total freedom of the press to C.I.A. agents and counterrevolutionaries, particularly so long as it preserves and encourages the extensive freedom that does exist. Also, Americans must not forget that the State Department, the ambassador to the United Nations, and the Cuban exiles have all lied about United States actions and internal conditions in Cuba. It is the height of hypocrisy to condemn the Revolution, from a lofty, moral pedestal, because it does not allow United States agents to circulate these lies in Cuba.

On the other hand, I think that we have to be troubled and on guard when there are *any* ideological qualifications on freedom. Who is to be the final judge of whether another man's ideas are counterrevolutionary? Is it to be simply a matter of who has the power? Once advocacy of counterrevolution is considered beyond the protection of civil liberties, there will always be persons ready to argue that all those who differ from them are counterrevolutionaries. This was the method by which a wide range of dissenters were hounded, imprisoned, and exterminated under Stalin, and a terrible tyranny entrenched itself.

Conscription. I shall write later about the relationship of non-violence to the Revolution. But I find it deeply disturbing, even within the framework of conscientious armed defense, that military conscription was passed in Cuba in December 1963. The Cubans say that conscription was necessary in order to distribute equitably the burden of military defense against the persistent attacks, to put such defense on an efficient footing, and to prevent the frequent disruptions of industry and agriculture which took place when the burden of response rested on the volunteer militia. The Cuban arguments are reasonable, and those who foster armed attacks or threaten invasion are not in a position to criticize Cuba for having responded in traditional fashion to such perils. But the tragedy of counterrevolution is that it tends to poison the revolutionists when it cannot overcome them directly. Steps, such as conscription, that seem necessary, or at least reasonable, when they are taken, turn out later to have been turning points in which the unique character of the Revolution was subverted. Certainly conscription strengthens the power of the state over all its citizens and weakens the spirit of voluntary participation. Once the principle is established that the state can commandeer a man's time and labor (which is what conscription means, no matter how content today's draftees may be to have been selected by impartial lot instead of by volunteer processes), what is to stop someone from suggesting conscription of cane-cutters, compulsory classes in Marxism-Leninism, etc.? The spirit of voluntary dedication to the advancement and defense of the Revolution is still so strong in Cuba that conscription alone will not alter the people's relationship to the government, but it is an unfortunate step in the wrong direction.

Although I have pointed out the existence of certain flaws and sources of potential danger, it would give a false impression if I did not end as I began, by stating that in Revolutionary Cuba, more than any other place I have ever been, the people and the government have succeeded in making common cause. The people enjoy a life of freedom, daily satisfaction, social solidarity, and practical brotherhood such as most adults in the United States have long since decided is impossible of attainment. Perhaps we should ask the Cubans if they will send us a Peace Corps to instruct us in the ways of practical idealism, before *all* the humanity is squeezed out of us. We could call off the blockade and send them some of our surplus food and machinery, in exchange. We were revolutionists in 1776. Perhaps, with the aid of Cuba, we could become revolutionists again.

Barbara Deming

Two Issues or One?

The man took a leaflet and read a few lines. "This is the Nashville, Tennessee to Washington, D. C. Walk for Peace," it began; " 'Since 650 B. C. there have been 1,656 arms races, only sixteen of which have not ended in war. The remainder have ended in economic collapse.' " He looked up. "Are you walking with that nigger?" he asked.

This kind of discussion of our message had been anticipated by the Committee for Nonviolent Action, when it decided that the walk should be integrated. "Token integrated," somebody later commented. Of thirteen young men and women committed to walk the whole distance, Robert Gore was the only Negro, though we hoped others might join before Washington. Whether they did or not, it was assumed that in the many talks about war and peace we would attempt to provoke along the way, we were sure to be asked a good many times whether we would be happy to see Robert married to our sisters. Before we headed south, we discussed the question of just how distracting our obvious attitude to race relations might be, and the proper way to cope with the problem. Events then proved our tentative conclusions to have been utterly inadequate.

Most of those advising us felt that battle on the two issues simply could not be combined. Of course we ought never to deny our belief in racial brotherhood; but Robert's presence was enough to confirm it. We should try to avoid talking about it; we were there to talk about *peace*. And it would be folly to seek to associate ourselves too closely with the people down there who were struggling for integration. Many people would then shy away from us. And they, the Negroes, could be harmed by it even more than we. They had enough of a burden to bear, already, without our giving their opponents added ammunition—the charge of their being "unpatriotic."

I supposed that the advice was practical, but it depressed me. I think we all left the meeting feeling unsatisfied—wondering a little why, then the walk *was* to be integrated. We'd talked about the fact that this could lead us into danger. The South was unpredictable, it was stressed: we might not run into any trouble at all; on the other hand, we just might all get killed. In a cause we were not to appear to be battling for?

I had felt for a long time that the two struggles—for disarmament and for Negro rights—were properly parts of the one struggle. The same nonviolent tactic joined us, but more than this: our struggles were fundamentally one—to commit our country in act as well as in word to the extraordinary faith announced in our Declaration of Independence: that all men are endowed with certain rights that must not be denied them. *All* men, including those of darker skin, whom it has been convenient to exploit; including those in other countries, with whose policies we quarrel; among those rights which are not to be questioned, the right to be free to pursue happiness, and among them the right not to be deprived of life. In short, the Christian faith, still revolutionary, that men are brothers and that—no matter what—our actions must respect the fact. The only mode of battle that does, implicitly, respect this fact is that of nonviolence, and I had heard that for more and more of those in the civil rights as well as in the peace movement, the very attempt to practice it had implanted a corresponding faith, however tentative. But of course it is possible to hold a faith and yet not recognize all its implications, to be struggling side by side with others and yet be unaware of them. Perhaps it wasn't realistic to think of joining ranks.

We started out, in Nashville, with only a wistful look in the direction of the integration movement. We marched past a sit-in demonstration at a "Simple Simon's" and "smiled in." We didn't even picket for a few minutes; didn't pause in our marching. "There they are"—we turned our heads. We caught a glimpse of a row of young people at a counter—a glimpse, as in a flash photograph, of young heads held in a certain proud and patient fashion; and then we had marched past. A few

steps away, in front of a movie theatre, several adolescent
toughs loitered—faces furtive, vacant. Did they plan trouble?
In a minute, we were out of sight. It felt unnatural, I think, to
all of us.

That afternoon we held a small open meeting at Scarritt
College for Christian Workers. Two Negro leaders were
among those present—James Lawson and Metz Rollins. Members of the group staging the sit-in—the Student Nonviolent
Coordinating Committee—had been invited; but none came.
Was this because they *were* shy of association with us? Or was
it perhaps because, as one walker suggested, they felt that we
should have done more to demonstrate solidarity with them?
Rollins inclined his head, smiled. "It may well be."

Lawson spoke that afternoon. In the course of his talk, he
remarked, "There is a clearcut relation between the peace walk
and what some of us are seeking to do in the emerging nonviolent movement in the South. Some people have tried to classify
our effort here as one that is of and for and by the Negro. They
have tried to define the struggle for integration as a struggle to
gain the Negro more power. I maintain that it is not the case.
Go among the common ordinary people . . . for the 'leading
Negroes' are not the leaders of this movement. . . . Listen to
their prayers and to their speech. They are constantly thinking
not in terms of civil rights but in terms of the kingdom of God
on earth, the brotherhood of all men. . . . What is behind it is
an effort to build a community for all of us . . . 'the beloved
community.' I say that this work is related to the work for
peace. . . . It might be a prototype to speak to the whole world.
. . . And the peace walk is related to the task of building
community here. . . . The movements are related to each other,
in a sense are one and the same enterprise."

I took down the words he spoke, in my notebook, nod-
ding, "Yes"; and at the same time, disregarding them—perhaps
because I was tired from the long drive south, and the process
of breaking myself in again to group life, to sleeping on the
floor, to packing up and moving each day; or perhaps because
the meeting room was very nearly empty: the peace movement
and the civil rights movement were certainly not visibly related here.

On Easter afternoon, we walked out of Nashville, heading out along Route 70N toward Knoxville. Two Fisk students, members of S.N.C.C., did appear just before starting time, to walk with us for a little while. Their presence was well noted. The signs we carried were unconventional: "If your conscience demands it, refuse to serve in the armed forces," ". . . refuse to pay taxes for war," "Defend freedom with nonviolence"; but more conspicuous than our signs, quite obviously, were the Negro students—while they remained with us—and after a while the single figure of Robert Gore. Robert carried the "lollipop" sign that simply labelled the walk: NASHVILLE TO WASHINGTON; but he was in himself our most provocative, most instantly legible sign—walking along very quietly; dressed, carefully, not in hiking clothes but sober sports jacket and slacks; head held high, a quiet tension in his bearing.

We encountered a certain amount of Southern courtesy— "Well, have a nice walk!"; and now and then expression of active sympathy—"God go with you!" "You mean you agree with us?" "I sure do!" But less friendly messages were of course more common—"Boo!", "Get out of here!" As we held out our leaflets, car windows were rolled up swiftly; some cars actually backed off from us in a rush; citizens on foot stepped quickly behind shop doors. Approaching a leaflet victim, one tried, by remaining very calm oneself, and looking him quietly in the eye, to prevent his flight, and infect him with corresponding calm; but the exercise was difficult. Soon the "hot rod gang" began to face us in the field. Parking their cars by the roadside, they would line up, leaning against them, awaiting our approach, assuming looks that were meant to kill—expressions glowering and at the same time pathetically vacant. We would offer leaflets, walk past; they would hop into their cars, speed past us, line up again by the roadside. And now the first warnings began to be delivered to us. I handed a leaflet to the manager of a garage, and to the Negro employee who stood beside him. "I hear they're going to shoot you a little farther down the line," the white man told me softly. "They don't like niggers there, you see." He turned and smiled fixedly into the eyes of the black man by his side—"That's what I hear." The Negro made no answer, returning the stare but allowing noth-

ing to come to the surface of his look—his shining eyes fathom-
less. The white man turned back to me. "I just hope you'll be
all right," he said—not pretending not to pretend. I told him,
as brightly as I could, "Keep hoping."

That first night we slept on the floors of a white church
near Old Hickory; the next night our "advance worker" had
arranged for us to stay in a Negro church in Lebanon. Lebanon was a small town which had lately seen much violence.
Fifteen months before, a young Negro minister, Reverend Cor-
dell Sloan, had been assigned to the town to try to build a
Negro Presbyterian church. He had felt called, as well, to try
to build a sit-in movement. This was the first small town in the
South in which the struggle had been taken up; and it involved
not college but high school students. Retaliation had been
vigorous. Just recently the headquarters of the group had been
demolished with rocks, while the Negroes themselves stood
pressed against the walls inside, and the police looked on. This
day, as we filed along the highway, a car slowed down in
passing, a young man leaned his head out: "You walking into
Lebanon?" "That's right." "Good place for you to be walking.
We're going to hang you all there." It was a bright beautiful
day. Fruit trees were coming into bloom; the purple redbud
was out. Horses and goats and litters of many-colored pigs ran
in mixed company through the long Tennessee fields. The
fields were vivid with flowering mustard. We marched along,
trying not to straggle out, but to keep fairly close together. Just
before mid-day a car approaching us suddenly whizzed into a
side-road and stopped; the doors flew open, and several men
leaped out. Well here it is, I thought; may we all behave well.
Then I saw that their faces were dark. They were students
from Lebanon, two of them come to walk into town with us.
More planned to join us later. They held out their hands for
signs to carry.

We stopped by the side of the road and shared a picnic
lunch. We bought a carton of milk at a nearby store, and in a
shy ritual gesture passed it from hand to hand, each drinking
from the spout. On the road again, we walked past an all-
Negro primary school, set high on a hill. The entire school
stood out in the yard, waving to us. I ran up the hill with

leaflets. A sweet-faced teacher asked me—so softly that I could hardly catch the words: "How many colored are with you?" I told her that two of the young men she saw were from Lebanon. "I thought I recognized J. T.," she said; and in her voice, in her face, was a contained, tremulous pride and excitement. A few miles further on, more students waited by the road to join us; a little further on, more; and at the town's edge, still more. As we stepped onto the sidewalks of the town, more of us were black than white.

A car sped by, an arm jerked out of the window and slung an empty coke bottle. The youngest of the team, Henry Wershaw, gave a little cry: he had been hit in the ankle. He was able soon to limp on. We kept close ranks, to be ready for worse than that; but everyone was stepping lightly; the mood among us was almost gay. One small boy, Sam, strode with us, eyes sparkling. A pretty young woman named Avis, in a light-colored summer dress, almost skipped along the street. The citizens of the town, as usual, stepped back from us in dread; withdrew behind their doors and peered out, through the glass panes, in amazement and dread, as the unarmed troop of us passed. There were several among us who bore the marks of violence at the hands of townspeople. The skull of one of the young Negroes showed, beneath his close-cropped hair, an intricate tracery of scars: he had been hit with a wrench during one of the sit-ins. There were others walking, too, who had suffered such blows; and none had ever struck back. They walked along the street now, lighthearted, as if secure, faces extraordinarily bright, while those who had, in one way or another, condoned the blows struck, drew back, in the reflex of fear. Before we headed south, the women had been cautioned against walking in public next to a Negro man; it might make things dangerous for him. At any rate, we were told, best to take our cue from the man himself. I had carefully made no move to walk next to any of these students. But now one after another, as we moved through the town, stepped alongside me, to introduce himself, to exchange a few words—free of caution. They had made their choice, had entered a fight, and if one was in it, then one was in it—ready to take what might come. At lunch one of them talked about this a little: "When you see those hoodlums arriving, you just divorce yourself from your body—prepare your body for anything: spit, fists, sticks, anything—"

Police cars had begun to drive past us at frequent intervals; but our friends remarked that we mustn't assume that they were there for our protection. During recent trouble, one woman had asked an officer whether the police intended to protect them from the mob. "We're hired to protect the city, not individuals," had been his reply. We headed for the town square now, preparing ourselves for "anything." We walked through uneventfully. Within our hearing, an officer in a squad car pulled up next to a car full of young toughs and told the driver, "Not today, Hank, not today." We turned the corner and limped the final block to Picketts Chapel Methodist Church.

In the white churches where we had stayed so far, we had had the use of the church kitchen in which to fix our meals, from supplies we carried about with us; once the pastor's wife had kindly fixed us sandwiches and lemonade; and evenings, after supper, as many as five members of the congregation had sometimes dropped in to ask questions. This day, as we sat in the churchyard easing our feet, women began to appear from the four points of the compass, carrying bowls and platters; all who had walked were soon summoned into the room behind the church to a feast: fried chicken, garden peas, turnip greens, two kinds of potato salad, three kinds of pie. After we had sat down together to eat, we were invited into the church itself; word of a meeting had been spread through the community; the door kept opening, and soon the church had filled up.

The shape this meeting took swiftly dissolved any remaining anxieties about the harm we might do to the integrationists and to ourselves if we sought association with them. Reverend Sloan spoke first—a thin handsome man with gentle but stubborn demeanor, and the luminous wide eyes of a man who is almost blind but who sees what it is that he wants to do. "I hope the town never gets over what it saw today," he began. What the town had seen of course, as we walked through its streets together, was the first integrated gathering that had ever occurred in Lebanon. The white community had seen, and the Negro community had seen, too, the brotherhood of which Sloan preached made visible—turned fact. "I hope it gets into its system, I hope it gets to the bone," said Sloan. It was clear that he meant both white community and Negro. We learned, at the end of the meeting, that this was the largest audience he had ever had there. He had made great headway with students, but adults had been largely apathetic. Because of the drama of our arrival, many adults were present tonight, gazing about them in quiet astonishment, and he was addressing them particularly.

He spoke of the struggles in which he and his followers had been involved; he spoke of the opposition they had encountered—sprayed with insecticides, hit with ketchup bottles, threatened with pistols, run down with lawn mowers, "Name it, we've had it." "The proficient, efficient, sufficient police" had been on the scene. He smiled wryly. "We like to get killed." Many had been arrested. He asked those who had been to jail to stand. A large number stood. The leader of the peace walk, Bradford Lyttle, here interrupted to ask those among the peace walkers who had been to jail to stand, too; and an equal number rose. "Let no one be afraid of going to jail," the minister urged; "It has become an honor. . . . It's easy to say, isn't it? But come and try it." They shouldn't be afraid, he repeated; they should be afraid of being slaves any longer. "The only thing I'm afraid of is going back into the old way of living again. We've gone too far." He reminded those in the audience who had not been fighting that when freedom came, they too would enjoy it—unless perhaps they'd feel too guilty to enjoy it. They had better begin to get the feeling of it right now. Then he got very specific about the ways in which they could help, and the ways in which they had been doing the movement harm.

After he had spoken, Bradford Lyttle spoke about the work of the C.N.V.A. He spoke at ease, his words briefer than they often were—so much obviously could be assumed to be understood by this audience. He felt very strongly, he told them, that America was in a desperate situation today. Here were the most prosperous and happily situated people who

had ever lived, on the verge of giving up their souls—for we
were professing ourselves quite willing to murder hundreds of
millions of other human beings to try to preserve our own
standards of life. Many Americans were beginning to demonstrate in protest—to name themselves *un*-willing. He urged
them to join the protest. C.N.V.A. believed in disarming unilaterally, and in training for defense through nonviolent resistance. Heads nodded. No one stood up to hurl the familiar
challenge: Are we supposed to lie down and let the Russians
walk right over us? Of all the signs we carry, the sign that
usually remains the most abstract for those who read it is
"Defend freedom through nonviolent resistance"; but when the
students of Lebanon walked through their town carrying that
banner, the message could not remain abstract. If our walking
beside them had made visible for the community the substance
of what Reverend Sloan had been preaching, their walking
beside us had made visible the substance of what Bradford
Lyttle preached. Forty-five people in that audience came forward to put their names on C.N.V.A.'s mailing list.

Reverend Sloan called for a collection to be taken up for
both causes. Many who had little enough to spare opened their
purses. Some who had never given before gave this night. We
stood and clasped hands and sang the hymn that has become
the theme song of the movement in the South: "We shall overcome some day! . . . Black and white together. . . . We shall
live in peace!" The words seemed to belong to both our causes.

The next day we were scheduled to walk to the small
town of Carthage, set on the bluffs of the Cumberland River.
A number of the people who had walked into town with us the
day before turned up to see us on our way. Reverend Sloan
was among them, and a leader among the students, Bobby,
and Sloan's right-hand man, a tall, very homely newspaper reporter, Finley, a man of wit and feeling; and quite a few
others. We expected to be escorted to the town's edge and I
rather think they had expected to walk only this far, themselves; but most of them ended by walking with us all the way
to Carthage. Passing motorists again leaned out of their cars to
shout threatening or vile remarks. "Let not your hearts be
troubled," Reverend Sloan advised, in his soft, rather lilting

voice. He and Finley left for a while to ride up ahead with Bradford and find a place for us to stay that night. They found it at Braden Methodist Church, where Sloan knew the assistant minister, Beulah Allen. "How could we turn you out?" she said to Bradford. "You can never tell when the stranger will be the Lord."

After we had entered Carthage with our banners, Sloan and Finley and Bobby took a little stroll about its streets. The walk had now linked them dramatically with *that* town; and who knows when their battle may not be taken up there?

Again, this evening, women of the community appeared, arms laden; a feast was spread for us in the church basement. Again, after dinner together, we moved into the "sanctuary"; and again the church filled up. It was the first integated meeting that had ever taken place here, too. That night, the women in our group slept in the house of Beulah Allen's sister, Dona. As we tiptoed through her room, Dona's old mother woke, and Dona introduced us. "Honey, they look white," Dona's mother whispered to her. "Mama, they are," said Dona. "Lord bless us!" said the old lady.

Braden Methodist Church was set up on a little rise just above the large town square, and as we gathered noisily first in the basement and then in the church proper, a good many of the white people of the town and of the country round the town gathered in the square and stood glaring up. A few of them had thrown some rotten fruit and vegetables, as we sat outside before dinner; a few had walked past, holding empty coke bottles—but not quite bringing themselves to throw those. During the meeting, the door would open and shut, open and shut, as more and more of the Negro community kept arriving; and one was never quite sure that some of the crowd below might not be arriving at last. But again there were a lot of cops around, and again they had decided to keep order. The crowd just stood, until past midnight, glaring up at the small frame building which resounded with our talk and laughter and singing and prayer. Dona reported to us afterward that she had gone outside once and found several white boys loitering and had asked them in. "They don't understand," she explained to us; "They've never even been outside

the county." If the resistance movement had not yet taken root
among the Negroes of Carthage, they hardly needed to be introduced to the idea of nonviolence. They had found it long
ago in the New Testament.

This meeting was above all an old-fashioned prayer meeting. Bradford Lyttle talked again briefly—drawing a picture of
the world-wide nonviolent movement. And he issued a rather
shy invitation to them to walk with us the next day. Reverend
Sloan then rose and declared that he would be less shy about
it: he would simply tell them that they *should* walk with us.
Robert Gore asked Beulah Allen if he could say a few words
from the pulpit, and he spoke of how the message of Jesus—to
love one's enemies—was a strange message, a revolutionary
one. "That's right," came from the audience—"Amen!" But it
was Beulah Allen who led the meeting, and who spoke the
prayers. I think few of us had ever before this evening felt that
we were being prayed for. The days we were now approaching
on the walk promised to be the most trying. We were about to
enter Cumberland County, where—we had been told by both
friends and antagonists—no Negro was supposed to remain
after nightfall. The last Negro family that had tried to build
had been burned out; the last Negro who had tried to walk
through the county had been found dead by the side of the
road. Beulah Allen had heard these stories too. She stood sol-
idly before the altar rail, spread out her arms, raised up her
voice—half in a piercing shout, half in a song—and addressing
God as though He were indeed there just above us, just beyond the roof—"Heavenly FATHER! . . . Heavenly FA-
THER!"—she asked Him to give us courage, and also a good
night's sleep that night, asked Him to teach all of us, including
the people out there in the square, and the people along the
road we were going to walk, how best to behave. The words
themselves vanish now in my memory, having entered too
deeply that evening into my flesh. I looked about me, and the
other walkers, too, were sitting up, stock still. We had all of us
heard, before, theatrical versions of such prayer—intended
sometimes to be funny or sometimes to be endearing; and
Beulah's prayer retained for us of course something of the

extravagance of theatre; but now we were in the play; we
were at the heart of it, amazed.

Again we sang together. Dona, accompanying us at the
upright piano, hit the keys with a heavily-pouncing, laboring
but joyful, heart-felt emphasis of her own. The rhythm was
always almost jazz, and as we nodded our heads, tapped our
feet, our weariness and the nudging fears we'd kept down all
the past days dissolved. Again, at Reverend Sloan's prompting,
we sang the integration hymn—reaching out and taking
hands: "We shall overcome some day!" "Now this is difficult,"
Reverend Sloan said, with a flickering smile, and prompted,
"Black and white together some day." He prompted, "We are
not afraid *today*." At the end of the meeting, Beulah Allen
gave us a blessing, and exclaimed, "It's been so sweet!" At that
moment, I recalled the words of James Lawson about "the
beloved community." It seemed that we had been living in that
community this past hour.

The next morning I learned to my astonishment that our
evening's meeting had not caused the breach between us and
the white community that might have been supposed. I entered
one of the shops on the square to buy some things, expecting
to be served with glum hostility. The young woman behind the
counter—who clearly knew who I was—was full of both curiosity and warmth. She chattered eagerly about the peculiar
weather they had been having this past year, and "It's the
times, I think," she ventured. I asked whether she felt that
atomic tests were disrupting the weather, and she nodded:
"There's One who is more powerful; we forget that." As I left,
"I hope you come back and see us again," she said.

In the course of the next few days, we walked into
mythical Cumberland County and walked out of it, unharmed.
Two Quaker couples who bravely put us up received middle-
of-the-night telephone calls, threatening "roast nigger for
breakfast"; one night the fire department arrived in the yard,
summoned by false alarm; one night local high school students
swarmed up to the house—but when invited in, sat and talked
until late, quietly enough, their curiosity about us obviously
deeper than their hostility. (As they left, they were arrested by
the police as eager to protect them from us as to protect us

from them.) It was actually at the edge of the county, the first
night after we left Carthage, that we had our nearest
brush with violence. Reverend Sloan and Finley and Bobby
and others had walked with us again this third day, but
had taken their final leave of us at a little one-room Negro
church by the side of the road, way out "nowhere," between
towns. No one was in the church, but we had been told
that we could spend the night there. We had crawled into
our sleeping bags, scattered out on the floor between the
pews, and were listening sleepily to the small country
noises in the air, when abruptly the ruder sound of rocks
hitting the building brought us full awake. Two of the men
stepped outside and called into the dark, inviting the besiegers
to come and talk to us about it. The hail of rocks stopped and
the people rustled off into the dark. We could hear the crickets
again for a while and then the barrage began again; a rock
came crashing through one of the windows. Another two
stepped outside, this time carrying flashlights aimed at themselves, to show the strangers where they were and that they
were unarmed. We could hear their voices and we could hear
the stones still flying and suddenly we heard a small gasping
cry. Eric Weinberger had been hit on the side of the head and
knocked off his feet. He staggered up, and called to them
again, "It's all right. You hit me in the head, but it's all right.
But now why don't you come and talk with us?"—and seven or
eight young men finally emerged out of the dark and con-
sented to talk. They were young workingmen from around
there. They talked for a good while, and finally they said that
well, they might perhaps agree with some of the things we said
about war and peace, but they couldn't understand our walking around with a nigger, and all sleeping in the same building
with him. And then one of them asked the time-worn question: "Would you let a nigger marry your sister?" The question
was posed to Sam Savage, who is a Southerner himself. When
he answered that yes, he would; the decision would, after all,
be hers to make—they exclaimed in sudden anger and disgust:
well he was no real Southerner then, and there was no use
talking about anything further; and they stamped off into the
dark. At which point, one might have said that the advice we

had been given before starting out on the walk had now been proved to be correct: the two issues of race relations and of war and peace could not be discussed together. However, there is a final chapter to this story. After a short time, the young men returned, wanting to talk further. The talk this time went on until the one who had done the most arguing remarked that they must be up early to work and had better get some sleep. But would we be there the next evening? he wanted to know. (We had of course, unfortunately, to move on.) As they left, he shook hands with Sam, who had said that yes, he'd let his sister marry a black man. It is my own conviction that these men listened to us as they did, on the subject of peace, just *because* Robert Gore was travelling with us. It made it more difficult for them to listen, of course; it made the talk more painful; but it also snatched it from the realm of the merely abstract. For the issue of war and peace remains fundamentally the issue of whether or not one is going to be willing to respect one's fellow man.

Martin Luther King, Jr.

Our Struggle*

The segregation of Negroes, with its inevitable discrimination, has thrived on elements of inferiority present in the masses of both white and Negro people. Through forced separation from our African culture, through slavery, poverty, and deprivation, many black men lost self-respect.

In their relations with Negroes, white people discovered that they had rejected the very center of their own ethical professions. They could not face the triumph of their lesser instincts and simultaneously have peace within. And so, to gain it, they rationalized—insisting that the unfortunate Negro, being less than human, deserved and even enjoyed second class status.

They argued that his inferior social, economic and political position was good for him. He was incapable of advancing beyond a fixed position and would therefore be happier if encouraged not to attempt the impossible. He is subjugated by a superior people with an advanced way of life. The "master race" will be able to civilize him to a limited degree, if only he will be true to his inferior nature and stay in his place.

White men soon came to forget that the Southern social culture and all its institutions had been organized to perpetuate this rationalization. They observed a caste system and quickly were conditioned to believe that its social results, which they had created, actually reflected the Negro's innate and true nature.

In time many Negroes lost faith in themselves and came to believe that perhaps they really were what they had been told they were—something less than men. So long as they were

* April, 1956.

prepared to accept this role, racial peace could be maintained. It was an uneasy peace in which the Negro was forced to accept patiently injustice, insult, injury and exploitation.

Gradually the Negro masses in the South began to re-evaluate themselves—a process that was to change the nature of the Negro community and doom the social patterns of the South. We discovered that we had never really smothered our self-respect and that we could not be at one with ourselves without asserting it. From this point on, the South's terrible peace was rapidly undermined by the Negro's new and courageous thinking and his ever-increasing readiness to organize and to act. Conflict and violence were coming to the surface as the white South desperately clung to its old patterns. The extreme tension in race relations in the South today is explained in part by the revolutionary change in the Negro's evaluation of himself and of his destiny and by his determination to struggle for justice. *We Negroes have replaced self-pity with self-respect and self-depreciation with dignity.*

When Mrs. Rosa Parks, the quiet seamstress whose arrest precipitated the nonviolent protest in Montgomery, was asked why she had refused to move to the rear of a bus, she said: "It was a matter of dignity; I could not have faced myself and my people if I had moved."

The New Negro

Many of the Negroes who joined the protest did not expect it to succeed. When asked why, they usually gave one of three answers: "I didn't expect Negroes to stick to it," or, "I never thought we Negroes had the nerve," or, "I thought the pressure from the white folks would kill it before it got started."

In other words, our nonviolent protest in Montgomery is important because it is demonstrating to the Negro, North and South, that many of the stereotypes he has held about himself and other Negroes are not valid. Montgomery has broken the spell and is ushering in concrete manifestations of the thinking and action of the new Negro.

We now know that:

We Can Stick Together. In Montgomery, 42,000 of us

have refused to ride the city's segregated buses since December 5. Some walk as many as fourteen miles a day.

Our Leaders Do Not Have to Sell Out. Many of us have been indicted, arrested, and "mugged." Every Monday and Thursday night we stand before the Negro population at the prayer meetings and repeat: "It is an honor to face jail for a just cause."

Threats and Violence Do Not Necessarily Intimidate Those Who Are Sufficiently Aroused and Nonviolent. The bombing of two of our homes has made us more resolute. When a handbill was circulated at a White Citizens Council meeting stating that Negroes should be "abolished" by "guns, bows and arrows, sling shots and knives," we responded with even greater determination.

Our Church Is Becoming Militant. Twenty-four ministers were arrested in Montgomery. Each has said publicly that he stands prepared to be arrested again. Even upperclass Negroes who reject the "come to Jesus" gospel are now convinced that the church has no alternative but to provide the nonviolent dynamics for social change in the midst of conflict. The $30,000 used for the car pool, which transports over 20,000 Negro workers, school children and housewives, has been raised in the churches. The churches have become the dispatch centers where the people gather to wait for rides.

We Believe in Ourselves. In Montgomery we walk in a new way. We hold our heads in a new way. Even the Negro reporters who converged on Montgomery have a new attitude. One tired reporter, asked at a luncheon in Birmingham to say a few words about Montgomery, stood up, thought for a moment, and uttered one sentence: "Montgomery has made me proud to be a Negro."

Economics Is Part of Our Struggle. We are aware that Montgomery's white businessmen have tried to "talk sense" to the bus company and the city commissioners. We have observed that small Negro shops are thriving as Negroes find it inconvenient to walk downtown to the white stores. We have been getting more polite treatment in the white shops since the protest began. We have a new respect for the proper use of our dollar.

We Have Discovered a New and Powerful Weapon—Nonviolent Resistance. Although law is an important factor in bringing about social change, there are certain conditions in which the very effort to adhere to new legal decisions creates tension and provokes violence. We had hoped to see demonstrated a method that would enable us to continue our struggle while coping with the violence it aroused. Now we see the answer: face violence if necessary, but refuse to return violence. If we respect those who oppose us, they may achieve a new understanding of the human relations involved.

We Now Know That the Southern Negro Has Come of Age, Politically and Morally. Montgomery has demonstrated that we will not run from the struggle, and will support the battle for equality. The attitude of many young Negroes a few years ago was reflected in the common expression, "I'd rather be a lamp post in Harlem than Governor of Alabama." Now the idea expressed in our churches, schools, pool rooms, restaurants and homes is: "Brother, stay here and fight nonviolently. 'Cause if you don't let them make you mad, you can win." The official slogan of the Montgomery Improvement Association is "Justice without Violence."

The Issues in Montgomery

The leaders of the old order in Montgomery are not prepared to negotiate a settlement. This is not because of the conditions we have set for returning to the buses. The basic question of segregation in intra-state travel is already before the courts. Meanwhile we ask only for what in Atlanta, Mobile, Charleston and most other cities of the South is considered the Southern pattern. We seek the right, under segregation, to seat ourselves from the rear forward on a first come, first served basis. In addition, we ask for courtesy and the hiring of some Negro bus drivers on predominantly Negro routes.

A prominent judge of Tuscaloosa was asked if he felt there was any connection between Autherine Lucy's effort to enter the University of Alabama and the Montgomery non-violent protest. He replied, "Autherine is just one unfortunate girl who doesn't know what she is doing, but in Montgomery it looks like all the niggers have gone crazy."

Later the judge is reported to have explained that "of course the good niggers had undoubtedly been riled up by outsiders, Communists and agitators." It is apparent that at this historic moment most of the elements of the white South are not prepared to believe that "our Negroes could of themselves act like this."

Miscalculation of the White Leaders

Because the Mayor and city authorities cannot admit to themselves that we have changed, every move they have made has inadvertently increased the protest and united the Negro community.

[1955]

Dec. 1   They arrested Mrs. Parks, one of the most respected Negro women in Montgomery.

Dec. 3   They attempted to intimidate the Negro population by publishing a report in the daily paper that certain Negroes were calling for a boycott of the buses. They thereby informed the 30,000 Negro readers of the planned protest.

Dec. 5   They found Mrs. Parks guilty and fined her $14. This action increased the number of those who joined the boycott.

Dec. 5   They arrested a Negro college student for "intimidating passengers." Actually, he was helping an elderly woman cross the street. This mistake solidified the college students' support of the protest.

Two policemen on motorcycles followed each bus on its rounds through the Negro community. This attempt at psychological coercion further increased the number of Negroes who joined the protest.

In a news telecast at 6:00 P.M., a mass meeting planned for that evening was announced. Although we had expected only 500 people at the meeting, over 5,000 attended.

Dec. 6   They began to intimidate Negro taxi drivers. This led to the setting up of a car pool and a resolution to extend indefinitely our protest, which had originally been called for one day only.

Dec. 7   They began to harass Negro motorists. This encouraged the Negro middle class to join the struggle.

Dec. 8   The lawyer for the bus company said, "We have no intention of hiring Negro drivers now or in the foreseeable future." To us this meant never. The slogan then became, "Stay off the buses until we win."

Dec. 9   The Mayor invited Negro leaders to a conference, presumably for negotiation. When we arrived, we discovered that some of the men in the room were white supremacists and members of the White Citizens Council. The Mayor's attitude was made clear when he said, "Comes the first rainy day and the Negroes will be back in the buses." The next day it did rain, but the Negroes did not ride the buses.

At this point over 42,000 Montgomery Negroes had joined the protest. After a period of uneasy quiet, elements in the white community turned to further police intimidation and to violence.

[1956]

Jan. 26   I was arrested for traveling 30 miles per hour in a 25-mile zone. This arrest occurred just 2 hours before a mass meeting. So, we had to hold seven mass meetings to accommodate the people.

Jan. 30   My home was bombed.

Feb. 1   The home of E. D. Nixon, one of the protest leaders and former State President of the NAACP, was bombed. This brought moral and financial support from all over the state.

Feb. 22   Eighty-nine persons, including the 24 ministers, were arrested for participating in the nonviolent protests.

Every attempt to end the protest by intimidation, by encouraging Negroes to inform, by force and violence, further cemented the Negro community and brought sympathy for our cause from men of good will all over the world. The great appeal for the world appears to lie in the fact that we in Montgomery have adopted the method of nonviolence. In a world in which most men attempt to defend their highest values by the accumulation of weapons of destruction, it is morally refreshing to hear 5,000 Negroes in Montgomery shout "Amen" and "Halleluh" when they are exhorted to "pray for those who oppose you," or pray "Oh Lord, give us strength of body to keep walking for freedom," and conclude each mass meeting with: "Let us pray that God shall give us strength to remain nonviolent though we may face death."

The Liberal Dilemma

And death there may be. Many white men in the South see themselves as a fearful minority in an ocean of black men. They honestly believe with one side of their minds that Negroes are depraved and disease-ridden. They look upon any effort at equality as leading to "mongrelization." They are convinced that racial equality is a Communist idea and that those who ask for it are subversive. They believe that their caste system is the highest form of social organization.

The enlightened white Southerner, who for years has preached gradualism, now sees that even the slow approach finally has revolutionary implications. Placing straws on a camel's back, no matter how slowly, is dangerous. This realization has immobilized the liberals and most of the white church leaders. They have no answer for dealing with or absorbing violence. They end in begging for retreat, lest "things get out of hand and lead to violence."

Writing in *Life*, William Faulkner, Nobel prize-winning author from Mississippi, recently urged the NAACP to "stop now for a moment." That is to say, he encouraged Negroes to accept injustice, exploitation and indignity for a while longer. It is hardly a moral act to encourage others patiently to accept injustice which he himself does not endure.

In urging delay, which in this dynamic period is tantamount to retreat, Faulkner suggests that those of us who press for change now may not know that violence could break out. He says we are "dealing with a fact: the fact of emotional conditions of such fierce unanimity as to scorn the fact that it is a minority and which will go to any length and against any odds at this moment to justify and, if necessary, defend that condition and its right to it."

We Southern Negroes believe that it is essential to defend the right of equality now. From this position we will not and cannot retreat. Fortunately, we are increasingly aware that we must not try to defend our position by methods that contradict the aim of brotherhood. We in Montgomery believe that the only way to press on is by adopting the philosophy and practice of nonviolent resistance.

This method permits a struggle to go on with dignity and without the need to retreat. It is a method that can absorb the violence that is inevitable in social change whenever deep-seated prejudices are challenged.

If, in pressing for justice and equality in Montgomery, we discover that those who reject equality are prepared to use violence, we must not despair, retreat, or fear. Before they make this crucial decision, they must remember: whatever they do, we will not use violence in return. We hope we can act in the struggle in such a way that they will see the error of their approach and will come to respect us. Then we can all live together in peace and equality.

The basic conflict is not really over the buses. Yet we believe that, if the method we use in dealing with equality in the buses can eliminate injustice within ourselves, we shall at the same time be attacking the basis of injustice—man's hostility to man. This can only be done when we challenge the white community to re-examine its assumptions as we are now prepared to re-examine ours.

We do not wish to triumph over the white community. That would only result in transferring those now on the bottom to the top. But, if we can live up to nonviolence in thought and deed, there will emerge an interracial society based on freedom for all.

Robert F. Williams

Can Negroes Afford to Be Pacifists?*

In 1954 I was an enlisted man in the United States Marine Corps. As a Negro in an intergrated unit that was overwhelmingly white, I shall never forget the evening we were lounging in the recreation room watching television as a news bulletin flashed on the screen. This was the historic Supreme Court decision that segregation in the public schools is unconstitutional. Because of the interracial atmosphere, there was no vocal comment. There was for a while complete silence. I never knew how the Southern white boys felt about this bulletin. Perhaps I never will, but as for myself, my inner emotions must have been approximate to the Negro slaves' when they first heard about the Emancipation Proclamation. Elation took hold of me so strongly that I found it very difficult to refrain from yielding to an urge of jubilation. I learned later that night that other Negroes in my outfit had felt the same surge of elation.

On this momentous night of May 17, 1954, I felt that at last the government was willing to assert itself on behalf of first-class citizenship, even for Negroes. I experienced a sense of loyalty that I had never felt before. I was sure that this was the beginning of a new era of American democracy. At last I felt that I was a part of America and that I belonged. That was what I had always wanted, even as a child.

I returned to civilian life in 1955 and the hope I had for Negro liberation faltered. I had returned to a South that was determined to stay the hand of progress at all cost. Acts of violence and words and deeds of hate and spite rose from every quarter. An attitude prevailed that Negroes had a court decree from the "Communist inspired court," but the local

* September, 1959.

racist had the means to initiate the old law of the social jungle called Dixie. Since the first Negro slaves arrived in America, the white supremacists have relied upon violence as a potent weapon of intimidation to deprive Negroes of their rights. The Southerner is not prone to easy change; therefore the same tactics that proved so successful against Negroes through the years are still being employed today. There is open defiance to law and order throughout the South today. Governor Faubus and the Little Rock campaign was a shining example of the Southern racists' respect for the law of the land and constituted authority.

The State of Virginia is in open defiance of federal authority. States like my native state of North Carolina are submitting to token integration and openly boasting that this is the solution to circumvention of the Supreme Court decisions. The officials of this state brazenly slap themselves on the back for being successful in depriving great numbers of their colored citizens of the rights of first-class citizenship. Yes, after having such great short-lived hope, I have become disillusioned about the prospect of a just, democratic-minded government motivated by politicians with high moral standards enforcing the Fourteenth Amendment without the pressure of expediency.

News Blackout

Since my release from the Marine Corps I could cite many cases of unprovoked violence that have been visited upon my people. Some, like the Emmett Till case, the Asbury Howard case and the Mack Parker incident, have been widely publicized. There are more, many many more, occurring daily in the South that never come to the light of the press because of a news blackout sponsored by local racist officials.

Laws serve to deter crime and to protect the weak from the strong in civilized society. When there is a breakdown of law and the right of equal protection by constituted authority, where is the force of deterrent? It is the nature of people to respect law when it is just and strong. Only highly civilized and moral individuals respect the rights of others. The low-mentality bigots of the South have shown a wanton disregard for the well-being and rights of their fellow men of color, but there is one thing that even the most savage beast respects, and that is force. Soft, polished words whispered into the ears of a brute make him all the more confused and rebellious against a society that is more than he can understand or feel secure in. The Southern brute respects only force. Nonviolence is a very potent weapon when the opponent is civilized, but nonviolence is no match or repellent for a sadist. I have great respect for the pacifist, that is, for the pure pacifist. I think a pure pacifist is one who resents violence against nations as well as individuals and is courageous enough to speak out against jingoistic governments (including his own) without an air of self-righteousness and pious moral individuality. I am not a pacifist and I am sure that I may safely say that most of my people are not. Passive resistance is a powerful weapon in gaining concessions from oppressors, but I venture to say that if Mack Parker had had an automatic shotgun at his disposal, he could have served as a great deterrent against lynching.

"Turn-the-other-cheekism"

Rev. Martin Luther King is a great and successful leader of our race. The Montgomery bus boycott was a great victory for American democracy. However, most people have confused the issues facing the race. In Montgomery the issue was a matter of struggle for human dignity. Nonviolence is made to order for that type of conflict. While praising the actions of those courageous Negroes who participated in the Montgomery affair, we must not allow the complete aspects of the Negro struggle throughout the South to be taken out of their proper perspective. In a great many localities in the South Negroes are faced with the necessity of combating savage violence. The struggle is for mere existence. The Negro is in a position of begging for life. There is no lawful deterrent against those who would do him violence. An open declaration of nonviolence, or turn-the-other-cheekism, is an invitation that the white racist brutes will certainly honor by brutal attack on cringing, submissive Negroes. It is time for the Negro in the South to reappraise his method of dealing with his ruthless oppressor.

In 1957 the Klan moved into Monroe and Union counties.

In the beginning we did not notice them much. Their numbers steadily increased to the point wherein the local press reported as many as seventy-five hundred racists massed at one rally. They became so brazen that mile-long motorcades started invading the Negro community. These hooded thugs fired pistols from car windows, screamed, and incessantly blew their automobile horns. On one occasion they caught a Negro woman on the street and tried to force her to dance for them at gun point. She escaped into the night, screaming and hysterical. They forced a Negro merchant to close down his business on direct orders from the Klan. Drivers of cars tried to run Negroes down when seen walking on the streets at night. Negro women were struck with missiles thrown from passing vehicles. Lawlessness was rampant. A Negro doctor was framed to jail on a charge of performing an abortion on a white woman. This doctor, who was vice-president of the N. A. A. C. P., was placed in a lonely cell in the basement of a jail, although men prisoners are usually confined upstairs. A crowd of white men started congregating around the jail. It is common knowledge that a lynching was averted. We have had the usual threats of the Klan here, but instead of cowing, we organized an armed guard and set up a defense force around the doctor's house. On one occasion, we had to exchange gunfire with the Klan. Each time the Klan came on a raid they were led by police cars. We appealed to the President of the United States to have the Justice Department investigate the police. We appealed to Governor Luther Hodges. All our appeals to constituted law were in vain. Governor Hodges, in an underhanded way, defended the Klan. He publicly made a statement, to the press, that I had exaggerated Klan activity in Union County—despite the fact that they were operating openly and had gone so far as to build a Klan clubhouse and advertise meetings in the local press and on the radio.

Cringing Negro Ministers

A group of nonviolent ministers met the city Board of Aldermen and pleaded with them to restrict the Klan from the colored community. The city fathers advised these cringing, begging Negro ministers that the Klan had constitutional rights to meet and organize in the same way as the N. A. A. C. P. Not having been infected by turn-the-other-cheekism, a group of Negroes who showed a willingness to fight caused the city officials to deprive the Klan of its constitutional rights after local papers told of dangerous incidents between Klansmen and armed Negroes. Klan motorcades have been legally banned from the City of Monroe.

The possibility of tragedy's striking both sides of the tracks has caused a mutual desire to have a peaceful coexistence. The fact that any racial brutality may cause white blood to flow as well as Negro is lessening racial tension. The white bigots are sparing Negroes from brutal attack, not because of a new sense of morality, but because Negroes have adopted a policy of meeting violence with violence.

The Screams of the Innocent

I think there is enough latitude in the struggle for Negro liberation for the acceptance of diverse tactics and philosophies. There is need for pacifists and non-pacifists. I think each freedom fighter must unselfishly contribute what he has to offer. I have been a soldier and a Marine. I have been trained in the way of violence. I have been trained to defend myself. Self-defense to a Marine is a reflex action. People like Rev. Martin Luther King have been trained for the pulpit. I think they would be as out of place in a conflict that demanded real violent action as I would in a pulpit praying for an indifferent God to come down from Heaven and rescue a screaming Mack Parker or Emmett Till from an ungodly howling mob. I believe if we are going to pray, we ought to pass the ammunition while we pray. If we are too pious to kill in our own self-defense, how can we have the heart to ask a Holy God to come down to this violent fray and smite down our enemies?

As a race, we have been praying for three hundred years. The N. A. A. C. P. boasts that it has fought against lynching for fifty years. A fifty-year fight without victory is not impressive to me. An unwritten anti-lynch law was initiated overnight in Monroe. It is strange that so-called Negro leaders have never stopped to think why a simple thing like an anti-lynch law in a supposedly democratic nation is next to impossible to get passed. Surely every citizen in a republic is entitled not to be lynched. To seek an anti-lynch law in the present situation is to seek charity. Individuals and governments are more inclined to do things that promote a general welfare and well-being of the populace. A prejudiced government and a prejudiced people are not going to throw a shield of protection around the very people in the South on whom they vent pent-up hatreds as scapegoats. When white people in the South start needing such a law, we will not even have to wait fifty days to get it.

Stop Lynching with Violence

On May 5, 1959, while president of the Union County branch of the National Association for the Advancement of Colored People, I made a statement to the United Press International after a trial wherein a white man was supposed to have been tried for kicking a Negro maid down a flight of stairs in a local white hotel. In spite of the fact that there was an eyewitness, the defendent failed to show up for his trial, and was completely exonerated. Another case in the same court involved a white man who had come to a pregnant Negro mother's home and attempted to rape her. In recorder's court the only defense offered for the defendant was that "he's not guilty. He was just drunk and having a little fun." Despite the fact that this pregnant Negro mother was brutally beaten and driven from her home because she refused to submit, and a white woman neighbor testified that the woman had come to her house excited, her clothes torn, her feet bare, and begging her for assistance, the court was unmoved. The defendant's wife was allowed to sit with him throughout the trial, and his attorney asked the jury if they thought this white man would leave "this beautiful white woman, the flower of life, for this Negro woman." Some of the jurymen laughed and the defendant went free. This great miscarriage of justice left me sick inside, and I said then what I say now. I believe that Negroes must be willing to defend themselves, their women, their children and their homes. They must be willing to die and to kill in repelling their assailants. There is no Fourteenth Amendment, no equal protection under the law. Negroes *must* protect them-

selves, it is obvious that the federal government will not put an
end to lynching; therefore it becomes necessary for us to stop
lynching with violence. We must defend ourselves. Even
though I made it known that I spoke as an individual American citizen, I was suspended by the N. A. A. C. P. for advocating violence. The N. A. A. C. P. was so fearful of the consequence of this statement that I heard about my suspension
over the radio before I got an official notice. The radio an-
nouncer tried to give local Negroes the impression that the
N. A. A. C. P. advocated turn-the-other-cheekism. The thing
that struck me most was not the suspension, but the number of
letters and telegrams I received from Negroes all over America who showed a readiness to fight. The Negro on the street
who suffers most is beginning to break out of the harness of
the nonviolent race preachers. The fact that the N. A. A. C. P.
had to issue a statement saying, "The N. A. A. C. P. has never
condoned mob violence but it firmly supports the right of Negroes individually and collectively to defend their person, their
homes and their property from attack" is a strong indication of
the sentiment among the masses of Negroes. How can an individual defend his person and property from attack without
meeting violence with violence? What the N. A. A. C. P. is
advocating now is no more than I had advocated in the first
place. I could never advocate that Negroes attack white people
indiscriminately. Our branch of the N. A. A. C. P. in Union
County is an interracial branch.

King Cashes in on War

It is obvious that the Negro leadership is caught in a terrible
dilemma. It is trying to appease both white liberals who want
to see Negro liberation given to us in eye-dropper doses and
the Negro masses who are growing impatient and restive
under brutal oppression. There is a new Negro coming into
manhood on the American scene and an indifferent government must take cognizance of this fact. The Negro is becoming
more militant, and pacifism will never be accepted wholeheartedly by the masses of Negroes so long as violence is
rampant in Dixie. Even Negroes like King who profess to be
pacifists are not pure pacifists and at times speak proudly of

the Negro's role of violence in this violent nation's wars. In a speech at the N. A. A. C. P. convention, he said, "In spite of all of our oppression, we have never turned to a foreign ideology to solve our problems. Communism has never invaded our ranks. And now we are simply saying we want our freedom, we have stood with you in every crisis. For you, America, our sons died in the trenches of France, in the foxholes of Germany, on the beachheads of Italy and on the islands of Japan. And now, America, we are simply asking you to guarantee our freedom." King may not be willing to partake in expeditions of violence, but he has no compunction about cashing in on the spoils of war. There are too many Negro leaders who are afraid to talk violence against the violent racist and are too weak-kneed to protest the warmongering of the atom-crazed politicians of Washington.

Some Negro leaders have cautioned me that if Negroes fight back, the racist will have cause to exterminate the race. How asinine can one get? This government is in no position to allow mass violence to erupt, let alone allow twenty million Negroes to be exterminated. I am not half so worried about being exterminated as I am about my children's growing up under oppression and being mentally twisted out of human proportions.

We live in perilous times in America, and especially in the South. Segregation is an expensive commodity, but liberty and democracy, too, have their price. So often the purchase check of democracy must be signed in blood. Someone must be willing to pay the price, despite the scoffs from the Uncle Toms. I am told that patience is commendable and that we must never tire of waiting, yet it is instilled at an early age that men who violently and swiftly rise to oppose tyranny are virtuous examples to emulate. I have been taught by my government to fight, and if I find it necessary I shall do just that. All Negroes must learn to fight back, for nowhere in the annals of history does the record show a people delivered from bondage by patience alone.

Dave Dellinger

Are Pacifists Willing to Be Negroes?

Robert F. Williams makes a strong case for a negative answer
to the question many Negroes are asking these days [1959]:
Can Negroes afford to be nonviolent? The Montgomery bus
protest, which was once hailed as a portent of greater victories
to come, is fast becoming an icon for pacifist devotions. In
Alabama and Mississippi, in North Carolina and Virginia, in
Little Rock and Tallahassee, the organized movement for
liberation is virtually at a standstill. In almost any southern
town, the individual Negro who dares to assert his dignity as a
human being in the concrete relationships of everyday life
rather than in the privileged sanctuary of the pulpit is in danger of meeting the fate of Mack Parker or Emmett Till.

    In such a situation, it would be arrogant for us to criticize
a Robert Williams for arming in defense of himself and his
neighbors. Gandhi once said that although nonviolence is the
best method of resistance to evil, it is better for persons who
have not yet attained the capacity for nonviolence to resist
violently than not to resist at all. Since we have failed to reach
the level of effective resistance, we can hardly condemn those
who have not embraced nonviolence. Nonviolence without
resistance to evil is like a soul without a body. Perhaps it has
some meaning in heaven but not in the world we live in. At
this point, we should be more concerned with our own failure
as pacifists to help spread the kind of action undertaken at
Montgomery than with the failure of persons like Williams
who, in many cases, are the only ones who stand between an
individual Negro and a marauding Klan.

    When nonviolence works, as it sometimes does against
seemingly hopeless odds, it succeeds by disarming its opponents. It does this through intensive application of the insight

that our worst enemy is actually a friend in disguise. The nonviolent resister identifies so closely with his opponent that he feels his problems as if they were his own, and is therefore unable to hate or hurt him, even in self-defense. This inability to injure an aggressor, even at the risk of one's own life, is based not on a denial of the self in obedience to some external ethical command but on an extension of the self to include one's adversary. "Any man's death diminishes me."

But it is a perversion of nonviolence to identify only with the aggressor and not with his victims. The failure of pacifists with respect to the South has been our failure to identify with "a screaming Mack Parker" or with any of the oppressed and intimidated Negroes. Like the liberals, we have made a "token" identification to the point of feeling indignant at lynching and racist oppression, but we have not identified ourselves with the victims to the point where we feel the hurts as if they were our own. It is difficult to say what we would be doing now if Emmett Till had been our own son or if other members of our family were presently living in the South under the daily humiliations suffered by Negroes. But it is a good bet that we would not be in our present state of lethargy. We would not find it so easy to ask them to be patient and long-suffering and nonviolent in the face of our own failure to launch a positive nonviolent campaign for protection and liberation. The real question today is not, can Negroes afford to be pacifists, but are pacifists willing to be Negroes?

This question is particularly pointed in the South, and those of us who live in the North should not feel overconfident as to how we would act if we lived there. But the tragic fact is that in the South the bulk of the members of the Society of Friends and of other pacifist groups live down to the rules of segregation, much as other people do. Only a few scattered individuals, like Carl and Anne Braden in Louisville, Kentucky, and a few intentional communities, like Koinonia in Americus, Georgia and the Highlander Folk School in Monteagle, Tennessee break significantly with the pattern of segregation. So long as this pattern is maintained, a temporary absence of overt violence only means the appearance of peace when there is no peace. Human beings must love one another, or they will learn to hate one another. Segregation is incompatible with love. Sooner or later, segregation must erupt into violence, and those white persons who conform to the practice of segregation are as surely responsible as those of either color who bring out the guns.

Robert Williams makes a bad mistake when he implies that the only alternative to violence is the approach of the "cringing, begging Negro ministers," who appealed to the city for protection and then retired in defeat. The power of the police, as the power of the F. B. I., the courts, and the Federal government, is rooted in violence. The fact that the violence does not always come into bloody play does not alter the fact that the power of the government is not the integrating power of love but the disintegrating power of guns and prisons. Unfortunately, too many of those who hailed the precedent of the Montgomery bus protest have turned away from its example and have been carrying on the fight in the courts or by appeals to legislators and judges.

In Montgomery, it was Rosa Parks, Martin King and their comrades who went to jail, not the segregationists. The power of the action lay partly in the refusal of the participants to accept defeat when the power of the local government was stacked against them, partly in their refusal to cooperate with the evil practice (riding in segregated buses) and partly in the spirit of dignity and love expressed in the words and actions of King.

It would be foolhardy for a white Northerner to present a blueprint for a specific large-scale action which would apply the lessons of Montgomery to other situations in the South. But it is significant that the Montgomery action developed when a single woman, Rosa Parks, found herself psychologically unable to comply with an order to get in the back of a bus.

Those of us who are white will never experience the indignities that are imposed from birth to burial on our colored brothers. But the least we can do while working for another Montgomery is to refuse to conform to segregation wherever we are. At home and when travelling in the South, we can refuse to eat in segregated restaurants, to stay in segregated hotels, to shop in segregated stores, or to use "White Only" toilets. We can refuse to attend segregated churches or send our children to segregated schools. These simple acts of identification and decency could turn out to be more revolutionary than we dare hope.

Martin Luther King, Jr.

The Social Organization of Nonviolence
(A Reply to Robert F. Williams)

Paradoxically, the struggle for civil rights has reached a stage of profound crisis, although its outward aspect is distinctly less turbulent and victories of token integration have been won in the hard-resistance areas of Virginia and Arkansas.

The crisis has its origin in a decision rendered by the Supreme Court more than a year ago which upheld the pupil placement law. Though little noticed then, this decision fundamentally weakened the historic 1954 ruling of the Court. It is imperceptibly becoming the basis of a *de facto* compromise between the powerful contending forces.

The 1954 decision required for effective implementation resolute Federal action supported by mass action to undergird all necessary changes. It is obvious that Federal action by the legislative and executive branches was half-hearted and inadequate. The activity of Negro forces, while heroic in some instances, and impressive in other sporadic situations, lacked consistency and militancy sufficient to fill the void left by government default. The segregationists were swift to seize these advantages, and unrestrained by moral or social conscience, defied the law boldly and brazenly.

The net effect of this social equation has led to the present situation, which is without clearcut victory for either side. Token integration is a developing pattern. This type of integration is merely an affirmation of a principle without the substance of change.

It is, like the Supreme Court decision, a pronouncement of justice, but by itself does not insure that the millions of Negro children will be educated in conditions of equality. This is not to say that it is without value. It has substantial importance.

However, it fundamentally changes the outlook of the whole
movement, for it raises the prospect of long, slow change without a predictable end. As we have seen in Northern cities,
token integration has become a pattern in many communities
and remained frozen, even though environmental attitudes are
substantially less hostile to full integration than in the South.

Three Views of Violence

This then is the danger. Full integration can easily become a
distant or mythical goal—major integration may be long post-
poned, and in the quest for social calm a compromise firmly
implanted in which the real goals are merely token integration
for a long period to come.

The Negro was the tragic victim of another compromise in
1878, when his full equality was bargained away by the Federal Government and a condition somewhat above slave status
but short of genuine citizenship became his social and political
existence for nearly a century.

There is reason to believe that the Negro of 1959 will not
accept supinely any such compromises in the contemporary
struggle for integration. His struggle will continue, but the
obstacles will determine its specific nature. It is axiomatic in
social life that the imposition of frustrations leads to two kinds
of reactions. One is the development of a wholesome social
organization to resist with effective firm measures any efforts to
impede progress. The other is a confused, anger-motivated
drive to strike back violently, to inflict damage. Primarily, it
seeks to cause injury, to retaliate for wrongful suffering. Sec-
ondarily, it seeks real progress. It is punitive—not radical or
constructive.

The current calls for violence have their roots in this latter
tendency. Here one must be clear that there are three different
views on the subject of violence. One is the approach of pure
nonviolence, which cannot readily or easily attract large
masses, for it requires extraordinary discipline and courage.
The second is violence exercised in self-defense, which all societies, from the most primitive to the most cultured and civilized, accept as moral and legal. The principle of self-defense,
even involving weapons and bloodshed, has never been con-

demned, even by Gandhi, who sanctioned it for those unable to master pure nonviolence. The third is the advocacy of violence as a tool of advancement, organized as in warfare, deliberately and consciously. To this tendency many Negroes are being tempted today. There are incalculable perils in this approach. It is not the danger or sacrifice of physical being which is primary, though it cannot be contemplated without a sense of deep concern for human life. The greatest danger is that it will fail to attract Negroes to a real collective struggle, and will confuse the large uncommitted middle group, which as yet has not supported either side. Further, it will mislead Negroes into the belief that this is the only path, and place them as a minority in a position where they confront a far larger adversary than it is possible to defeat in this form of combat. When the Negro uses force in self-defense he does not forfeit support—he may even win it, by the courage and self-respect it reflects. When he seeks to initiate violence he provokes questions about the necessity for it, and inevitably is blamed for its consequences. It is unfortunately true that however the Negro acts, his struggle will not be free of violence initiated by his enemies, and he will need ample courage and willingness to sacrifice to defeat this manifestation of violence. But if he seeks it and organizes it, he cannot win. Does this leave the Negro without a positive method to advance? Mr. Robert Williams would have us believe that there is no effective and practical alternative. He argues that we must be cringing and submissive or take up arms. To so place the issue distorts the whole problem. There are other meaningful alternatives.

The Negro people can organize socially to initiate many forms of struggle which can drive their enemies back without resort to futile and harmful violence. In the history of the movement for racial advancement, many creative forms have been developed—the mass boycott, sit-down protests and strikes, sit-ins—refusal to pay fines and bail for unjust arrests—mass marches—mass meetings—prayer pilgrimages, etc. Indeed, in Mr. Williams' own community of Monroe, North Carolina, a striking example of collective community action won a significant victory without use of arms or threats of violence. When the police incarcerated a Negro doctor unjustly, the aroused people of Monroe marched to the police station, crowded into its halls and corridors, and refused to leave until their colleague was released. Unable to arrest everyone, the authorities released the doctor and neither side attempted to unleash violence. This experience was related by the doctor who was the intended victim.

There is more power in socially organized masses on the march than there is in guns in the hands of a few desperate men. Our enemies would prefer to deal with a small armed group rather than with a huge, unarmed but resolute mass of people. However, it is necessary that the mass-action method be persistent and unyielding. Gandhi said the Indian people must "never let them rest," referring to the British. He urged them to keep protesting daily and weekly, in a variety of ways. This method inspired and organized the Indian masses and disorganized and demobilized the British. It educates its myriad participants, socially and morally. All history teaches us that like a turbulent ocean beating great cliffs into fragments of rock, the determined movement of people incessantly demanding their rights always disintegrates the old order.

It is this form of struggle—non-cooperation with evil through mass actions—"never letting them rest"—which offers the more effective road for those who have been tempted and goaded to violence. It needs the bold and the brave because it is not free of danger. It faces the vicious and evil enemies squarely. It requires dedicated people, because it is a backbreaking task to arouse, to organize, and to educate tens of thousands for disciplined, sustained action. From this form of struggle more emerges that is permanent and damaging to the enemy than from a few acts of organized violence.

Our present urgent necessity is to cease our internal fighting and turn outward to the enemy, using every form of mass action yet known—create new forms—and resolve never to let them rest. This is the social lever which will force open the door to freedom. Our powerful weapons are the voices, the feet, and the bodies of dedicated, united people, moving without rest toward a just goal. Greater tyrants than Southern segregationists have been subdued and defeated by this form of struggle. We have not yet used it, and it would be tragic if we

spurn it because we have failed to perceive its dynamic
strength and power.

Cashing In on War?

I am reluctant to inject a personal defense against charges by
Mr. Williams that I am inconsistent in my struggle against war
and too weak-kneed to protest nuclear war. Merely to set the
record straight, may I state that repeatedly, in public addresses
and in my writings, I have unequivocally declared my hatred
for this most colossal of all evils and I have condemned any
organizer of war, regardless of his rank or nationality. I have
signed numerous statements with other Americans condemning nuclear testing and have authorized publication of my
name in advertisements appearing in the largest circulation
newspapers in the country, without concern that it was then
"unpopular" to so speak out.

A. J. *Muste* and *Bayard Rustin*

Struggle for Integration—1960

Not many months ago the movement for liberation of Negroes in the South, which had been highlighted by the struggles in Montgomery and Little Rock, was in the doldrums. Instead of massive initiative being developed by the Negro people, their organizations and their leaders, it was those who opposed the democratization and humanization of American, and particularly of Southern, society who were organizing massive resistance.

The resistance to integration of the public schools and to recognition of the right of Negroes to the vote has, of course, not been free from outright violence on the part of extremists and brutality on the part of the police. In the main, however, it has not taken the form of naked and unabashed violence, as in an earlier period it might have done. For obvious reasons, white people and their agencies of government cannot operate in the United States in exactly the same way as in South Africa. Moreover, it would not have been easy to resort to naked violence against a movement which had Martin Luther King, Jr., an exponent and practitioner of the Gandhian philosophy and tactic of nonviolent direct action, as its symbol.

Southern resistance has mainly taken two forms. In the first place, there are the various ways in which legislative and judicial machinery is used to thwart the 1954 Supreme Court decision providing for public school integration. One of the architects of this policy is said to have boasted that segregationists would tie the movement for liberation up in "a century of legislation and litigation." They certainly did slow it down to not much more than a crawl, as the pattern of "token integration," which is actually a denial of integration, was established where simple refusal to do anything did not suffice.

The second form of resistance to basic change in the structure of Southern society was cultural or spiritual, which is not to say that it does not have massive political consequences. The weight of Southern thinking, sentiment, emotional reaction, has remained on the side of segregation, i.e. of inequality, i.e. of white supremacy. Most so-called progressive or liberal opinion, at least insofar as it achieves organized expression, is *for* segregation; but *against* closing the public schools rather than acquiescing in token integration; *against* mob violence; *against* crude but *not against* subtle defiance of the Supreme Court decision, and so on. But this is equivalent to saying that the basic human and political issue of equality, whether we are indeed a "new nation . . . dedicated to the proposition that all men are created equal," has been decided in the negative by the majority of Southerners, whether consciously and deliberately or passively and by default. This is indeed "massive" resistance.

There are certain negative factors also contributing to the slowing down of the Negro movement, which we can only list in passing. Firstly, there is no political democracy in the South, even to the extent that this obtains in other sections of the country. The South is dominated by a one-party political régime, which distorts, when it does not absolutely frustrate, anything like popular discussion of issues and consequent decisions. Secondly, Negroes have virtually no share in the control of law-enforcement machinery. Thirdly, the economic status of Negroes is inferior. This holds true of all but a small minority of individual Negroes. Equally important is the fact that Negro finance, business and industrial institutions are relatively weak and have to operate in an economy controlled by whites.

Fourthly, the labor movement in the South is woefully weak, and the labor movement in the country as a whole generally lacks social vision and militancy. It offers no substantial opposition to the nuclear-war policy of the Democratic and Republican parties, even when it does not wholeheartedly support that policy. It has been divided in its own mind over the race issue and lacked the vision and courage to mount a vigorous campaign to organize Southern Negroes and whites together in powerful unions, when Montgomery and the Supreme Court decision opened the way for such a move.

As we have said, the liberation movement was badly bogged down a few months ago. The leaders did not provide a strong program and clear initiative. During the disgraceful filibuster over the civil rights bill in the Senate, not a single move was made by any of the organizations to launch a stern and dramatic protest. Then the student sit-ins in one Southern city after another "bailed them out," if we may use that expression to state a sociological fact, not to cast slurs at individual leaders. These sit-ins were essentially spontaneous. They occurred, of course, in the context of the struggles, frustrations and disappointments to which we have referred. But, in the first place, neither Communists (who simply don't count in situations of this kind in the United States, whatever J. Edgar Hoover may believe or pretend to believe) nor anybody from the North, thought up and organized the sit-in demonstrations. Southerners who know such allegations are false but make them nonetheless are political scoundrels, and in the present world situation are playing with fire. Southerners who honestly think that such things as the sit-ins could not happen "spontaneously", i.e. simply because the more well-to-do, the best educated, the most disciplined and cultured—*essentially middle-class*—Negro students were fed up with racial discrimination, are the benighted victims of a caste-structured society and of mis-education and non-education, for which the white "Christian" churches in the South—it includes after all the "Bible Belt"—are chiefly responsible.

But it is even more important that the sit-ins were spontaneous in the sense that no organization, such as the N.A.A.C.P. or the Southern Christian Leadership Conference, thought them up and organized them. For the time being, it is the students who have given a lift to the organizations rather than the other way around. The sit-ins have conferred a fresh importance on such men as Roy Wilkins and Martin Luther King, Jr.—to use them as symbols—and have given them subject matter for their pronouncements.

Within a single week, each of these men recently issued a call to action. On May 2nd, according to the New York *Herald-*

Tribune of the following day, King, in Atlanta, confirmed a report that Negroes will go to registration places and voting places in the hundreds of thousands, refusing to move until satisfaction is obtained. He endorsed the statement of an associate that "the greatest progress of the American Negro in the future will not be made in Congress or in the Surpreme Court. It will come in the jails," as Negroes refuse to dissipate money and energy in raising bail and carrying on countless time-consuming legal battles, and instead choose jail, emulating the Indians in their nonviolent struggle for independence under Gandhi.

Shortly thereafter, Roy Wilkins, speaking at a conference of N.A.A.C.P. leaders, also in Atlanta, according to the New York *Times* of May 8th, announced on behalf of the N.A.A.C.P. a "wade-in" campaign on Southern beaches from Cape May, New Jersey, to Brownsville, Texas. Negroes, Wilkins pointed out, pay taxes to maintain the public beaches, "they get hot just like white folks do"; and they are going swimming "this summer." Along with this campaign, school desegregation, ending discrimination at lunch counters, and registration at the polls are to be vigorously pressed.

Revolutions, however, are not made by militant statements. Nor for that matter are they successfully carried out merely by a series of spontaneous demonstrations. Given the external conditions which made radical changes desirable and even necessary, success depends upon a creative integration of mass need and impulse, on the one hand, and great, dedicated leadership, on the other.

Whether, in the current Southern struggle, words are to be translated into competent and sustained action, is, with the exception of the issue of nuclear war, the most important question before the American people today. We used the word "revolution" advisedly a moment ago. If Negroes come out of the current struggles with their feet firmly set on the road to equality and recognized as human beings (without quibble or reservation) the whole structure of Southern society will be transformed. A "way of life," as the phrase goes, will cease to be. The people who have lived under it—whites and Negroes alike—will be liberated.

The transformation of the social structure will have all kinds of repercussions. The Democratic Party in the South will be shaken. In fact, in its present form and structure, it will disappear, which is not the least of the reasons why Southern Democratic politicians are so bitterly opposed to the integration movement and why they are so indifferent to the advantages that accrue to Communism from the persistence of discrimination in this country. These people would apparently rather see Communism triumph than pay the price of its defeat by abandoning their "way of life" and their power. There is no phonier political phenomenon today than Senator Eastland's Committee on Internal Security, with its "war" on Communism! It is needless to add that the demise of the Southern Democratic Party as now constituted will have repercussions elsewhere.

If the Negro liberation movement succeeds, this means that white and Negro workers in the South will accept each other as human beings, and will be organized into mass unions. This in turn means that the color line will be wiped out in all unions. Moreover, the organization of Southern labor and the accompanying impetus to organization elsewhere, will almost certainly lead to a much greater strengthening of the labor movement and (let us hope) a deeper transformation of its social vision than took place in the halcyon days of the upsurge of organization in the late Thirties and early Forties.

To cite another future possibility, liberation of Negroes in the South will require a great moral effort on the part of a people and will bring with it a great release of moral energy. This will be especially true if the movement remains nonviolent or—to speak more accurately—becomes deeply nonviolent in spirit, in program and in tactics, i.e. revolutionary in the profoundest and finest sense. If this happens, it will greatly affect the whole of American life, including our attitude toward war and our relations with the rest of the world.

Such things may happen. There is no "law" which says they must. Despite inspiring and heroic episodes in the liberation struggle, despite the emergence from time to time of appealing figures among adults or youth, no true revolution and renewal will take place without planning, without program, without leadership and discipline and sacrifice. If there is a vacuum so far as these items are concerned, vested interests among Negroes will assert themselves, as they are already doing in places where Negro teachers don't want public-school integration "hurried," although it has been delayed for a century, and Negro bishops don't want churches integrated, although this question should have been settled once and for all nineteen centuries ago. The politicians who want to see the *status quo* maintained in American life generally will stand ready to provide "leadership" that will direct discontent into safe channels. They will neutralize the one element—the Negroes of the United States, and especially of the South—who, driven by their immediate needs and grievances, may provide the driving force to break the crust of custom and of apathy and provide American life with *élan* and vision. Lacking this, American life may remain outwardly tolerable for a time. But for its own people it will be stale and frustrating.

Hard Facts the Leaders Must Face

Those who undertake a revolution, as is the case with those in the South who call for freedom and human equality for Negroes, are obligated to try at least to see it through. By definition, they have undertaken a job which cannot be accomplished entirely, or perhaps even mainly, through the existing social and political machinery. It is to a large extent the existing structures and mechanisms which prevent accomplishment, as we are freshly reminded by the passage of the much touted civil rights bill, allegedly to facilitate registration of Negroes. Action which is illegal under current definitions cannot be avoided.

Where does the power reside which can advance the movement for Negro liberation? As everyone sees at certain moments (during the Montgomery bus protest or lunch counter sit-ins), the power is in mass action by the Negro people. This is not merely a matter of numbers, though they are a factor. It is a matter of human solidarity, of the moral power that is generated when people who have been fragmented individuals for having accepted inferior status, are transformed, because together they demand freedom. It is this power which suddenly causes an imposing structure of custom, law, authority and force to crumble because people unitedly stop respecting it and conforming to it.

To assert that power derives from mass direct action is not to say that other means, such as legislative or judicial procedures, have no place. It is to say that without direct action, they are impotent, and may even be diversionary and enfeebling. It is to say that they must supplement and serve direct action, not vice versa.

Mass action is a mere gesture unless those who engage in it are prepared for mass arrests. These are almost certain to take place. At that point again, the logic of mass action has to be followed. Without claiming that in all cases accepting bail, pleading not guilty and standing trial, appealing cases to higher courts, paying fines, etc., must be rejected, these things cannot be the central policy of a mass movement. They eat up money, and place the movement for liberation in a defensive position. They are likely to stall mass action until, months or years later, the outcome of appeals is decided. It all amounts to acquiescing in the slow grinding of the machinery which is there precisely to prevent the changes the mass movement seeks. It is more effective to fill the jails, and use the money for the families of the volunteers than to throw it into the jaws of the legal mills.

The thesis that mass action leads to jail applies to leaders as well as to the rank and file. When you go to newly independent countries these days, in India or Africa, you find that practically every cabinet member, every leading labor unionist, writer and professional man, served one or more terms in prison for challenging the old régime. We are stating an obvious and often demonstrated fact, and not attempting to "tell somebody what to do," when we assert that leaders cannot expect students and workers to heed exhortations not to accept bail, not to pay fines, to go to jail, from leaders who do not follow their own advice.

The recognized leader of the movement for Negro liberation, the man who has become a symbol of the struggle and who evokes emotion so that people, Negro and white, identify with him (or react against him) is Martin Luther King, Jr.

King is a Southerner and his work has been and is in the South. It has been pointed out that this is the first time since Booker T. Washington's days that the leading Negroes have lived and operated in the South, because that is where the crucial battle is taking place, where Negroes can take mass action, and are driven to it because there is no alternative. This or that may happen to or be achieved by *individual* Negroes, but the Negro *people* will remain in bondage and humiliation unless the South's Negroes win freedom.

This factor—that leadership must be Southern and must be leadership of masses of people in motion—imposes itself upon the individuals and organizations in the field, as we see it. There is no escape from it. Individuals may have their rivalries, as they nearly always do. Organizations may have their established patterns, their vested interests, their competitions for funds, their ambitions. The individuals involved will, of course, have to deal with their respective conflicts. The various organizations in the field will have to resolve their conflicts and find ways of working together. God knows, there is no shortage of work to do. But it is not we—"outsiders," as it were —but the hard facts of the situation which say that Martin Luther King, Jr. and the Southern Christian Leadership Conference cannot escape the awful responsibility implied in this condition, that leadership has to be Southern. Equally, it is the tough political and social realities which say to the N.A.A.C.P. and any other organizations in the field and to their leaders that the crucial struggle is in the South, that the indispensable major instrument of that struggle is action which involves masses, and that leadership has to be indigenous to the South. This is not to say that *only* Southern Negroes can act, or that there are not other forms of action which are also necessary and tremendously helpful, if the condition we have mentioned is accepted and acted upon.

The Negro Church, N.A.A.C.P. and CORE

A second element in the strategy of the Southern struggle must be noted. Martin King is an ordained clergyman, and was the pastor of a local church when the Montgomery bus protest occurred and swept him up. We make no effort to explore the workings of this man's mind and spirit. That a preacher emerged as the leader of so formidable a social movement while remaining firmly rooted in the church as an institution— a very unusual development—is due to the special character of the Negro church, especially in the South. The fact that King's associates in the leadership of the broad movement and in the S.C.L.C. itself are also preachers, of course reinforces this point.

Psychologically, in spite of the "other-wordliness" expressed in familiar spirituals such as "Swing Low, Sweet Chariot," the church has been the channel for the expression of the Negroes' anguish under slavery and their unquenchable thirst for freedom and dignity, as evidenced in such spirituals as "Let My People Go." The church in the South has been the chief, almost the only, place where men of talent could arise. The leadership of preachers in the integration movement is a parallel to the leadership of the British unions, in their early period a century or more ago, by leaders trained as lay preachers in the Non-conformist chapels of England, Scotland and Wales. But perhaps the most important element is that economically the church is the one Negro institution which is basically independent of white control.

For all these reasons it is inevitable that a movement which involves Southern Negroes—and Negroes in motion— which is *their* movement and not something which is done for them by others, whether Negro or white, must be essentially church-centered and preacher-led.

On the one hand, organizations like N.A.A.C.P. and CORE can be immensely helpful if they accept this fact and build on it with real enthusiasm and, if one cares to put it in those terms, self-abnegation. If these organizations try to ignore or circumvent this element, to put up another symbol than the Negro preacher, to develop a rival center of power to that which is located in the church environment, vast harm may be done.

But this condition imposes very stern responsibilities on Martin Luther King Jr., on Abernathy, Lawson, Shuttlesworth, and others who might be named, and on the Negro churches in the South generally. Leaders have to lead. They have to de-

velop programs. A movement has to have structure and machinery, as was recognized when the Southern Christian Leadership Conference was set up. It is obvious that at least in
some cases leaders cannot at the same time carry on all the
manifold duties of parish ministers, even if they have "associates" and "assistants," and also discharge the duties involved in
S.C.L.C. leadership. It is our impression that this problem of
leadership and organizations has not yet been adequately
faced. Perhaps it will have to be faced and resolved soon if, for
example, the student sit-ins are not to prove another glorious
but isolated episode, rather than a serious action in a continu-
ous struggle, and if the movement for registration and the
greatly stepped-up exercise of the franchise is not to peter out.

We do not here enter into the very interesting question as
to what may be the internal development of the Negro church
as the nation moves toward an integrated society. What does
have to be noted here is that, central as the Negro churches are
at the moment, they do not by themselves constitute an adequate base even now, and that increasingly there must be
support from other social institutions.

This provides abundant opportunity for the organizations
especially devoted to the racial field that we have already
named. It also suggests the necessity for Negroes to have a
genuine voice in Southern political life and a share in civic
functions. Most importantly, it emphasizes the necessity for
close cooperation between the movement for integration and
the labor movement. For both it is essential that integrated
mass Southern unions be built. For the labor movement this
means that for the sake of its own future nationally it must
quickly increase its support of S.C.L.C. and the integration
movement generally. Most credit belongs to those unions and
union leaders, as yet far too few, who have seen this and have
given at least token financial, and thus moral, support to King
and others. In this field A. Philip Randolph has, of course,
for years been the prophet, the practical and imaginative
leader and the noble symbol. If the Negro Labor Congress
avoids becoming merely an instrument for Negro trade-union
office-holders to advance their own ambitions and instead
manages to carry on the great educational job which is re-

quired in the A.F.L.-C.I.O. to set in motion adequate support
of the Southern struggle for integration and a vigorous unioni-
zation campaign in the South, it will prove the crowning
achievement of Randolph's career.

Guerilla Warfare or Nonviolence?

We come now to the last major aspect of a viable approach to
the problem of liberation for the Negro people. We have referred to Martin Luther King Jr. and have pointed out that he
is and, so to speak, had to be a Southerner and a preacher.
Does anyone think that if he had been pastor of Wesley Methodist Church in Boston, Buffalo or Los Angeles, he would be in
the position in which he finds himself today? As we have said,
King is also an exponent and practitioner of nonviolent direct
action. Again, we need not dwell here on what Martin King's
personal faith is and how he came by it. Speaking politically,
nonviolence had to be and has to be the program of the
movement under discussion.

Sporadic resort to violence, in self-defense or even in retaliation, is understandable in some situations in the Deep South.
It is in fact inevitable that there should be such instances. But
the idea of solving the problem of Negroes in the South by
guerilla-war tactics is bizarre. It is hard to believe that anyone
who is capable of visualizing what it would lead to in practice
can seriously propose that Negroes and whites should engage
in a race for small arms and baby bombs. Moreover, if Southern Negroes are sufficiently united and determined to make
some kind of showing in armed conflict, they will have no need
of arms to make the present machinery of repression inopera-
tive.

But nonviolence is not a negative thing. It does not mean
the absence of violence, the renunciation of action, submission.
It means resort to a superior form of struggle, the tapping of
the reservoirs of moral force—"soul-force," as Gandhi called
it—which lie in human beings who individually and collectively assert their dignity as human beings and, being serenely
possessed of their own souls, refuse to strike back at those who
oppress and demean them but with equal resoluteness refuse
any longer to submit to oppression and humiliation. It is the

terrific moral force generated in those who are ready to die rather than submit longer to injustice. The big ultimate question is whether Southern Negroes in sufficient numbers have reached that point.

There is no time here for a detailed exposition of the philosophy of nonviolence, whether in a Christian, a Gandhian or any other form; but there is one aspect of this philosophy that seems to require interpretation for many involved in the integration struggle. Martin King exhorts his fellow-Negroes to "love your enemies," and there is reason to think a good many people, especially the young, misunderstand that phrase or simply do not get a coherent picture from it. It does not mean having a sentimental liking for people who spit on you. What is involved may be stated as follows.

The objective of the integration movement is to remove the present social structure, which makes some masters over others, which is so ordered that human beings whose skin is dark are humiliated, and human beings whose skin is light subject others to humiliation (which means that they, too, are humiliated). This system degrades everyone who lives under it. Community is impossible under such a structure. Suspicion and fear and neurosis are generated by it. Ultimately, the social fabric is torn asunder and individuals rush into hysteria. The objective is, then, to develop in the South, and elsewhere, a truly democratic social structure.

Everybody realizes that if such a society is to be possible, whites have to believe in the capacity of Negroes to be fully human. That is what it means for whites to "love" Negroes. To "hate" them is to refuse to recognize the Negro as fully human. Basically, this is what Southern whites, *operating in the social structure they still want to maintain,* are doing. Conversely, for Negroes to "love" white Southerners means to recognize that the whites have the capacity to be fully human. If this is not the case, no genuine new community, no democratic society, is possible in the South. Theoretically, a society in which the Negroes had subdued and dominated the whites might emerge. This is the nightmare which disturbs the sleep of some Southerners who are caught in the pattern of "white supremacy" and therefore unable to conceive of another basic pattern in which men live together as humans. But in fact a "black supremacy" régime is not remotely possible in the South, nor does any sane Negro want it. Therefore, Martin Luther King, Jr. is both spiritually and politically completely right in saying that Negroes must "love" white Southerners, i.e. believe in their capacity to be human. This faith will certainly find expression also in personal relations between individuals of both groups; but there is no genuine love in the personal and Christian sense, in spite of apparent exceptions, within a pattern of racial domination, among those who have not fundamentally broken out of that pattern.

All this finally means that in carrying on their relentless nonviolent struggle for their own liberation, *Negroes are liberating white Southerners.* This is the basic way in which the former express their "love" for the latter. White Southerners could not hand true freedom to Negroes, even if they wanted to. Nobody can bestow freedom on those who do not want it. And to "want" in this context does not mean to have a pale wish for freedom, but to have a hunger which can no longer be denied. It means to demand freedom and to be ready to die for it.

We are aware that we have left out of this discussion many items that would have to come into a comprehensive study, including most of what has to do with the problems and the rôle of Southern whites. But it remains true that the one great and indispensable element in that rôle is that they should recognize the "love" for them that is expressed in the nonviolent struggle for liberation; that Southern white society should therefore cease to fear this movement or try to dilute it, but should accept it and embrace it. If this is to say that love spells travail and that reconciliation is a painful process which involves not the covering up of issues and antagonisms but the bringing of them to the surface, this would simply mean that this struggle and its resolution has the same characteristics as all great human struggles and reconciliations.

David Wieck

The Invention of Responsibility

What we must do first of all is to extricate ourselves mentally from the *artificial* drama of which we have been witnesses [1957]. President Eisenhower has been criticized in the liberal press for his failure to act sooner, for his hesitation and post-ponement. As to the motivation of the President and his ad-visers, one must suspect a sympathy with the ancient racist patterns, conjoined with an ideology according to which the Chief-of-State must represent the whole of the State (the Law) and never a partisan faction; no doubt the Eisenhower group would be most pleased if the nine students would eliminate the whole difficulty by returning to the schools which the nine judges condemned to death. But this very procrastination, this very believe-no-evil policy, has had a remarkable subsidiary effect, an effect we ignore at our own risk, because the effect is on our thinking. The drama of good and evil, of right and wrong, was, by these dilatory policies, brought to such a pitch that *everyone* must have experienced relief that at last the agents of governmental violence had come to smite down, by the aura of their presence, the mob athwart the road to so-long-deferred emancipation.

The men of "good will" could hardly be unaffected by this drama. The crime of racist oppression was among the first of which we became conscious; later, we despaired of seeing it abolished in our life-times; now the victory is in sight, and we are terribly impatient for it. I too am impatient, and affected by the drama of "When will Eisenhower act?" For I acknowl-edge that I did not see how, after the Little Rock situation had so far degenerated, after the mob had received the protection of the National Guard and, inferentially, the encouragement of the President, after the failure of any independent force to gather and manifest itself in Little Rock—I could not see how, at this point, one could oppose the act of Federal violence against the mob. One branch of government was suppressing a mob incited by another branch of government; the soldiers were giving the adolescents the chance, within the school, to discover their way to each other. I care strongly about the outcome of the Little Rock struggle of Autumn '57, and it seemed to me that for the sake of this victory one had to tolerate what one would have given anything to avoid.

But it is obvious that analysis cannot stop here. The concrete possibilities in Little Rock on a certain date have their importance, but the crucial questions raised by this one instance are of a different, more embracive order, they put the Little Rock events in a different perspective. First of all, is the Little Rock pattern desirable, should it be repeated (as the NAACP seems to hope)? If one answers this negatively—as I shall—one faces the question of paramount importance: *are* there ways to avoid this pattern? Are there ways to promote the downfall of Southern racism without invoking or relying on the power of Federal violence? When I answer these questions, I am obliged to retrace my steps, and admit that my emotional reaction to the events in Arkansas was wrong.

I. Can we accept it as a "solution," that Federal troops be stationed, in fact or in threat, before every school-building in the South, until the Southern "white" communities accept the new pattern of education?

Against this solution there are powerful objections implicit in pacifism and in the libertarian, anti-State philosophy which I hold. But perhaps these considerations will appear to be too abstract, or too sectarian. I prefer, therefore, to approach the problem differently, by means of two questions which I believe will give conclusive answers.

The first, which I regard as the less important, is the strategic question: is it so certainly the case that the injunctions and the troops are going to open the route to the school-rooms of the South? Would it not be entirely in keeping with the past of the Eisenhower Administration—which is the custodian of the troops and to a certain measure of the judiciary—to bargain with Southern racism, to yield the deepest South in ex-

change for states like Arkansas which the racists cannot expect
to hold? This is very probably the strategy of the group for
which the Governor of Arkansas acts, and it is not a stupid
strategy. If the Federal government is, in an objective sense, a
kind of ally to the struggle against racism, it is the most uncertain kind of ally: not from conviction but from the pressure of
an immediate situation (especially as it bears on "prestige
abroad"). We do not know that this government will not, if
the Little Rock situation is repeated, announce at a certain
point that its methods are a failure, and reach toward a new
kind of peaceful co-existence with Southern racism.

I am not insisting that the Federal government *will* act in
a duplicitous manner: it is not possible to know this. What is
knowable is that the government may swing this way or that
way, depending on considerations extraneous to the issues involved. From this, the following conclusions: (1) There should
be an intensive search for methods to advance the integration
of the schools without the intervention of this ambiguous force
(the government). (2) There should be emphasis on reliance
upon the unambiguous forces, namely the Negroes and the
"whites" sympathetic to their cause, and opposition to the developing habit of reliance on government, of waiting for injunction and troops, of invoking the Federal agencies.

But considerations of strategy, though weighty, are not
really the ultimate ones. We have to ask ourselves: What view
do we take of the Southern "whites"? Do we regard them as
wild animals who have to be put on a chain? Or how do we
regard them? We are, I believe, in the presence of a critical
time in the evolution of the South. The march of events (including of course the Supreme Court decision) has undermined the faith of Southern "whites" in their ancient ways;
they feel that these are doomed (even the mobs have no confidence in their ultimate victory); they are becoming at last
uneasy about the conflict between ancient customs and the
Western ideals. But now they want to evade a full confrontation of the crisis in their minds and lives. The middle-of-the-
road Southerner, as I read him in the newspapers, *wants* to be
coerced into obedience. He wants to say, I am doing this because it is the law not because it is right; I have not changed

my mind, I bow to force. If the technique of military enforcement succeeds, it will be because the desire for this escape
from the existing moral dilemma has become more powerful
than the desire to go into the streets for a losing cause. It
seems to me crucial that these people be deprived, as much as
possible, of this easy way out. Not for the sake of punishment
—not in order to compel public acknowledgement of guilt. But
so that they may transcend the character which the Southern
style of life has imposed upon them.

I am concerned about these people, because I believe, as
did the Supreme Court in fact, that the Southern "whites" are
also victims of their own ways: that the terrible sullenness and
hatred that is the habitual mask of so many of them is as much
a degradation of humanity, and as much attributable to the
racist mores, as the masks of Southern "blacks": in each case,
personality has been the victim, and is maimed. And while I
care very much that Negroes be freed from these obscene
customs, I care also that the "whites" of the South attain the
possibility of liberation from their own past, by a full confrontation of that obscenity.[1]

From this analysis, it follows that reliance upon, support
of, acceptance of, Federal violence to enforce the new pattern
is not only dangerous, its effects are likely to be contrary to the
aims which persons of liberal and radical social beliefs claim to
share. Alternative forms of action are not only a desideratum,
but the search for them is a necessity.

The direct action movement against racism finds itself,
therefore, at a critical point. It is tempted with surrender of
initiative and responsibility to a government which now represents itself as friendly; but it is exactly at this point that this
movement most needs to affirm and strengthen its consciousness of its role and its latent power. In the light of this
analysis, Little Rock must be regarded as a lost opportunity,

---

[1] It will be seen that, from the viewpoint of this critique, the pacifist critique is not adequate. A "nonviolent army," in the Gandhian sense, if its
coercion were successful, would not have a different effect than that of
paratroopers with fixed bayonets. What should be averted, *to the degree
it is possible*, is *any* reliance upon *any* form of coercion that will permit
the people of the South to evade confronting the problem of living
together as human beings.

rather than an exception to the pacifist or libertarian reliance on direct action.

II. Now, it is customary, when one subjects one line of action to criticism, to propose an alternative. I am not going to propose a specific alternative, if only because I am a "white" Northerner, whose relationship to the case is emotional rather than personal, and who cannot expect to know what is the *exactly appropriate action* in the given circumstances; there is nothing that requires such constant inventiveness as a method of direct action. But within these limitations certain remarks are possible.

The Montgomery demonstration stands, it seems to me, as the prototype for action. Consider what it means: this action does not compel the non-Negro population to do anything against its will; it does nothing except state, by the most appropriate action, the unwillingness of these people to suffer the indignity they are asked to suffer. It confronts the "white" population with the facts: they are now required to *choose*, to choose whether to continue in their old ways, but no longer with any illusions that the Negroes "like it," and no longer with the possibility of ignoring what they are doing; or whether to take the positive step of acceptance. It is a method possessing beauty, dignity and efficaciousness. The problem would be, I should think, to look for analogies in the school situation.

The long-run effectiveness of such methods—assuming they are not turned into mere techniques for provoking Federal intervention—is predicated upon the belief that there is already occurring in the Southern "white" community the shift of belief referred to earlier. I am aware that the degree to which it has occurred is debatable and a question of judgment. In Little Rock, at least, there are abundant signs that this shift has been considerable. The shame of Little Rock—really—was not that a thousand persons gathered from everywhere to surround a school-building, but that another thousand, or two, or five, who *might* have come to the school to demonstrate their disagreement with the mob, did not come. This was shameful. They read about it in the newspapers, and accepted no responsibility; they preferred the anonymity of the Center; they preferred the disgrace upon their city; they preferred to let the injunction and the troops settle it; they preferred to accept identification with a mob which no longer truly represented them. The question asks itself: How are they to be persuaded to accept responsibility? And the further question: If there are ways to induce them—or some few of them, for it would not take many—to accept this responsibility, is it not worth doing, even if it takes a little longer? (When I speak of what may take a little longer, I am not speaking of *in*action; on the contrary.)

I repeat, I am not proposing a particular tactic—I do not believe I have a right to. But I will offer a concrete illustration of the type of alternative that I have in mind. Suppose, instead of trying to precipitate Federal intervention, and defense of the right of their children to go to the schools, the Negro parents kept their children *out of all schools* until the local community will take responsibility for itself, until the *local community*—not the National Guard, not the local police, but the weight of local opinion—will stand up to the mob and the politicians that foment mobs? Do we really believe that an action of this type would not have a profound effect?

Dave Dellinger and *Bayard Rustin*

Mississippi Muddle

It is customary to ask these days [1962] whether Governor
Barnett and his cohorts learned anything from the Civil War.
It is perhaps more relevant to ask whether the rest of us did.
For if it is freedom for the Negro we desire, and a society in
which skin color becomes as minor a social and economic consideration as the color of one's eyes or hair, then the actions of
the Federal government in the Mississippi crisis can give us
little joy. Kennedy has proven that the Federal government
has the military power to install one Negro on the campus of a
previously segregated State University and to conduct him to
and from classes. (Even this hollow accomplishment may be
lost if Meredith falls from a sniper's bullet, as easily could
happen, or succumbs to a case of nerves, as any but the most
hardy would do under such pressures.) He has also proven
that there are certain extreme circumstances in which the Federal government will intervene, however belatedly and apolo-
getically, on the side of its beleaguered and oppressed Negro
citizens. This appears to be the greatest source of comfort for
many Negroes and Northern liberals who feel reassured that
the government supports them in their struggle for elementary
justice. (By contrast, Southern liberals, as we shall see later,
found themselves isolated and betrayed by its moral equivoca-
tions and last-minute "military invasion" and therefore had an
entirely different reaction.) Big Brother has overpowered the
bully, and after so many previous disappointments it is hard
not to feel encouraged.

In fact, (as both Kennedys went to great pains to point
out) Kennedy did not intervene on behalf of integration but
only in defense of Federal authority in a situation where the
unyielding militancy of both Meredith and Barnett had pushed

the conflict to a point where the supremacy of the Federal government over the States was involved. "This is far more fundamental than the question of whether Meredith is white or colored, or whether the University of Mississippi is segregated," said Bobby. "The system of government in the United States means nothing if the law is disregarded." But where does that leave those of us who believe that a man's conscience is a higher authority than the law? What of the Freedom Riders and the members of the sit-in movement (not to mention the long history of slave revolts and those who, throughout the years in between, conscientiously broke the law in their desperate struggle for elementary human rights)? The law itself would not have advanced even at the snail's pace it has except for the illegal intransigence of those who were obeying a higher law, and what of an Adolph Eichmann, who argued that he did what he did because it was the law? The relevance of this example is underlined by the fact that Kennedy climaxed his nationwide television speech with a jingoistic appeal: "Let us preserve both the law and the peace, and then, healing those wounds that are within, we can turn to the greater crimes that are without and stand united as one people in our pledge to man's freedom."

What needed affirming in this case was not the sanctity of the Federal law or our supposed common devotion to the Cold War but the inalienable rights of Negroes to man's full measure of freedom. At no point did Kennedy appeal to the students, the moderates, or anyone, to join the Twentieth Century, to recognize the rights of their fellow human beings, to rise to the moral challenge. He went to great lengths to flatter "Mississippi and her university [which] are noted for their courage, for their contribution of talent to the affairs of this nation (sic). . . . This is the State which had four Medal of Honor winners in the Korean War alone." (We wonder if their courage was any greater—or half so relevant—as that of James Meredith, which went completely unmentioned. Always Meredith was a "private party" to an annoying suit, never a fellow human being for whom anyone was asked to have any sympathy or even respect.) He apologized for the fact that the government had to support Meredith: "Even though this gov-

ernment had not been originally a party to the case" (this
theme was emphasized over and over again) "my responsibility was . . . inescapable. . . . I deeply regret the fact that any
action by the executive branch was necessary." He spoke as if
all Mississippians were white racists who would disapprove of
Meredith's admission to the university but must be constrained
to go along with it to preserve the sanctity of the law. Nowhere did he mention or speak to that half of the state's population which is colored and has a somewhat different perspective, which would like to be able to contribute *their* talents to
the affairs of this country. He made no appeal of any kind to
that besieged minority of white persons who are not stridently
racist and who are capable of responding to ethical and
humanitarian leadership.

Paradoxically enough, in the 1960 election campaign,
speaking in New York on October 12th, Kennedy uttered his
own epitaph: "There is more power in the Presidency than to
let things drift and then suddenly to call out the troops." Earlier in the same speech, he promised: "Moral and persuasive
leadership by the President to create the conditions in which
compliance with the constitutional requirements of school desegregation takes place; this is the kind of leadership I intend
to give." In view of his subsequent behavior, these fine phrases
may be dismissed as "campaign oratory" which Kennedy
lacked either the sincerity or perhaps the courage to live up to.
But it seems to us that the important question is not whether
Kennedy was sincere but whether, given the complexities of
political power in the United States and the moral debilitation
inherent in the Cold War, anyone else in the Presidency could
have acted significantly better. It comes down to a question of
whether any politician can get into "power" and stay there
without forming a whole network of compromising alliances,
and a whole complex of psychological attitudes which effectively shear him of valid power, which prevent him, in other
words, from exerting imaginative, problem-solving leadership
—in the South, in Latin America, or anywhere else.

In the first place Kennedy is politically beholden to both
the upsurging integrationists and the die-hard segregationists.
He won election only by a deft and deceptive campaign in

which he wooed both the Negro and the Dixiecrat vote. He has had to pay off men like Senator Eastland of Mississippi and Governor Patterson of Alabama, for their electoral support, by dispensing patronage in such a way as to strengthen their hand against that of the moderates. He has had to play the Negro and the Dixiecrat off against one another, constrained somehow to convince *both* of them that he is doing everything possible for him under the circumstances of the other's intransigency. (We wonder what would happen if some Republican had managed to tape his private conversations with Senator Eastland—or for that matter his phone conversations with Governor Barnett during the ten days when they were dickering on the phone—and played them in Harlem; or conversely, if a tape of his conversations in the White House with Martin Luther King, Jr. were played in Mississippi. Ordinarily, of course, the "assurances" are given by assistants, who can be disavowed, if necessary, but still there is an interesting project here.)

Secondly, when a man's whole life is taken up with the power moves of H-bomb diplomacy, in a desperate Cold War struggle to outchicken and outmaneuver Khrushchev and to hold the line in Vietnam, Berlin and Latin America in opposition to the needs and aspirations of the people, he loses the ability to think and act in ethical or humanistic terms. When the time came for creative action in Mississippi, Kennedy could not break out of the trap which he and the men around him had forged for themselves by the methods they have used (and the outlook they have developed) all over the world. Although the President must always seek to maintain a humanitarian public image, he can no more be expected to heal the wounds of Southern racism than the C.I.A. might be expected to develop a humanitarian plan for land reform in Latin America, or the F. B. I. to defend civil liberties. I. F. Stone was quite right when he pointed out in criticism of the President's "synthetic pep-talk" that "The fight cannot be won until the South is made to feel that integration is not just some ruling by a Supreme Court accidentally filled with Negro-lovers but a movement which springs from the deepest ideals of this nation and the most irrepressible aspirations of human beings everywhere." But the President—any President—will be the last person to take the lead in such a fight. Someday when Negro and white integrationists and just-plain-fair moderates have done the job, the President or, more likely, some Presidential aspirant will "lead the battle," but not before.

Having failed utterly to pave the way for desegregation, having, in fact, made compliance less likely by his alliance with the Southern Democrats and his opportunistic handling of racial problems (his failure, for example, to carry through on his campaign pledge to stop discrimination in federally assisted housing by "a single stroke of the pen"), was not Kennedy nonetheless right to call in the troops? Did he not, in the last analysis, come through for integration? Is he not "on our side"? To answer these questions we must consider what some of the nonviolent alternatives were, first for the President and then for those concerned to achieve real and lasting integration.

A far better approach for the President, even at the last minute, would have been to fly to Mississippi and personally escort Meredith into the University. He could have met with university officials, student spokesmen, and local and religious leaders. He could have addressed the student body and introduced Meredith to them. Instead of appealing irrelevantly to the pure-white military heroes of the past (as he did on television), he could have found some enlightened Mississippians to join him in person. He could conceivably have brought "moderates" from Charlotte, North Carolina, Atlanta, Georgia, or Memphis, Tennessee, three Southern cities where integration of the schools was carefully prepared for and has been proceeding with remarkable success. (Charlotte has even had a desegregated swimming pool for two years, without any untoward incidents.) How much more inspiriting it would have been for these people to be invited to stand beside the President in a moral struggle for decency and human rights rather than be put in the unenviable position of seeming to support his armed invasion on behalf of Federal law against Mississippi law.

This course of action would have been far less drastic or costly, far more reconciling and effective, than the actual sequence of events: his ingratiating but unconvincing television speech, the sending in of five hundred marshals and twenty-three thousand troops, and the resulting necessity for maintaining a semi-permanent military occupation of Oxford. *Liberation* and a number of other periodicals proposed a personal intervention by the President in the Little Rock crisis of 1958, as did CORE and other organizations. The idea has been so widely discussed that it is impossible for the President and his advisers not to have heard of it.

Ironically, much of the strength of Governor Barnett's position in his advocacy of a bad cause is that he made just such a straightforward personal identification with his beliefs. He personally barred Meredith's path and personally refused to accept his registration. This effectively dramatized his opposition and won a begrudging, if temporary, respect from many who are horrified by what he stands for. It succeeded in partially obscuring the ugly realities of the hooded violence, the anonymous brutality, and the pitiless economic pressure by which the Negro is kept "in his place" in Mississippi. Though in the end Barnett hedged a little rather than go to jail (or pay a large fine), it is hard to say whether it was Barnett or Kennedy who was more anxious to avoid this eventuality. Kennedy, typically, dreaded any clear-cut personalization of the issue on either side, preferring an abstract, token, Pyrrhic victory and trying desperately to arrange a political save-face for everyone that would not basically challenge the *status quo*. To be brutally honest, Kennedy rose to prominence, first in the political sewers of Boston and later on the national scene, by making sharper deals than his opponents—usually by having more money and connections behind him. After all these years, and with the 1964 campaign ahead of him, how can he change his pattern now? Was it not "more important" that he be in the White House in 1964 than the two lives that were lost on September 30th should have been saved—or that actual integration be advanced peacefully? So he wheeled and dealed for ten days after Governor Barnett had committed himself on television to uncompromising opposition. This created a moral vacuum that was falsely filled by the opposition. Hodding Carter, editor of the *Delta Democrat-Times,* in Greenville, Mississippi, has written in the *Nation:*

> When it finally became obvious that a total effort by the Executive branch would be necessary to make good the court orders, the job had become infinitely more difficult than it would have been earlier in the game. The extremists had been given a week to bestir themselves and rally public opinion. . . . With each seeming success, with each rejection of James Meredith by the Governor or Lt. Governor Paul Johnson, more Mississippians allowed themselves to be convinced that this time the line was going to be successfully drawn.

To make matters worse, Kennedy then compounded his ineptitude by having Meredith smuggled onto the campus on a Sunday, when most of the students were away, and under cover of darkness, once again giving the moral and psychological advantage to his opponents, who could claim, correctly, that they had been tricked. Even when there are not larger issues or deep-seated prejudices involved, college students will often riot when they feel they have been tricked by their elders. It is not without reason that nonviolence stresses the pragmatic as well as the moral necessity for openness and honesty in the social struggle.

Can we rightfully say, then, that Kennedy is, after all, on our side? Did he not follow, rather, the way of the politician, who is actually on no one's side? Did he not follow, rather, the lazy-man's way of the military, which offers no enlightenment, no principled opposition (in fact at the early stages aids the enemy, as Churchill aided Hitler, as Roosevelt aided Stalin, as Kennedy still aids Eastland) and then mindlessly rushes in at the last minute with troops to "save the situation." If Kennedy had made a personal commitment to integration, if he had gone to Mississippi in the manner we have suggested, he would be in a position to move ahead now to seek further, more thorough-going advances throughout the South. As it is, the likelihood is that, even without a real victory for integration, he must now backtrack to mend political fences ruptured by the "invasion" of Mississippi to prevent a Dixiecrat walkout

in '64, to minimize the gains of the Republican party in the
South, to unify the country "against the greater crimes that
are without."

Hodding Carter reports from Mississippi:

> Governor Barnett. . . is the most popular political
> figure the state has known since the leader of the lost
> cause [Jefferson Davis], himself a Mississippian. . . . The
> Democratic Party here, as anything but a hollow shell,
> has been destroyed. There may be candidates . . . who
> will run as Democrats, but they will be Democrats in
> name only. If they are to be elected, they will have to
> run as Ross Barnett Democrats, as Mississippi Democrats
> or as States'-rights Democrats.

And Frank R. Ahlgren, editor of the Memphis *Commercial
Appeal,* says (*U.S. News and World Report*):

> In Memphis we went about it in a planned way. They
> did it in Dallas, too. Atlanta had a little fanfare. But we
> planned it carefully. We integrated our schools and stores,
> eating places and so on, without big incidents. . . . [In
> Mississippi] violence has been done, and it's going to
> intimidate some of the more forward-looking people who
> might move others along with them toward integration.
> . . . And then, it's alienated a lot of people who would
> otherwise tolerate integration. Now they say "To hell with
> them; they've invaded us."

But let us not play any longer the popular game of figur-
ing out what Kennedy should have done. Let us rather put
forward a philosophy and strategy by which the rest of us can
act.

It is often said that the strength of nonviolence lies in its
emphasis on converting the opposition by love—and for many
conscientious persons who are unwilling to tolerate oppression
and discrimination any longer this supposed strength becomes
an apparent weakness because they imagine that nonviolence
is limited to logical persuasion, moral exhortation, and heroic
self-sacrifice and is therefore socially irrelevant except in

marginal situations. How can anyone, for example, win over a Southern racist by such methods? How would we go about it at the University of Mississippi? By letting James Meredith be killed—in the hope that this would shame and humiliate the segregationists? By standing beside him ourselves, unarmed and helpless before the mob and preaching love as we fell victim to its assault? This is not what happened in the Montgomery bus boycott, the student sit-ins, or the Freedom Rides, though transforming love and heroic self-sacrifice were present in all these actions. The integrationists acted in such a way as to confront the white Southerners with a hard choice—a choice they did not want to make but couldn't avoid. In Montgomery, for example, the boycott of the buses made it economically unfeasible for the company to keep them running. When arrests, intimidation and argument failed to get the Negroes back on the buses, the people of Mongomery had to choose between having no buses at all and having them integrated. Similarly, where the sit-inners succeeded in integrating Southern restaurants, they were able to do so because they implemented the logic and morality of their case by putting their bodies in the restaurants in sufficient numbers and with enough perserverance so that the owners were faced with the choice of closing down entirely or opening on an integrated basis. In the end it was the combination of many pressures which won more and more people over to the position that the facilities would be better open and integrated than "segregated" and shut—businessmen who were losing money, customers who were being seriously inconvenienced, absentee owners whose other restaurants were being picketed or boycotted, wavering moderates who were impressed or inspirited by the dignity and heroism and love of the nonviolent resisters.

In the case at issue there are several steps that could have been taken to supplement the moral and educational appeals with similar pressures. If the National Collegiate Athletic Association can "suspend" colleges that engage in excessive recruiting of athletes, the various professorial and educational authorities could impose sanctions on colleges that engage in discriminatory negative recruiting of scholars. If students were denied accreditation for courses taken at a Jim Crow college or denied entrance to a wide list of graduate schools, if teachers found they were to be denied offers to teach at other universities, they would soon become pressure groups from within for integration. Since the town of Oxford is economically dependent on the University, and what cultural prestige the state has centers in the University, there are many persons who would have been given cause to rethink the extent of their commitment to segregation if nonviolent pressures had been exerted to weaken the value of a Mississippi degree, to cut down the flow of funds, even to shut down the University if necessary. The Federal government has continued to supply funds to the University and to a variety of other state agencies in Mississippi during the eight years since the Supreme Court declared segregated schools unconstitutional—just as it continues to supply funds to the states of Alabama and South Carolina, which have absolutely no integrated schools. If funds had been progressively withheld, those employed in the various agencies affected or benefiting from their services would have found it less glamorous to hold out against the advance of the Twentieth Century. If proper nonviolent pressures had been applied, many of those who have now moved defensively and self-righteously backwards in reaction to the sending of Federal troops would have been enabled to move forward—first to acquiesce in a gradually evolving situation and then to undergo profound changes of outlook. Instead of being a hero defending their way of life against an overriding Federal government, the governor would have been put in the uncomfortable position of disrupting the daily life of countless Mississippians.

There is a profound lesson in the Mississippi muddle for all of us. When radicals, liberals, moderates, religious groups, "decent people" fail to take positive action on the local level in support of exploited or abused groups, the Federal government is ultimately forced to intervene and the issue becomes falsely posed as a conflict between the forces of local reaction and the "progressive" or "humanitarian" Federal government. The temptation for shortsighted men and women of good will is to rely on the Federal government to take up the slack created by their own failure to act responsibly and in social solidarity. But in the long run the Federal government must act in accord with its own nature, which is that of a highly centralized political, military, industrial, and financial bureaucracy. Kennedy's failure to advance the cause of integration in Mississippi was not primarily a personal failing, but symbolizes the institutional inability of the Federal government to act creatively and imaginatively in conflict situations, to sow love where there is hate, peace where there is discord, and integration where there is segregation. These are obligations which we cannot pass on to any outside agency, particularly one whose ultimate faith is in military methods and which characteristically subordinates all considerations, including the very survival of the species, to the prosecution of the Cold War.

Bayard Rustin

The Meaning of Birmingham

Since the signing of the Emancipation Proclamation in 1863, the struggle for justice by Afro-Americans has been carried out by many dedicated individuals and militant organizations. Their ultimate aim, sometimes stated, often not, has always been total freedom. Many forms of strategy and tactics have been used. Many partial victories have been won. Yet the gradual and token "progress" that many white liberals pointed to with pride served only to anger the black man and further frustrate him. That frustration has now given way to an open and publicly declared war on segregation and racial discrimination throughout the nation. The aim is simple. It is directed at all white Americans—the President of the United States, his brother, Robert, the trade-union movement, the power élite, and every living white soul the Negro meets. The war cry is "unconditional surrender—end *all* Jim Crow now." Not next week, not tomorrow—but *now*.

This is not to say that many have not felt this way for decades. The slave revolts, the occasional resorts to violence in recent times, the costly fifty-year struggle that the National Association for the Advancement of Colored People has carried on in the courts, the thousands arrested throughout the South since the Montgomery bus boycott—all reveal an historic impatience and a thirst for freedom. What *is* new springs from the white resistance in Birmingham, with its fire hoses, its dogs, its blatant disregard for black men as people, and from the Afro-American's response to such treatment in "the year of our Lord" 1963.

For the black people of this nation, Birmingham became the moment of truth. The struggle from now on will be fought in a different context. Therefore, to understand the mood, tac-

tics and totality of the black people's relentless war on Jim
Crow, we must grasp fully what is taking place in this Southern industrial city.

For the first time, every black man, woman and child,
regardless of station, has been brought into the struggle. Unlike the period of the Montgomery boycott, when the Southern
Christian Leadership Conference had to be organized to stimulate similar action elsewhere, the response to Birmingham has
been immediate and spontaneous. City after city has come into
the fight, from Jackson, Mississippi, to Chesterton, Maryland.
The militancy has spread to Philadelphia, where the "city fathers" and the trade-union movement have been forced to
make reluctant concessions. It has reached the old and established freedom organizations. For example, Roy Wilkins, executive secretary of the N.A.A.C.P., who only a year ago, from a
platform in Jackson, Mississippi, criticized the direct-action
methods of the Freedom Riders, was arrested recently for leading a picket line in that very city, after hundreds of N.A.A.C.P.
members had been arrested in a direct-action struggle.

Before Birmingham, the great struggles had been waged
for specific, limited goals. The Freedom Rides sought to establish the right to eat while traveling; the sit-ins sought to win
the right to eat in local restaurants; the Meredith case centered
on a single Negro's right to enter a state university. The Montgomery boycott, although it involved fifty thousand people in a
year-long sacrificial struggle, was limited to attaining the right
to ride the city buses with dignity and respect. The black
people now reject token, limited or gradual approaches.

The package deal is the new demand. The black community is not prepared to engage in a series of costly battles—first
for jobs, then decent housing, then integrated schools, etc., etc.
The fact that there is a power élite which makes the decisions
is now clearly understood. The Negro has learned that,
through economic and mass pressures, this élite can be made
to submit step by step. Now he demands unconditional surrender. It is significant that in city after city where the spirit of
Birmingham has spread, the Negroes are demanding fundamental social, political and economic changes. One can predict
with confidence that in the future the scope of these demands

will be widened, not narrowed, and that if they are not met in the North as well as in the South, a very dangerous situation will develop. Federal troops may well become a familiar sight in the North as well as the South, since the black community is determined to move vigorously and fearlessly and relentlessly ahead.

Absence of Fear

Gandhi used to say that the absence of fear was the prime ingredient of nonviolence: "To be afraid is to be a slave." A. J. Muste frequently says that to be afraid is to behave as if the truth were not true. It was the loss of all fear that produced the moment of truth in Birmingham: children as young as six paraded calmly when dogs, fire hoses and police billies were used against them. Women were knocked down to the ground and beaten mercilessly. Thousands of teen-agers stood by at churches throughout the whole county, waiting their turn to face the clubs of Bull Connor's police, who are known to be among the most brutal in the nation. Property was bombed. Day after day the brutality and arrests went on. And always, in the churches, hundreds of well-disciplined children eagerly awaited their turns.

While these youngsters, unlike Meredith, had the advantage of operating in groups, and while Meredith's ordeal must have been the most difficult borne by any freedom fighter short of death—the children of Birmingham, like no other person or group, inspired and shamed all Afro-Americans, and pulled them into a united struggle.

E. Franklin Frazier wrote in the past of the Negro bourgeoisie. He told of the efforts of the Negro upper classes to ape white people, of the exploitation of Negroes by wealthy members of their own race and of the absence of identity among Negroes. But had Frazier been alive to see Birmingham he would have discovered that the black community was welded into a classless revolt. A. G. Gaston, the Negro millionaire who with some ministers and other upper-class elements had publicly stated that the time was not ripe for such a broad protest, finally accommodated himself, as did the others, to the mass pressure from below and joined the struggle. Gaston owns

much property, including a funeral parlor and the motel that
eventually became the headquarters for the Birmingham campaign. The bombing of his motel was one cause of the outbreak of rioting on the part of elements that had not come into
the nonviolent struggle.

On the basis of the behavior of the black business community in the cities where protests have emerged since Birmingham, one can confidently predict that future struggles will
find the Negro bourgeoisie playing a major role in social
change and nonviolence. They know that unless they join in
the struggle they will lose the business of their fellow Negroes,
who are in no mood to tolerate Uncle Tom-ism.

Black people have waited a hundred years for the government to help them win their rights. President after President has made commitments before election and failed to use
the executive power he possesses after election. Congress
today, dominated by Southern Democrats, cannot pass any
meaningful civil-rights legislation. The Supreme Court, from
1954 to 1963, took a gradualist approach, thereby putting its
stamp of approval on "with all deliberate speed," which spells
tokenism.

So the black people have looked elsewhere for allies, hoping to discover some major power group within American society which would join them not only in the struggle for Negro
rights, but also in the struggle for a more democratic America.
The trade-union movement and the churches have issued radical pronouncements but in fact have done precious little and
on occasion have even blocked progress. Thus the black population has concluded that the future lies in casting not just a
ballot, what Thoreau called "a piece of paper merely," but the
total vote—the human person against injustice.

This is not to say that black people are not deeply appre-
ciative of those few independent radicals, liberals and church
people who have offered time, money and even their lives.
They have nothing but admiration for people like Jim Peck,
who was brutally beaten in Mississippi and Alabama during
the Freedom Rides, Barbara Deming, who was arrested in
Birmingham, Eric Weinberger, who fasted for a month in Alabama jails, and William Moore, the slain postman. One can be

thankful that the number of such *individuals* is increasing. However, social change of such magnitude requires that major power groups in our society participate as meaningful allies.

The Body Against Injustice

The use of the "black body" against injustice is necessary as a means of creating social disruption and dislocation precisely because the accepted democratic channels have been denied the Negro.

In practice, it works like this: having urged the social institutions to desegregate to no avail, having pleaded for justice to no avail, the black people see that the white community would rather yield to the threats of the segregationist (in the name of law and order) than change the social system. And so Negroes conclude that they must upset the social equilibrium more drastically than the opposition can. They place their bodies against an unjust law by sitting in a restaurant, or a library, playing in a park or swimming in a pool. The segregationists, frequently joined by the police, attack. Arrest and brutality follow. But the black people keep coming, wave after wave. The jails fill. The black population boycotts the stores. Businessmen begin to lose money.

At this point the white community splits into two groups. On one side are the political and law-enforcement agencies, supported by the arch-segregationists, who fearfully resort to indiscriminate violence as a stop-gap measure. Then the more enlightened section of the community, including many business leaders, begin to act for the first time. They sense not only the rightness of the Negroes' demands but their inevitability. They realize that police violence may bring both a violent response from unorganized elements of the black population and increased economic reprisals. Thus the business community, previously having sided with the forces of reaction, at first quietly and then openly sue for discussion and negotiation with the Negro community, an approach they had earlier dismissed when it was proposed by Negro leaders.

This method of massive nonviolence has many dangers. The greatest threat is that violence, which has been smoldering beneath the surface for generations, will inevitably manifest itself. But the creative genius of people in action is the only safeguard in this period and it can be trusted to bring about, ultimately, a better community, precisely because the tactic of mass action is accompanied by nonviolent resistance. The protesters pledge themselves to refrain from violence in word and deed, thereby confining whatever inevitable violence there may be in the situation to an irreducible minimum.

The genius of this method and philosophy lies in its ability to destroy an old unjust institution and simultaneously create a new one. For finally the white community is forced to choose between closing down the schools, restaurants, parks, buses, etc., and integrating them. Faced for the first time with a choice that can impose discomfort, inconvenience and economic turmoil on the white community, that community discovers that it would prefer integrated institutions to no public institutions at all.

It is therefore clear that we can now expect, following Birmingham, a more sympathetic ear from the power structure, in both the North *and* the South.

Financial Tenderness of Segregation

Loss of money to retail stores throughout the country, the reluctance of many industries to move to Little Rock during the school integration struggle, the fear of capitalists to invest in Mississippi and Alabama now, and the disrupting of the economy in Birmingham have caused big businesses, including steel, to take a second look at the "Negro problem."

The nation gives Robert Kennedy credit for the fact that the real rulers of Birmingham sat down with representatives of the black revolution. But knowledgeable people realize that it was the withdrawal of black purchasing power in a city which is almost half black, and the militant, unconditional surrender policies of the nonviolent struggle that turned the tide.

Again, Birmingham is a turning point in that all significant elements of the power structure have now acknowledged that the white community must recognize the true nature of the black revolution and its economic consequences.

Therefore, in city after city, following Birmingham, the real powers have moved to convince the politicians that they should negotiate. Chain store, moving picture, hotel and restaurant executives have recently sought out representatives of the black community to ask for negotiations leading to nationwide desegregation. This is new. It is a consequence of the handwriting they see on the wall. They see it in police brutality and the bombed-out homes and business establishments. They see it in the eyes of Birmingham's children.

The tragedy is that the trade-union movement, the churches and educational institutions which lay claim to freedom and justice, reveal that they have learned nothing from the Battle of Birmingham. This is especially sad since the great battle lies ahead. And this battle the black population is now prepared to wage. This is going to be the battle for jobs.

Negroes are finally beginning to realize that the age of automation and industrialization presents them with peculiar problems. There is less and less of a market where the unskilled can sell his labor. Inadequate, segregated schools increase the problem. The negative attitude of the trade unions compounds it further. The Cold War economy, geared to armaments production (perhaps the most automated of all industries) is throwing millions out of work, but the minority groups are being hit hardest. For every white person unemployed, there are close to three Negroes without jobs.

In general, the unemployed, whether white or black, are not yet prepared to take radical action to demand jobs now. However, unemployed black people are prepared to move in conjunction with the rest of the black community and its many white supporters, within the context of the broad civil-rights upheaval. Since their most immediate ends are economic, their banner will be "Dignity of work with equal pay and equal opportunity." This agitation on the part of Negroes for jobs is bound to stimulate unemployed white workers to increased militancy. There will be sit-downs and other dislocating tactics. Nonviolent resistance will have to be directed against local and federal governments, the labor unions, against the A.F.L.-C.I.O. hierarchy and any construction plant or industry that refuses to grant jobs. Such mass disturbances will probably soon take place in the major industrial centers of the country and it is likely that they will be more vigorous in the North

than they have been in the South. And they will have incalculable effects on the economic structure.

The great lesson of Birmingham is at once dangerous and
creative; black people have moved to that level where they
cannot be contained. They are not prepared to wait for courts,
elections, votes, government officials, or even Negro leaders.
As James Baldwin said in an interview published in the New
York *Times* for June 3rd [1963]: "No man can claim to speak
for the Negro people today. There is no one with whom the
power structure can negotiate a deal that will bind Negro
people. There is, therefore, no possibility of a bargain." The
black people *themselves* are united and determined to destroy
all unjust laws and discriminatory practices, and they want
total freedom, including equal economic opportunity and the
right to marry whom they damned well please. They know
that at a time when the Kennedy brothers were fighting hard
to maintain an aura of leadership and control of the civil-rights
movement, the children of Birmingham, using methods of nonviolent resistance, restored the leadership to the black community. This was, as reported in the June 6th issue of *Jet*, a
"terrible licking" for the federal government. If *kids* can revitalize the civil rights movement in Birmingham, the least we
can do is to act like men and women and fight now to provide
them with a decent future.

The mood is one of anger and confidence of total victory.
The victories to date have given added prestige to the method
of nonviolent resistance. One can only hope that the white
community will realize that the black community means what
it says: *freedom now.*

Barbara Deming

Notes After Birmingham

Home

Home. A world calm and beautiful. Everything is familiar, yet I have the sensation of staring at an illusion which I cannot quite bring into focus. Another world still catches at me. I live both here and there—until the two worlds can be one.

Part of Me Now Lives in That Other World

Part of me now lives in the stark undecorated room at the Negro Y.W.C.A. in Memphis where I stayed on my way home. A CORE fieldworker has been living there—Mary Hamilton, who took me under her wing in Birmingham. Typed field reports spread on the spare cot. A room for a while, but not home. Her few things tucked away at random. Now she is on another mission, and will live in Chattanooga; a minister has opened his house to her and to several other "soldiers." The night I stayed there, two or was it three people shared a couch-bed; others, curled in blankets or in sleeping bags—long, restive cocoons—scattered themselves about the dining room and living room floors.

Part of me lives in the bombed house of A. D. King, in Birmingham. His wife sits staring into the next room which had collapsed like a tent the moment after she had run from it—toward her children's room—at a strange sound. Her eyes shining, she tells the neighbors who have gathered, "He led me out of that room. I'll praise Him and serve Him, praise Him and serve Him, all the rest of my life!" Two police officials wander through the shambles. A Negro minister asks them, "What are you looking for? It was you who did this." "It wasn't us!" one of the cops answers quickly. "Well, it was your boss." A tall Negro sings out, "That's right. Speak the truth, Reverend!" The cop's eyes, meeting mine for a moment, turn away.

And I live in my room at the Gaston Motel—headquarters for the movement. The motel too has been bombed now. King's eleven year old daughter sits up most of the night there, waiting for her father. He is going about the streets, with others, trying to calm the Negroes of the district who have begun to riot against the police. We can hear his voice, at intervals, raised above the garbled voices of the rioters. They, too, suspect the police of having been involved in the bombings. I urge the little girl to lie down and rest, like the other woman who has taken shelter with us. But she insists that she'd rather sit in the big chair by the door. She seems very calm, her hands quiet in her lap. I beg her one further time to lie down on the bed, and then she tells me softly: "I don't want to lie down because I might fall asleep, and then I might dream about the bombing."

Towards dawn, her father picks her up. Mary Hamilton comes in from the streets to get a little rest. I've gone to sleep on the soft carpet on the floor, so that others, more tired than I, can use my bed. I wake. Some noise in the courtyard has drawn Mary to the window again. She stands, holding the curtains, peering out—her whole body arched, tense, her head, thrust forward, turning quickly to the left, the right.

Having Entered This World That Is Theirs, I Live in It Too Now. But I Am Able to Leave

What a queer feeling to be able to travel in a few minutes from this world into quite another world—as they cannot. The day I leave Birmingham, I simply drive out of it, in a taxi cab.

Most of the day I spend in hiding. Who knows whether or not it is necessary? The violence of a few Negroes the night before has provided the police with an excuse to be even more violent themselves. The state police, in particular—rushed in by the governor—roam the district, clubbing people at random. I walk down to the motel's office to use the telephone there and have just lifted the receiver when I see several white men moving into the drive. I leave the phone and duck into what remains of the room behind the office. I stand in the corner of the wrecked room, waiting—letting the dust of fallen plaster settle on me there—when, through the jagged opening

torn by the bomb in the wall across from me, I see the figure of
another white man, stooping to examine something. I hurry
out of that room into a bathroom around the corner, and sit on
the tiled floor for almost an hour, until I figure that the way is
clear. Then I stay in my room. "You're learning to be smart,"
Mary Hamilton tells me.

I have begun, even before this day, to feel a sudden unpleasant catch in my stomach every time I step out onto the
street and see a white man. What is he going to do? So now I
know what it is like. Now I am a Negro. Except that I can
drive away from it.

The cab drives round the last police guard set up at an
intersection, and rolls smoothly through the streets—eerily—on
out toward the airport. At the airport, a traveler holds the
door open for me with a little bow. The building is hung with
gracious signs: "It's nice to have you in Birmingham." The
clerk at the counter where I buy a pencil and a newspaper tells
me the price of the pencil in gentle murmuring tones, and as
she hands me my change grants me a honeyed smile. Wait, I
am moved to say to them, you don't intend those smiles for me.
I am not the person you think; or rather, you do not think me a
person. You taught me this my first day in Birmingham.
Nigger-lover, nigger.

The First Day. Scene in the Park

The city authorities are turning the high-pressure hoses on a
group of demonstrators who have marched peacefully, two by
two, out of the Pilgrim Baptist Church—driving them into the
park nearby. The playing hoses make a sound like machine
gun fire. The water pressure can be turned up to over two
hundred pounds. By the end of the day, bark has been
stripped from many of the trees in the park, and the clothes
have been stripped from some of the people. A small crowd of
onlookers, white people, screams with glee as the water knocks
the demonstrators to the ground, tumbling them like objects.
Yes, they are not people but dark objects which the water can
drive this way and that! Hurrah! Soon there is a high wailing
of sirens and several police cars drive up and the big dogs are
led out on leashes. The onlookers give a cheer. Bull Connor is

directing the scene, a cigar in his mouth, a sweaty gray straw hat on his head. He doesn't put the dogs into action for a while. He lets them squat in the corner of the park, as a promise. Their masters lean over and pat them now and then, with boyish smiles—good fellowship between them. Bull Connor keeps trying to keep the onlookers—including newsmen —out of the park itself. He explains himself, finally, in a loud voice: "I don't want anybody here to get hurt."

The Demonstrators Give the Lie to Bull Connor's Words

They are not bodies. They are dark objects which the water tumbles at will. But as one's heart leaps, the demonstrators prove this to be a lie. Some of the young boys and girls manage to leap high in the air above the spurting water—holding up their limp but still recognizable signs: "Freedom!" And they manage to stand. They do it by clasping hands, by holding one to another. More run to join them against the water's force. Two young girls, glancing at each other, find their courage, take hands and run to join the rest. They manage to stand.

In the Church

And in the church that evening they shatter his lie. Many people have gathered, after the arduous day; they pack the church to bursting. The leaders review for them what has taken place: they're not to think that the demonstration in which they took part has been the only demonstration this day; many different groups of them have kept the city officials busy. Plans for the next day are revealed. And everybody sings. Again they join strength to strength—they join their voices; and the song swells and shakes the walls. It shakes the ground under my feet. Sitting in the midst of this rush of sound, I know myself—with awe—to be at the wellspring of that which is human—which insists that it is, which at long last is sure that it is, and affirms it: "Freedom! Freedom! Freedom! Freedom!" One woman, a newcomer, looks about her, dazzled, eyes wide. Has she not thought freedom possible? It exists, within these walls, here and now.

The Newsmen Stand Across the Street

Each day the people gather in the churches—before the demonstrations and after them. The newsmen stand across the
street. Bull Connor doesn't like to see them going into the
meetings—though he has his own "reporters" there—so they
stand on the curb. "No sense asking for trouble," one explodes
to me, when I question this. "A reporter's job is to get his copy
in, not to wave any fucking banners." (Not even the banner:
freedom of the press.) "Connor must wish he could keep us
away altogether," says one reporter. "Without this publicity,
the demonstrations would stop." At the distance he keeps, how
little he understands the demonstrations. Their purpose: to
assert a certain truth and to hold to it. If the newspapers didn't
report them, the force of that truth would be diminished—but
would remain. The truth is also for the Negroes themselves.

One part of the truth which they are grasping: We have
no right to be ashamed of anything. "Our hair is not like
white folks'? What's wrong with kinky hair? Let's talk about
that. For too long the white man has told us that our hair is
bad because it's kinky, and our noses are bad because they're
thick, and our lips are bad, they're blubbery, and we've
giggled; and it's time we stopped this. We've got to change
all the values. Hear me." It's James Forman talking.

Another part of the truth: the Negro has helped to bring
this city and this nation into being. "Once Birmingham was
nothing but wilderness. Who cut the trees, dug the ditches
and laid the streets, built the skyscrapers? . . . We don't want
to take over, either. We just want to live as brothers. . . . But
we're not going to go back to Africa until the Englishman goes
back to England, the Italian goes back to Italy, the German
goes back to Germany, and the white man gives this country
back to the Indians." (Delighted laughter. "Talk to us,
Ralph!") Reverend Ralph Abernathy is talking.

And Reverend James Bevel is talking: "I want everybody
to listen to me. Everybody listen." He's talking to the children,
telling them not to go back to school—to march off to jail
instead. "You get an education in jail, too. In the schools
you've been going to, they haven't taught you to be proud of

yourselves and they haven't taught you good history—they haven't taught you the price of freedom. . . . The white man has brainwashed us, tricked us; but Mr. Charlie's brainwashing is washing off now. . . . And the most important thing in the struggle is all to stay together. This is why we've been enslaved all these years: our parents didn't have enough love for one another to suffer for one another. We've got to start learning to love one another enough to say: as long as one Negro kid is in jail, we all want to be in jail. If everybody in town would be arrested, everybody would be free, wouldn't they?"

Forman is talking again: "This is a great day, people. Let's talk about it. Let's try to understand what's going on." There is the noise of sirens outside, and uproar of the crowd. Some of the children run to the windows. "Now this is the thing that can cause confusion," he says. "Let's be orderly. Let's not worry about what's going on outside. The important thing that's happening is happening right in here."

This is so. The words in one of their songs run: "The truth shall make us free." Within these walls, the truth they affirm is making them free. The same truth that will carry them out into the streets.

And now Martin Luther King is speaking: "They can handle violence; but we have a weapon that they can't handle. They don't know what to do with us when we are nonviolent; they are confused. You don't need to strike them in return, or curse them in return. Just keep going. Just keep presenting your body as a witness to the truth as you see it. Don't get tired. Don't get bitter. Are you tired?" The answer comes in a great shout: "NO!"

One Part of the Truth Is Out

The reporters stand across the street, assigned to report the truth—though they stand rather far away from it. The cops and the firemen stand there assigned to break it up, to douse it. For it doesn't match the official truth. This truth has been expressed to me by the soft-voiced lady in the white piqué dress who sat next to me on the plane: "Most of them are quite content, quite content. When my mother died last Spring, two Negro women called me at once. 'We've heard about Muddy. We're coming to take care of you this week' . . . They wouldn't take a penny." The other part of her truth, oddly enough: "My friends are putting floodlights in their backyards—afraid. They're ready enough to murder us in our sleep, you know."

The demonstrators have taken out of their pockets anything that could possibly be called a weapon—"even a nailfile, even a spoon." They march out of the church, two by two, holding up their signs: WE WANT FREEDOM! The firemen maneuver the heavy hoses into position. "It's a strange thing," one of the leaders has said, back in the church, "They have the idea that water can put out all fire. They don't seem to know that there's a certain type of fire water can't get to."

A group of children has emerged now from a side door of the church. Firemen drag a length of hose in their direction. The children are singing bravely but their voices waver a little. Mary Hamilton hurries over to join them. She dances in front of them, clapping her hands to their song with fierce gaiety. The song gains spirit. Moving from foot to foot, she stamps the off-beat of the tune, on the beat striking her hands together with the motion of cymbals. Sometimes she faces the children and sometimes she faces the sweating fireman. The fireman is hypnotized by her; aims the hose but can't quite seem to get the water turned on. Then all of a sudden the children vanish back into the side door—will-o'-the-wisp. They'll be out another door a little later on.

All through the city the firemen drag their hoses, trying to douse this fire. But the demonstrators spring up first in one place and then in another—WE WANT FREEDOM!—then in another, then in another—WE WANT FREEDOM!—assembling, then spreading out from half a dozen churches across the town. Sometimes they picket, sometimes they march, sometimes they sit in. The water doesn't quench their truth, so the cops begin to try to put it away. They stuff the demonstrators into paddy wagons and rush them off to jail. The cars go rocketing through the streets of the city, from every direction —hands waving through the bars, the Negroes calling at the top of their voices: WE WANT FREEDOM! WE WANT FREEDOM! WE WANT FREEDOM! The city couldn't have provided them with a better public address system. The citizens of Birmingham stand on the sidewalks, eyes opening wide.

Another Part of the Truth

The demonstrators sing gaily as they ride off to jail: "*Every-body* wants freedom! Bull Connor wants freedom! Our mayor wants freedom! The driver wants freedom!" They like to announce in church: "Now we'll all pray for Bull Connor." They are being playful. But they are also serious. At the meetings they make it plain: "We're struggling not to save ourselves alone. . . . This fight is for the freedom of the white man also—to free him from fear and from hate. . . . We're going to have to teach him."

The press—standing across the street—misses these words. The demonstrators come marching out of the church; the hoses are turned against them, and the water drives them this way and that; they are mingled with onlookers from the neighborhood. Some of the onlookers lose their heads, and the bottles and the stones begin to fly. A riot is reported. It's not made clear that the demonstrators themselves have remained nonviolent throughout. ("Negroes have been throwing bottles and cussing for the last hundred years and it hasn't ended segregation. We're going to *peacefully* protest, and we're going to break it down this way.") WE WANT FREEDOM!—that part of the truth is out. But another part of the truth has been blurred: THIS FIGHT IS FOR THE FREEDOM OF THE WHITE MAN ALSO.

The Freedom of the White Man Also

I recall the contorted faces of whites in the crowds. I recall the puckered face of the lady on the plane. "Martin Luther King? A dreadful man!" She draws away from me; her chin is trembling.

I recall my own distress—own sharp sense of a distance between black and white hard to travel.

On my way to Birmingham, S.N.C.C. has arranged hospitality for me at the house of an old Negro lady. I arrive rather late at night along with one of their field workers, Ruby Dee Smith. The old lady, in her nightgown, opens the door to us, and stares and stares at me; fetches herself a glass of milk with bits of bread in it and, spooning it slowly into her mouth, stares again, trying to believe what she sees. What have we done that she must stare like that—unable to believe that I am there?

Dick Gregory's mournful words return to me: "Whitey has made so many mistakes. Oh yes."

I stand on the lawn of A. D. King's bombed house and suddenly notice another old lady, close by, staring at me—not in amazement, this time, but in dread. Her finger is pointed at me. Too aghast to be able to speak, she just stares and points. Am I not one of them, the enemy—"whitey"? I put my hand on her shoulder: "I am a friend, a friend." Her look stays with me.

I stand in the church. The congregation has risen to sing "We shall overcome some day". They have linked hands. Have I the right to reach out and to take hands, too? I am not sure, not sure. I stand self-conscious.

They Sing: "The Truth Shall Make Us Free Some Day . . . Black and White Together, We Shall Live in Peace"

The truth is that distance between us is unreal. I have always known it. But the distance nevertheless has been there.

The evening that I arrive in Birmingham, at a mass meeting, I decide that I want to join the demonstration the next day. There *is* no distance between us; I know it; and I wish to affirm the fact. Then on the way back to the motel afterwards I suddenly lose my nerve. First, the recognition jumps at me that the jail will be segregated. I won't go marching off to it black and white together; I'll be marched, quite by myself, into a cell with other whites who may well feel like beating me up. I struggle with this fear. I manage to come to terms with it for a moment. Other fears leap up in me, to reinforce it. Even if I get through the days in jail—what will happen to me when I come out? I won't be welcome in this city. Will anyone be there to set me on my way home? Or will I be forgotten by my fellow demonstrators—on my own? A sense of stark abandonment enters my soul. I give up the plan.

Then, over the next days, the people I move among give me their courage. There is a contagion to it, and I catch it; it is simple as that. I catch it through closeness. They make me one of them.

The afternoon of my second full day there I enter one of

the churches for a meeting. I go in through a side door, and
I'm no sooner inside than word is passed that Guy Carawan,
the folk singer, has been arrested for trying to enter; Bull
Connor has decided to allow no white people in the meeting.
So I keep in the wings, wondering what is going to happen
now. A. D. King is headed up to the podium, to speak, and as
he passes the place where I'm standing he comes toward me
and takes my hand in his, with extraordinary gentleness. We've
never met before. "I'm A. D. King," he says very softly.
"Happy to see you, but I thought you might be interested to
know that they've just arrested Guy Carawan." His voice is
altogether calm, and the calm enters me from him, as the
warmth of his hand passes to my hand. Some of the people
standing there gather closely round me and move me, hidden
in their midst, up into the balcony where Connor's spies are
unlikely to come. Then at the end of the meeting they gather
round me and move me to a back door. One of the students,
"Meatball," will bring a car up to the door and smuggle me
out. But when I reach the door, he has not yet been able to
maneuver the car there, through the thick of other cars. And
suddenly someone calls out in a whisper: "Bull Connor is just
outside!" A tall thin man, a stranger to me, hurries close, assuming a comic falsetto: "Don't you worry, honey! We'll get
you out! Won't let Bull Connor get you! Bull Connor out
there!" His piping voice imitates a childish panic—so charm-
ingly that my panic evaporates. "Here, we'll wrap you up,
honey." Someone has borrowed a thin black cape from someone else. They wrap it round me. "Here, push your hair up
under—Here!" and the tall man claps a man's straw hat on my
head. The car has drawn close at last. They gather round me,
chattering, and lead me out—I am an old man—and thrust me
down onto the floor of the car. Several of them jump in, chattering, laughing, and we head for somebody's house. After
we've driven for a while, "Here, you can sit up now, but put
my hat on you," a woman called Jimmie tells me. I pull a large
purple velvet cloche down to just over my eyes. We enter the
district where a friend of hers lives. "Now you're safe as a
rabbit in a briar patch."

They have wrapped me in their own clothes; they have

smuggled me into their briar patch. They have wrapped me in their gaiety and their courage. I am not any longer the same. It is my third morning in Birmingham. Almost a thousand children have gathered in the church—bringing their toothbrushes and their rubbers, ready to go to jail. James Forman is talking to them. He tells them, "The reason they were able to defeat your parents is that they'd take one out, they'd pick on one, and all the rest would just stand and look. We have to learn to stay together." He looks about and sees several white faces. Joan Baez is there, to sing with the children for a few minutes; and another young white woman is present, a friend of hers; and I am sitting there. Forman tells them, "If they come in here today and try to arrest any of our white friends, tell them at that moment, 'Take all of us!' Don't hesitate. We'll stand and say, 'Take all of us!' " His words touch me like a blessing. I know I am one of them, and because of that, I know I have the strength finally to go off to jail—even by myself. After a few groups have lined up and marched out onto the street, I stand up to join the next one. I stand next to one of the few mothers who have come that day—a large gentle woman who has brought her three-year-old son. I put my hand on her shoulder. I'm trembling a little bit. "Don't be afraid," she tells me. I tell her I won't be. Then each of us takes one of the little boy's hands. The children begin to sing. And it's time to walk out onto the street.

On the Killing of Children

Eighteen days after the triumphant March on Washington, the civil rights movement faced its biggest crisis since it became a movement. Four little girls were murdered by a bomb blast in Birmingham's Sixteenth Street Baptist Church. Within a few hours, Birmingham police had shot a fifth youth in the back, and two teenagers, returning from a segregationist rally, at which they had been given a pistol, had shot another boy, 12-year-old Vergil Ware, who was riding peacefully on the handlebars of his brother's bicycle, on his way home from a Sunday outing.

Both bombings and police brutality against Negroes are commonplace in Birmingham. Only a few weeks earlier, after the second bombing of Negro attorney Arthur Shore's residence, police had shot 20-year-old John Coley, when a crowd gathered outside Shore's house to protest the bombings. On that occasion, the bullets had apparently been intended for civil rights leader Fred Shuttlesworth. Eyewitnesses report that: "At least one section of armed white men driving through the crowd saw Coley and yelled: 'Kill that nigger Shuttlesworth! That's the nigger Shuttlesworth there. . . .' Then shots began tearing through the crowd and Coley, who was looking in the opposite direction, hit the ground face down. Blood gushed from a huge hole in the back of his neck —and he never moved again." (Muhammad Speaks, Sept. 27th, 1963.)

But the fact that the girls were killed while attending Sunday school, and that six children were killed in one day, led to extensive news coverage and shocked people around the world, as the other killings have not.

After the initial shock and horror, integrationists responded with a variety of calls to action, some of them ill-considered and rapidly abandoned, but all of them revealing a new sense of urgency and determination, a new readiness to embrace more radical and unconventional methods than before the bombing. The failure of either the white South or the Kennedy Administration to react at all adequately to the infamy of the latest bombing and to the ensuing bestiality of the police seemed to drive home the lesson that there is no sense holding back in order to get help from either source.

One lone voice cried out in the wilderness of white Birmingham. Charles Morgan, 33-year-old Birmingham attorney, stood up at a meeting of the Young Men's Business Club, the day after the bombing, and delivered a searing, though compassionate, indictment of all white Birmingham.

The ten chairmen of the March on Washington called for a National Day of Mourning, on Sunday, September 22nd. Mass meetings were held in numerous cities throughout the country. James Baldwin and James Farmer talked to more than ten thousand people outside the Department of Justice Building, in Foley Square, New York City. Another featured speaker was Bayard Rustin. He received an ovation when he began his remarks by saying:

"This is not a zoo, and therefore I intensely resent the New York Police Department's having horses here today. I can assure you that they may run over fifty young students with horses [as they had done at a protest two days earlier] but they will not do it here. . . . We know how to run a disciplined revolution, and I dare them to send horses to another demonstration that we have."

Charles Morgan, Jr.

The Popularity of Hatred

September 16th, 1963

Four little girls were killed in Birmingham yesterday. A mad, remorseful, worried community asks: "Who did it? Who threw that bomb? Was it a Negro or a white?" The answer should be: "We all did it." Every last one of us is condemned for that crime and the bombing before it and the ones last month, last year, a decade ago. We all did it.

A short time later, white policemen kill a Negro and wound another. A few hours later, two young men on a motor bike shoot and kill a Negro child. Fires break out and, in Montgomery, white youths assault Negroes.

And all across Alabama, an angry, guilty people cry out their mocking shouts of indignity and say they wonder *why? who?* Everyone then "deplores" the "dastardly" act.

But, you know, the "who" of "who did it?" is really rather simple. The "who" is every little individual who talks about the "niggers" and spreads the seeds of his hate to his neighbor and his son. The jokester, the crude oaf whose racial jokes rock the party with laughter. The "who" is every governor who shouted for lawlessness and became a law violator. It is every senator and every representative who in the halls of Congress stands and with mock humility tells the world that things back home aren't really like they are. It is courts that move ever so slowly and newspapers that timorously defend the law. It is all the Christians and all their ministers who spoke too late in anguished cries against violence. It is the coward in each of us who clucks admonitions. We are ten years of lawless preachments, ten years of criticism of law, of courts, of our fellow man, a decade of telling school children the opposite of what the civics books say. We are a mass of intolerance and bigotry, and stand indicted before our young. We are cursed by the failure of each of us to accept responsibility, by our defense of an already dead institution.

Yesterday, while Birmingham, which prides itself on the number of its churches, was attending worship services, a bomb went off and an all-white police force moved into action, a police force which has been praised by city officials and others at least once a day for a month or so. A police force which has solved no bombings. A police force which many Negroes feel is perpetrating the very evils we decry. And why would Negroes think this?

There are no Negro policemen; there are no Negro sheriff's deputies. Few Negroes have served on juries; few have been allowed to vote; few have been allowed to accept responsibility or granted even a simple part to play in the administration of justice. Do not misunderstand me. It is not that I think that white policemen had anything whatsoever to do with the killing of these children or previous bombings. It's just that Negroes who see an all-white police force must think in terms of its failure to prevent or solve the bombings and think perhaps Negroes would have worked a little bit harder. They throw rocks and bottles and bullets. And we whites don't seem to know why the Negroes are lawless. So we lecture them.

Birmingham is the only city in America where the police chief and the sheriff in the school crisis had to call its local ministers together to tell them to do their duty. The ministers of Birmingham, who have done so little for Christianity, call for prayer at high noon in a city of lawlessness and, in the same breath, speak of our city's "image." Did those ministers visit the families of the Negroes in their hour of travail? Did many of them go to the homes of their brothers and express their regrets in person or pray with the crying relatives? Do they admit Negroes into their ranks at the church?

Who is guilty? A moderate mayor elected to change things in Birmingham and who moves so slowly and looks elsewhere for leadership? A business community which shrugs its shoulders and looks to the police or perhaps somewhere else for leadership? A newspaper which has tried so hard of late, yet finds it necessary to lecture Negroes every time a Negro home is bombed. A governor who offers a reward but mentions not his own failure to preserve either segregation or law and order? And what of those lawyers and politicians who counsel people as to what the law is not when they know full well what the law is?

Those four little Negro girls were human beings. They have lived their fourteen years in a leaderless city; a city where no one accepts responsibility; where everybody wants to blame somebody else. A city with a reward fund which grew like Topsy as a sort of sacrificial offering, a balm for the conscience of the "good people." The "good people" whose ready answer is for those "right wing extremists" to shut up. People who absolve themselves of guilt. The liberal lawyer who told me this morning: "Me? I'm not guilty," then proceeding to discuss the guilt of the other lawyers, the ones who told the people that the Supreme Court did not properly interpret the law. And that's the way it is with the Southern liberals. They condemn those with whom they disagree for speaking, while they sit in fearful silence.

Birmingham is a city in which the major industry, operated from Pittsburgh, never tried to solve the problem. It is a city where four little Negro girls can be born into a second-class school system, live a segregated life, ghettoed into their own little neighborhoods, restricted to Negro churches, destined to ride in Negro ambulances, to Negro wards of hospitals or to a Negro cemetery. Local papers, on their front and editorial pages, call for order and then exclude their names from obituary columns.

And who is really guilty? Each of us. Each citizen who has not consciously attempted to bring about peaceful compliance with the decisions of the Supreme Court of the United States, each citizen who has ever said "they ought to kill that 'nigger,'" every citizen who votes for the candidate with the bloody flag; every citizen and every school board member and school teacher and principal and businessman and judge and lawyer who has corrupted the minds of our youth; every person in this community who has in any way contributed during the past several years to the popularity of hatred, is at least as guilty, or more so, than the demented fool who threw the bomb.

What's it like living in Birmingham? No one ever really has and no one will until this city becomes part of the United States.

Birmingham is not a dying city; it is dead.

James Baldwin

We Can Change the Country

Before I say anything else, I have an announcement to make. I want all of you, and your wives and your children and your brothers-in-law and everyone you know, to resolve as of this moment that you will buy no presents for Christmas. And when I say no presents, I mean not a nail file, not a tooth brush, and I want you to tell your children, as of this moment and on Christmas Day, that the reason there is no Santa Claus this year is because we have lost the right—by the murder of our brothers and sisters—to be called a Christian nation. And until we regain that right, we cannot celebrate the birth of the Prince of Peace. And I am very serious about this for two reasons: A) Morally, I think this nation should be, for the foreseeable future, in mourning. B) One must face the fact that this Christian nation may never have read any of the gospels, but they do understand money.

We are not—we who are on the barricades in this unprecedented revolution—in the position of someone in the Congo or someone in Cuba. That is, we cannot take over the land. The terms of this revolution are precisely these: that we will learn to live together here or all of us will abruptly stop living. And I mean that. This is not, and never has been, a white nation. I am not a pupil or a ward of Senator Eastland. I am an American. My forefathers bled and suffered and died to create this nation, and if my forefathers had not dammed all those rivers and picked all that cotton and laid all that track, there would not be an American economy today.

We are living, at the moment, through a terrifying crisis, and let me try to put it in the cruelest and most abrupt terms that I can. Let us say that a hundred years ago, when I was technically emancipated from the land and given over to the landlords and the bosses—let us say that I was happy in my place and that I loved doing all that singing and dancing down on the levee. Now I, and my father and my grandfather, to say nothing of my grandmother and her mother, never for a moment believed that we were singing and dancing down on the levee because we were so happy, and not for a moment does any black man that I've ever encountered believe that he really was what the country said he was. But what has happened is that the country (by the country I mean our government and most of our citizens) believes that I was happy in my place. They believe it so strongly that now they have the courage to ask what does the Negro want? Well, I know what the Negro wants, and any man who is able to walk and talk knows what the Negro wants. If you know what *you* want, then you know what *I* want.

It is the American Republic—repeat, the American Republic—which created something which they call a "nigger." They created it out of necessities of their own. The nature of the crisis is that I am not a "nigger"—I never was. I am a man. The question with which the country is confronted is this: Why do you need a "nigger" in the first place, and what are you going to do about him now that he's moved out of his place? Because I am not what you said I was. And if my place, as it turns out, is not my place, then you are not what you said you were, and where's your place? There has never been in this country a Negro problem. I have never been upset by the fact that I have a broad nose, big lips and kinky hair. *You* got upset. And now you must ask yourself why. I, for example, do not bring down property values when I move in. You bring them down when you move out.

Now there are several concrete and dangerous things that we must do to prevent the murder—and please remember there are several million ways to murder—of future children (by which I mean both black and white children). And one of them, and perhaps the most important, is to take a very hard look at our economic structure and our political institutions. For example, the North (for as long as I've been in the North, and I was born in the North) has prided itself on not being like the Southern racists. In the North they don't have signs up saying "white" and "colored." No one tells you where you can and cannot go. In the North, you have to find that out day by day, by what we call trial and error. But the moment you go anywhere near what The Man is really concerned about—I mean his pocketbook—what happened in Birmingham happens in New York.

New York is a segregated city. It is not segragated by accident; it is not an act of God that keeps the Negroes in Harlem. It is the real estate boards and the banks that do it. And when you attack that, that's where the power is. For example, I ask all of you to ask yourselves what would happen if Harlem refused to pay the rent for a month. We've got to bring the cat out of hiding. And where is he? He's hiding in the bank. We've got to flush him out. We have to begin a massive campaign of civil disobedience. I mean nationwide. And this is no stage joke. *Some laws should not be obeyed.*

Secondly, when I talk about our political institutions, there is no reason for any American to continue to be victimized by what we still refer to as the Republican and Democratic parties. Speaking for myself, I cannot imagine voting for any Republican, because the party contains Goldwater. I can't imagine voting for any Democrat, because that party contains Eastland. It is important to bear in mind, or to recover the notion, that we are responsible for our government and the government is responsible to us. The government is supposed to represent *us*. It is time that the government knew that if the government does not represent us, if it insists on representing a handful of nostalgic Southern colonels, the government will be replaced.

For a very long time, we have operated on the theory of

the lesser of two evils. For example, I myself was so terrified of that salesman called Nixon that I allowed myself to be stampeded into the Kennedy camp. And I believe that was done, if you remember, by a phone call to Martin Luther King, when he was in jail. That swung the Negro vote. Well, the man has been in power for quite some time. If we care about this country—and not only the area of civil rights—it is time to serve notice on our representatives that they are under the obligation to represent us and that they cannot be said to represent us if they continually betray twenty million citizens. It is time to let the government know that we will no longer accept this peculiar, pathetic excuse: "We have no right to act." If they can invade Cuba, they can act. It is time to say, and unequivocally, that I—speaking now for myself, Jimmy Baldwin, and speaking for myself as though I were white even—I don't see any reason why I should invade Havana. I would much rather invade Miami.

The moral leaders of the Free World are in great trouble. This is not a free country, and if you doubt me, when you leave here, walk or ride up to 125th Street and walk through those streets and ask yourself what you'd feel like if you lived there, why you lived there if you did, and why it looks like a concentration camp. I mean the police walking two by two and three by three. Ask yourself what chances you would have if you lived there, to get theft or fire or life insurance. Now, this, as I said, is not an act of God. It is an act of the nation and it began not quite a hundred years ago when the North signed a bargain with the South: they would take me out of the cotton fields and lift me over to the factories, where I've been ever since. If you doubt me, check it out with your labor unions. Ask yourself why the Puerto Ricans and the Negroes are pushing carts in the garment center and nobody else.

Now we are here not only to mourn those children, who cannot really be mourned. We are here to begin to achieve the American Revolution. It is time that we the people took the government and the country into our own hands. It is perfectly possible to tap the energy of this country. There is a vast amount of energy here, and we can change and save ourselves. We don't have to be at the mercy forever of these sordid political machines. It is possible to create a third party, you know.

And finally, let me leave you with this: the government pretends it has no right to arrest Governor Wallace, but I know that governors have been impeached. The F.B.I. has not been able to find a single bomber. In Alabama alone, fifty bombings and not one culprit—not yet. The F.B.I. can't find them. Let me tell you why they can't find them. They can't afford to. They stay at the homes of the people who did the bombings. And when they come into town they investigate the students. We are the guilty party. When they come into Birmingham and Mississippi, they don't investigate the Ku Klux Klan or the White Citizens' Council or the mayor. They investigate the people in the streets. . . .

If I had done one tenth of what General Edwin Walker has done in Mississippi, if I had been inciting a mob to murder children, I would be in jail. When Robert Williams armed the Negroes in Monroe, North Carolina, the Justice Department hounded him out of this country on charges of kidnapping and called him—I've seen the posters in the post office myself—a psychopathic, dangerous, armed kidnapper. Well, General Edwin Walker is white and Robert Williams is black, and that is the reason one is in Cuba and the other is—probably working in the Justice Department. If we don't now move, literally move, sit down, stand, walk, don't go to work, don't pay the rent, if we don't now do everything in our power to change this country, this country will turn out to be in the position, let us say, of Spain, a country which is so tangled and so trapped and so immobilized by its interior dissension that it can't do anything else.

We have already paid a tremendous price for what we've done to Negro people. We have denied, and we are paying for the denial of the energy of twenty million people. No society can afford that. The future is going to be worse than the past if we do not let the people who represent us know that it is our country. A government and a nation are not synonymous. We can change the government, and we will.

James Farmer

Guilty Bystanders

Brothers and sisters, I could not take my eyes off that inscription on the building to the side: "The true administration of justice is the firmest pillar of good government." The true administration of justice in Birmingham, Alabama, in Mississippi, in Louisiana, and in Georgia. The deaths of the six children were not the first atrocities which have been committed against persons who are merely asking for freedom. I saw state troopers in Gadsden, Ala., with their fearsome electric cattle prods, prodding children and old men and women. I saw people who had been arrested for peacefully asking for freedom, jailed and beaten. "The true administration of justice is the firmest pillar of good government." There in Louisiana, in Plaquemine, horses used as weapons. I understand the same thing happened in New York yesterday. In Plaquemine, children were trampled by horses. One girl still lies in a hospital after having been stepped upon by a horse ridden by a state trooper. . . .

The bigots all over the South have seen a green light and they are pulling out their violence and their brutality. They are trying to stop you—they are trying to stop all of us in the fight for freedom. We have not been stopped by dogs. We have found that when the dogs bite our people in Birmingham or in Mississippi, we bleed all over the country. We have found that the fire hoses that roll women over in the streets merely build up the demand for freedom in New York, and Chicago, and California. They have tried to stop us with injunctions and restraining orders. There in Louisiana, before and during and after the days I spent in jail, I was served with one restraining order after another—issued, my friends, not by a state court, but by a federal court of the United States of America. That didn't stop us. After all, we've been under a restraining order for three hundred and fifty years now. They are not going to stop us with the bombs either. . . .

Thus far, this has been a very cheap revolution. We have not suffered much in the revolution. Not many people have died. A few have been beaten, a few have been jailed, but the long haul lies in front of us, and many more people will suffer before it is over. That suffering, yes, is bound to come. Wallace is to blame, but Wallace is not alone to blame. I accuse the Department of Justice and the President of the United States for their inactivity. They must share the blame with the demented fool who threw that bomb. The Department of Justice says that it has no statutory authority to get troops into Birmingham, and yet the Administration refuses to push for Part Three, which would grant statutory authority to the Department of Justice to move. They cannot have it both ways: they cannot say we are on the side of the angels, but we don't have the authority, out of one side of the mouth, and then out of the other side of the mouth say we need no further authority. If the Federal Government cannot protect its citizens today, my friends, the Federal Government ought to say so. It should say so to the world, and it would be a horrible admission. They have the authority and the right and we demand that troops go into Birmingham and wherever the rights of citizens are being trampled upon.

Now you are here, of course, to mourn and to grieve for the death of our little children. But mourn not the blessed dead. Mourn rather the tortuous living. Mourn the agonized babies of black skin who have a life expectancy in our country that is ten years less than babies of lighter skin. They too are being killed. Mourn the babies unborn who have less of a chance to be born alive, for their skins are black and their mothers, in many cases, undernourished, for they're poor and work too hard. It is a bomb of prejudice and bigotry that is killing them. Mourn our children in Harlem and in Bedford-Stuyvesant. Oh, you don't hear the bomb blast, but mourn those who must live with cockroaches and with rats. Mourn those who are victimized by disease germs. The slumlords who allow such conditions to go on are just as guilty as the fools and beasts of Birmingham. Mourn too the child of black skin, who when he grows up may get the training for a job but will not be able to work at that job; instead, will be confined to pushing a broom and a mop. Mourn him too, for the bomb is killing him. Yes, my friends, the bomb is bigger than Birmingham. The bomb is as big as our country. Mourn not those alone. Grieve too for the Negro who says: I have it made. I will get me a car as big as your house and have me a good time and die. Mourn him. He helped to throw the bomb too. Mourn those of us who have not registered and do not vote in New York City. We too are helping to make the bombs—the bombs of the future. On Election Day, the man who is not registered and who stands on a street corner thinking thoughts far away —that man with idle hands is manufacturing the bombs for a hundred Birminghams. Mourn him. Mourn all of us who have not been involved in this fight. Oh, you come to a rally. You will go home after the rally is over. But have you done your bit for the children of Birmingham? The best thing you can do for the children of Birmingham is to become an intimate part of this movement. . . .

We all share the guilt. The guilt is America's. Every Negro who has walked into a segregated waiting room shares the guilt for the continuation of Jim Crow. An African friend of mine was asked, "What do you think of the American Negro?" His answer was, "What does the American Negro think of himself?" So what *do* you think of yourselves, my brothers and sisters, black and white? What do you think of yourselves when you allow Jim Crow to go on, and accept segregation? What do you of white skins think of yourselves when a Negro moves into your neighborhood or your apartment house? You don't throw a bomb, like the beasts of Birmingham, but you pack your bags and silently steal away into the night. How long will it go on? How long will this nation tolerate segregation and discrimination, which kills little children in Birmingham? I'll tell you how long. As long as you let it. As long as you try to be an innocent bystander in a time of great social upheaval. There are no innocent bystanders now. If you are a bystander, you are guilty. If you are a bystander, you are helping the bigots in their evil deeds. You are helping to preserve the *status quo*. You are helping to cut ten years off the lives of one-tenth of our population. You are helping to kill babies who have not yet been born. The call is *Freedom Now*, and I believe, my friends, that I will live to see the day when the six children of Birmingham who gave their lives will be leading a giant movement throughout this country of black and white, of persons who say "we have had enough!—bring an end to Jim Crow!" and if the Administration will not move, then the Administratoin will be replaced.

Theodore Roszak

Children as Hostages

Four children are dead in Birmingham, Alabama, victims of as yet unknown killers, men who murdered out of a hate as blind as it was fierce. What shall we call such an act? Not a crime. For it was more and worse than that. The victims were too special and wholly undeserving, the act too grotesquely irrational. Tragedy? Surely not. For that is too comfortably impersonal, too consolingly fatalistic. Not a crime, not a tragedy. Atrocity is the word, the black and brutal word we need to describe this massacre of the innocent.

Who is to blame? The bomb throwers, of course. They primarily. But, we are told by those who would have us know that their own moral insight is deep and unobscured, "We are *all* to blame . . . the system as a whole . . . white society at large is at fault." Four children are dead in Birmingham, victims of indiscriminate violence, and we are asked to understand that the whole of the white community is implicated. For what we have done and left undone. For inaction and long indifference, as much as for any act of bigotry we have ever committed or condoned.

All this is true. But the truth goes deeper than I suspect its speakers realize. The truth goes deeper than James Baldwin or Martin Luther King may realize when they sweepingly accuse white society at large of this atrocity; deeper, I think—and this is a hard thing to say—than many leading members of the Negro community suspect, than even the parents of the victims know.

To condemn society at large for such atrocities has become a cliché. "Society is responsible." . . . how often have each of us said it? Like all clichés, there is point and validity to the remark. But it has become worn and imprecise with too much usage. Like all clichés, it comes to mind too quickly and blocks further thought. It is true . . . as far as it goes. But we must go further. There must be no clichés about these four children. We must understand exactly what their murder means.

I am disturbed by the limited grasp of this situation which even the best and noblest minds in our society seem to have. In response to the deed, James Baldwin calls for rent strikes in Harlem and proposes a Christmas-buying boycott. Again, these things may be good, as far as they go. But we must go further. For what has happened in Birmingham is *not* a matter simply of civil rights in Alabama. It is not simply a matter of race relations throughout America. And it will do no ultimate good to confine our thinking, our mourning and active atoning for this in that narrow compass.

This is what happened in Birmingham: let us be clear about it. Men, twisted by fear and savage with anger, struck out in what they must have thought was their own defense: the defense of values and institutions in which they believed. Threatened, they turned to violence. Desperate, they were prepared to be indiscriminate in perpetrating that violence. Hate-filled, they were willing to destroy even the innocent by an act of wholesale terror. And yet, how deliberately they must have planned the act, how methodically they must have gathered the dynamite and fashioned the bomb. Desperation and hatred were in them, but a cold desperation, a cunning hatred. And what must their hope have been in doing this thing? That the act would frighten and drive off those who threatened them . . . that it would stop them, cow them, *deter* them. And the blacker and madder the act, the more blindly destructive, the greater would be its deterrent value.

This describes the atrocity committed in Birmingham. But is it not clear that it describes much more: a world in which children everywhere are held hostage to the hatreds and desperations of organized society? Thus, it describes, in all its essential horror, the political condition that we call the Cold War.

This is what we must realize, what the Negro community especially must understand. Even as white society has mur-

dered these children, believing, mistakenly, that it thus defends itself, so American society as a whole, the white and
colored communities together, steel themselves day by day to
the murder of millions of children . . . in the name of national
defense.

To be sure, the innocence of the world extends beyond
children—to whole populations of men and women. I don't
wish to be misunderstood. But innocence is nowhere so clear,
so all-embracing, so indisputable as in the community of children. Yet these especially are the targets of the deliberate
cruelty upon which the major political powers rely for what
they call "defense." And in the evil men intend against children, the moral failure of our time thrusts itself irrepressibly
through every rationalization. There is nothing that pardons it,
justifies it, alleviates its wickedness.

So then, where does the real mockery lie in John Kennedy's response to Birmingham? Not simply in the fact, as
James Baldwin observes, that he sends an ex-soldier and an ex-
football coach to "investigate" the scene of the crime. But
rather that a man who continues to arm this country against
hundreds of millions of children, a man who has never
questioned his decision to do this, should now indulge himself
in the reactions of one shocked and grief-stricken by the deaths
of four children. How can we believe him? How can we believe in the grief of any member of our society, if that grief
does not lead him to denounce and reject, not only the in-
humanity of racism, but the enormity of the balance of terror?

I put the question to the Negro community and its leaders: what can it be, ultimately, but a futility to expect this
society, the colored and white within it, so acquiescent in the
preparation for thermonuclear war, to take moral resolve from
the deaths of four children? The cause of these Negro children
is the cause of the endangered children of the entire world, a
cause which dissolves the distinction between "foreign" and
"domestic" affairs.

It is distressing that in their response to this atrocity so
many Negro leaders seem unaware of this fact. Or leave it
unexpressed. As if it might distract us from the main issue.
Where should these children be mourned? Not only in the

streets of Birmingham and Harlem. There, to be sure. But not *only* there. Clearly, these children must be mourned at every missile base and radiation laboratory and munitions factory and submarine yard in America: wherever child-killing is planned and its weapons perfected. Mourned there as if the attack upon their young lives stemmed from there as much as from the headquarters of the Ku Klux Klan or the White Citizens Council. Surely no experience we have known thus far as a people more clearly manifests the essential one-ness of the peace and civil rights issues. Is it not clear: they must be understood as a single goal, a single struggle?

The words that are most vivid in my mind as I write this are those of James Baldwin: an address he delivered in New York shortly after the atrocity. It was a fine address, charged with revolutionary implications, a frontal attack on the whole order and ethos of white America. And still it left unexpressed (I ask, why?) the indissoluble ethical alliance of race relations with the cause of peace. As if it made sense to confine one's dissent from the American social order within the national boundaries. But the evil is so very much greater. It extends to the international system which our society participates in sustaining: a system which predicates its stability upon the threat of genocide. It is impossible for me to understand how any critique of our society that purports to be radical, that strives to mobilize productive action can ignore this fact and settle for less than rubbing our collective noses in all the dirt. There are other and more destructive forces than the bombs of the Ku Klux Klan to protect our children from.

A. J. Muste

Rifle Squads or the Beloved Community

Everyone who is at all informed about the civil rights struggle seems agreed that the summer of 1964 will be critical and quite possibly tragic. The present situation is a product of forces which have been piling up for years and even centuries. The changes that will come about if integration is achieved will be profound in all spheres of American life—the political patterns, the economy, the culture, the ethos. The issues which are faced by individuals and organizations are highly complicated and emotion-laden. Yet all sorts of individuals and groups (including advocates and practitioners of "nonviolence") have to act—do act and make decisions these days—without adequate information to guide them and for the most part able to calculate the consequences only tentatively and partially. It is clearly important that we try to discern such guidelines to action as may be available.

The Georgia Council on Human Relations, with headquarters in Atlanta, has just issued a pamphlet entitled "Albany, Georgia—Police State." This city was the scene of bitter episodes in the civil-rights struggle in 1961 and 1962 and of an encounter between the Albany authorities and people, on the one hand, and the Quebec-Washington-Guantánamo Peace Walk, on the other, early in 1964. The pamphlet begins as follows:

> The white majority in Albany is living in a dream—a one hundred year old, segregated dream. In the dream, everybody dwells contentedly. Negroes are happy in their child-like singing and dancing. Whites are loving, understanding and paternal. Listen to some white people in Albany talk:
> "We love our Nigras and they love us."

> *"We're making a lot of progress here. I can't tell you how much we've done for our colored folks."*
>
> *"Many's the Monday morning I've gone downtown to get our yardman, Joe, out of jail. I take care of my own."*
>
> *"My maid told me herself: 'Oh, no ma'am, I don't want to be integrated. I wouldn't be happy in with all the white folks.'"*

I can testify on the basis of my own recent visits to Albany and other Southern cities that attitudes and statements such as those listed here are to be found even among religious and other leaders. Moreover, the parochialism which sees the situation essentially in terms of annoyance with Negroes who suddenly don't keep their place and become "aggressive" and with liberal dreamers or radical and "Communist" subverters who mislead Negroes is not confined to the South. Many people have no realization of the fact that we live in a world upheaval which is "happening" to all of us, white and Negro alike, much as a natural phenomenon like a hurricane or tidal wave asks no by-your-leave and makes no distinctions based on character, color or anything else. To change the metaphor, there is no awareness that on one level various people and groups are playing parts which they did not freely choose in a drama which they did not write and are not directing. The one thing we are powerless to do is to wish away the problem. Change and disturbance are as certain as "death and taxes."

In this context it is pertinent to point out that in so far as one can speak of "responsibility" in such historic developments, the white peoples of West Europe and North America have brought the present situation upon themseves and the rest of mankind. These people developed the technology which made large-scale industry possible and revolutionized agriculture. For several centuries, they spread their rule over the world by direct or indirect conquest, while preaching doctrines of freedom, equality and even love. They are now developing automation. The white nations are still the dominant military and nuclear powers. They made the mistake of engaging, mostly among themselves, in two colossal World Wars during the present century, as a result of which their hold over colonial peoples was broken.

The psychological aspect of white conquest should constantly be kept in mind these days. One of the great chasms in the world is that between the peoples who have known humiliation as peoples and those who have not, but instead have humiliated others. The white peoples are the ones who shoved other peoples, especially the colored, off the sidewalk in Western and in Asian and African countries alike, but no one could push the white master off the sidewalk anywhere.

The tide began to turn some time ago and is now flowing strongly in the other direction. The colored peoples are asserting themselves; the white people are having to make room and to abandon theories and practices of superiority. This is never easy, and seldom if ever has backing down from a position of superiority and domination to one of something near equality been done gracefully. But there come times when it has to be done.

We may here remind ourselves that it is a part of American tradition to hold that freedom cannot be handed to people on a silver platter, that real men and women stand up for their rights. "Don't tread on me" is thought of as a typical American slogan. To be ready to defend your own house and shoot the man who invades it and would perhaps insult or attack your women folk is commonly considered a laudable attitude, especially in the South. Are not Negroes following in this American tradition when they resent being patronized, when they do not have the "feel" of being free until they have taken hold of freedom? One often hears men of standing say that it would be different if Negroes asked (begged?) for their rights, but that "we're not going to be bullied into granting them—don't push us." In much the same way, many Englishmen, of the time of George III, thought of the colonials as upstarts and insolent boors for "demanding" rights and independence. There are many generations of humiliation and oppression behind the upsurge among Negroes and the belligerence now asserting itself. The results are not invariably pleasant. They are often bizarre and in some cases horrible, as revolutions always are. Perhaps we could at least not be so surprised that the familiar accompaniments of mass change manifest themselves in the United States today. We might even take some satisfaction in the realization that once more people are "demanding" that beautiful thing, freedom, and their leaders saying: "Let my people go." Perhaps whites could derive a measure of intellectual objectivity and reduce the intensity of their anger by realizing that these things are "happening" to us (as similar surprises, mysteries and disturbances have happened to others in revolutionary periods) rather than being "inflicted" by some mad or evil persons who live in the Negro section or flood out of New York's Harlem to tie up highways to the New York World's Fair.

Who Is Obstructing Whom?

There are a couple of other cases that might be mentioned of a tendency on the part of whites to apply a double standard and find reprehensible among Negroes what they condone or even practice themselves. Take the resentment of Southern senators and a good many citizens in all sections of the country against what are stigmatized as illegal, undemocratic and obstructionist tactics on the part of Negroes and their allies in the civil rights struggle. The senators are presently engaged in the obstructionist tactic of a filibuster. It is usually possible for men in positions of power with the machinery of government in their hands, working to maintain the *status quo*, to obstruct measures they oppose, in a respectable and outwardly legal fashion. Southern senators do not have to display themselves on the street in Washington or in the states where their civil rights senatorial colleagues live. They do not have to commit "trespass," or distribute leaflets on the streets, or "disobey an officer's command." But the results in the Senate today and the shocking business of their being elected to Congress by a small minority of voters in direct violation of the Constitution—are no less obstructionist and undemocratic, and all the more effective. People who have not realized this and worked to change it are not in a position to press the issue of obstructionism against the civil rights movement.

Another case in point is that of ordinances in Southern cities and towns, which limit civil liberties and are patently contrary to decisions laid down by the Supreme Court. The only recourse citizens (of whatever color) who want to exercise their democratic rights are supposed to have is to take each unconstitutional ordinance all the way to the Supreme Court, only—in many cases—to have a slightly altered but no less repressive ordinance adopted. In Mississippi a whole series of measures has been enacted for the avowed purpose of preventing or indefinitely delaying change in the racial pattern. Yet a good many people—and not all by any means poorly educated or simple-minded—have a more negative and intense reaction toward the proposed "stall-in" at the World's Fair (which I am not endorsing at this point) than to the colossal and enduring "stall-in" which is being staged in Mississippi.

A word needs to be said about the attitudes people take toward violence and nonviolence. Many act as if they thought Negroes have a peculiar obligation to be nonviolent, and especially in the civil rights struggle, the struggle for emancipation, Freedom Now. Yet in the very sections of Georgia and other states where any but the most pacific, not to say submissive, conduct on the part of Negroes seems shocking, and one frequently hears discourses on how readily Negroes resort to violence in their day-to-day life, one finds little espousal of pacifism or nonviolence. There is less concern than in some other sections of the country about the nuclear arms race and the danger of nuclear war. There is only a most embryonic peace movement. The Peace Churches are almost nonexistent. The military virtues are extolled. And, of course, one encounters practically no opposition to the location of missile bases and various other military installations in this region.

Until one has faced these facts, one is in no position, either politically or morally, to speak to the Negro community or the civil rights movement. This is preeminently true of those of us who advocate nonviolence.

Self-Defense

Turning now to the relevance of nonviolence in face of an undoubtedly growing tendency among Negroes to be suspicious of it and to feel that the movement has to become more militant and resort to more "realistic" tactics, it seems to me at the outset that there is a confusion around the use of the so-called "right to self-defense" and the call to exercise it, which ought to be cleared up. If one is talking in terms of legality and prevailing mores, then the right of an individual to defend himself, his home, his famliy, even to shoot a man who threatens to shoot or otherwise injure him and his family, undoubtedly exists in American and Western society. So long as that is the case, the Negro should have the right to self-defense as well as the white man. The pamphlet by the Georgia Council on Human Relations, referred to at the beginning of this article, states: "Everywhere in the streets of Albany you see white men carrying fire-arms. 'If you are white and can see to sign your name to the application, you are given a permit, no questions asked,' a white businessman observed. Of course, no Negroes need apply."

But the problem now before American society and in particular before Negroes is not so simply or automatically disposed of. For one thing, it is not generally assumed that a good community or one where people can live peacefully is one where all or even many citizens go about with guns in their belts or in their homes. Quite the contrary. As a matter of fact, Malcolm X and other "leaders" who call on Negroes to exercise the right of "self-defense" are not talking about that "right" as commonly understood. I suspect that some of them at least are aware of this and use the term as a demagogic and manipulative device. If they are not aware that this is the case, then they are not qualified to be leaders. People who do not know what an explosive or a poison is should not handle explosives or poisons.

What is meant in the present context is only in a small degree that an individual Negro should have a gun and under circumstances of great danger use it against another individual, white or Negro, who attacks him or his family. What is meant is that Negroes generally around the country should provide themselves with firearms and organize rifle clubs wherever there are conflict situations and the agencies which are supposed to provide safety for citizens and enable them to exercise elementary rights fail to do so for Negroes. This tactic is thought to hold good more particularly where whites are armed and have bullied and very likely actually injured or killed Negroes. It is this reasoning which has to be evaluated, not a simple case of "self-defense" or a spontaneous action of one individual toward another in a tense moment.

I have more than once heard it said by Negroes who are reluctantly turning to the idea that "nonviolence" may not be enough, that if in a couple or a few cases Negroes were to use force, or even threaten it seriously, this would cool down the Citizens Council people and white hoodlums. It would also convince the wielders of power in the South that it was no longer possible to keep Negroes down or to delay integration.

It seems to me conceivable that a shooting in some local situation might have what could be called a questioning or catalytic effect in that isolated local instance. But, putting pacifist considerations aside for a moment, one cannot realistically think of the problem raised by the tendency to become belligerent and violent in these isolated local terms. What is virtually certain to happen (and is indeed expected by people like Malcolm X and those who go along with him in greater or less degree) is a summer series of mass demonstrations and rioting in which Negroes will "fight back." Whitney Young, Jr., executive director of the National Urban League, commented on the restraint exercised up to now by Negroes as follows in recent testimony before a Congressional Committee:

> I think Negro citizens in the face of the years of provocation, in the face of the historic abuse, have shown an amazing restraint and an amazing loyalty. This from a people who have so little reason to have this kind of faith, who have all the provocation, the abuse, the murders, the years of want, of poor housing, of rats biting their children.

I trust I have made it abundantly clear that in a sense things "happen" to people, even the things they themselves do in situations of social turmoil, and that it is absurd to expect that Negroes will be an exception. But this does not absolve individuals and especially leaders from the necessity of making choices as to tactics and not simply being the pawns of historic forces or social hysteria. On this level and in this context the current trend away from nonviolence is certainly subject to suspicion and criticism.

One basic question that exponents of this trend have not, in my opinion, seriously faced is whether Negroes basically and eventually want to be part of American society. I do not necessarily mean society as it is now constituted and organized, though truth compels us to face the fact that this is probably just what large numbers of Negroes want. However, as I see it, a desegregated American society would be pretty radically different from the one we now have. Now I believe that whether in an America radically transformed or not, Negroes as a people want to live in the United States; they don't want to migrate and they don't seriously want to live in a Negro nation-state in some corner of American soil. Parenthetically, the desire of Negroes to control their own movement and not to have it run by whites is legitimate. In this as in other instances, demagogues use nationalist appeals or proclamations of Negro racial superiority to overcome social inertia and evoke a response from those who rightly want to be free from various forms of white domination or patronizing. At the same time, they run the risk of helping to precipitate tragedy.

If, for example, Negroes do want to be eventually a genuine part of the American community, then they will have to live in a community to which whites also belong. To create or think lightly of deepened rifts between the races, of psychological wounds which may take long to heal in numerous cities and towns, of polarized enmities, seems clearly dangerous and may be laying the groundwork for eventual elimination of that multiracial or *truly* integrated society which is the object of the civil rights movement and the goal of the Negro community. The race problem is psychological and social, not merely one of economic or political structure. It is necessary that the reality and shame, the deep roots, of the present rift be exposed and not slurred over. But this can only be for the purpose of obliterating the rift, not for deepening it or making it permanent and utterly rigid.

Federal Intervention

Even in a more narrowly political sense there is a problem here which has hitherto received too little attention. Important sections of the Negro movement look to Federal action, and spe-

cifically the intervention of Federal troops, to contribute at
critical moments to the advance of the integration movement.
Many seem to have espoused a strategy which will lead to the
intervention of Federal troops on a mass scale in Mississippi
this summer. The wisdom of this dependence on Federal agencies and especially Federal armed force can be questioned on
various grounds. But in the present context it seems clear that
the civil rights movement cannot expect the support of the
very Federal agency that is supposed to hold society together
at a critical moment, to keep the situation from getting utterly
out of hand and the society from falling apart—and this is
precisely what the civil rights movement looks to in a desperate situation like Mississippi—and at the same time itself work
for the (temporary?) breakdown of the society, or more accurately, accept it as inevitable.

To put it in another way, it is one thing for the Federal
troops to intervene eventually in order to protect Negroes from
police brutality and/or vigilante violence. A quite different
situation will exist if it even appears that whites have to be
protected from Negro violence born of frustration and intolerable emotional pressures.

To cite a case which to my mind illustrates the perils of
dependence on Federal intervention, whether military or not,
the Johnson Administration is certainly going to try to have a
civil rights bill adopted and then avoid creating a bad image of
the United States in the minds of other nations and colored
peoples throughout the world. But I do not see how anyone
can for a moment entertain the thought that the Administration
will welcome a call to send Federal troops to Mississippi or
anywhere else during an election campaign; or that one can
assume confidently that it will decide to do so at all.

What Kind of Revolution?

There is another aspect of strategy to which very little if any
serious consideration has as yet been given. There is no doubt
that those who have been denied freedom and equality have to
desire them, and struggle for them in a way that will "disturb"
society, or else things will remain as they are (or get worse).
This involves "social dislocation." But when tactics are devised

—and the proposed stall-in in connection with the opening of the World's Fair seems to me probably to fall in this category —with a view to creating inconvenience and disturbance in general, as an outlet for pent-up emotion, then a vast problem is opened up. The same problem is raised when people like Malcolm X ridicule "nonviolent revolution" as spurious and contend that in a real revolution blood has to flow.

A phase of traditional revolutions has been disintegration of an old order in various ways and by various means. One of the most important factors in the disintegration of Czarist society in 1917 was Lenin's counsel to the Russian soldiers to "vote with your feet" and go home. He told them that the defeat of "their own nation" in war was a lesser evil. Now there is sense of a kind in general dislocation in such a situation, *provided* that there is an element in the situation that wants to take power, and may perhaps be able to, and is ready to undertake building a new society and a new center of power. The Bolsheviks were in that position in 1917.

Assuming for the sake of argument that such an overturn were desirable, who are the elements that are to accomplish this in the United States today? Malcolm X and his followers? Even moderately informed people know that the civil rights issue, the economic or job issue and the Cold War issue are linked together. They know that without labor and other elements joining in the struggle even integration as such cannot be achieved. But any such cooperation of various elements exists today only in the most embryonic sense. To base the tactics of the civil rights movement on the assumption that a traditional revolution is imminent in the United States is either mad or criminal. In the present state of things there has to be some fairly obvious connection between a demonstration and a specific not infinitely remote goal.

In general, there is no coherent or generally recognized theory as to how or whether a revolution like the historic ones can take place in a country like the United States in the nuclear age. For all thoughtful people, and certainly for those who espouse nonviolence, or at least conceive of its possible relevance, the question of what "revolution" means in our time is posed.

The traditional revolution centers around the transfer of power from one class or social element to another, and results in the setting up of a new power structure. It is well to remind ourselves at this moment when a good many seem to think that nothing "real" is taking place except where there is shooting, that in their early stages traditional revolutions were often remarkably free from violence. Essentially, the old order collapsed and the new element moved in to fill a vacuum. The large-scale violence was likely to come when counter-revolutionary efforts were staged.

It is also the case that revolutions were in their beginnings idealistic. They were to bring in a new order of "liberty, fraternity, equality" or "a class-less and warless world." In no sense did the masses realize in the early stages that a new power structure to dominate society was going to be set up. There would not have been sufficient emotional motivation for the great venture and arduous labors of revolution if people had not believed that liberation and not just another variety of bondage was in sight.

The Beloved Community

The believers in nonviolence (and at least some who do not think of themselves in those terms) do not see the task of our age as that of a seizure of power by a new social element and the setting up of a new power structure. They see the task of our age as that of building the beloved community. No one can have a fairly close contact with the civil rights movement and the people in it, including the young people, without feeling that, in spite of all contrary appearances and even realities in the movement, deep near its center is this aspiration for a beloved community and the faith that this is what they are working for and already in a sense realizing now. "O, Freedom, Freedom over me." "Deep in my heart I do believe that we shall overcome some day"—not overcome the white man, but overcome that which stands in the way of man, each man.

In the meantime, regardless of whether or not one embraces nonviolence either as revolutionary strategy or as a way of life, all the available evidence points to the conclusion that nonviolence as basic strategy should not be abandoned by the civil rights movement. Rather, mistakes should be corrected and new possibilities of developing nonviolent action should be diligently explored and experimented with. It seems essential that the decision to adhere to nonviolence be a firm one and that it be clearly and openly proclaimed. The present situation, where there is considerable difference of opinion in various sections of the movement and a tendency for many of the adherents of nonviolence to weaken in their stand, while the advocates of "self-defense" and "true revolution" are (or seem to be) certain of their stand and aggressive in their attitude, is the worst possible. If the latter are right, their strategy should be generally accepted. Some of them might be shocked if it were accepted. If their policy is not adopted, those who reject it should not be intimidated by its advocates.

There is no space here to make detailed suggestions as to tactics. Moreover, the civil rights movement has in the leaders of the Student Nonviolent Coordinating Committee, CORE, and in Bayard Rustin, persons who are brilliant and masterful in this field. Three general suggestions do seem to me worth recording.

In the first place, the opponents of nonviolence tend to gain a following among the more depressed and poverty-stricken elements in the Negro ghettos. There are a number of reasons for this, but one of the main ones is that the "nationalists" and others pay attention to these elements and at least appear to offer programs they think can improve their condition. I think more attention to them, as against what might be called Negro white-collar elements, might produce results. Rent strikes and unemployed actions would presumably appeal to them more than actions related to education or electing Negroes to Congress or even voter registration.

Secondly, there are indications that training for nonviolent action is being taken more seriously than it has been, but much more needs to be done immediately in this field.

Thirdly, while there is a tendency in parts of the white community to polarize into a hostile or disillusioned position because of alleged "extremist" action by Negroes, there are also many who become increasingly troubled and eager to help. Very large sections of the nation are capable of experiencing deep moral revulsion against racism and segregation, especially when Negro nonviolent demonstrators are brutally treated, as was shown in relation to the Birmingham struggle. In my view, that moral revulsion may have been the main factor in at last impelling Kennedy to submit a civil rights bill and the House actually to adopt a stronger one than Kennedy's. It is my impression that the nonviolent movement may have been distracted from paying sufficient attention to the involvement of whites on this moral ground.

In closing as in beginning an analysis of this kind, attention must be focused on the white community. I referred earlier to the chasm between the peoples who have known humiliation as peoples and those who have not, but have humiliated others. The latter are the West Europeans and the Americans. The chasm has for the most part kept the colored and white peoples separated from each other. It is so no longer. The chasm is going to be bridged somehow. From the side of white men a bridge of understanding, repentance, reconciliation and love might be thrown across the chasm. If this is not done, a bridge of pent-up frustration, vengeance, hate may be thrown across it by the majority of the human race. Those who over centuries dug the chasm would hardly be in a position to quarrel with the effect. But this would not be building the beloved community either. It would be opening another familiar cycle of domination and eventual corruption. This might prove suicidal for all in the nuclear age.

Therefore, Negroes of whom love cannot be "demanded" by whites—love is in any case not subject to demand—may nevertheless give it. Those who have so long known what it is to be shoved off the sidewalk by whites may possibly understand what it means to the latter to be shoved into the street. If by discrimination and hate Negroes are driven to discrimination and hate, what, after all, have they done to themselves? There is no virtue or healing in following a bad example. There are Negroes who know this: whites are not needed to teach it to them. It was in Jackson, Mississippi last year that the widow of Medgar W. Evers said to her fellow-Negroes at a Memorial service for her slain husband: "You mustn't hate; you must love."

The poet Mark Van Doren was asked recently to read his poem entitled "Born Brother?" to a gathering of writers. He first exclaimed: "Ah, yes. Equality—the greatest of all doctrines and the hardest to understand." Then he read:

> *"Equality is absolute or no.*
> *Nothing between us can stand*
> *we are the sons*
> *Of the same sire, or madness*
> *breaks and runs*
> *Through the rude world."*

The venerable Jewish philosopher, Martin Buber, referring mainly to relations between nations, uttered an appeal some years ago, which is applicable in a peculiarly poignant way to the race situation. He spoke of those in whatever camp who "carry on the battle against the anti-human," and said: "Those who build the great unknown front shall make it known by speaking unreservedly with one another, not overlooking what divides them but determined to bear this division in common."

IV

The Center Is Man

"What matters to us is what happens to the individual human being — here and now"

Editors of *Liberation*
"Tract for the Times"

Arnold Sachar

To Live as Men

It is hardly easy to say that one can become sick of living in the land of his own birth. The burden one assumes in the face of such a confession is astonishment, animosity and implicit self-denial. And this is true because most people feel a profound residual loyalty to whatever body of institutions, *mores* and codes they have become attached. Indeed, this complex age makes men of even special vision strangely timid. In a sense, the world is organized in a manner at once intricate and efficient. It makes people ashamed to betray and question the seemingly omnipotent social machine. Self-denial occurs in the face of one's own discontent for yet another, very particular reason. Individuals feel an almost mystical bond to the culture into which they grow, for they are intimately related to people who share their symbols, language and geography. This is a fact which one can neither escape nor deny.

It is in his culture that a man first learns to seek community, advancement and esteem; he can never yield in this desire. Briefly, men understand human life most intimately in the terms of their own culture. This fact came home to me with great force on the day that the President of the United States was murdered. I was, and am still, a severe critic of the man and that for which he stood. Indeed, he was perpetuating much in this culture that I take to be socially and humanly disastrous.

I would have expected in all honesty that my feeling toward him, even in a moment of tragedy, would be profoundly ambivalent and confused. But no, my first gush of feeling was one of frank patriotic indignation. How could some bastards murder the President of the United States?

I am a writer by impulse and duty. Tragic and massive

events tend to bring people of my order to creative excitement and ingenuity. But somehow I had the feeling that people who were abrupt to ponder publicly the death of the President were vulgar, shallow and dense. In a way, I hated to feel this about them, for some who are of relatively mediocre bent took the occasion to say some decent things about our generally wretched condition. But my own feeling was, for a time, lonely and rootless. I asked myself questions like, What does power mean? What does history mean? What do I come to? Why has this strange, sophisticated, wrong-headed man named Kennedy been shot? But also, How awful it is to be without a President!

This situation of mine testified grimly to the incoherent outlines of our civilization; and one must take the chance of apprehending this if he dares to say an important critical word. But still, I am sick of my culture. It is venal, empty and awful. One must be sturdy to know what is deeply wrong and endure. There are rhetorical rituals with which I persistently define the sickness of the society. I say that people do dull, mechanized work, have guilty sex, authoritarian schools, monolithic, tasteless mass entertainments and ugly, forlorn communities. Some people deny the truth of my statements. However sane or sick such people may be, I am somehow shocked by their absence of vision. I can hardly believe that they have physical organs, have been born on this earth and know they will die.

Others tell me that I am, in principle, correct, but then, one can't do much about it. After all, it is the way God made things. And that settles the matter.

I then point to practical solutions. I say that we can control our lives in a real and productive manner. We can humanize our work, release our sexuality, imaginatively and autonomously plan our committee, make our schools interesting, open and permissive and escape from the awful shadow of constant Cold War. I am then met with astonished, grateful responses. "We need honest, sensitive people in this world after all." But now there comes a strange, embarrassed, inexplicable silence. Nobody responds in a way that is authentic and real, i.e., to say that we must unite in an independent, unsentimental spirit and make a world which is peaceful, free and livable for man.

This is where acute pain and disaster set in. One looks for roots and connection in his own culture. One wishes to have a great President, love his own people and know where he is in this his only world.

All day one puts up with rigid faces, mechanical postures and incredible dishonesty. People devise extraordinarily complex patterns and rituals. It is not the tyranny of machines alone that is expressed when it is pointed out that almost everything we do seems to be haunted by offices, examinations, dollar bills, radio stations and grotesque, convoluted courtesy. People rarely know how to speak to each other in civil, direct English. The act of intimate human conversation has become heroic. Often when one says a gracious hello to someone, he acts as if he had been put upon. One would never think that such a man was once a lively, laughing, playing child.

In this dreary context, then, there is needed some indication of empathy, passion, accord. But instead, even those close to the point of it become inarticulate and aloof. One becomes sick. The spirit is drained. Hope is weakened. One sometimes feels at an inevitable loss. One can almost imagine the sense behind the genocidal Cold War of the governments and their ridiculous hydrogen bombs. But I am determined not to let this sickness overtake me. I must see deeply into the fact that now I have neither Kennedy, Johnson nor anyone else.

One would wish for a great country and a great President. But we have a sick and wayward people. They cannot even grieve decently over the terrible tragedy of a dead President. They must defame it with routine politics, sentimental eulogy and vulgar inhibition of natural grief. There are people in their midst who are the victims of great injustice. Yet, our people are not even human enough to understand let alone correct this. They conduct business, ride trains and take tests in vapid complacency. This, when crying, poor children quiver in their cities without steam-heat, medical care and food. This, when children suffer in dreary schools in a stultified, ignoble, status-ridden environment. This, when men endure abuse and indignity because of the color of their skin. When men suffer in spiritual and social anguish everywhere, in offices, cars, factories and homes. When, finally, all of mankind can be wiped out in the morning, in the name of nothing. And their intellectuals sit in their universities and engage in sterile, humiliating abstractions. They act as if there were no world around them. The teachers cower like mice and students follow the pattern with extraordinary, robot-like precision. Are they not ashamed? Do they not hate themselves?

Enough.

I and those who see with me cannot, for the time being, take any false hope. We have vital and delicate work to do. We must pray for, struggle with and redeem our own people in a sad, peculiar time. We will falter, age and mourn. In strength and courage we can live on. We may never achieve connection with our culture, but we will have lived and died as men.

David McReynolds

Man Beckons to Man

One of the chief vices of our culture—and perhaps of any culture—is the desire to prove how sophisticated we are. We are determined to let the world know that we are too smart to be taken in by the con man. It is a vice radicals have accepted with a vengeance.

We know the score—the inside story. We know about the cops, the courts, the governments, the unions, the churches, and our own souls—they are all corrupted. We have been around. We are wised up. You won't catch us talking about utopia and the brotherhood of man. Someone might call us naive. Instead we talk about social ownership of the means of production and effective social planning. Sometimes in the silence of the night we remember how deeply we want to love people—but we don't dare say it in public: someone might snicker. (As Lenin is reputed to have said: "One would like to pet the people, but they bite.")

We are afraid to try the hard thing. We go on picket lines, are arrested, serve prison terms. But what is really hard, and what we are afraid to do, is to trust people, to try loving them. All of them. Even Dave Beck. Even Henry Luce. Even William Z. Foster (of the Communist Party).

I have been a good anti-Communist radical, and better than most. I am a sharp fellow. I know where the political lines fall, how far one goes and when to stop, the conditions under which to support joint action and the conditions under which to oppose it. I know why we must oppose united fronts. I know Communists can't be trusted, just as I know that talk about the "mutual interest" of employers and employees is a snare and a delusion. I know all these things—and many, many more—because I am a wise and sophisticated person.

My wisdom, however, has palled on me. My political sophistication has begun to frighten me. I begin to suspect that none of our political lines make sense if you start with the individual man. People—individual men and women—are not first of all and basically Communists or reactionaries, Marxists or militarists. First of all they are people. The other things are shadows beside this reality.

To believe that the truth of the political label is still truth when you pin it on the individual man or woman is as stupid, as arrogant, and as pompous as are the lines traced by nations across the face of this green earth. You look at a map and there the lines are, the political boundaries all marked out in black. But if you go to the land and look at it you find that the earth is alive and real and that the lines are nowhere to be seen. Sometimes you find barbed wire thrown up, wounding the natural dignity of the land. But you know it will rust in time, fall away.

Just so with people. And we radicals, we say it. We say we believe in HUMANITY and that means everybody. Everybody except: Dave Beck, Henry Luce and William Z. Foster.

I'm a weak man, and I admit I don't trust Mr. Beck or Mr. Luce or Mr. Foster. But I want to. I am a petty man, and when I look I still see the political lines. But I would rather see the man, the individual, the human soul. In the words of Kenneth Patchen:

> It would take little to be free.
> That no man hate another man,
> Because he is black;
> Because he is yellow;
> Because he is white;
> Or because he is English;
> Or German;
> Or rich;
> Or poor;
> Because we are everyman.

> ———

> Because the white man and the black man,
> The Englishman and the German,

Are not real things.
They are only pictures of things.
Their shapes, like the shapes of the tree
And the flower, have no lives in names or signs;
They are their lives, and the real is in them.
And what is real shall have life always.

Don't misunderstand me—I believe in the class struggle. I know you don't wage revolutions without analyzing society. But if it is true that you can't wage revolutions in a mist of good will, nor end terror by a kind word, it is just as certain that no revolution is ever going to be worth the heartache it takes to accomplish it if we don't learn to infuse our sharpest analysis with a compassion for every individual man and woman.

It was about a year ago that I began to question the wisdom of being "wise." I had been asked to take the anti-Communist side in a small discussion before some 30 people. One of the speakers was from the Communist Party. While the Communist spoke I checked my pulse rate out of curiosity and found it had hit 160. Oh yes, I believe in discussion and in free speech, and I spoke well that day. But I so basically considered that member of the Communist Party to be my enemy that to sit in the same room with him raised my pulse to 160.

My talk having been militantly anti-Communist, I was greatly surprised the next evening when I got a phone call from the C.P. speaker. He had, he said, been greatly impressed with my talk. He hadn't known, he said, that members of the Socialist Party felt as antagonistic toward Washington as toward Moscow, or that we supported the civil liberties of Communists, etc. In short, he said, he would like to have another discussion.

Being wise in the ways of the world in general and the Communist Party in particular, I asked myself: "Who does he think he's kidding?" I said to myself: "He only wants a discussion as a tactic leading to joint action—he thinks we are suckers." But because I believe in discussion as a principle—and not because I thought for a moment it would achieve anything where Stalinists were concerned—I agreed. And then, as the phone conversation came to an end, and as we concluded our tentative arrangements for further discussion, this man said: "You know, it is very hard for us to trust you." I laughed a little nervously and said I guessed he knew I didn't find it easy to trust him either.

That night I thought about his statement on the phone and it bothered me. There we were, on opposite sides of the political fence, unable for sound political reasons to trust each other. But both of us wanting to see a world where the rain wouldn't be radioactive.

Recently that haunting moment on the phone came back with added force when I learned the man involved—who I was so sure had wanted the discussion only for tactical reasons —had resigned from the C.P. Perhaps the man so "wise" that he *assumes* the worst elements always motivate his adversary is not really wise at all, but an immature person who hasn't found the courage to trust, who is afraid to love, who has lost the faith to believe.

I am not arguing for gullibility, for a tolerance of evil, or a blindness to injustice. I am arguing for the importance of learning not to attach the evil to individual men and women. I am arguing for somehow finding the courage to act in a decent, quiet, human way toward people who may not respect us for it. St. Paul once said he was willing to be a fool for Christ. Perhaps there is no job harder or more important for radicals than this willingness to appear foolish. Let Foster, Luce or Beck think they've conned us into something. What they think about us is not as important as what we feel about them.

Don't get me wrong—I propose to struggle as hard as I know how against what these gentlemen represent politically. But I am determined that in the future I will *try to believe* that even in the midst of the social struggle we are not personal enemies, that more important than Mr. Eastland's vicious racism is his potential to act like a decent human being. This is what is hard about carrying on a social revolution. There *are* classes. There *are* vested interests. *There is a social struggle.* The plight of those committed to a social revolution is nowhere more clearly or movingly expressed than in these lines from Bertolt Brecht's poem "To Posterity":

Indeed I live in the dark ages!
A guileless word is an absurdity . . .
He who laughs
Has not yet heard
The terrible tidings.

———

For we knew only too well:
Even the hatred of squalor
Makes the brow grow stern.
Even anger against injustice
Makes the voice grow harsh. Alas, we
Who wished to lay the foundations of kindness
Could not ourselves be kind.

Saying that every man is "basically decent" is part of being really sophisticated. But we have not believed it. When confronted with the concrete situation our pulse goes up to 160 and our words are barbed so that everyone will know we are too wise to trust our enemy.

It is impossible for us to trust fully or to love fully, because we are caught up in a social conflict in which we must choose sides and, as humans, that act of choosing destroys our ability to see all men impartially. But it remains extremely important for us to sense the tragedy of our situation, rather than to rejoice in our sophistication at learning how an exploitative society corrupts men and women. This grief in the face of our weakness, this constantly frustrated and frustrating desire to trust all our fellow men and to love them—this will, in the long run, be far more important for the transformation of the social order than the jaded recognition of the corruption in the men and institutions around us and in ourselves.

James Baldwin

The Artist's Struggle for Integrity

[The following is the text of a speech given at Community Church, New York City, February, 1963:]

I really don't like words like artist or integrity or courage or nobility. I have a kind of distrust of all those words because I don't really know what they mean, any more than I really know what such words as democracy or peace or peace-loving or war-like or integration mean. And yet one is compelled to recognize that all these imprecise words are attempts made by us all to get to something which is real and which lives behind the words. Whether I like it or not, for example, and no matter what I call myself, I suppose the only word for me, when the chips are down, is that I am an artist. There is such a thing. There is such a thing as integrity. Some people are noble. There is such a thing as courage. The terrible thing is that the reality behind these words depends ultimately on what the human being (meaning every single one of us) believes to be real. The terrible thing is that the reality behind all these words depends on choices one has got to make, for ever and ever and ever, every day.

I am not interested really in talking to you as an artist. It seems to me that the artist's struggle for his integrity must be considered as a kind of metaphor for the struggle which is universal and daily of all human beings on the face of this globe to get to become human beings. It is not your fault, it is not my fault, that I write. And I never would come before you in the position of a complainant for doing something that I must do. What we might get at this evening, if we are lucky, is what the importance of this effort is. However arrogant this may sound, I want to suggest two propositions. The first one is that the poets (by which I mean all artists) are finally the only people who know the truth about us. Soldiers don't. Statesmen don't. Priests don't. Union leaders don't. Only poets. That's my first proposition. We know about the Oedipus Complex not because of Freud but because of a poet who lived in Greece thousands of years ago. And what he said then about what it was like to be alive is still true, in spite of the fact that now we can get to Greece in something like five hours and then it would have taken I don't know how long a time.

The second proposition is really what I want to get at tonight. And it sounds mystical, I think, in a country like ours, and at a time like this when something awful is happening to a civilization, when it ceases to produce poets, and, what is even more crucial, when it ceases in any way whatever to believe in the report that only the poets can make. Conrad told us a long time ago (I think it was in *Victory*, but I might be wrong about that): "Woe to that man who does not put his trust in life." Henry James said, "Live, live all you can. It's a mistake not to." And Shakespeare said—and this is what I take to be the truth about everybody's life all of the time—"Out of this nettle, danger, we pluck this flower, safety." Art is here to prove, and to help one bear, the fact that all safety is an illusion. In this sense, all artists are divorced from and even necessarily opposed to any system whatever.

Let's trace it, just for kicks, for a minute. And I'll use myself. I won't say "me," but it's my story. The first thing an artist finds out when he is very, very young (when I say young I mean before he is 15, that is to say, before, properly speaking, he or she can walk or talk, before he or she has had enough experience to begin to assess his or her experience)— and what occurs at that point in this hypothetical artist's life is a kind of silence—the first thing he finds out is that for reasons he cannot explain to himself or to others, he does not belong anywhere. Maybe you're on the football team, maybe you're a runner, maybe you belong to a church, you certainly belong to a family; and abruptly, in other people's eyes—this is very important—you begin to discover that you are moving and you can't stop this movement to what looks like the edge of the

world. Now what is crucial, and one begins to understand it
much much later, is that if you were this hypothetical artist, if
you were in fact the dreamer that everybody says you are, if in
fact you were wrong not to settle for the things that you cannot for some mysterious reason settle for, if this were so, the
testimony in the eyes of other people would not exist. The
crime of which you discover slowly you are guilty is not so
much that you are aware, which is bad enough, but that other
people see that you are and cannot bear to watch it, because it
testifies to the fact that they are not. You're bearing witness
helplessly to something which everybody knows and nobody
wants to face, least of all the hypothetical misfit who has not
learned how to walk or talk and doesn't know enough about
experience to know what experience he has had.

Well, one survives that, no matter how. By and by your
uncles and your parents and church stop praying for you. They
realize it won't do a bit of good. They give you up, and you
proceed a little further and your lovers put you down. They
don't know what you're doing either and you can't tell them
'cause you don't know. You survive this and in some terrible
way, which I suppose no one can ever describe, you are compelled, you are corralled, you are bull-whipped into dealing
with whatever it is that hurt you. And what is crucial here is
that if it hurt you, that is not what's important. Everybody's
hurt. What is important, what corrals you, what bull-whips
you, what drives you, torments you, is that you must find some
way of using this to connect you with everyone else alive. This
is all you have to do it with. You must understand that your
pain is trivial except in so far as you can use it to connect with
other people's pain; and in so far as you can do that with your
pain, you can be released from it, and then hopefully it works
the other way around too; in so far as I can tell you what it is
to suffer, perhaps I can help you to suffer less. Then, you
make—oh fifteen years later, several thousand drinks later, two
or three divorces, God knows how many broken friendships
and an exile of one kind or another—some kind of breakthrough, which is your first articulation of who you are, that is
to say, your first articulation of who you suspect we all are.

Let me put it another way. When I was very young (and

I am sure this is true of everybody here), I assumed that no one had ever been born who was only five-feet-six-inches tall, or been born poor, or been born ugly, or masturbated, or done all those things which were my private property when I was 15. No one had ever suffered the way I suffered. Then you discover, and I discovered this through Dostoevski, that it is common. *Everybody* did it. Not only did everybody do it, everybody's *doing* it. And all the time. It's a fantastic and terrifying liberation. The reason it is terrifying is because it makes you once and for all responsible to no one but yourself. Not to God the Father, not to Satan, not to anybody. Just you. If you think it's right, then you've got to do it. If you think it's wrong, then you mustn't do it. And not only do we all know how difficult it is, given what we are, to tell the difference between right and wrong, but the whole nature of life is so terrible that somebody's right is always somebody else's wrong. And these are the terrible choices one has always got to make.

All right, I said the cat survived all that, and—this is a very crucial thing—you know dirty socks can make you feel like nothing but a dirty sock. You walk into a room and somebody says, "What do you do?" And you say "I write." And they say, "Yeah, but what do you *do*?" And you wonder, what *do* you do? And what's it for? Why don't you get a job. And somehow you can't, and finally you learn this in the most terrible way because you try. You're in the position of someone on the edge of a field, and it's cold in the field, and there's a house over there, and there's fire in the house, and food and everything you need, everything you want, and you make all kinds of efforts to get into the house. And they would let you in; they would let you in. They're not being cruel. They recognize you as you come to the door, and they *can't* let you in. You get in, let us say, for five minutes and you can't stay. When I was much younger, people said to me, this is very serious and not just a confession, I'm not just being self-indulgent—"All right, you were working, now stop working. Forget it! Have a drink. Why are you so serious all the time? You can't write all the time, Jimmy. Relax." Have you ever had anyone tell you to relax?

All right, you get through all that and you make your first

breakthrough, people have heard your name—and here comes
the world again. The world you first encountered when you
were 15. The world which has starved you, despised you. Here
it comes again. This time it is bearing gifts. The phone didn't
ring before—if you had a phone. Now it never stops ringing.
Instead of people saying, "What do you do?", they say "Won't
you do this?" And you become, or you could become, a Very
Important Person. And then, and this is a confession, you find
yourself in the position of a woman I don't know who sings a
certain song in a certain choir and the song begins: "I said I
wasn't gonna tell nobody but I couldn't keep it to myself."
You've come full circle. Here you are again, with it all to do all
over again, and you must decide all over again whether you
want to be famous or whether you want to write. And the two
things, in spite of all the evidence, have nothing whatever in
common.

Now what is it at the point that the artist, since I must put
it this way, begins to come of age, that he cannot keep to
himself? This is the trickiest part of the whole argument. I was
having lunch today with a very good friend of mine and a
friend of his—and they're both artists. The friend of the friend
is a man I admire very much but the other one is a cat I really
dig. My friend is an actor and there's a role which we all know
he ought to play. In fact, we all know—anyone who loves
him—that he has no choice but to play it sooner or later and
we all know that he's a little afraid to. And God knows he
should be. But he knows he's got to do it. And his friend was
saying to him—and I paraphrase it very awkwardly—you must
remember that most people live in almost total darkness. It is
true, said this friend, that we drink too much, we suffer from
stagefright and you may get an ulcer or die of cancer, and it is
true that it is all very very hard and gets harder all the time.
And yet people, millions of people whom you will never see,
who don't know you, never will know you, people who may try
to kill you in the morning, live in a darkness which—if you
have that funny terrible thing which every artist can recognize
and no artist can define—you are responsible to those people,
to lighten, and it does not matter what happens to you. You
are being used in the way a crab is useful, the way sand

certainly has some function. It is impersonal. This force which you didn't ask for, and this destiny which you must accept, is also your responsibility. And if you survive it, if you don't cheat, if you don't lie, it is not only, you know, your glory, your achievement, it is almost our only hope—because only an artist can tell and only artists have told since we have heard of man, what it is like for anyone who gets to this planet to survive it. What it is like to die, or to have somebody die, what it is like to be glad. Hymns don't do this, churches really cannot do it. The trouble is that although the artist can do it, the price that he has to pay himself and that you, the audience, must also pay, is a willingness to give up everything, to realize that although you spent twenty-seven years acquiring this house, this furniture, this position, although you spent forty years raising this child, these children, nothing, none of it belongs to you. You can only have it by letting it go. You can only take if you are prepared to give, and giving is not an investment. It is not a day at the bargain counter. It is a total risk of everything, of you and who you think you are, who you think you'd like to be, where you think you'd like to go—everything, and this forever, forever.

Now I, if I may put it this way, and all my tribe, if I may put it that way, find this very hard to do and it's very hard on my mother, on my sisters and my brothers and all my friends, and it's very hard on me and I may fail in the next two seconds. But then one has got to understand, that is I and all my tribe (I mean artists now), that it is hard for me. If I spend weeks and months avoiding my typewriter—and I do, sharpening pencils, trying to avoid going where I know I've got to go—then one has got to use this to learn humility. After all, there is a kind of saving egotism too, a cruel and dangerous but also saving egotism, about the artist's condition, which is this: I know that if I survive it, when the tears have stopped flowing or when the blood has dried, when the storm has settled, I do have a typewriter which is my torment but is also my work. If I can survive it, I can always go back there, and if I've not turned into a total liar, then I can use it and prepare myself in this way for the next inevitable and possibly fatal disaster. But if I find that hard to do—and I have a weapon which most people don't have—then one must understand how hard it is for almost anybody else to do it at all.

And this is where the whole question in my own private, personal case of being an American artist, of being not yet 65 years old, and of being an American Negro artist in 1963 in this most peculiar of countries begins to be a very frightening assignment. One is dealing all the time with the most inarticulate people that I, in any case, have ever encountered, and I don't hesitate to say the most inarticulate group of people we are ever likely to encounter, I or anybody else, for a very long time, at least in this century. Inarticulate and illiterate and they're very particular and difficult to describe away, unlettered in the language, which may sound a little florid but there's no other way that I can think of to say it, totally unlettered in the language of the heart, totally distrustful of whatever cannot be touched, panic-stricken at the very first hint of pain. A people determined to believe that they can make suffering obsolete. Who don't understand yet a very physiological fact that the pain which signals a toothache is a pain which saves your life. This is very frightening. It frightens me half to death, and I'm not talking now merely about race, and I'm certainly not talking merely about Southerners. I am talking really about two-thirds of my public and technical allies. People who believe that segregation is wrong. People who march on picket lines who yet have overlooked something else and are still under the illusion, I think, that what they've overlooked has something to do with social questions and in my particular case anyway that it has something to do with Negroes. I would like to live long enough—don't misunderstand me, but I would like to live long enough—to see that word or the use to which it's put struck from the American vocabulary. In effect, there is no Negro problem. The problem is that one is still in a kindergarten, an emotional kindergarten, and the Negro in this country operates as some weird kind of gorilla who suddenly is breaking up all the blackboards. I am tired not only of being told to wait, but of people's saying "What should I do?" They mean, "What should I do about the Negro problem; what should I do for you?" There is nothing you can do for me. There is nothing you can do for Negroes. It must be done for you. One is not attempting to save twenty-two million people. One is attempting to save an entire country, and that means an entire civilization, and the price for that is high. The price for that is to understand one's self. The price for that, for example, is to recognize that most of us, white and black, have arrived at a point where we do not know what to tell our children. Most of us have arrived at a point where we still believe and insist on and act on the principle, which is no longer valid, that this is such and such an optimum, that our choice is the lesser of two evils, and this is no longer true. Gonorrhea is not preferable to syphilis.

The time has come, it seems to me, to recognize that the framework in which we operate weighs on us too heavily to be borne and is about to kill us. It is time to ask very hard questions and to take very rude positions. And no matter at what price. It is time, for example, for one example, to recognize that the major effort of our country until today (and I am talking about Washington and all the way down to whoever heads the Women's Christian Temperance Union) is not to change a situation but to *seem* to have done it. It is spectacular for example, to have been forced ultimately to bring in the entire whatever-it-was—militia, U.S. Marshals—to get James Meredith into school, and from a certain point of view, which I do not at all share, I can see that one could say that no other country would have done it. It's escaped everybody's notice that no other country would have had to. It is easy to admire the sit-in students in the South, and nothing is more delightful than to talk to Martin Luther King, whom I very much admire. But it is too easy to admire a Christian minister, especially if you take no responsibility for what's happening to him or to those people that he tries to represent. It is hard to begin to understand that the drift in American life towards chaos is masked by all these smiling faces and all these do-good efforts.

Nat Hentoff

The Humorist as Grand Inquisitor

The basic division in current American and British topical satire is between Lenny Bruce and all the others. The "others," of course, are themselves diversified, but each on his own skillfully self-protecting way stops short of revealing the marrow of his audiences and of himself. Bruce, on the other hand, is a danger to many of our most fundamental defenses and self-evasions. He is also a danger to himself, as is illustrated, on a surface level, by his several arrests for "obscenity." This past March, he was convicted on such a charge in Chicago and was sentenced to a year in jail in addition to a $1,000 fine. The case is being appealed. Bruce has also provoked physical assault, having once been thrown through a plate glass window by one of the more exacerbated members of his audience.

Even without external abrasions, because of the persistent tensions endemic to his nightly act of self-exposure, Bruce is coming closer and closer to the possibility of quite literally destroying himself.

The difference between Bruce and the others is almost palpably evident before one of his performances even begins. The expectancy in the nightclub is laced with anxiety. How far will he go *tonight?* Anyone in the audience who has seen Bruce before knows that he—the listener—is soon about to be the target, but he doesn't know exactly where the shock is going to be applied. The nervousness affects Bruce's most enthusiastic partisans as well. By what new vulgarism is he going to embarrass *us?* And will we be able *this time* to understand why he used those words or will we be self-condemned as squares for not digging his message all the way? Bruce, in sum, continually puts his audiences on trial; and there is never a final passing grade because the examinations continue during the next show, the next night, and the next time he comes through town.

By contrast, an audience for Mort Sahl, Shelley Berman, Jonathan Winters, Nichols and May, *The Second City*, *The Premise* or *Beyond the Fringe* is expectant, but pleasurably so. After all, they are about to be invited to witness to their own superior sophistication by laughing at the anti-Establishment impieties of the performers. They know by experience—an experience that goes back among the elders to W. C. Fields, Will Rogers and Fred Allen—that for all the seeming irreverence of what they hear, the impieties will be "safe."

As Albert Hunt, a British journalist, has observed about nearly all current political satire, "the attacks tend to hit at the way events are reported—at the fatuity of television interviews, the meaninglessness of newspaper headlines—rather than at the absurdity of the events themselves." Similarly, when the bright young jongleurs parody elements of our other mores—sex, religion, familial relations—they may crease the skin but they do not draw blood. There are, of course, occasional exceptions, as in a *Second City* sketch in which a Puerto Rican in New York gently but mercilessly dissects a "sensitive" social worker who has come to "help" him by trying to impose upwardly mobile middle class values on this man who, first of all, is blocked by the society which the social worker represents from substantially enjoying the putative harvest of those values. More to the revolutionary point, the Puerto Rican already has found his own non-aggressive, non-competitive, essentially non-materialistic way of being, and has no need of what are for him irrelevant and spirit-corroding "rewards."

These exceptions, however, are rare. As a whole, the topical satirists do not question the foundations of our society. They simply caricature surface oafishness and hypocrisy; they do not attempt to subvert. Therefore, of course, they do not get in trouble with the police. Unlike Bruce's basing points, the clubs at which they appear do not find their licenses suspended. And they are invited on prime time television to cozen millions more into seeing themseveles as "in," as aware of the way things really are. Being entertained by those satirists across the chasm from Bruce is like walking through a gallery of fun house mirrors. Your reflection goes through a succession of grotesqueries, but you know perfectly well that once you're outside, you'll still be your comfortable, familiar, rather stale self. After an encounter with Bruce on one of his more demonic nights, however, you may look at the mirror with gnawing doubt that you indeed know who you are, or rather, what you really feel. About sex. About justice. About Negroes. About being a Jew.

It is reasonably easy to describe the professional characteristics of the other satirists by stringing together their more trenchant lines and quick descriptions of their more carefully outrageous skits. Conveying the particular impact of Bruce, however, is almost as difficult as verbalizing about Thelonious Monk, Ornette Coleman or those few other jazzmen who move in a distinctively personal nimbus and who have to be seen and directly felt to be fully believed.

Bruce too is a presence. His lunging gestures, nakedly mobile features (not a kaleidoscope of artful masks as with the others), and his almost ominous range of vocal texture (from a growling mumble to the fierce clarity of a Harlem street corner agitator)—all these color and punctuate and weight what he actually says.

His Basic Premise

The closest approximation of Bruce I've yet read is by George Melly in the *New Statesman*: "His basic premise, though he never states it directly, is that the only moment when we might be considered possible is when we are making love (unlike him, I shan't use the real word). His method is to leave the lovers unseen and desperate on either side of the stage, and to attack with inventive and hysterical rage everything which is keeping them apart. The judge, the policeman, the politician, the racialist, the priest at the moment of absolution, the 'decent' citizen for whom the sexual act is 'dirty,' the whole disgusting crew who hang morons and test bombs. He is a black humorist in the authentic tradition. He never tells us what he loves. We have to deduce that from what he hates . . . What elevates him above any other satirist I have seen or heard is that he never suggests that it is 'the others' who are the pris-

oners. It is this assumption which makes all our local satire so
cozy. Lenny Bruce offers no such comfort. Even his tiring
obsession with his own Jewishness is to the point: here is one
more limitation. He is in prison, and as he talks it is impossible
not to grasp that we are in prison too. Even so the effect of
what he does is positive. On our behalf he scrawls on the
white-washed wall the dirty and defiant words. The rest is up
to us."

I would disagree with Melly that Bruce believes that the
only moment when we might be considered possible is when
we are making love. He does, however, insist that we must be
capable of the quality of contact with another which makes
love possible before we can talk with anything more than easy
charity-giving of love for "mankind" or for the Negroes or the
"disadvantaged"—and similar liberal pieties. It is quite true, as
Jonathan Miller of *Beyond the Fringe* has said, that for Bruce,
"the marrow of the human condition is not political or otherwise social, but is rather that soft, fleshy thing concerned with
sex, privacy, and the body."

Bruce, though extremely intelligent (a non-Establishment
psychiatrist I know expects that he would test close to the
genius level) is not an intellectual in the sense of being well
read and otherwise concerned with the morphology of ideas.
He is a ruthlessly astute observer, but he functions on a much
more instinctual, unblocked emotional level than the vast
majority of the citizenry, especially the intellectuals. "In an
aesthetic sense," he once said, "if you could graph me I'd be
pretty shallow because I'm very concerned with the physical.
First attraction is not intellectual, ever, with me."

Accordingly, for example, Bruce would be swiftly bested
in an argument with, let's say, the tacticians of *Realpolitik*. But
it is his emotions, spurting from his unabashed appreciation of
"that soft, fleshy thing concerned with sex, privacy and the
body," which propel him to wonder aloud how a Jew can
mourn the murdered in the concentration camps while having
expunged all feeling of personal guilt (if it ever existed) for
the killing-by-long-distance that was Hiroshima and who can,
furthermore, support national leadership based on peace-
through-terror. He is convinced, moreover, that there is some-

thing pitifully wrong with a society which gives more respect to a gunner's mate than a whore. "It's perverse," he explains, surprised that he has to explain, "to give more respect to men who kill you than to ladies who at least play at loving you."

On stage, Bruce lists and examines our "dirty words"—in Jewish as much as in English, because he is indeed tiringly obsessed with his Jewishness—which are so pervasively used in talking about the act of love. And in the course of his antic etymology, he wonders quite rightly how many in his audience are blocked sexually, to a greater or lesser extent. Most, of course are (see Dr. Marie Robinson's *The Power of Sexual Surrender*).

Bruce's specialty is a continuing analysis of the results of what he calls the "*zug gornisht*" (say nothing) culture—the destructive power of what has been repressed and therefore transmogrified. A corollary preoccupation is the psychopathology of the way we punish to "rehabilitate." (What do we do with homosexuals in this society? We throw them in prison with other men.") And sometimes we punish for the digestive pleasure of vengeance. Bruce often cites the killing of the Rosenbergs as a particularly gratuitous act of communal savagery. Essentially apolitical, Bruce does not attempt in *National Guardian* fashion to construct a case for the Rosenbergs' innocence. Innocent or guilty, he says, in what way did their punishment fit their crime and what does their punishment tell us about ourselves? He might have added: what does their end tell us of the vast majority of Establishment Jews who did not protest the Rosenbergs' execution?

Bruce is consistent in that he does not adopt a *zug gornisht* approach to his ambivalence about his own Jewishness. He changed his name from Schneider, but makes no secret of it. Because he is a Jew, he feels himself an outsider in the country at large and admits to envy of the stance, features and easy sense of power of the Anglo-Saxon élite whom he also mocks. He is obsessively interested in whether the girls he meets are Jewish, and is surprised and rather chagrined when he has guessed wrong. He has, in short, not "worked out" the problem of alienation felt (though not always admitted) by many non-religious American Jews of his age (thirty-seven) and older. But neither does he pretend to himself to have worked it out. He shows zestful disrespect for "Frank-Lloyd-Wright *shuls*" and for those puffy Reform rabbis who confuse a community center with a commitment to religion as a way of feeling and doing. Bruce is hung up on being a Jew, and he may always be; but he doesn't try to con himself out of his aching rootlessness.

Aside from their effectiveness as italics in his monologues, it may well be that Bruce's use of so many Yiddishisms in his performances is an attempt to "belong" to some tradition, if only through the osmosis of having been raised among Jews. But it doesn't work. He is acutely alone, and because he is furthermore able—in fact, compelled by temperament and use of experience—to see through the *zug gornisht* culture, he finds few people with whom he can achieve even transitory companionship on a basis of non-evasion of feeling. He seems most at ease with the night people—prostitutes, show business workers, hustlers of various kinds, and jazz musicians. At least they are only on the periphery of the anti-life power structure and some actively work to undermine it for their own non-revolutionary reasons. And because of the perspective the more sensitive and sensitized of the night people acquire of "responsible" citizens "relaxing," these nocturnal observers also possess what Jonathan Miller has described as Bruce's "sharp, harsh, fire-lit view of human nature."

The Perfectibility of Man

Yet Bruce is not yet a cynic or a pessimist. The underside of the ardor of his condemnation is a faith, however ingenuous, in the perfectibility of man. He would agree with the sternest of the Neo-Orthodox Christian theologians (as well as with existential psychoanalysts) that there is much in man that is ugly, viciously and fearfully irrational, and self-destructive. But without a political or religious system on which to lean, Bruce remains innocent of fatalism or despair. As an Episcopalian minister said in a note to him: "Thank you for caring so much about life."

In so far as he does have a conscious philosophy, it is solipsism: "You don't know anything about anybody but you.

Just you live in that thing. You always live alone. You're always in there, even with your wife. That's why when I'm out there working, I'm only working to me. That's why I won't, I can't, sell out. That is, so long as I stay honest with myself. And that's why I can't stay with any set bits, any set routines. I'm somebody different each time out. I keep changing. I'm not bragging about this, but I—well, it *exists,* that's all I'm telling you."

Bruce *does* continue changing, testing his feelings and perceptions, and that's why every Bruce performance is so unpredictable. In his solipsism, his coruscatingly negative jeremiads, his commitment to improvisation and his uncontrollable restlessness, Bruce is a distillation of the unfocused rebelliousness among more and more of the young. They protest segregation and testing and the hollowness of their parents, but they cannot yet say what they are for, what new society they desire. They are only *against,* but that at least is a beginning, and many of them regard Bruce as one of their primary guides to the bleakness of the society which they want to dislocate.

The satisfactions of Bruce as the nay-sayer are insubstantial; for as he attacks and interrogates, he is affirming his own loss of roots and his own unfulfilled needs. But he is at least alarmingly alive in his rage and yearning. It is his thrust to *be* which attracts to Bruce the more radically dissident of the young. They listen as he says: "What has the word 'prostitute' come to mean? An out-of-town buyer wants a hundred-dollar prostitute. He makes the call, and some *schmuck* writer with a beard will come up to his room."

The young listen, and the message they get from Bruce is that they will have to be constantly on guard to avoid the so easy—and so diversified—slides to whoredom in this society. Moreover, he provides a galvanic antidote to the currently prevalent image of "success" personalized in the dehumanized pragmatism of the Kennedys. Since he has no "answers" himself, Bruce can only function as this kind of itinerant, solitary figure of warning. It is not an ignoble function, and it certainly sets him far apart from those topical satirists whose essential vacuity is indicated by the fact that they would be entirely at ease in a White House-sponsored telethon for a National Cultural Center; in a symposium headed by David Susskind or Max Lerner or Henry Luce; and as the official entertainment for an annual banquet of the National Conference of Christians and Jews.

Bruce is more likely to feel in context with the absolutist resisters of the Committee for Nonviolent Action, the unpolitic and radically uncompromising workers for integration in the Student Nonviolent Coordinating Committee in the South, and perhaps with Jimmy Hoffa. ("I'd nominate him as the Christian of the year. He hires ex-convicts.")

Ad Hoc Committee

The Triple Revolution: Cybernation—
Weaponry—Human Rights

This statement is written in the recognition that mankind is at a historic conjuncture which demands a fundamental reexamination of existing values and institutions. At this time three separate and mutually reinforcing revolutions are taking place:

The Cybernation Revolution: A new era of production has begun. Its principles of organization are as different from those of the industrial era as those of the industrial era were different from the agricultural. The cybernation revolution has been brought about by the combination of the computer and the automated self-regulating machine. This results in a system of almost unlimited productive capacity which requires progressively less human labor. Cybernation is already reorganizing the economic and social system to meet its own needs.

The Weaponry Revolution: New forms of weaponry have been developed which cannot win wars but which can obliterate civilization. We are recognizing only now that the great weapons have eliminated war as a method for resolving international conflicts. The ever-present threat of total destruction is tempered by the knowledge of the final futility of war. The need of a "warless world" is generally recognized, though achieving it will be a long and frustrating process.

The Human Rights Revolution: A universal demand for full human rights is now clearly evident. It continues to be demonstrated in the civil rights movement within the United States. But this is only the local manifestation of a world-wide movement toward the establishment of social and political régimes in which every individual will feel valued and none will feel rejected on account of his race.

We are particularly concerned in this statement with the first of these revolutionary phenomena. This is not because we underestimate the significance of the other two. On the contrary, we affirm that it is the simultaneous occurrence and interaction of all three developments which make evident the necessity for radical alterations in attitude and policy. The adoption of just policies for coping with cybernation and for extending rights to all Americans is indispensable for the creation of an atmosphere in the United States in which the supreme issue, peace, can be reasonably debated and resolved.

Interaction of Three Revolutions

The Negro claims, as a matter of simple justice, his full share in America's economic and social life. He sees adequate employment opportunities as a chief means of attaining this goal: the March on Washington demanded freedom *and* jobs. The Negro's claim to a job is not being met. Negroes are the hardest hit of the many groups being exiled from the economy by cybernation. Negro unemployment rates cannot be expected to drop substantially. Promises of jobs are a cruel and dangerous hoax on hundreds of thousands of Negroes and whites alike who are especially vulnerable to cybernation because of age or inadequate education.

The demand of the civil rights movement cannot be fulfilled within the present context of society. The Negro is trying to enter a social community and a tradition of work-and-income which are in the process of vanishing even for the hitherto privileged white worker. Jobs are disappearing under the impact of highly efficient, progressively less costly machines.

The United States operates on the thesis, set out in the Employment Act of 1946, that every person will be able to obtain a job if he wishes to do so and that this job will provide him with resources adequate to live and maintain a family decently. Thus job-holding is the general mechanism through which economic resources are distributed. Those without work have access only to a minimal income, hardly sufficient to provide the necessities of life, and enabling those receiving it to function as only "minimum consumers." As a result, the goods and services which are needed by these crippled consumers, and which they would buy if they could, are not produced. This in turn deprives other workers of jobs, thus reducing their incomes and consumption.

Present excessive levels of unemployment would be multiplied several times if military and space expenditures did not continue to absorb ten per cent of the gross national product (i.e., the total goods and services produced). Some six to eight million people are employed as a direct result of purchases for space and military activities. At least an equal number hold their jobs as an indirect result of military and space expenditures. In recent years, the military and space budgets have absorbed a rising proportion of national production and formed a strong support for the economy.

However, these expenditures are coming in for more and more criticism, at least partially in recognition of the fact that nuclear weapons have elmiminated war as an acceptable method for resolving international conflicts. Early in 1964, President Johnson ordered a curtailment of certain military expenditures. Defense Secretary Robert McNamara is closing shipyards, airfields, and army bases, and Congress is pressing the National Aeronautics and Space Administration to economize. The future of these strong props to the economy is not as clear today as it was even a year ago.

The Nature of the Cybernation Revolution

Cybernation is manifesting the characteristics of a revolution in production. These include the development of radically different techniques and the subsequent appearance of novel principles of the organization of production; a basic reordering of man's relationship to his environment; and a dramatic increase in total available and potential energy.

The major difference between the agricultural, industrial and cybernation revolutions is the speed at which they developed. The agricultural revolution began several thousand years ago in the Middle East. Centuries passed in the shift from a subsistence base of hunting and food gathering to settled agriculture.

In contrast, it has been less than two hundred years since the emergence of the Industrial Revolution, and direct and accurate knowledge of the new productive techniques has reached most of mankind. This swift disseminaton of information is generally held to be the main factor leading to widespread industrialization.

While the major aspects of the cybernation revolution are for the moment restricted to the United States, its effects are observable almost at once throughout the industrial world and large parts of the non-industrial world. Observation is rapidly followed by analysis and criticism. The problems posed by the cybernation revolution are part of a new era in the history of all mankind but they are first being faced by the people of the United States. The way Americans cope with cybernation will influence the course of this phenomenon everywhere. This country is the stage on which the Machines-and-Man drama will first be played for the world to witness.

The fundamental problem posed by the cybernation revolution in the United States is that it invalidates the general mechanism so far employed to undergird people's rights as consumers. Up to this time economic resources have been distributed on the basis of contributions to production, with machines and men competing for unemployment on somewhat equal terms. In the developing cybernated system, potentially unlimited output can be achieved by systems of machines which will require little cooperation from human beings. As machines take over production from men, they absorb an increasing proportion of resources, while the men who are displaced become dependent on minimal and unrelated government measures—unemployment insurance, social security, welfare payments. These measures are less and less able to disguise a historic paradox: that a growing proportion of the population is subsisting on minimal incomes, often below the poverty line, at a time when sufficient productive potential is available to supply the needs of everyone in the United States.

The existence of this paradox is denied or ignored by conventional economic analysis. The general economic approach argues that potential demand, which if filled would raise the number of jobs and provide incomes to those holding them, is underestimated. Most contemporary economic analysis states that all of the available labor force and industrial capacity is required to meet the needs of consumers and industry and to provide adequate public services: schools, parks, roads, homes, decent cities, and clean water and air. It is further argued that demand could be increased, by a variety of standard techniques, to any desired extent by providing money and machines to improve the conditions of the billions of impoverished people elsewhere in the world who need food and shelter, clothes and machinery and everything else the industrial nations take for granted.

There is no question that cybernation does increase the potential for the provision of funds to neglected public sectors. Nor is there any question that cybernation would make possible the abolition of poverty at home and abroad. But the industrial system does not possess any adequate mechanisms to permit these potentials to become realities. The industrial system was designed to produce an ever-increasing quantity of goods as efficiently as possible, and it was assumed that the distribution of the power to purchase these goods would occur almost automatically. The continuance of the income-through-jobs link as the only major mechanism for distributing effective demand—for granting the right to consume—now acts as the main brake on the almost unlimited capacity of a cybernated productive system.

Recent administrations have proposed measures aimed at achieving a better distribution of resources, and at reducing unemployment and underemployment. A few of these proposals have been enacted. More often they have failed to secure Congressional support. In every case, many members of Congress have criticized the proposed measures as departing from traditional principles for the allocation of resources and the encouragement of production. Abetted by budget-balancing economists and interest groups, they have argued for the maintenance of an economic machine based on ideas of scarcity to deal with the facts of abundance produced by cybernation. This time-consuming criticism has slowed the workings of Congress and has thrown out of focus for that body the inter-related effects of the triple revolution.

An adequate distribution of the potential abundance of goods and services will be achieved only when it is understood that the major economic problem is not how to increase production but how to distribute the abundance that is the great potential of cybernation. There is an urgent need for a fundamental change in the mechanisms employed to insure consumer rights.

Facts and Figures

No responsible observer would attempt to describe the exact pace or the full sweep of a phenomenon that is developing with the speed of cybernation. Some aspects of this revolution, however, are already clear:

> The rate of productivity increase has risen with the onset of cybernation.
>
> An industrial economic system postulated on scarcity has been unable to distribute the abundant goods and services produced by a cybernated system or potential in it.
>
> Surplus capacity and unemployment have thus co-existed at excessive levels over the last six years.
>
> The underlying cause of excessive unemployment is the fact that the capability of machines is rising more rapidly than the capacity of many human beings to keep pace.
>
> A permanent impoverished and jobless class is established in the midst of potential abundance.

Evidence for these statements follows:

> 1. The increased efficiency of machine systems is shown in the more rapid increase in productivity per man-hour since 1960, a year that marks the first visible upsurge of the cybernation revolution. In 1961, 1962, and 1963, productivity per man-hour rose at an average pace above three and a half per cent—a rate well above both the historical average and the post-war rate.

Companies are finding cybernation more and more attractive. Even at the present early stage of cybernation, costs have already been lowered to a point where the price of a durable machine may be as little as one-third of the current annual wage-cost of the worker it replaces. A more rapid rise in the rate of productivity increase per man-hour can be expected from now on.

2. In recent years it has proved impossible to increase demand fast enough to bring about the full use of either men or plant capacities. The task of developing sufficient additional demand promises to become more difficult each year. A thirty-billion-dollar annual increase in gross national product is now required to prevent unemployment rates from rising. An additional forty-to-sixty-billion-dollar increase would be required to bring unemployment rates down to an acceptable level.

3. The official rate of unemployment has remained at or above five and a half per cent during the Sixties. The unemployment rate for teenagers has been rising steadily and now stands at around fifteen per cent. The unemployment rate for Negro teenagers stands about thirty per cent. The unemployment rate for teenagers in minority ghettoes sometimes exceeds fifty per cent. Unemployment rates for Negroes are regularly more than twice those for whites, whatever their occupation, educational level, age or sex. The unemployment position for other racial minorities is similarly unfavorable. Unemployment rates in depressed areas often exceed fifty per cent.

These official figures seriously underestimate the true extent of unemployment. The statistics take no notice of underemployment or featherbedding. Besides the five and a half per cent of the labor force who are officially designated as unemployed, nearly four per cent of the labor force sought full-time work in 1962 but could find only part-time jobs. In addition, methods of calculating unemployment rates—a person is counted as unemployed only if he has actively sought a job recently—ignore the fact that many men and women who would like to find jobs have not looked for them because they know there are no employment opportunities. Underestimates for this reason are pervasive among groups whose unemployment rates are high—the young, the old, and racial minorities. Many people in the depressed agricultural, mining and industrial areas, who by official definition hold jobs but who are actually grossly underemployed, would move if there were prospects of finding work elsewhere. It is reasonable to estimate that over eight million people are not working who would like to have jobs today as compared with the four million shown in the official statistics.

Even more serious is the fact that the number of people who have voluntarily removed themselves from the labor force is not constant but increases continuously. These people have decided to stop looking for employment and seem to have accepted the fact that they will never hold jobs again. This decision is largely irreversible, in economic and also in social and psychological terms. The older worker calls himself "retired"; he cannot accept work without affecting his social-security status. The worker in his prime years is forced onto relief: in most states the requirements for becoming a relief recipient bring about such fundamental alterations in an individual's situation that a reversal of the process is always difficult and often totally infeasible. Teenagers, especially "drop-outs" and Negroes, are coming to realize that there is no place for them in the labor force, but at the same time they are given no realistic alternative. These people and their dependents make up a large part of the "poverty" sector of the American population.

Statistical evidence of these trends appears in the decline in the proportion of people claiming to be in the labor force—the so-called labor-force-participation rate. The recent apparent stabilization of the unemployment rate at around five and a half per cent is therefore misleading: it is a reflection of the discouragement and defeat of people who cannot find employment and have withdrawn from the market rather than a measure of the economy's success in creating jobs for those who want to work.

4. An efficiently functioning industrial system is assumed to provide the great majority of new jobs through the expansion of the private-enterprise sector. But well over half of the new jobs created during the period 1957-1962 were in the public sector—predominantly in teaching. Job creation in the private sector has now almost entirely ceased except in services; of the four million three hundred thousand jobs created in this period, only about two hundred thousand were provided by private industry through its own efforts. Many authorities anticipate that the application of cybernation to certain service industries, which is only beginning, will be particularly effective. If this is the case, no significant job creation will take place in the private sector in coming years.

5. Cybernation raises the level of the skills of the machine. Secretary of Labor Willard Wirtz has recently stated that the machines being produced today have, on the average, skills equivalent to a high school diploma. If a human being is to compete with such machines, therefore, he must at least possess a high school diploma. The Department of Labor estimates, however, that on the basis of present trends as many as thirty per cent of all students will be high school dropouts in this decade.

6. A permanently depressed class is developing in the United States. Some thirty-eight million Americans, almost one-fifth of the nation, still live in poverty. The percentage of total income received by the poorest twenty per cent of the population was 4.9 per cent in 1944 and 4.7 per cent in 1963.

Secretary Wirtz recently summarized these trends: "The confluence of surging population and driving technology is splitting the American labor force into tens of millions of 'haves' and millions of 'have-nots.' In our economy of sixty-nine million jobs, those with wanted skills enjoy opportunity and earning power. But the others face a new and stark problem—exclusion on a permanent basis, both as producers and

consumers, from economic life. This division of people threatens to create a human slag heap. We cannot tolerate the development of a separate nation of the poor, the unskilled, the
jobless, living within another nation of the well-off, the trained
and the employed."

Need for a New Consensus

The stubborness and novelty of the situation that is conveyed
by these statistics is now generally accepted. Ironically, it continues to be assumed that it is possible to devise measures
which will reduce unemployment to a minimum and thus
preserve the overall viability of the present productive system.
Some authorities have gone so far as to suggest that the pace
of technological change should be slowed down "so as to allow
the industrial productive system time to adapt."

We believe, on the contrary, that the industrial productive
system is no longer viable. We assert that the only way to turn
technological change to the benefit of the individual and the
service of the general welfare is to accept the process and to
utilize it rationally and humanely. The new science of political
economy will be built on the encouragement and planned expansion of cybernation. The issues raised by cybernation are
particularly amenable to intelligent policy-making: cybernation itself provides the resources and tools that are needed to
ensure minimum hardship during the transition process.

But major changes must be made in our attitudes and
institutions in the foreseeable future. Today Americans are
being swept along by three simultaneous revolutions while
assuming they have them under control. In the absence of real
understanding of any of these phenomena, especially of technology, we may be allowing an efficient and dehumanized
community to emerge by default. Gaining control of our future
requires the conscious formation of the society we wish to
have. Cybernation at last forces us to answer historic questions: What is man's role when he is not dependent upon his
own activities for the material basis of his life? What should be
the basis for distributing individual access to national resources? Are there other proper claims on goods and services
besides a job?

Because of cybernation, society no longer needs to impose

repetitive and meaningless (because unnecessary) toil upon the individual. Society can now set the citizen free to make his own choice of occupation and vocation from a wide range of activities not now fostered by our value system and our accepted modes of "work." But in the absence of such a consensus about cybernation, the nation cannot begin to take advantage of all that it promises for human betterment.

Proposal for Action

As a first step to a new consensus it is essential to recognize that the traditional link between jobs and incomes is being broken. The economy of abundance can sustain all citizens in comfort and economic security whether or not they engage in what is commonly reckoned as work. Wealth produced by machines rather than by men is still wealth. We urge, therefore, that society, through its appropriate legal and governmental institutions, undertake an unqualified commitment to provide every individual and every family with an adequate income as a matter of right. This undertaking we consider to be essential to the emerging economic, social and political order in this country. We regard it as the only policy by which the quarter of the nation now dispossessed and soon-to-be dispossessed by lack of employment can be brought within the abundant society. The unqualified right to an income would take the place of the patchwork of welfare measures—from unemployment insurance to relief—designed to ensure that no citizen or resident of the United States actually starves.

We do not pretend to visualize all of the consequences of this change in our values. It is clear, however, that the distribution of abundance in a cybernated society must be based on criteria strikingly different from those of an economic system based on scarcity. In retrospect, the establishment of the right to an income will prove to have been only the first step in the reconstruction of the value system of our society brought on by the triple revolution.

The present system encourages activities which can lead to private profit and neglects those activities which can enhance the wealth and the quality of life of our society. Consequently national policy has hitherto been aimed far more at the welfare of the productive process than at the welfare of people. The era of cybernation can reverse this emphasis. With public policy and research concentrated on people rather than processes we believe that many creative activities and interests commonly thought of as non-economic will absorb the time and the commitment of many of those no longer needed to produce goods and services. Society as a whole must encourage new modes of constructive, rewarding and ennobling activity. Principal among these are activities, such as teaching and learning, that relate people to people rather than people to things. Education has never been primarily conducted for profit in our society; it represents the first and most obvious activity inviting the expansion of the public sector to meet the needs of this period of transition.

We are not able to predict the long-run patterns of human activity and commitment in a nation when fewer and fewer people are involved in production of goods and services, nor are we able to forecast the overall patterns of income distribution that will replace those of the past full employment system. However, these are not speculative and fanciful matters to be contemplated at leisure for a society that may come into existence in three or four generations. The outlines of the future press sharply into the present. The problems of joblessness, inadequate incomes, and frustrated lives confront us now; the American Negro, in his rebellion, asserts the demands—and the rights—of all the disadvantaged. The Negro's is the most insistent voice today, but behind him stand the millions of impoverished who are beginning to understand that cybernation, properly understood and used, is the road out of want and toward a decent life.

The Transition[1]

We recognize that the drastic alterations in circumstances and in our way of life ushered in by cybernation and the economy of abundance will not be completed overnight. Left to the ordinary forces of the market, such change, however, will in-

[1] This view of the transitional period is not shared by all the signers. Robert Theobald and James Boggs hold that the two major principles of the transitional period will be 1) that machines rather than men will take up new conventional work openings and 2) that the activity of men will be directed to new forms of "work" and "leisure." Therefore, in

volve physical and psychological misery and perhaps political chaos. Such misery is already clearly evident among the unemployed, among relief clients into the third generation and more and more among the young and the old for whom society appears to hold no promise of dignified or even stable lives. We must develop programs for this transition designed to give hope to the dispossessed and those cast out by the economic system, and to provide a basis for the rallying of people to bring about those changes in political and social institutions which are essential to the age of technology.

The program here suggested is not intended to be inclusive but rather to indicate its necessary scope. We propose:

1. A massive program to build up our educational system, designed especially with the needs of the chronically undereducated in mind. We estimate that tens of thousands of employment opportunities in such areas as teaching and research and development, particularly for younger people, may be thus created. Federal programs looking to the training of an additional hundred thousand teachers annually are needed.

2. Massive public works. The need is to develop and put into effect programs of public works to construct dams, reservoirs, ports, water- and air-pollution facilities, community-recreation facilities. We estimate that for each billion dollars per year spent on public works a hundred and fifty thousand to two hundred thousand jobs would be created. Two billion dollars or more a year should be spent in this way, preferably as matching funds aimed at the relief of economically distressed or dislocated areas.

3. A massive program of low-cost housing, to be built both publicly and privately, and aimed at a rate of seven hundred thousand to a million units a year.

4. Development and financing of rapid-transit systems,

---

their opinion, the specific proposals outlined in this section are more suitable for meeting the problems of the scarcity-economic system than for advancing through the period of transition into the period of abundance.

urban and interurban, and other programs to cope with
the spreading problems of the great metropolitan centers.

5. A public-power system built on the abundance of
coal in distressed areas, designed for low-cost power to
heavy industrial and residential sections.

6. Rehabilitation of obsolete military bases for community or educational use.

7. A major revision of our tax structure, aimed at re-
distributing income as well as apportioning the costs of
the transition period equitably. To this end an expansion
of the use of excess-profits tax would be important. Subsidies and tax-credit plans are required to ease the human
suffering involved in the transition of many industries
from manpower to machine-power.

8. The trade unions can play an important and significant role in this period in a number of ways:

a. Use of collective bargaining to negotiate, not only for
people at work but also for those thrown out of work by
technological change.

b. Bargaining for perquisites, such as housing, recreational facilities, and similar programs, as they have
negotiated health and welfare programs.

c. Obtaining a voice in the investment of the unions'
huge pension and welfare funds, and insisting on investment policies which have as their major criteria the social
use and function of the enterprise in which the investment is made.

d. Organization of the unemployed, so that these voiceless
people may once more be given a voice in their own
economic destinies, and strengthening of the campaign
to organize white-collar and professional workers.

9. The use of the licensing power of government to
regulate the speed and direction of cybernation to minimize hardship; and the use of minimum-wage power as
well as taxing powers to provide the incentives for moving as rapidly as possible toward the goals indicated by
this paper.

These suggestions are in no way intended to be complete or definitively formulated. They contemplate expenditures of several billions more each year than are now being spent for socially rewarding enterprises, and a larger role for the government in the economy than it has now or has been given except in times of crisis. In our opinion, this is a time of crisis, the crisis of a triple revolution. Public philosophy for the transition must rest on the conviction that our economic, social and political institutions exist for the use of man and that man does not exist to maintain a particular economic system. This philosophy centers on an understanding that governments are instituted among men for the purpose of making possible life, liberty, and the pursuit of happiness and that government should be a creative and positive instrument toward these ends.

Change Must Be Managed

The historic discovery of the post-World War II years is that the economic destiny of the nation can be managed. Since the debate over the Employment Act of 1946, it has been increasingly understood that the Federal Government bears primary responsibility for the economic and social well-being of the country. The essence of management is planning. The democratic requirement is planning by public bodies for the general welfare. Planning by private bodies, such as corporations, for their own welfare does not automatically result in additions to the general welfare, as the impact of cybernation on jobs has already made clear.

The hardships imposed by sudden changes in technology have been acknowledged by Congress in proposals for dealing with the long- and short-run "dislocations" in legislation for depressed and "impacted" areas, retraining of workers replaced by machines, and the like. The measures so far proposed have not been "transitional" in conception. Perhaps for this reason they have had little effect on the situations they were designed to alleviate. But the primary weakness of this legislation is not ineffectiveness but incoherence. In no way can these disconnected measures be seen as a plan for remedying deep ailments but only, so to speak, as the superficial treatment of surface wounds.

Planning agencies should constitute the network through which pass the stated needs of the people at every level of society, gradually building into a national inventory of human requirements, arrived at by democratic debate of elected representatives.

The primary tasks of the appropriate planning institutions should be:

—to collect the data necessary to appraise the effects, social and economic, of cybernation at different rates of innovation;

—to recommend ways, by public and private initiative, of encouraging and stimulating cybernation;

—to work toward optimal allocations of human and natural resources in meeting the requirements of society;

—to develop ways to smooth the transition from a society in which the norm is full employment within an economic system based on scarcity, to one in which the norm will be either non-employment, in the traditional sense of productive work, or employment on the great variety of socially valuable but "non-productive" tasks made possible by an economy of abundance; to bring about the conditions in which men and women no longer needed to produce goods and services may find their way to a variety of self-fulfilling and socially useful occupations;

—to work out alternatives to defense and related spending that will commend themselves to citizens, *entrepreneurs* and workers as a more reasonable use of common resources;

—to integrate domestic and international planning. The technological revolution has related virtually every major domestic problem to a world problem. The vast inequities between the industrialized and the underdeveloped countries cannot long be sustained.

The aim throughout will be the conscious and rational direction of economic life by planning institutions and democratic control.

In this changed framework the new planning institutions will operate at every level of government—local, regional and federal—and will be organized to elicit democratic participation in all their proceedings. These bodies will be the means for giving direction and content to the growing demand for improvement in all departments of public life. The planning institutions will show the way to turn the growing protest against ugly cities, polluted air and water, an inadequate educational system, disappearing recreational and material resources, low levels of medical care, and the haphazard economic development into an integrated effort to raise the level of general welfare.

We are encouraged by the record of the planning institutions both of the Common Market and of several European nations and believe that this country can benefit from studying their weaknesses and strengths. A principal result of planning will be to step up investment in the public sector. Greater investment in this area is advocated because it is overdue, because the needs in this sector comprise a substantial part of the content of the general welfare, and because they can be readily afforded by an abundant society. Given the knowledge that we are now in a period of transition it would be deceptive, in our opinion, to present such activities as likely to produce full employment. The efficiencies of cybernation should be as much sought in the public as in the private sector, and a chief focus of planning would be one means of bringing this about. A central assumption of planning institutions would be the central assumption of this statement, that the nation is moving into a society in which production of goods and services is not the only or perhaps the chief means of distributing income.

The Democratization of Change

The revolution in weaponry gives some dim promise that mankind may finally eliminate institutionalized force as the method of settling international conflict and find for it political and moral equivalents leading to a better world. The Negro revolution signals the ultimate admission of this group to the American community on equal social, political and economic terms. The cybernation revolution proffers an existence qualitatively richer in democratic as well as material values. A social order in which men make the decisions that shape their lives becomes more possible now than ever before; the unshackling of men from the bonds of unfulfilling labor frees them to become citizens, to make themselves and to make their own history.

But these enhanced promises by no means constitute a guarantee. Illuminating and making more possible the "democratic vistas" is one thing; reaching them is quite another, for a vision of democratic life is made real not by technological change but by men consciously moving toward that ideal and creating institutions that will realize and nourish the vision in living form.

Democracy, as we use the term, means a community of men and women who are able to understand, express and determine their lives as dignified human beings. Democracy can only be rooted in a political and economic order in which wealth is distributed by and for people, and used for the widest social benefit. With the emergence of the era of abundance we have the economic base for a true democracy of participation, in which men no longer need to feel themselves prisoners of social forces and decisions beyond their control or comprehension.

Donald G. Agger, Dr. Donald B. Armstrong, James Boggs, Louis Fein, W. H. Ferry, Maxwell Geismar, Todd Gitlin, Philip Green, Roger Hagan, Michael Harrington, Tom Hayden, Robert L. Heilbroner, Ralph L. Helstein, Frances W. Herring, Hugh B. Hester, Alice Mary Hilton, Irving Howe, Everett C. Hughes, H. Stuart Hughes, Gerald W. Johnson, Irving F. Laucks, Stewart Meacham, A. J. Muste, Gunnar Myrdal (with reservations), Linus Pauling, Gerard Piel, Michael D. Reagan, Bayard Rustin, Ben B. Seligman, Robert Theobald, John William Ward, William Worthy.

Dave Dellinger

Revolution and Water

More important than the development of machines that think like men is the development of men who think like human beings. If the first process can encourage the second, so much the better. And this is exactly what is happening, at least in the case of the authors of "The Triple Revolution." For in the process of analyzing the increasing uses of cybernation they come out, in effect, for a more extensive application of humanism. They try to face head on the implications of the well known fact that machines are rapidly catching up to man in brain power (as they have long since surpassed him in muscle power) and end by making a proposal which would restore man to his natural eminence as a person. They give him back his human heart, which has been all but denied him by competitive economics and poverty in the midst of affluence.[1]

The authors try to speak gruffly, as scientists. Or perhaps because of the decline of the humane currents that once enriched this country's public outlook and their fear that to speak openly as humanitarians would be to impart a political "kiss of death" on their proposal, they edge up to it by establishing the inability of our economic system to function in the age of cybernation under any other arrangement. But when all is said and done, their basic proposition is only a skip and a jump from the economic philosophy of the early Christians ("And there was neither rich nor poor among them") and of Karl Marx ("From each according to his ability, to each according to his need"), though it is, of course, not more than remotely related to that of present-day Communism.

[1] Every year six million children under 16 die in Brazil, which has a total population of only seventy million, but the wealth, power, and paranoia of the United States will not tolerate the continuation in office of even moderate reformers like Janio Quadros and Joao Goulart.

Their central proposition is forthright and unambiguous:

> . . . the traditional link between jobs and incomes is
> being broken. The economy of abundance can sustain all
> citizens in comfort and economic security whether or not
> they engage in what is commonly reckoned as work. . . .
> We urge, therefore, that society, through its appropriate
> legal and governmental institutions, undertake an un-
> qualified commitment to provide every individual and
> every family with an adequate income as a matter of right.

If such a "sensible and rather obvious" proposition can be
put forth for the serious consideration of the President and
Congress by the thirty-two prominent and, in most cases, non-
utopian social thinkers who have done so, then perhaps Paul
Goodman's recent proposals have more political relevance than
he seems to think. For if our being dependent on a paying job
in order to receive anything but the barest income actually
inhibits the functioning of the economic system (as the Ad
Hoc Committee on the Triple Revolution maintains), then what
is so impractical about "supposing people actually did the
things which really absorbed them, which they felt they were
getting something out of and which they kept doing for long
hours"? The Ad Hoc Committee asserts that "society no longer
needs to impose repetitive and meaningless (because unnecessary) toil upon the individual" and Goodman goes on to discuss just how meaningless and unproductive most people's
work *and* consumption are, under a system which all but requires the kinds of work and consumption which maximize
private profits. To be sure, the categories of meaningless and
unnecessary occupations can no longer be limited to "repetitive" work, such as adding columns of figures all day or tight-
ening nuts on an assembly line. What about dreaming up the
"imaginative" ads that appear in the *New Yorker*, researching
consumer resistances and susceptibilities, serving as a tax consultant or a stock-market analyst, preparing competitive and
often deceptive packaging for basically identical low-quality
products? What about collecting tolls at bridges and on highways, or the billing, bookkeeping and collecting of fares and
fees for a wide variety of goods and services that could just as
well be free to the public? Some experiments have indicated

that it would be actually cheaper—as well as a lot more pleasant—to provide free public transportation for metropolitan
areas than to maintain the fee-collecting and traffic- and
parking-control systems now in operation.

The conventional response to the idea that people should
be able to spend their lives doing what they want to do and
receive the material decencies of life without charge is that it
wouldn't work. People just wouldn't want to do the right
things. They have to be coerced, if not by the old-fashioned
alternatives of a future hell or heaven, then at least by a system of more immediate material rewards and punishments. Of
course, this is the kind of incentive system which people have
been conditioned to live by, and if it were suddenly discarded
there would undoubtedy be a certain amount of "goofing off."
But we predict that it wouldn't take very long for most people
to settle down and discover, in many cases for the first time,
that the satisfactions of useful or challenging work are more
fulfilling than those supposedly derived from either nonpro-
ductive idleness or alienated work and the putative rewards of
status or luxury that, in theory at least, fall to the hard-working
and conscientious.

Even today, a large proportion of the most valuable work
in the fields of scientific discovery, mechanical invention, medical research, education, architecture, literature and the other
arts, community planning, valid civic improvement, etc., is motivated not by lust for material gain or fear of poverty but by a
desire for the pleasures associated with such activity. Where
the aim of monetary success has been compelling in these
fields it has been more apt to diminish rather than improve
the quality of the performance. Some foundations—and even
certain corporations as well—have discovered that to give a
man money, freedom, and facilities leads to more valuable work
than tying him to time-clocks and promised results. In general,
there has been somewhat more recognition of man's natural
joy in learning (cf. educational experiments, ranging all the
way from the Summerhill School for children to certain experimental colleges) than of his natural fulfillment in productive
work. But the do-it-yourself craze, the widespread use of work
therapy for the mentally ill and the "prematurely" retired, the

popularity of community arts-and-crafts programs, the reliance in rural areas on voluntary fire departments and emergency squads, even the familiar puttering of the suburbanite in his back yard—all point, even within the framework of a monetary culture, to the natural attractiveness of useful work.

And in the society implicitly projected by the Ad Hoc Committee's major thesis, it would be harder and harder to distinguish between the learning process and the work process.

In any event, it is perfectly possible—and according to the committee, increasingly necessary—to take a few concrete steps in the direction of what would really constitute a "free economy" without knowing fully what man might turn out to be like in the absence of selfish economic incentives. Already our society is to a great extent committed in theory to the proposition that no child should be permitted to starve, suffer medical neglect, or be denied an elementary school education regardless of whether or not his parents are unemployed, lazy, profligate, or criminal. We have been committed for years to the principle of free public museums, parks, libraries, roads (if not highways, any more), fire protection, and sewage disposal in most cities. Would it be so utopian to propose adding a few key items to the list of goals and services to which all people are supposed to have free and equal access?

Our chief disappointment with the Ad Hoc Committee's document is its failure to do just that. It unaccountably refrains from following up its major contention that the job-wage nexus is obsolete in today's world and must be abolished in favor of comfort and security for all as a natural right. Instead it offers a program of transitional steps which are not really steps in the desired direction at all—at least not as outlined. For the most part they seem designed to fulfill the old-fashioned, Keynesian (and even pre-Keynesian) pump-priming function whose inadequacies they have pointed out a few paragraphs earlier.

It is laudable to advocate expanding the educational system, public works, low-cost housing, urban and interurban rapid transit systems, and public power—and liberals have been advocating such measures, often with some success, for generations. But what do such measures have to do with providing an adequate income for all, regardless of employment status? Why is there not even a hint that the new and expanded facilities should be made available to all without charge. Why concern oneself with "subsidies and tax-credit plans to ease the human suffering involved in the transition of many industries from manpower to machine power" instead of complete freedom from taxation for all *persons* whose income is below an agreed-upon level of minimum decency, with the minimum to be progressively raised? What about such elementary steps as providing substantial family allotments for each child, a practice observed for years in less affluent Canada and many European countries? What about providing free milk, as a beginning, for, let us say, everyone under 16? With the age to be progressively raised in the future? What about free medical care, including visits to the doctor, surgery and hospitalization? Or free prescriptions? (The United States fell even further behind a number of other Western countries in infant-mortality and life-expectancy rates during the very period in which it was forging ahead in cybernation, death-dealing weaponry, and—corporate profits.)

One could debate about which or how many of these suggestions to get behind this year. But if one really accepts the committee's major proposal as a practical and legitimate goal, one should make proposals that begin to move in its direction.

We are too grateful for the committee's analysis and major formulation to quibble over details. Nor do we think that our own comments have more than begun to touch on the issues that must be discussed and explored. For instance, there is a whole series of questions concerning the possibility of decentralizing function and control, and safeguarding local and individual freedom. For the moment, however, we have only one more comment. Perhaps it is even more important that this document be placed in the hands of the Negroes, the unemployed, the underemployed, the poor, and everyone whose job is insecure because of automation or who is fed up with meaningless and unnecessary work than that it be perused by the President and other members of the Establishment. For there is one lesson from the civil rights movement that the committee did not go into. It is that the motive power and dynamic for needed social change come not from the top but rather from those who are victims of the way things are.

"The Triple Revolution" opens up new vistas for today's victims, both black and white. United behind a program of the kind we have been discussing, they could do more than either the present civil rights movement or the President and Congress is apt to do to formulate and put into practice an up-to-date version of the old American dream of dignity, equality, and freedom for everyone.

Robert Theobald

Cybernation and Human Rights

My use of the word cybernation instead of automation does not stem from a desire to *seem* to be saying something new. On the contrary, I use the word cybernation because it represents something quite different from automation. Automation was the process by which you could take a block of metal, put it in at one end of a series of machines and it would come out at the other, as a finished engine block, without the need for human intervention. Automated machinery could do some things fast and well; nevertheless, its potential to organize people out of work was limited because it was inflexible.

Cybernation, however, is highly flexible and will become more so as time passes. Cybernation is the process of linking a computer, which is effectively a machine which will make decisions, and using it to control automated machinery. These interlocking machine-systems can often be controlled by a few people sitting at computers, while the requirements for other workers are very small, for not only will the machines do all the work but the latest ones are being built practically to repair themselves. The potential to organize human beings out of work in order to increase the efficiency of machine-systems is already large and rapidly growing. In other words, the present type of change in technology cannot be considered merely a continuation of the organizational process of the last one hundred and fifty years—it means something completely new which is quietly taking place all around us. Cybernation involves a production revolution which has two major consequences. First, in the field of production it is challenging and will increasingly challenge the supremacy of man's mind, and it will do this just as surely as the industrial revolution challenged and overcame the supremacy of man's muscle. In the relatively near future the machine-systems will take over all repetitive physical and mental production tasks and huge numbers of people will be thrown out of work. It has been estimated by some authorities that as little as 10% or even 2% of the labor force will be required for conventional work in the future.

The idea that we can continue to aim at finding a job for everybody is obsolete. A large proportion of those born in the fifties and sixties have no prospect of ever holding an ordinary job. There is no role in today's economy for those teen-agers who are high-school dropouts and there is increasingly little place for those over fifty-five.

Such a picture seems bleak to many: they seem afraid that there will not be enough toil to go round. To me, on the other hand, it appears like the lifting of the curse of Adam, for it will no longer be necessary for man to earn his bread in the sweat of his brow. Machines could perform the productive toil and men could receive the resulting abundance, for machines would not only take over all the toil, they would also make it possible to turn out effectively unlimited quantities of both goods and services. U Thant, Secretary General of the United Nations, has expressed it in the following terms:

> The truth, the central stupendous truth, about developed countries today is that they can have—in anything but the shortest run—the kind and scale of resources they decide to have. . . . It is no longer resources that limit decisions. It is the decision that makes the resources. This is the fundamental revolutionary change—perhaps the most revolutionary mankind has ever known.

There is no need—and no excuse—for poverty in the America of the second half of the twentieth century. Why, then, does it exist, and what can be done? Before I discuss this I want to present a few figures which will show that there is already too much unemployment, that there is the ability to produce more goods and services, and that we will have more unemployment and more ability to produce additional goods and services in coming years.

First, unemployment rates have remained around or

above the excessive rate of 5.5% during the sixties. (The last few months have seen a decline to 5.1%.) The unemployment rate for teenagers has been rising steadily, reaching 17% in 1963; the unemployment rate for Negro teenagers was 27% in 1963, while the unemployment rate for teenagers in minority ghettoes often exceeds 50%. Unemployment rates for Negroes are regularly above twice those for whites, whatever their occupation, educational level, age or sex. The unemployment position for other racial minorities is also unfavorable.

These official figures seriously underestimate the true extent of the unemployment problem. In 1962, in addition to the percentage of the labor force who were officially unemployed, nearly 4% of the labor force wanted full-time work but could only find part-time jobs. Methods of calculating unemployment rates—a person is only unemployed if he has actively sought a job recently—ignore the existence of a large group who would like to find jobs but who have not looked for them because they know there are no employment opportunities. Underestimation for this reason is particularly severe for people in groups whose unemployment rates are high—the young, the old and racial minorities. Willard Wirtz, Secretary of Labor, has stated that at least 350,000 young men between 14 and 24 have stopped looking for work. Many people in the depressed agricultural, mining and industrial areas, who officially hold jobs but who are actually grossly under-employed, would move if there were real prospects of finding work elsewhere. It is therefore reasonable to estimate that around eight million people are looking for jobs today as compared to the 3.6 million shown in the official statistics.

Even more serious is the fact that the number of people who have voluntarily removed themselves from the labor force is not static but increases continually. For these people the decision to stop looking for employment and to accept the fact that they will never hold a job or will not hold a job again is largely irreversible, not only in economic but also in social and psychological terms. The older worker calls himself "retired"; he cannot accept work without affecting his social security status. The worker in prime years is forced onto relief: in most states the requirements for becoming a relief recipient bring about such fundamental alterations in an individual's total material situation that a reversal of the process is always difficult and often totally infeasible. The teenager knows that there is no place for him in the labor force but at the same time is unaware of any realistic alternative avenue for self-fulfillment.

Statistical evidence of these trends appears in the decline in the proportion of people claiming to be in the labor force. The recent apparent stabilization, and indeed decline, of the unemployment rate is therefore misleading: it is primarily a reflection of the discouragement and defeat of people who cannot find employment rather than a measure of the economy's success in creating enough jobs for all those who want to find a place in the labor force.

Second, we could produce far more goods and services if we would only find more ways to allow people to buy them—for the past eight years there has been the potential to produce some sixty billion dollars of additional goods and services. We are able every year to produce at least another thirty billion dollars of additional goods and services; this will rise to forty billion dollars per year before the end of the sixties, fifty billion dollars during the first half of the seventies, and at least sixty billion dollars well before the end of the seventies. We will be able to produce an additional one hundred and fifty billion dollars of extra goods and services every year by the end of the century. The children born in 1964 will only be about half way through their lives at this time. I should add that these estimates are certainly conservative.

Third, the forward movement of cybernation is raising the skill level of the machine. If a human being is to compete with such machines, he must *at least* possess a high school diploma. The Department of Labor has estimated, however, that on the basis of present trends as many as thirty per cent of *all* students will be high school drop-outs in this decade.

Fourth, a permanently depressed class is developing in the United States. Scattered throughout the land, some thirty-eight million Americans, or almost one-fifth of the population, are living in a condition of chronic poverty which is daily becoming more evident to the rest of the nation. The percentage of total income received by the poorest 20% of the population has

fallen from 4.9% to 4.7% since 1944. Movement out of the ranks
of the poor is increasingly difficult, for it depends on an adequate education, while conscription of new and apparently
permanent recruits continues.

The best summary of the effects of these trends was perhaps made by the Secretary of Labor at the beginning of 1964:

> The confluence of surging population and driving tech-
> nology is splitting the American labor force into tens
> of millions of "haves" and millions of "have-nots." In
> our economy of sixty-nine million jobs, those with wanted
> skills enjoy opportunity and earning power. But the others
> face a new and stark problem—exclusion on a permanent
> basis, both as producers and consumers, from economic
> life. This division of people threatens to create a human
> slag-heap. We cannot tolerate the development of a sepa-
> rate nation of the poor, the unskilled, the jobless, living
> within another nation of the well-off, the trained and the
> employed.

Is it surprising that the news media are full of reports of violence? There is no need to remind you of these reports nor of
the climate which has created them—we all live too close to
these problems. But I want to discuss with you the response, or
rather the reaction, which is growing among many people. I
will quote from the police chief, William H. Parker, in Los
Angeles. This report appeared in the magazine *U. S. News and
World Report* in April, 1964, in the form of a question and
answer interview.

> *Question:* Has the crime picture changed much in [the
> last 37 years]?
> *Answer:* Not only has the crime picture changed, but
> the entire attitude of the American people toward crime,
> I think, has undergone quite a definite change. I think
> there is a tendency to accept crime as part of the Amer-
> ican scene, and to tolerate it.
> *Question:* Do you mean that people now feel that
> wrong-doing is normal?
> *Answer:* More than that—they seem to think that we

must have a certain amount of crime not only because
of man's inherent weakness, but because we are enlarg-
ing upon the scope of individual liberty.

Question: America might have a choice, eventually, between a criminal state and a police state.

Answer: I believe that will become the option before us
if crime becomes so troublesome that we are no longer
able to control it.

But Chief Parker did not mention what is to me the most
serious aspect of the present situation. He did not deal with
the passive apathy of individuals recently demonstrated in several notorious cases in the New York area. In one of these, at
least 38 people failed to call the police although they became
progressively more aware that a woman was being murdered
in the street below their windows. He did not deal with the
fact that there is now a desire to witness violence, to participate vicariously, as when a crowd of forty interested spectators
remained indifferent to the appeals of an 18-year-old bruised
and bloodied office worker as she tried to escape from a rapist.
(Only the accidental arrival of two policemen eventually re-
sulted in her rescue.)

It is understandable, if regrettable, when those accidently
present at the scene of a crime or disaster flee through fear. It
is incomprehensible as rational behavior when they remain as
interested spectators or even active participants. During an
attempted suicide which took place in Albany recently, numerous spectators participated in this novel type of sports-event,
urging the mentally-disturbed youth to jump to his death and
betting on the outcome. Two comments reported in the New
York *Times* are hardly believable: "I wish he'd do it and get it
over with. If he doesn't hurry up we're going to miss our last
bus." And another: "I hope he jumps on this side. We couldn't
see him if he jumped over there."

I believe this indifference to violence, and indeed increasing encouragement of it, are products of a society which is
rapidly coming to regard inter-race conflict as inevitable; a
society which fails to challenge the individual to anything
more than economic goals and responsibilities and which has

now deprived many people of even an opportunity to achieve
the self-respect which would result from reaching these economic goals. Although we are confronted with the symptoms
of incipient total breakdown in our society, we are unwilling to
face reality. We refuse to recognize that the survival of American values depends on fundamental changes which will reverse
the process toward alienation. We refuse to recognize that the
economically poor and the culturally alienated, who are the
young and the minorities, have and should have little interest
in the goals our society presently espouses. Instead of looking
for the new and better society that cybernation makes possible
we continue the drift into a worse society: we then propose
that the way to arrest this drift is through measures which
must necessarily be categorized as movements toward a centralized authoritarian state: teen-age curfews and all-day
seven-day-a-week retention of children within the confines of
the school plant.

Some Proposals

Now I want to set out a program which might suffice to reverse
the drift toward a centralized authoritarian state.

    The first necessity is to guarantee every individual within
the United States a decent standard of living whether he can
find work or not. We should provide every individual with an
absolute constitutional right to an income adequate to allow
him to live with dignity. No governmental agency, judicial
body or other organization whatsoever should have the power
to suspend or limit any payments by this guarantee. Such an
absolute constitutional right to an income will recognize that in
an economy where many jobs already represent make-work in
any social, and indeed economic, sense and where the requirements for workers will decrease in coming years, it is nonsensi-
cal to base the right to an income on an ability to find a job.

    Many people have attacked this proposal, but their argu-
ments have failed to convince me. I remain quite sure that the
guaranteed income is the first necessary step if we are to
achieve the new and better society made possible by cybernation, that it is the only practical means of preserving our fundamental goal of individual freedom, the only method of al-

lowing the individual to make his own decisions and pursue his own interests. The guaranteed income is not one of many solutions to the problems of cybernation: on the contrary it is the economic prerequisite for the solution of the real problems of the second half of the twentieth century, many of which have not yet even begun to be discussed in realistic terms.

The first of these problems is education. One of the key principles of the cybernated era is that society must make an unlimited commitment to produce the conditions in which every individual can develop his full intellectual potential. The acceptance of this principle would make me highly optimistic for the long run. I believe that we have so far developed only a tiny proportion of the potential of most human beings. I believe that acceptance of an absolute right to an income and complete education would allow a flowering of the spirit and mind whose dimensions cannot even be guessed today.

If we are to achieve the complete education of every individual, we must recognize that the student is "working" at least as relevantly as the man in the factory. The time has come when we must introduce the concept of a student salary, starting possibly at 14 and increasing with age, payable to all students attending school or university. This salary would be tangible proof of the recognition by society of the value of this young individual and its acceptance by the child would be a recognition by him of his obligation to the society which has accorded him this right.

Society must not only be concerned with the individual's mental abilities but also with his physical health. We must develop a system which will ensure that everybody can obtain the best medical care—both preventive and curative. Income levels should be seen as totally irrelevant to rights to health and life.

Rights to an income sufficient to live with dignity, to the opportunity to develop oneself fully and to obtain meaningful activity are only extensions of present values, although many people will be shocked by the direction of the proposed extension. However, the coming of the cybernated society not only forces us to live up to past ideals but it also requires the development of new human rights. I want to talk about the need for three rights which seem highly important to me. (There are others which should be mentioned if space permitted.)

The first of these new human rights is for the individual to be provided with guarantees about the quality of all the goods he purchases. It has always been a fundamental principle of marketing in the Western world that the purchaser should discover the quality, condition and quantity of the goods he is purchasing. The seller simply offers a product and it is held to be the responsibility of the purchaser to inform himself as to whether it is satisfactory. This is the famous legal doctrine of *caveat emptor* (let the buyer beware).

Today, the consumer cannot reasonably be expected to examine a television set or any other complex product to discover if it is well made: the makers of many types of goods have recognized this fact and have steadily lengthened their periods of guarantee. We now need to take the next step and acknowledge that the total responsibility for determining whether a product is satisfactory lies with the seller and not with the buyer. Each seller should become responsible for the claims made on behalf of his product and should be forced to refund some multiple of the purchase price if the product does not meet his claims. In some cases, when injury to the purchaser results, the seller should be liable for damages. The manufacturer will therefore have a direct financial interest in living up to the claims made for his product.

In upper Manhattan, we are all used to the shoddy-goods salesman with the foot in the door on a Sunday afternoon or late on a weekday evening. We fail to translate our momentary irritation into terms of national waste. The proposed human right would not only minimize the time wasted by the individual in purchasing repair or replacement: it would also meet desirable social criteria. The time and money the manufacturer saves by selling unsatisfactory products is wasted many times over by the troubles of the user. We need a productive system which will turn out goods which will render the services for which they were designed with the minimum possible number of breakdowns.

In addition, the long-run necessity, if mankind is to survive on this planet, is maximum economy in the use of raw materials. Every pressure should therefore be placed on the manufacturer to maximize the life of the product. This measure would be a first step in this direction.

The second new human right is the right to buy from any seller. Originally the buyer and seller were in close human contact and they naturally wished to choose to whom they would sell and from whom they would buy. Today, business desires to move goods and services at a profit without entangling social problems. As a result it is not only desirable but also necessary for society to state that in return for the right granted the businessman to sell goods and services, he has the obligation to serve all comers. Those who do not want to accept the obligation to sell to all comers should not be granted the right to sell at all.

It is, of course, *only* the establishment of such a principle in law which will provide a completely satisfactory answer to present discrimination practices. It is an answer which must be eventually passed as a constitutional amendment: it must be clearly recognized that private property ceases to be private *just as soon as* the individual or company makes the decision to sell to the public.

It would be naive, of course, to expect that these new rights, and many others, could be effectively established without a major reform in our legal system. Today, the government has all the resources in a criminal case: the private individual, unless he is wealthy, has no opportunity to hire legal talent of comparable skill. In a civil case, the large corporation controls enough funds to hire a battery of lawyers; the private individual rarely has enough resources to match this ability to spend. We require a new institution: the public defender. Public defenders would be paid by the government and would have the power of government officials but their responsibility would be to take the cases of the private individual whose interests they felt had been unjustly damaged by the use of private and governmental power. They would possess enough resources to challenge the large institution effectively. A system similar to this has already been established in Scandinavia, and Justice

Goldberg of the Supreme Court has proposed it be introduced into the United States.

The third new human right is that every individual should have the right to receive information undistorted by desires to mislead for the purposes of private gain. This is, in today's world, a very novel proposal for it means that society must develop effective sanctions against individuals and groups who distort information deliberately. That such a proposal seems novel is perhaps a good measure of the degree of malfunction in our society. The framers of the American Constitution intended that the right of free speech and a free press should be a method of achieving free debate, not a justification of deliberate distortion with consequent fragmentation of the society.

What types of distortion am I condemning? I condemn the advertisers who play on the weakness of the individual in order to increase their sales. I condemn the propagandists of any country who unhesitatingly distort the unfavorable and bury the undesirable news. I condemn the academics who distort the truth as they see it in order to gain reputations or power. On the other hand, I do not condemn but resolutely uphold the right of the individual to put forward all the truth as he sees it, however unpalatable it may be. I believe, indeed, that we must smooth the path of individuals who are willing to dissent, for the costs of disagreement with existing social norms are always high. The granting of an absolute constitutional right to an income will be helpful here.

Indeed, I go further. The existence of lively controversy which allows the discovery of the truth in constantly changing circumstances is one of the prime necessities of today. Only a lively democracy can lead to the adoption of appropriate policies to deal with changing situations. Concentration of power in the hands of a few not only is against our past ideals but also fails to meet present necessities.

I would like to suggest that this is, in fact the major role which has been played by the civil rights movement in recent years, and particularly in recent months. The attention of the civil rights groups themselves, and of outside observers, has been concentrated on the degree of success or failure achieved in striving for stated goals. There is a considerable feeling that they have consistently fallen short of their goals and this has been called failure. This is an excessively naive view of social change. Very few commentators discuss the real success of the civil rights movement—the fact that it has, almost single-handed, wrested America out of the apathy in which it was mired and forced it to face the problems of unemployment and inadequate education, the problems of poverty, and the long-run dangers of cybernation. The drive of the civil rights movement is forcing America to re-examine itself and to recognize that the rights of the Negro cannot be achieved without fundamental social and economic change. The civil rights movement has provided America with another chance, and possibly its last one, to recognize that in conditions of abundance every citizen both can and should be provided with the means to obtain enough food, clothing, shelter, education and health care: in effect to be a first class citizen.

Martin Luther King has taken this theme and proposed in his new book ". . . that the United States launch a broad-based and gigantic Bill of Rights for the Disadvantaged." He adds: "It is a matter of simple justice that the United States, in dealing creatively with the task of raising the Negro from backwardness, should also be rescuing a large stratum of the forgotten white poor. A Bill of Rights for the Disadvantaged could mark the rise of a new era, in which the full resources of the society could be used to attack the tenacious poverty which so paradoxically exists in the midst of plenty."

How can this goal be achieved? Clearly the civil rights movement must be joined by other supporting groups. Only if all those who are concerned with the improvement of our society unite to bring about major change will it be possible to achieve the pace of development in social values which will allow us to benefit from technology and consequent abundance rather than be destroyed by it.

The civil rights and labor movements stand, indeed, at a crossroads. They can become the rallying point for true social change, for demands which in any other period of history would clearly have been Utopian but which are today completely practical and indeed essential. The decision to take the route proposed would deprive the civil rights movement of the

432]   ROBERT THEOBALD

support of some sections. It would alienate those who are only concerned with obtaining justice for the Negro, who refuse to recognize that justice for the Negro cannot be secured in a society which does not secure justice for all its citizens; in the same way that present injustice to the Negro is progressively involving injustice to others. In addition, this decision would deprive the unions of the support of those who are concerned solely with people who still are, or might become, union members.

If we plan and carry out the necessary actions our common future has a brighter aspect but we must face up to the unkind fact that much of the potential benefit from cybernation and abundance will be reaped not by us but by our children. We are in many ways the truly lost generation: we are torn adrift from the certainties by which our parents still lived and we will never fully understand the new set of apparent certainties which will seem totally natural to the children growing up today. These children, in their turn, will never understand how we could have allowed our defunct concepts of economics to prevent us from providing everybody with food, clothing, shelter, education, and health care.

In one sense, we will remain chained to our past, unable to enter the promised land. But our generation, and *only* our generation, can bring humanity to this promised land. The challenge is uniquely ours: if we fail to rise to it we will destroy our values, the values of our children and very possibly the whole world. If we succeed we have laid the groundwork for the Great Society.

Paul Goodman

Getting into Power*

Part I

The spirited candidacy of Stuart Hughes for Senator—like an actualization of Leo Szilard's courageous plan to finance and organize a national party for peace—makes it useful to review the ambiguities involved in this kind of politics.

"War is the health of the State"—modern history teaches no other lesson, whether we think of the weird personal, fanatic, and dynastic wars of the Sixteenth and Seventeenth Centuries or the economic and geopolitical wars of recent generations. The sovereign national States have lived and grown by preparing for war and waging war; and as the Powers have aggrandized themselves, they have become more crashingly destructive. I do not mean that men have not also used simpler social organizations, feudal, tribal, free city, in order to kill one another *en masse,* but centralized sovereign power, radiating from baroque capitals, has proved to be the ideal executive of murderous will. In our own nation, at present, it would be impossible to describe the economy without regarding war-making as a crucial factor; the foreign relations of the United States are carried on entirely in terms of bellicose power-blocs, and either to expand "influence" or to hang onto it; and to mention my own field where I can speak at first hand, our primary education and heavily State-subsidized higher educa tion have become regimented to apprentice-training for war, more directly if less sickeningly than the psychological national regimentation endemic in French and German schooling. (The Russians go in for both the technological and psychological aspects.)

* October, 1962.

This solidifying of national sovereign bellicosity is at present all the more irrational, and of course all the more necessary if the sovereigns are to maintain themselves, since the cultural, technological, economic, and communications relations of the world are now overwhelmingly supra-national. (What a pity that, partly to combat colonialism and partly out of the emulative stupidity and cupidity of their Western-trained leaders, peoples of Africa and Asia are adopting the same fatal and outmoded style.)

The only possible pacifist conclusion from these facts is the anarchist one, to get rid of the sovereignties and to diminish, among people, the motivations of power and grandiosity. This means, regionally, to decentralize or centralize directly in terms of life-functions, empirically examined. My own bias is to decentralize and localize wherever it is feasible, because this makes for alternatives and more vivid and intimate life. It multiplies initiative. And it is safer. On the basis of this weakening of the Powers, and of the substitution of function for power, it would be possible also to organize the world community, as by the functional agencies of the United Nations, UNICEF, WHO, somewhat UNESCO; and to provide *ad hoc* cooperation like the International Geophysical Year, exploring space, or feeding the Chinese.

Rigidly applied, this logic would seem to make pacifist State politics absurd. It is not in the nature of sovereign power to decree itself out of existence. (Thus, it is absurd for picketers of the White House to petition Mr. Kennedy as the President, rather than to sermonize him as a man or lecture him as a boy.) Also, such politics confuses the basic issue, that *pacifism is necessarily revolutionary*. A moment's recollection of the defection of the French and German Socialist deputies from their pacifism in 1914 will show that this confusion is not trivial. Nevertheless, the attitude of the General Strike for Peace[1] is as follows: in November we shall urge people actively and explicitly to refuse to vote, to strike against voting, except for candidates who are unambiguously committed to immediate action to relax the Cold War, for instance Stuart Hughes or Robert Kastenmeier. Our reasoning is that, in our increasingly

[1] Mike Harrington, a Socialist, has recently pointed out in the *New Leader* that the GSP "suffers from an anarchist tinge."

monolithic society and economy, any anti-war activity is likely to exert a revolutionary influence willy-nilly. And secondly, as Professor Hughes himself has said, the machinery of an electoral campaign *can* be a powerful means of education, especially by compelling mention of what the mass-media ordinarily refuse to mention. We wish to cooperate with pacifist activity of *every* kind, whether SANE, Quaker, Third Party politics, or Committee for Nonviolent Action, because although "objectively" we are in a revolutionary situation in that the Powers-that-be are certainly bent on destroying themselves and everything else, nevertheless people do not take this seriously and there is an almost total lack of practical will to make the necessary reorganization of society. To say it grimly, unlike 1914, people do not even have political representatives to betray them.

Personally, what I enjoy about Professor Hughes' campaign is that often, when the students were out getting signatures to put him on the ballot, people would say, "Do you mean he is *neither* a Democrat *nor* a Republican? Then give me the pen!" (It is said, by people from Massachusetts, that this response is peculiarly appropriate to the ordinary local politics of Massachusetts; but I take this as local boasting.) In the deadly routine that the Americans have sunk into, the mere possibility of an *alternative* is a glorious thing. Especially if there is the framework of a permanent organization. Also such a campaign must be a remarkable experience for Hughes himself, to confront many people who do not at all have the same assumptions. And it gives some concrete activity to his phalanx, the New England professors of the Council of Correspondence. The students of Brandeis, Harvard, etc. are also busy with it; but on them this *kind* of political involvement might be, in my opinion, more ambiguous, and that is why I am writing this essay.

Part II

For let me turn to an issue much deeper and more fateful for pacifism than these questions of strategy and tactics. This is the assumption, now appallingly unanimous among the ordinary electorate, professional politicians, most radicals, and even political scientists who should know better, that politics is essentially a matter of "getting into power," and then "deciding," directing, controlling, coercing, the activities of society. The model seems to be taken from corporations with top management, and there is something prestigious about being a "decision-maker." (Even C. Wright Mills was mesmerized by this image; but, as I tried to show recently in *Commentary*, in such a set-up less and less of human value is really decided by any responsible person, though plenty of disvalue is ground out by the set-up itself.) It is taken for granted that a man wants "power" of this kind, and it is quite acceptable for people like Joseph Kennedy and his sons to work toward it, even though this is directly contrary to the political ideal that the office and its duties seek the man rather than the man the office. It is axiomatic that a Party's primary purpose is to get into power, although this was not the original idea of "factions," in Madison's sense, which were functional but divisive interest groups. More dangerously still, it is taken for granted that a nation wants to be a Great Power, and maintain itself so at any cost, even though this may be disadvantageous to its culture and most of its citizens.[2]

And following the popular Leviathan like a jolly-boat, the political-sociologists devote their researches to the analysis and simulation of power struggles, as if this were their only possible subject; and as advisers, they take part in the power struggles, rather than helping to solve problems. Unfortunately, the thinking of Hughes and Szilard seems to share some of this assumption about the paramountcy of "getting into power"—just as Dave Riesman is always hounding people who are in "power." And frankly, when I question such a universal consensus, I wonder if I am on the right planet. Nevertheless, these persons are deluded. They are taking a base and imprac-

[2] Recently Robert Frost, who has been losing his horse-sense since becoming the friend of the President, told the Russians in Moscow that a nation must be "great . . . in order to protect the language, the poetry." Yet in this century a majority of the greatest writers of English have been Irish, e.g. Yeats, Synge, Joyce, Shaw. So Rilke and Kafka were Czech and wrote, natively, German. As the Jews have long known, it is best to share in a world-language and culture and to be free of the prejudices, hypocrisy, and foolishness of Great Powers.

tical, and indeed neurotic, state of affairs as if it were right and inevitable. The state of affairs is impractical because, finally, no good can come of it; though of course, since it *is* the state of affairs, it must be transiently coped with and changed. Unless we remember much more clearly than we seem to, what this "power" is, our behavior in the madhouse cannot be prudent and therapeutic. So with chagrin I find myself forced to review elementary political theory and history.

Living functions, biological, psychosociological, or social, have very little to do with abstract, preconceived "power" that manages and coerces from outside the specific functions themselves. Indeed, it is a commonplace that abstract power—in the form of "will power," "training," "discipline," "bureaucracy," "reform-schooling," "scientific management," etc.—uniformly *thwarts* normal functioning and debases the persons involved. (It has a natural use, in emergencies, when not high-grade but minimal low-grade behavior is required.) Normal activities do not need extrinsic motivations, they have their own intrinsic energies and ends-in-view; and decisions are continually made by the on-going functions themselves, adjusting to the environment and one another.

We may then define the subject of normal politics. It is the constitutional relations of functional interests and interest groups in the community in which they transact. This is the bread-and-butter of ancient political theory and obviously has nothing to do with sovereignty or even power—for the ancients the existence of Power implies unconstitutionality, tyranny. But even modern authors who move in a theory of "sovereignty," like Spinoza, Locke, Adam Smith, Jefferson, or Madison, understand that the commonwealth is strongest when the functional interests can seek their own level and there is the weakest exercise of "power." For example, Spinoza tries to play power like a fish, Jefferson to de-energize it, Madison to balance it out.

Let us now quickly sketch the meaning of the recent transcendent importance of "power" and "getting into power," as if otherwise communities could not function.

First, and least important, there is the innocuous, nonviolent, and rather natural development of a kind of abstract

power in an indigenous (non-invaded) society. The functions
of civilization include production, trade and travel, the bringing up of the young in the mores; also subtle but essential
polarities like experimentation and stability; also irrational and
superstitious fantasies like exacting revenge for crime and protecting the taboos. Different interests in the whole will continually conflict, as individuals or as interest-groups; yet, since all
require the commonwealth, there is also a strong functional
interest in adjudication and peace, in harmonizing social invention or at least compromise. It is plausible that, in the interests
of armistice and adjudication, there should arise a kind of
abstract institution above the conflicts, to settle them or to
obviate them by plans and laws; this would certainly be
Power. (This derivation is plausible but I doubt that it is historical, for in fact it is just this kind of thing that lively primitive communities accomplish by quick intuition, tone of voice,
exchange of a glance, and suddenly there is unanimity, to the
anthropologist's astonishment.) Much more likely, and we
know historically, abstract power is invented in simple societies in emergencies of danger, of enemy attack or divine
wrath. But such "dictatorship" is *ad hoc* and, surprisingly,
lapses. Surprisingly, considering that power corrupts; yet it
makes psychological sense, for emergency is a negative function, to meet a threat to the pre-conditions of the interesting
functions of life; once the danger is past, the "power" has no
energy of function, no foreground interest, to maintain it. To
give a very late example: it seemed remarkable to the Europeans, but not to the Americans, that Washington, like Cincin-
natus, went home to his farm; and even the Continental Congress languished. There were no conditions for "power."

(Indeed—and this is why I have chosen the example—in
the last decades of the Eighteenth Century, in many respects
the Americans lived in a kind of peaceful community anarchy,
spiced by mutinies that were hardly punished. The Constitution, as Richard Lee pointed out, was foisted on them by trickery, the work of very special interest groups; it would have
been quite sufficient simply to amend the Articles.)

Altogether different from this idyl is the univeral history
of most of the world, civilized or barbarian. Everywhere is
invasion, conquest, and domination, involving for the victors

the necessity to keep and exercise power, and for the others the necessity to strive for power, in order to escape suffering and exploitation. This too is entirely functional. The conqueror is originally a pirate; he and his band do not share in the commonwealth, they have interests apart from the community preyed on. Subsequently, however, piracy becomes government, the process of getting people to perform by extrinsic motivations, of penalty and blackmail, and later bribery and training. But it is only the semblance of a commonwealth, for activity is directed. Necessarily, such directed and extrinsically-motivated performance is not so strong, efficient, spontaneous, inventive, well-structured, or lovely as the normal functioning of a free community of interests. Very soon society becomes lifeless. The means of community action, initiative, decision, have been preempted by the powerful. But the slaveholders. exploiters, and governors share in that same society and are themselves vitiated. Yet they never learn to get down off the people's back and relinquish their power. So some are holding on to an increasingly empty power; others are striving to achieve it; and most are sunk in resignation. Inevitably, as people become stupider and more careless, administration increases in size and power; and conversely. By and large, the cultures that we study in the melancholy pages of history are pathetic mixtures, with the ingredients often still discernible: There is a certain amount of normal function surviving or reviving—bread is baked, arts and sciences are pursued by a few, etc.; mostly we see the abortions of lively social functioning saddled, exploited, prevented, perverted, drained dry, paternalized by an imposed system of power and management that preempts the means and makes decisions *ab extra*. And the damnable thing is that, of course, everybody believes that except in this pattern nothing could possibly be accomplished: if there were no marriage-license and no tax, none could properly mate and no children be born and raised; if there were no tolls there would be no bridges; if there were no university charters, there would be no higher learning;[3] if there were no usury and no iron law of wages, there would be no capital; if

[3] In my forthcoming *The Community of Scholars*, which is an anarchist critique of the colleges, I try to show how certain centers of learning were doing beautifully before they officially "existed" at all.

there were no mark-up of drug prices, there would be no scientific research. Once a society has this style of thought, that every activity requires licensing, underwriting, deciding by abstract power, it becomes inevitably desirable for an ambitious man to seek power and for a vigorous nation to try to be a Great Power. The more that have the power-drive, the more it seems to be necessary to the others to compete, or submit, just in order to survive. (And importantly they are right.) Many are ruthless and most live in fear.

Even so, this is not the final development of the belief in "power." For that occurs when to get into power, to be prestigious and in a position to make decisions, is taken to be the social good itself, apart from any functions that it is thought to make possible. The pattern of dominance-and-submission has then been internalized and, by its clinch, fills up the whole of experience. If a man is not continually proving his potency, his mastery of others and of himself, he becomes prey to a panic of being defeated and victimized. Every vital function must therefore be used as a means of proving or it is felt as a symptom of weakness. Simply to enjoy, produce, learn, give or take, love or be angry (rather than cool), is to be vulnerable. This is different, and has different consequences, from the previous merely external domination and submission. A people that has life but thwarted functions will rebel when it can, against feudal dues, clogs to trade, suppression of thought and speech, taxation without representation, insulting privilege, the iron law of wages, colonialism. But our people do not rebel against poisoning, genetic deformation, imminent total destruction.

Rather, people aspire to be top-managers no matter what the goods or services produced. One is a promoter, period; or a celebrity, period. The Gross National Product must increase without consideration of the standard of life. There is no natural limit, so the only security is in deterrence. The environment is rife with projected enemies. There is a huddling together and conforming to avoid the vulnerability of any idiosyncrasy, at the same time as each one has to be one-up among his identical similars. Next, there is excitement in identifying with the "really" powerful, the leaders, the Great Nations, the decision-makers, dramatized on the front page. But these leaders, of course, feel equally powerless in the face of the Great Events. For it is characteristic of the syndrome that as soon as there is occasion for any practical activity, toward happiness, value, spirit, or even simple safety, everyone suffers from the feeling of utter powerlessness; the internalized submissiveness now has its innings. Modern technology is too complex; there is a population explosion; the computer will work out the proper war-game for us; they've got your number, don't stick your neck out; "fall-out is a physical fact of our nuclear age, it can be faced like any other fact" (*Manual of Civil Defense*); "I'm strong, I can take sex or leave it" (18-year-old third-offender for felonious assault). In brief, the underside of the psychology of power is that Nothing Can Be Done; and the resolution of the stalemate is to explode. This is the Cold War.

I have frequently explored this psychology of proving, resignation, and catastrophic explosion (Wilhelm Reich's "primary masochism"), and I shall not pursue it again. It is filling the void of vital function by identifying with the agent that has frustrated it; with, subsequently, a strongly defended conceit, but panic when any occasion calls for initiative, originality, or even animal response. Here I have simply tried to relate this psychology to the uncritical unanimous acceptance of the idea of "getting into power in order to . . ." or just "getting into power" as an end in itself. There is a vicious circle, for (except in emergencies) the very exercise of abstract power, managing and coercing, itself tends to stand in the way and alienate, to thwart function and diminish energy, and so to increase the psychology of power. But of course the consequence of the process is to put us in fact in a continual emergency, so power creates its own need. I have tried to show how, historically, the psychology has been exacerbated by the miserable system of extrinsic motivation by incentives and punishments (including profits, wages, unemployment), reducing people to low-grade organisms no different than Professor Skinner's pigeons; whereas normal function is intrinsically motivated toward specific ends-in-view, and leads to growth in inventiveness and freedom. Where people are now directly in feelingful contact with what is to be done, nothing is done well and on time; they are always behind and the emergency becomes chronic. Even with good intentions, a few managers do not have enough *mind* for the needs of society—not even if their computers gallop through the calculations like lightning. I conclude that the consensus of recent political scientists that political theory is essentially the study of power-maneuvers, is itself a neurotic ideology. Normal politics has to do with the relations of specific functions in a community; and *such a study would often result in practical political inventions that would solve problems*—it would not merely predict elections and solve nothing, or play war-games and destroy mankind.

Let me sum up these remarks in one homely and not newsy proposition: Throughout the world, it is bad domestic politics that creates the deadly international politics. Conversely, pacifism is revolutionary: we will not have peace unless there is a profound change in social structure, including getting rid of national sovereign power.

After this pedantic excursion, let me return, for a paragraph, to Professor Hughes. He does not have the psychology that Nothing Can Be Done, for he is doing something with immense energy. Indeed, his most valuable service, in my opinion, is to show that even in the framework of routine politics, there is a possible alternative mode of proceeding. (Adlai Stevenson, by contrast, never seemed to believe this.) Also, he obviously has no wish to "get into power" except precisely to stop the arms race and relax the Cold War. His campaign is primarily educational; and even if he were elected, I think, he would not feel that he has "power" but a splendid public forum. (This is the line of Kastenmeier and the Liberal Project Congressmen.)

Yet we cannot overlook the deep contradiction between peace and "getting into power" at all. With the strong background support of the unusually courageous New England professors, the hard work of politically renascent youth, and the total disgust of many of the electorate in the face of our insane policies, Professor Hughes has been able to by-pass the demoralizing and stupefying demands of the political club-

house, or the emasculating horse's-ass-making requirements of
rising to an important nomination through respectable channels. Nevertheless, the program with which he now appears
before the electorate—I presume he means it sincerely—is inadequate to the needs of the situation. In foreign affairs, it is
the kind of compromising that has no future. As a domestic
program it is valueless, as if he had not put his mind to this as
immediately important; yet it is just in this, in my view, that he
could shake and begin to revive our people. And suppose he
(or Szilard's candidates) were elected: he could hardly take a
Constitutional oath to proceed to ring down the flag. Of course
he has no such purpose, but nothing less will serve.

Concretely, our system of government at present com-
prises the military-industrial complex, the secret para-military
agencies, the scientific war-corporations, the blimps, the horses'
asses, the police, the administrative bureaucracy, the career
diplomats, the lobbies, the corporations that contribute Party
funds, the underwriters and real-estate promoters that batten
on Urban Renewal, the official press and the official opposition
press, the sounding-off and jockeying for the next election, the
National Unity, etc., etc. All this machine is grinding along by
the momentum of the power and profit motives and style long
since built into it; it *cannot* make decisions of a kind radically
different than it does. Even if an excellent man happens to be
elected to office, he will find that it is no longer a possible
instrument for social change on any major issues of war and
peace or the way of life of the Americans. Indeed, as the
members of the Liberal Project have complained, office does
not give even a good public forum, for the press does not
report inconvenient speeches.

So we must look, finally, not to this kind of politics, but to
direct functioning in what concerns us closely, in order to
dispel the mesmerism of abstract power altogether. This has,
of course, been the thinking of radical pacifism. The civil disobedience of the Committee for Nonviolent Action is the direct
expression of each person's conscience of what it is impossible
for him to live with. The studied withdrawal and boycotting
advocated by the General Strike for Peace is a direct counter-
ing of the social drift toward catastrophe that occurs just be-

cause we cooperate with it. (The same holds for refusal in what is one's "private" important business, like the Women's Strike against poisoned milk or young men's refusing the draft.) Best of all, in principle, is the policy that Dave Dellinger espouses and tries to live by, to live communally and without authority, to work usefully and feel friendly, and so *positively to replace an area of power with peaceful functioning.* (Interestingly, even a critical and purgative group like *The Realist* is coming around to this point of view—with a hard row to hoe among urban poor people.) Similarly, one can work in foreign lands as a citizen of humanity, trying to avoid the Power blocs and their aims; e.g. the Friends Service. The merit of all these activities is that they produce a different kind of human relations and look to a different quality of life. This is a global and perhaps impossibly difficult task. But think. There is no history of mankind without these wars, which now have come to the maximum: can we have any hope except in a different kind of human relations?

It will be said that there is no time. Yes, probably. But let me cite a remark of Tocqueville. In his last work, *L'Ancien Régime,* he notes "with terror," as he says, how throughout the Eighteenth Century writer after writer and expert after expert pointed out that this and that detail of the Old Régime was unviable and could not possibly survive; added up, they proved that the entire Old Régime was doomed and must soon collapse; and yet *there was not a single man who foretold that there would be a mighty revolution.*

Theodore Roszak

The Disease Called Politics*

I have just finished reading a remarkable little publication: the first (and perhaps only) edition of the *Journal for the Protection of All Beings*. This is the brain-child of Lawrence Ferlinghetti, David Meltzer, Michael McClure, with contributions from Allen Ginsberg, Gregory Corso, Norman Mailer, Kenneth Patchen . . . need I say more?

The expressed purpose of the journal is to give "normally apolitical men" a chance to talk about (if not to) "the world politics has made." What emerges from this venture is something quite delightful. But what exactly can you call it? Visionary politics, perhaps (the journal calls itself a "visionary and revolutionary review") . . . or better still, the politics of the Loony Left. That sounds unkind, I guess. But isn't there a poem by Jack Kerouac somewhere that describes his *Weltanschauung* as a "kind of old-new Zen lunacy"? I mean "loony" in that spirit.

Clearly nobody who makes any difference in the world will be reading this blend of *satori* and wacky satire. How likely is it you'll come across the *Journal* in Dean Rusk's portfolio? About as likely as finding a copy of William Blake in Napoleon's saddle-bags. No, the *Journal* will not be circulating where *Foreign Affairs* or *The Economist* circulate. And that's too bad. Because the Loony Left has something to say and says it with a kind of zany dignity all its own.

What does it mean, after all, when Allen Ginsberg recommends "Socialist-Co-op Anarchism" plus peyote as a solution to the Cold War? Or when Norman Mailer suggests that Castro should have gotten Ernest Hemingway to tell Jack Kennedy that it's O.K. what Fidel is doing in Cuba? Or when

* March, 1962.

William Burroughs pontificates, "If there is any political move that I would advocate it would be an alliance between America and Red China, if they'd have us."?

It means that from somebody's point of view the political scene is pretty weird, so weird that you have to be half-cracked to take it seriously. The *Journal* therefore refuses to approach politics on politics' own terms, abasing itself in fear and trembling before the blunt, brute fact that there are matters of life and death for the human race involved here. That may make politics terrifying, but it doesn't make it any less mad nor any more worthy of our respect.

So here we have at last a political journal which recognizes the basic nature of the political environment in which we live: namely, that it is pathological. The Protectors of All Beings are unabashed visionaries and they are playing at politics, spoofing them and shaming them, out of the knowledge that our world is not beset by problems to be solved, but rather by a disease to be cured. Our society, which celebrates the intellect quite as much as it exploits it, finds this hard to admit. But sixty years after the Freudian breakthrough how can we deny that intellect is but a small floating island atop a sea of unreason? And so, too, what passes for political policy and controversy in our world is largely the rationalization of pathological premises. To recognize this is not an excuse to stop thinking; but it is the beginning of wisdom.

We need only withdraw for a time from the melee of modern politics to become dizzyingly aware of the madness that governs our society. A moment's honest objectivity is enough, a moment's unwillingness to accept the age-old conventions and clichés of the politicians and political pundits. Within the past year we have seen the American President and Soviet Premier, without any significant dissent from their societies, threaten the extermination of Western civilization over an issue as abstract as access rights to a half-city which functions for both men as no more than an article of prestige. We have seen both men applauded for their courage and firmness in doing this, and for their responsible leadership in delegating the fate of mankind to a handful of uncontrolled tank commanders in the streets of Berlin. Or again, we have seen the British Labour Party complimented throughout the West for disavowing its desire to disarm Britain unilaterally. In this way, so the saying goes, "Labour has proved its fitness to govern." This is interesting indeed. A party proves its "fitness to govern." by turning its society into an aircraft carrier for a distant nation that can not conceivably defend it, by loading its landscape down with missiles that invite annihilating attack, but which will never have the chance to leave their launching pads, in short, by exposing its society as fully as possible to total destruction. And in our own country scientists of great repute appear before approving audiences of intellectuals to predict that the day is not far off when our security will be insured by fifty thousand trucks speeding across our highways carrying portable ballistic missiles, each truck under the exclusive control of a second lieutenant. This is called "stabilized deterrence." Its oceanic counterpart, in the form of the Polaris submarine, is already well on toward completion. In this way a society that prides itself fanatically on its democratic principles systematically delegates the power and authority to wage suicidal warfare to unknown, unelected soldiers and sailors.

We live in a world in which a fraction of what Russia and America eagerly spend in a decade for armaments could solve to the satisfaction of the most outrageously greedy disputants every outstanding issue of economic injustice and social inequality in the world—*if* these issues were, any of them, subject to rational economic and social adjustment.

Such a sum of money could surely resettle the Palestinian refugees, buy *Union Minière* out of the Congo, buy off the French oil interests in Algeria and relocate the *colons;* it could even move the city of West Berlin lock, stock, and barrel into West Germany, or indeed rebuild it there in greater splendor. Needless to say, it could readily industrialize and thus pacify the underdeveloped countries of Asia, Africa and Latin America, where destitution breeds anger and vengefulness. What I'm saying is that the wealth now exists and is simply going to waste that could save the peace, by, in effect, bribing all sides of all disputes—the just and the unjust alike—to relinquish their claims in return for compensation: they could name their

own prices. An expensive proposition? Yes, indeed. But what is
peace worth? I should hope at least as much as all these terrible weapons are worth.

"How naive!" "A fantastic notion!" "Life isn't that simple!"
"You just can't do things like that!"

Of course not. But it is interesting to raise the possibility in
order to see *why* we can't.

Obviously because ever so many things get in the way . . .
so many vested interests and special privileges. The existing
system works so nicely to the advantage of so many people.
How does it work to their advantage? Why, by making the
rich richer and the powerful more powerful. Why should they
give up a good thing? Why should power elites permit themselves to be bought off and retired?

Perhaps because they are rich *enough* . . . perhaps because
they are powerful *enough* . . . perhaps because their greed for
profit and power now threatens to destroy them utterly. But
then what sort of an answer is this? What does it mean to talk
about being "rich *enough* . . . powerful *enough* . . ."? It sounds
almost as if we were asking what the rational end of having
money or power or privilege is. Clearly, in the world of politics
we simply accept the drive for power or profit as given. It is a
rule of the game that this drive is unrestricted by any goal. It is
an insistent demand for More.

Ah! then sanity is on the side of those who resist this
demand. Perhaps . . . but *how* shall we resist it? By demanding
justice! But how shall we achieve justice?

Well, surely not by letting off or buying off the despots
and exploiters—even if we can afford to. Surely not by answer-
ing their evil with forgiveness! Justice means expropriating the
expropriators. It means driving the rascals out. It means . . .
retribution. And what place does retribution make for peace-
through-bribery? (The good Marxist recognizes that at once as
an old Revisionist heresy; the anti-Communist recognizes it as
appeasement.) Instead, we must pit against the power of the
wicked the power of the righteously indignant. Power against
power, that is the way.

Though relatively few have recognized the fact, the
thermonuclear bomb has revolutionized the social sciences.

What the bomb has done is to throw into sharp relief the irrationality of our political behavior. In the past the unlimited and demonic character of man's pursuit of power—whether it was the power of empire, of wealth, of retribution—was obscured by the limited destruction this pursuit could produce. The thrust stopped well short of total annihilation; it seemed to make some kind of sense.

But against the backdrop of universal extermination, the old games begin to lose their respectability. The ruthless drive for profit—for profit beyond the call of any conceivable need or caprice—is not simply criminal, but criminally insane. And the demand for retribution, though it cost the blood of innocent and guilty alike, is no longer justice, but a cruel fanaticism. Surely it is time that we asked what long-hidden pathological compulsion breeds such violent lust for power, for wealth . . . and perhaps even for justice.

But these questions are not being widely asked; the problem seems not even to be widely recognized. Instead, the leaders of China proudly offer the lives of hundreds of millions to revenge themselves upon the imperialists. And the Algerian rebels butcher and terrorize their own people in pursuit of justice. And in our own country Herman Kahn's *On Thermonuclear War*, the complete nonsense book, represents the style in political sophistication. Here we have a book which urges us to undertake an annual military budget of two to three hundred billion dollars for the next generation, and which seriously recommends embalming and burying in concrete our civilization in the name of civil defense. But it is this book, with this vision of the future, that is read with admiration by men of great political intelligence.

What must be recognized is that the next political failure of the Western world will mean the annihilation of all classes of society, high and low, East and West. Therefore, if Russia and the West continue their present course, they will, despite the ideologies they loudly propound ("mediocre and ferocious ideologies," Camus has called them—and so they are), they will end by destroying forever the values they claim to cherish. It is not the victimized proletariat alone that will bear the brunt of Capitalism's next war; nor will Communist missiles discriminate between exploiter and exploited. After the next war there will be neither property nor property rights, humans nor human rights; the means of production and their owners, both capitalist and proletarian, will all be so much ashes.

And still the mad round continues, the downward spiral toward disaster. Let us face the facts: we are, as a species, behaving almost exactly as we would if we did not wish to survive. Which means that the grand ideologies and marvelous values men pretend to champion are not to be taken seriously. Behind the façade of words and policies and white papers and manifestoes lurks the dark truth. A suicidal pathology is at the root of our politics. How else are we to explain what men are doing all about us? We experience war-scare upon war-scare. But the feverish investors of our society, those supposed epitomes of rational self-interest, are not sent scurrying to the hills by these crises. Instead they stick fast to ground-zero, glued to their telephones, instructing their brokers, "Buy Martin!" "Buy Boeing! The boom is coming!"

William Burroughs has put it well in the *Journal for the Protection of All Beings:*

> *To concern yourself with surface political conflicts is to make the mistake of the bull in the ring, you are charging the cloth. That is what politics is for, to teach you the cloth.*

And Gregory Corso asks, "Who manipulates the cloth?" And the answer: "Death."

But what does it mean to say that death manipulates politics?

It means that politics is not the art of life. Politics does not sustain life or serve it. Rather politics is the organization of power, and power is the enemy of life. For the measure of power is its ability to make life what it would not be; to break, bend, control, crush, direct and destroy life. The end of power is the inhibition of growth, which is life. And whatever interferes with the growth of things and of men participates in death; whatever its credentials, it is in alliance with death. This is what power is, and nothing else.

All of which is another way of saying that politics is everything love is not. It is love that brings forth and nourishes life, that sustains it in its sufferings and mourns for its defeat. Love thrives in spontaneity, accepting this moment and the next for what they are now, not for what they can be used for later. Love resides in the immediacy of our experience; it is, like a child at play, the gentle enemy of order, of efficiency of organization.

So it is not love, after all, that makes the world go around. Love lets grow; but it is power that makes go. Love may be part of each man's history, but in the world at large, love has no history. The world belongs to politics, which is to say, the world belongs to death.

This is what we must come to understand. Our society's obsession with power is an obsession with death. It is ultimately a search for self-destruction. And that is why we continue again and again, in the name of this or that political principle, to aggravate the international situation, and to insist that the way of sanity is impossible. That is why, with the capacity at hand to make the life of mankind secure, clean, comfortable, and enjoyable for the first time in human history, we persist in saddling ourselves with tension, fear, discontent and hardship. And this in the name of empty, unexamined issues. As if we were ashamed to give our minds and bodies peace! There are even those who pretend that unhappiness is good: it creates culture. That may be so. But if it is, it means that culture is a disease and nothing better.

There is no other explanation: we edge toward the brink of war, not out of cunning, but out of a morbid fascination with the abyss. What after all is the ultimate display of power, but the extermination of the race? Those who control the means of power—or perhaps I should say, those who are most immediately controlled by them—is it not obvious that there is a certain relish and deep satisfaction they derive from their position? Does it not show through their words and gestures? What else are we to make of Khrushchev threatening the world with 100-megaton bombs, or of the square-jawed, steel-eyed generals who have made the word "destroy" one of the basic terms of our national vocabulary?: "We can destroy the enemy totally," "We can destroy the enemy ten times over . . ."

and not a tinge of regret or guilt in their voices. What was the slogan John Kennedy confessed was closest to his heart? "Power all the way." These men are ecstatically wallowing in a Faustian dream of omnipotence, which can only end as a nightmare of self-annihilation.

To be sure, politics has always been a neurotic business. The senseless shenanigans of kings and conquerors have always had the character of madness about them. We recognize that clearly enough when we see them at a distance. We can look back at the bloody intrigues of Louis XIV and Richard III, the violent empire-building of Cecil Rhodes and Bismarck and see the crazy brutality of their compulsive masculinity. Obsessed and driven men, all.

We forget that our own political squabbles will be seen by the future—if we permit there to be a human future—with all the estrangement and cynicism with which we look back upon the quarrels of Hapsburg and Valois, of the Red and the White Rose.

"If we permit there to be a human future." This is the great difference! This is what makes the politics of our time not neurotic, but psychotic. In the past, the mad game of the politicians took place as a *part* of life; they did not, they could not claim to be the *whole* of life. There was always the chance to escape to the sidelines, leaving the mad fellows to butcher one another. Spinoza ground his lenses and his philosophy to a delicate focus, while the political world was convulsed with agony. Beethoven could be deaf to Napoleon and all his nonsense while he brought forth his hymns to life.

But now the game of politics has expanded to the point of embracing the whole of life. It claims to be the only game. It wants us all, and it wants all of each of us; no out-of-bounds and no spectators. The extent of political control and destructiveness is becoming total, and therefore politics is becoming totally insane.

All of which, in the words of Gregory Corso, "sounds real doomy."

Is there a way out?

Clearly there will be no way out until the pathological becomes a category of our political understanding. Otherwise

we will, like the psychotic, try helplessly to save ourselves in
ways that only aggravate the illness. The policy of deterrence
is such an attempt, a crippled, pathological attempt to work
within the very political conventions that endanger our survival. That is why deterrence is bound to fail. There is no cure
for madness within the context of madness.

No, we must find our way to health by first acknowledging our sickness. We must call madness madness wherever we
see it. We must refuse to drain off our constructive energies,
energies of mind and heart and will and conscience, in dignify-
ing the insanity of our political existence; in making it an
object of allegiance and sacrifice to the point of bloodshed.
Those who strain to rationalize the irrationality of the political
world—the experts and analysts, the propagandists, the political scientists and historians, sunk in their state-papers and
documents and official correspondence—they do us the worst
disservice. They are stuck so deep in the ruts of political
convention that they cannot see over the edge. And so they
take pride in their very lack of vision, in what they call their
"hard-headed, pragmatic" approach. No naive idealists, they!

Rather, they are Lewis Mumford's "undimensioned fragmented minds." They do not think to the roots. Their souls
have been corrupted by intellectual caution and professional
prudishness. The so-called sick comedians do more good than
they, for through the throats of Lenny Bruce and Edward
Albee the morbid fascinations of our civilization are being
vomited into view.

Camus speaks of the virtues of *engagement*, of being "engaged in the density of history, where man's very flesh stifles."
But his advice here is wrong. History is the insanity of the
race. Rather than involving ourselves ever more in that madness, we must first find detachment. We must fight our way out
of the moiling, suffocating arena of politics so that we can with
distance recognize the essential sickness of the games that are
played there.

The *Journal for the Protection of All Beings*, with its wild
and wacky insults to respectable intellectuality, is a contribution to that recognition. It is not all we need, but it is an
important addition. The recent conference of the American

Psychological Association on the "psychopathology of nuclear war" is another. So too is the recent work of Norman O. Brown, who, in *Life Against Death*, has given us one of the most exciting books of our time. Drawing upon the deepest wisdom of the Freudian vision, he has spoken to our condition.

> *Mankind today [Brown tells us] is still making history without any conscious idea of what it really wants or under what conditions it would stop being unhappy; in fact what it is doing seems to be making itself more unhappy and calling that unhappiness progress . . . man [must] be ready to live instead of making history, to enjoy instead of paying back old scores and debts.*

And then there is Lewis Mumford to remind us:

> *We may well say of [modern] man, driving himself and all about him to destruction, what Captain Ahab says to himself, in a sudden moment of illumination . . . "All my means are sane: my motives and object mad." Without a positive concentration upon love in all its phases, we can hardly hope to rescue the earth and all its creatures from the insensate forces of hate, violence, and destruction that now threaten it.*

Here are voices that speak for life, men who have firmly and irreverently refused to meet the world of politics on its own dehumanizing terms.

They are not alone. They are part of an awakening, and hopefully vast Loony Left, made up of inscrutable poets and crackpot painters, of visionaries and folk singers and angry old philosophers, of marching mothers who want their babies' bones made of calcium not strontium, of kids from Yale scrambling aboard submarines in the New London Navy yard, of kids from Fisk singing on their way to jail. Each in his own unashamedly unorthodox way is calling into question the sanity of our political world. Here are the foolish things of this earth who confound the wise. For the essence of their politics is not power, but love: the sheer love of being alive. The future, if there is to be one, belongs to them.

Dallas Smythe

Mass Media and the Cold War

The mass media are, collectively, the social agency—the institution—which we have chosen to serve as society's agenda-
setter for human problems. Like the House Rules Committee,
the mass media set an agenda for our consideration, and what
they omit from this agenda does not thereby fail of consequences. In today's world, what we don't know *can* hurt us.
But in addition to setting our agenda, the mass media, through
the way in which they report or portray the problems—be it in
news and commentary or in drama and documentary—educate
us to support or oppose particular solutions for these problems.
      You are familiar with the fact that upwards of 90 per cent
of all the scientists who ever lived are alive and working today.
You know that the perfection of nuclear weapons has made
"national defense" meaningless and military establishments obsolete—for any institution which cannot perform its function is
obsolete, and admittedly no military establishment today can
protect its people from the destruction of nuclear war. These
are but two of the token signs of major changes which we live
with. It is useful, then, to take a long-time view of the social
perspective and to ask what are the dimensions of the social
process changes which we tend to see as fragments.
      As Kenneth E. Boulding has said in "Post-Civilization," we
are now living in the second great change in the history of
man. The first great change was when man developed cities
and ultimately aggregated population in them to form national
states—a change which produced what we know as "civilization." Before that, as Boulding says, man had puttered along in
an astonishingly stationary state for half a million years or so.
The second great change—the one we are living through now
after some fifteen thousand years of civilization—is the transi-

tion from a system based on cities and national states to one
based on world and regional organization. The beginnings of
this post-civilization system appear in the United States, Western Europe and the Soviet Union. The change is evidenced by
a number of profound events:

1. *The diminution in the importance of agriculture.*
Under civilization, the great bulk of the population had
to work in agriculture to support the society; in post-
civilization, as few as ten per cent in agriculture is sufficient, because of the efficiency of technology and capital
in that area.

2. *The provision of a potential condition of affluence
—a decent standard of life for all people.* The application of technology virtually prohibits great inequalities
in consumption, because of the built-in mandate of industrial technology, including automation, to find uses
for its productive capacity. (As Veblen remarked, "Invention is the mother of necessity.")

3. *The extension of the life-span from about a twenty-
five-year expectation under civilization to seventy years
or higher.* The population explosion is another aspect
of this event, and we find that Malthusianism must now
be replaced by an ecological view of the adjustment of
population to resources plus technology on a world scale.

4. *The growing recognition of the present obsolescence
of the national state as the principal institution for adjusting international relations.* As Pope John XXIII said in
Pacem in Terris, the old system of national states is "no
longer capable of facing the task of finding an adequate
solution to the problems. . . . And this is not due to a lack
of good will or of a spirit of enterprise, but because of a
structural defect which hinders them. . . . Today the
universal common good poses problems of world-wide
dimensions. . . ."

5. *The obsolescence of warfare between national states.*
Not only is nuclear warfare terminal, rather than instru-
mental to policy, but nuclear deterrence as an instrument
of policy is inherently and inevitably unstable.

6. *The power of the mass media of communications over public opinion.* We had a demonstration in October 1962 of the ease with which public opinion could be managed into support of a possible nuclear war. In this country there is not only the capacity to wage a nuclear war, there is enough ideological intolerance, there are enough death-wishers, to bring us to one, if the power process permits control of the mass media for such an end. The power of the mass media to trigger disaster in the existing cold-war situation, however, is only matched by its power to educate public opinion leaders and the public to the inevitability and wisdom of the great, current historical change in which we live. As between the two goals of destruction and construction, the mass media, like nuclear deterrence, are unstable, and must inevitably in time elect one or the other goal.

Aldous Huxley, impatient with our slowness to realize and to act on the clear implications of history for the future, says:

> *Committing that sin of overweening bumptiousness which the Greeks called* hubris, *we behave as though we were not members of earth's ecological community, as though we were privileged and, in some sort, supernatural beings and could throw our weight around like gods. But in fact, we are among other things animals—emergent parts of the natural order. If our politicians were realists, they would think rather less about missiles and the problem of landing a couple of astronauts on the moon, rather more about hunger and moral squalor and the problem of enabling three billion men, women and children, who will soon be six billions, to lead a tolerably human existence, without, in the process, ruining and befouling their planetary environment. . . .*
>
> *Power politics, nationalism and dogmatic ideology are luxuries that the human race can no longer afford. Nor, as a species, can we afford the luxury of ignoring man's ecological situation. . . . The beginnings of ecological politics are to be found in the special services of the United Nations Organization (UNESCO, the Food and*

*Agriculture Organization, the World Health Organiza-
tion, the various Technical Aid Services) . . . In a world
where political problems are thought of and worked upon
within a frame of reference whose coordinates are nationalism and military power, these ecology-oriented organizations are regarded as peripheral. If the problems
of humanity could be thought about and acted upon
within a frame of reference that has survival for the
species, the well-being of individuals, and the actualization of man's desirable potentialities as its coordinates,
these peripheral organizations would become central.*[1]

The task is put in practical perspective when we realize
that as Boulding says, "If the human race is to survive, it will
have to change its ways of thinking more in the next 25 years
than it has done in the last 25,000." It is not only the historical
process of world ecology which the mass media should recognize for what it is; there are also some assumptions concerning
the relation of us and our mass media to that process which
should be re-examined. The sequence implicitly is: what will
"we" (the developed nations, or more narrowly, we the American innovators) say to "them" (the developing nations, or our
allies or adversaries in the Cold War)? At best this assumption
is a half-truth; at worst it implies authoritarianism and *hubris*.
It would be more realistic to assume that communications is a
reciprocal process in which feedback is always at least as important as the purpose of the communicator.

We also have a pervasive assumption that the machine-
based agencies or institutions which conduct "public information" in the developed countries are indeed "informing" the
public, and that those publics are more rational, less superstitious and more worthy of emulation than the publics in the
developing countries. Again, we manifest *hubris*. In the "free
world," communication agencies are engaged in public "formation" rather than "information." The power to influence the
press is the basis of political and economic power. (Alfred
Sauvy remarks that the freedom to inform is now the counter-

[1] "The Politics of Ecology" (Center for the Study of Democratic Institutions, 1963).

part of what was once the freedom to build castles.) As regards the developing countries, we often overlook the possibility that the individuals there may be better informed about their own social systems than the ill-informed citizens of industrially developed nations.

Still another implicit assumption in the way Americans look at the rest of the world is that our way of life, our way of using technology, should be imitated, especially by the developing countries. We assume, in other words, the moral validity of a kind of Twentieth Century technological and cultural imperialism, which would subordinate the developing nations to our hegemony. In the non-Soviet world, there are about four hundred million people with an average income of a thousand dollars a year, and about a billion people with an average income of about a hundred dollars a year. We in the industrially developed West use about three-fourths of the world's energy; we draw on the natural resources, the science, the manpower of the whole world for our transient, personal pleasures. We propose as the solution for the problems of hunger, disease, lack of housing and clothing for the great majority of the earth's population an extension of our own system, which relies on an economy of wants, guided by the want-creators of Madison Avenue. Is it too much to say that the hungry, diseased, ill-housed, ill-clad majority of the earth's population want an economy addressed to their needs—and that they hardly require an economy which rests on creating wants for goods?

We assume that technology, our version of political democracy, and capitalism will work for anyone anywhere in the world just as they did for us. But we are perennially being shocked and disappointed when the turn of historical events abroad denies this naive hope. For in other parts of the world other people are going through what we went through in the Nineteenth Century. They are applying new technologies to rich resources, but they are finding their own political forms in ways which make *them* optimistic (just as ours did for us). And they are finding economic organization in one or another form of socialism which permits growth on terms they will accept—i.e., faster growth than capitalism offers them: what took us a hundred and fifty years to accomplish, they plan to do in fifteen. What differentiates their political and economic experience from ours is that their emergence from feudalism is taking place in the Twentieth Century, when the new forms demonstrated by the Soviet Union and China are available for imitation.

Of course these revolutions take place without the civil liberties and freedom of the press which we prize so much. They mean much tyranny and suffering. But tyranny and suffering accompanied our Revolution of 1776, and the growth of the factory system in the Industrial Revolution of the Eighteenth and Nineteenth Centuries meant horrible suffering. The current hardships in these revolutionary régimes, being self-imposed, are weighed lightly against the future benefits which the current investments of energy are intended to produce. Moreover, this choice is more easily made by peoples who have lived as serfs or slaves and at the physical threshold of existence for millennia. Even a cup of rice every day and a bare roof overhead looks like fantastic progress to people who previously were starved and shelterless.

What our mass media seem to perceive generally as a great "closing-in" of history on our future—a "no-win situation," or as President Kennedy has repeatedly put it "a long twilight struggle"—is regarded by most of the people in the world as a great "opening-up" of history. We are riding a system—or a system is riding us, whichever you prefer—which does not serve the needs of those peoples and which therefore is of declining significance in the world as a whole. E. H. Carr says:

> Indeed, if I were addicted to formulating laws of history, one such law would be to the effect that the group— call it a class, a nation, a continent, a civilization, what you will—which plays the leading role in the advance of civilization in one period is unlikely to play a similar role in the next period, and this for the good reason that it will be too deeply imbued with the traditions, interests, and ideologies of the earlier period to be able to adapt itself to the demands and conditions of the next period.

Thus it may very well happen that what seems for one group a period of decline may seem to another the birth of a new advance.[2]

Our mass media generally lump together in undiscriminating denunciation all the different political forms which call themselves Socialist or Communist. This reflects a bias which can only blind our public to the situation in the world. Robert Heilbroner, who is no radical, remarks that:

> *Our magazines and newspapers, public speeches and books are quick to point up the inevitable failings of socialism, and never weary of calling to our attention the cruelties and repressions of communism. But such denunciations, far from arming us against or clarifying our understanding of socialism and communism, only serve to muddy our minds. They obscure the fact that the literature of social protest is one of the most moving and morally searching of all chronicles of human hope and despair. To dismiss that literature unread, to vilify it without the faintest conception of what it represents, is not only shocking but dangerously stupid.*[3]

The Mass Media

What can we say of the domestic scene, including specifically the mass media, as we survey the social process? Television, radio, and large-circulation newspapers and magazines practice mass production of communications with the aid of complex technology and very large capital investment. Most of the financial support for these mass production media of communications comes from advertising. If one asks what is the essential function of these media, the answer can only be: to induce Americans to buy the commodities and services which are produced by our consumer-goods industries; to train us, from infancy on, to be dutiful consumers. In this they enjoy the cooperation of our school system and other institutions. The point I want to make now is that this function of marketing the output

[2] *What Is History?* (Alfred A. Knopf, 1962).
[3] *The Future As History* (Harper & Row, 1959).

of American industry which the mass media perform is essential to the operation of the American economy. If media advertising were to vanish overnight, the output of America's consumer goods could not be sold. It is equally obvious that the mass production of communications would come to an abrupt halt if the flow of advertising revenues were suddenly to stop.

In this context, what is the product which the mass media create? The answer is that it is the probability that large numbers of viewers, listeners or readers will be "delivered" to the advertiser, i.e., available and receptive to the presentation of the advertiser's message. In fact the viewers, listeners or readers are packaged and sold much as is any other product, in terms of price per unit. In the present case the basis of the offer is "so and so many millions of households (or adult males, or adult females, or teenagers) at such and such a cost per thousand." Some confused people seem to feel that the fact that broadcast stations do not own their radio frequency assignments (and indeed that the public owns the airways) means that audience ratings should somehow measure the service provided to the viewing and listening public. That is not possible under the existing American broadcasting system, unless such service is equated with training for consumership. If the prime product of the mass media of communications is the selected, receptive audience, made available to the advertiser for its regular exercise in consumership training, what can one say is the role of the entertainment, the information, the educative content of the mass media (apart from advertising)? This material, which formerly was the prime product of the press, now has the role of the free lunch in the old-time saloon, to quote A. J. Liebling; or if you are a marketing expert, you might prefer the analogy to the role of the "loss leader" items, which the supermarket features at a non-profit price in order to attract the customer into the store.

This answer to the question of the role of the entertainment, the informational and the educative content of the mass media seems to be almost obsolete now, however. For increasingly the line between the advertising *context* and the non-advertising *content* of the mass media is being blurred and lost. I refer to the delivery of commercial announcements by

actors or news commentators, and the systematic "star" build-
ups accorded the Betty Furnesses. But beyond this I refer to
what might be called "institutional payola," or as it is otherwise known, the "tie-in" industry.

About now, one or more of you may want to ask: what's
wrong with making a buck? And what's wrong with enjoying
the American standard of living? What's wrong with materialism? Let me take the third question first. As to materialism,
Raymond Williams, the Cambridge professor, says that the
materialism in our capitalist mass production society is both
excessive and insufficient. I like his distinction between "use"
and "consumption." If we buy soap for its cleansing properties,
this is use. If we buy it as a means to becoming an attractive
sexual object, this is consumership. If we buy clothes for comfort, grace and durability, this is use. If we buy them because
they are the mode set this year by "Jackie," this is consumership. According to Williams, capitalist mass production injects
intangible and essentially irrelevant values into our materialism: it perverts materialism.

Our preoccupation with materialist objectives in this sense
has a direct bearing on how our mass media relate to the
nuclear age. For the whole thrust of our consumership is to
direct our attention and our resources to the pursuit of individual satisfactions, individual pleasures. We still judge our
educational system, our parks, all of our public works according to "use" standards. But because they are not subject to
styling and mass production marketing for profit, these public
works get starved, while our private sector is gorged with our
resources. And when it is pointed out that private self-gratifica-
tion is a standard for resource allocation which is dangerously
unrealistic for Americans to pursue in the nuclear age, no less a
person than the president of General Motors frankly says that
under the "free enterprise system," social goods and services
are a mere "by-product" of individual consumption. He calls
critics of the unbridled devotion of our resources to private
pleasure in the private sector "hair-shirt philosophers" who
consider "the American Way" to be a "sinful way." For myself,
I would not answer the question: What's wrong with making a
buck in cultural industry? by referring to sin (although in our

increasingly churched society, I am not aware that sin is altogether beneath notice). I would answer it on policy grounds, and therefore moral grounds: that somewhere the line must be drawn between private exploitation of and public care for public concerns.

It seems evident that the mass media and cultural industry have gone a long way towards making political candidates into commodities. Richard Nixon, in an unguarded moment in 1957, told the TV and Radio Executives Club of New York that "the public buys names and faces and not platforms" and that a candidate for public office has to be merchandised in much the same way as any TV product. No wonder that after the first of the so-called debates, he and his campaign managers were more concerned over the way his face appeared on the screen than with what he said. The TV networks suggested that the debates were in the tradition of the famous Lincoln-Douglas debates. Of course, this is ridiculous. There was no opportunity for systematic presentation of the candidates' views on the range of issues which confronts us all today. The format for these encounters, instead, was borrowed from the quiz shows; all that was missing was the isolation booth and the bank officer with the questions. Rather than the $64,000 question, there was a series of questions, leading symbolically to the power, perquisites and responsibility of the Presidency. And, as Walter Lippmann put it,

> *If the political quiz show becomes the accepted format . . . the temptation to rig the show is in many cases almost certain to become too strong to be resisted. As in the quiz shows the prize is too great and temptation is too strong and corruption is too easy.*

"Equal Time"

Before leaving the Great Debates of 1960, I should touch on their meaning for the TV industry in relation to Section 315 of the Communications Act. Under this section, a station which sells time to one candidate for office must be willing to sell equal time to all other candidates. The broadcast industry has repeatedly in recent years tried to get this provision revised, in order to free itself of the obligation to broadcast speeches by minority-party candidates to an equal extent with those of the two big candidates. Despite the rhetoric and confusion over this issue, it is really simple and important. Are we to freeze into law the conditions which will permit only the present Republican and Democratic parties to gain a hearing? We have had three-party elections in the past, but it is difficult to imagine how a third party could arise if the present policy on political broadcasts should be changed as the industry desires. The Great Debates of 1960 were produced under a temporary suspension of this aspect of Section 315, and clearly, the networks and industry hoped to "sell" a revision of the section by the hoopla attending these programs. But such debates probably will not be regularly repeated in future elections. Thus, the president of one network said that it is unlikely that Kennedy, as a candidate for re-election in 1964, would be willing to enter into a series of TV debates with his opponent.

Even before the campaigns start, however, the political conventions are thoroughly assimilated to the commodity aspects of TV. They are put in the framework of advertising sponsorship—which a study for the Brookings Institution called a "compromising . . . relationship." In "producing" the conventions, the implicit policy of the networks appears to be, not the transmission of a maximum of meaningful information, but "a maximum effect of excitement and interest." In a word, politics is to be produced and consumed as entertainment, as are the Game of the Week, the daily Westerns and the news. The conventions are played as a contest of personalities, with the outcome uncertain. Electoral votes in the nominating conventions are analogous to runs or points scored. And I predict that convention statistics will some day reach that stage of maturity in which the commentator will say that Mr. Jones, with 300 electoral votes, has broken the record for dark-horse candidates, batting from birthplaces west of the Mississippi river, for electoral votes tallied in his favor from the ten most populous states on the second roll call in a convention with two or more roll calls.

The mass media have debilitated the democratic process by allying themselves with advertisers, the military-industrial

complex (as Eisenhower called it) which limits and surrounds
the President, and the political parties through a bi-partisan
foreign policy. The process of making foreign policy in our
country is essentially as follows: Foreign-policy ideas start
from the administration—understanding this term to include in
addition to the President and the State Department, the huge
empires of bureaucratic and business-affiliated executives
known as the Department of Defense, and the small number
of huge corporations which dominate our armed-forces procurement. (A recent Senate study showed that 24 companies
received sixteen billion dollars in defense contracts or 70 per
cent of twenty-two billion dollars studied.) Whether we are
thinking of minor elements in foreign policy (such as the decision on the Skybolt weapon system) or of major ventures in
brinkmanship (such as the Cuban blockade last October), the
proposals stem from within the administration. In either case,
some sort of sanction, quaintly called "public opinion," is
needed to validate the proposals. Public opinion of the little
people as registered by polls is not what we mean: it is remote
from the decision-making process. We mean that the product
of the press itself is taken as a substitute for public opinion.
Crises may be manufactured by "managing the news," by
"using news as a weapon," by playing propaganda devices
with the cooperation of the mass media. Prime Minister Mac-
Millan in his famous "golf-links" interview in August 1961—an
interview at the height of the "Berlin Crisis" which the American press censored—indeed said that the 1961 Berlin crisis was
"all got up by the press." In the recent Cuban crisis, we had
another demonstration. Over a weekend, leaks to the press,
ominous rumors echoed by columnists and commentators on
TV and radio played on our anxieties and frustrations, and
activated local rumor circuits to panic proportions. When the
President presented his *fait accompli* over TV on that Monday
night, the press was ready to go all-out. The editorial opinion,
the commentators, and the columnists, not to mention the
"managed" stories in the news columns in the following days,
were the public opinion needed to support the policy. Congress, constitutionally elected to represent people and their
political views, finds itself hamstrung by bi-partisanship, which

excludes fundamentally alternative ways of looking on policy, manipulated by the lobbying from the military-industrial complex, and pressured by the mass media.

Reluctantly, I put a name to this process: it is a foreign-policy dictatorship, in which a self-perpetuating oligarchy (in mass media, administration and Congress), controls not only the very fact of our lives but also, through the brainrinsing of our attitudes, our minds. Is this too strong? Can anyone name one senator, one congressman, one public figure of any national reputation who dared publicly to oppose the administration's Cuban trip to the brink? Our constitutional system, once it is degraded by bi-partisan foreign policy, is incapable of distinguishing between criticism of administration policy and disloyalty.

We are fond of saying that the Russians are prisoners of an unrealistic ideology. But we are prisoners of an ideology which is rigid and blind to the reality of what is happening in the world. This ideological web of ours consists in clichés, half-truths and assumptions, all of them debatable and many of them false. Let me summarize them in clusters. The first has the theme that we are good, they are bad; being honest, we expect others to be honest too and if we deal with them they will trick us—otherwise known as the "Lone Ranger theory of history." The second has the theme that Communism is an international conspiracy; Communists never tell the truth but prefer Aesopian inversions. In reality, depending on where one lives—America, Russia, China, South America—either Communism or capitalism looks like a conspiracy—if one defines the real situation as one which requires war, hot or cold. The third cluster has the theme that most or all of our foreign-relations problems are caused by the Communists; therefore, anyone who resists Communism in foreign countries automatically deserves our support; counter-revolution or rollback anywhere in the world is good. The fourth cluster holds that the only appropriate response to foreign problems is military; we must be tough; armaments give us security; civil defense will protect us; you can't trust the Russians; and you shouldn't even think about the Chinese—maybe they'll go away, all six hundred and fifty million of them; better dead than Red. The fifth cluster centers on the theme that our policy on foreign problems must be authoritatively determined by the "judgment" of our Commander in Chief. The military know best, experts, if employed by the military, are always right—otherwise they are regarded not as "hard-nosed" but as "softheaded"; in a foreign affairs crisis, the press and Congress should discourage public debate; trust our leaders. We try to conceal the fact that this is a totalitarian doctrine by telling ourselves that a major difference between "us" and "them" is that we are pluralistic and free to think and say what we like, while they are monolithic and told what to think; that for us the individual is sacred; for them, only the system. And the sixth cluster centers on technique and opportunism. Technology, know-how and winning are the all-important values. In the name of law and order and freedom, we violate the rule of law internationally, as in the U-2 incident, as in the Bay of Pigs Cuban invasion attempt, as in the naval blockade and violation of Cuban air-space by our reconnaissance flights (which apparently still continue). Peace requires war; war means peace. We have high moral ends which justify our sometimes immoral means. What matters is preservation of our way of life—our standard of living and our Madison-Avenue-led privatized system of mass producing and distributing consumer goods. If NATO or SEATO members do not recognize the gravity of the Red menace, we will make the "judgment" for them to take any risks on their behalf.

Policy Changes

The implication of the foregoing is that some important policy changes should be made by the mass media, and perhaps some institutional changes may be required to accomplish the policy shifts. It is quite hopeless to expect that foreign policy or mass-media policy will change merely because new faces appear in Washington or New York. New faces, operating with obsolete policies or institutions, produce the same old results. The changes needed if we are to revitalize the democratic process seem to be three: 1. Restore a free market place of ideas in our mass media in regard to foreign affairs; i.e., break up the rigid cold-war ideological view of the world. 2. Restore partisanship

to foreign policy; i.e., make available at election time fundamentally alternative choices in foreign policy. 3. Reduce and
control the decision-making power of the military-industrial
complex; i.e., make Congress and the executive responsible to
the electorate again.

It seems to me that the place to begin is with the mass
media. Rather than think exclusively within the existing institutional frame of reference, I would think we should let our
imaginations roam over the possibilities of creating new mass
media enterprises. What could not be done, for example, if the
kind of radio station operated by the Pacifica Foundation in
Berkeley, New York and Los Angeles were expanded into a
nationwide FM radio network, with its own news staff? What
other kind of "yardstick" enterprise could be created in the
print media, to set a standard for the present giant enterprises
to emulate? Once we begin to pursue such questions as these
in the framework of the implications of world-wide ecology in
the nuclear age, it is safe to say that all manner of lesser issues
will take on fresh aspects, and their solutions seem obvious.

The mass media generally fail to inform our people of the
fact that we are in the process of de-emphasizing the national
state in this world; that a world-wide economic and political
organization must be built quickly to apply technology to resources equitably; that many parts of this organization will be
in countries employing one or another kind of socialistic organization; that in our own best interests as well as in the interests
of people all over the world, we must not only permit this
transition, we must help it and we must see the essential justice
and reason which calls it into being; that a measure of tolerance for diversity of institutions and attitudes which we have
never known or long since forgotten must be shown by our
people and our institutions. The mass media generally fail to
inform our people of the fact that we can't retreat into our
past; that we cannot live as if Nineteenth Century nationalism
was still a going concern: it isn't. That nuclear bomb President
Truman ordered dropped on Hiroshima signalled the end of
red-neck nationalism.

The mass media's failure is compounded with its unthink-
ing ideological rationalization of the cold-war alliance of the

military-industrial complex and the bi-partisan foreign policy
in terms which should shock us rather than brainrinse us. The
mindless, bureaucratic defense of the *status quo* by the mass
media rests on the blind substitution of their business function
of training Americans to consume, for their historic function of
helping us to identify our real problems, and informing us in a
free market place of ideas with information relevant to the
various possible ways of finding solutions to those problems.
While the monolithic inertia of our mass media in these direc-
tions is frighteningly powerful, we can take heart from the
realization that no concentration of institutional power has
ever been eternal or immune to change. Moreover, one must
assume that Americans, despite their long course of cold-war
brainrinsing, are human beings first and businessmen second.

Barbara Deming

Prison Notes

Part I

Albany city jail, Georgia. The cop locks the door on us and walks off. Now we're out of mischief. The barred steel door has banged shut; the big key has made a lot of noise; they have "put us away." People still believe there is some magic in the turning of a key.

He walks past some other cages, running his night stick, clattering, along the bars; and then we hear him make a curious little clucking noise to the prisoners—as though human speech were not quite appropriate to cross the distance between us. Magically, now, we are no longer quite of the same species.

As he goes, he glances down at his boots, and he puts his hand—as if to be sure of sometihng—upon his wide leather belt with its creaking tooled leather holster.

"Sonofabitch cop!" a prisoner rages, and grasps the bars and rattles them. "Oh goddam motherfucking sonofabitch! Wait till I get out of here tomorrow!"

I am reminded of the fairy tale of the miser Abu Kasem and his old slippers. One day they cause him embarrassment and he tries to throw them away. He isn't able to. He throws them out the window, he buries them in the garden, he tries to burn them, he travels to a distant country and drops them in a pond; but each time fate returns them to him, and each time in a way that causes him mischief. They are too much a part of him. If Kasem could not get rid of his old slippers—. But people persist in believing that they can put other people from them.

Yes, they manage to sound very reasonable to themselves as they talk of deterring others from crime. But the act of putting a man in jail remains essentially the act of trying to wish that man out of existence. From the moment of arrest one begins to feel against one's flesh the operation of this crude attempt at sorcery.

I remember suddenly the first time I was ever arrested, in New York City. As I begin to write about time I've served in Albany's jail, my earliest impressions of the world of jail crowd upon me.

A bitter March morning, 1962. The United States has just announced resumption of nuclear testing, and in protest I have sat down with a group of pacifists in front of the A.E.C. building on Hudson Street. A small group of us sit, expecting arrest; a larger group circles there, immune from arrest, in a simple picket line. The arrests are swift. Before we have time to shiver on the cold sidewalk, we are picked up and dumped into a paddy wagon waiting at the curb. We are dumped into the back, but we crowd that section, and one of the cops tells three or four of us to crawl over into the space up front in the wide cab. Up there, we can stare out the open door at our friends walking past, almost within our reach. And they could look in at us easily, exchange a few friendly glances. But not one of them does, though we sit there quite a long while before we are driven away, and they circle past us, circle past us again. With our arrest, we have become invisible, even to them. My friends are being dignified, of course. But there is more to it than that. When people are arrested, a kind of primitive awe can take hold of everybody involved. They are caught up in spite of themselves in the ritual act of denying our existence.

I remember the woman guard sitting outside the detention cell in which some of us were held before being taken to the Women's House of Detention—remember her uneasiness every time she noted in us signs of life.

She spies dangling from my lapel the lettered white ribbon we have all worn that morning: NO TESTS EAST OR WEST. She snatches for it. "No banners in here!" A little later she says that she can make one telephone call for each of us. One young woman in the group writes out a message to her sweetheart. She makes it, carefully, very brief, but her feeling for him is clear in it—it flies this banner. The guard gives a little start as she reads it, takes a pencil, swiftly edits. Nothing of the young woman's self now remains in the message.

Nobody has to print in a manual for guards that the prisoner must be wished out of existence for society's sake. This magic principle is grasped as if by instinct. Prison routine varies from place to place, but the one blind effort shapes it everywhere. Here is part of the routine of our "admission" that day:

A police woman takes us into a small room in the building where we're arraigned. She searches our handbags for sharp objects; we take off most of our clothing for her, unfasten the rest, as she peers at us. The guard outside the temporary detention cell examines our bags for a second time, removes a few more possessions. At the House of Detention, a third guard empties the bags, keeps every remaining article. We have packed a few things with which to keep ourselves decent: comb, toothbrush, deodorant, a change of underclothes. She takes them all—even, in my case, some pieces of Kleenex. "And if I have to blow my nose?" "Find something else to blow it on," she tells me cheerfully. She explains then: I might be smuggling in dope this way. I am led into a large shower room and told to strip. Another guard shakes out each piece of clothing. Hands on her hips, she watches me closely as I take my shower, and I struggle hard now for self-possession. Her stance reminds me a little of that of an animal trainer. Now she asks me to hold my arms wide for a moment, turn my back and squat. I ask the reason. She, too, is searching for dope—or for concealed weapons. One of my companions has been led in by another woman, and has stripped and is sitting on the toilet there. Her face is anguished. She explains her predicament to the guard: She is menstruating, but her extra sanitary napkins have been taken from her. "Just don't think about it," the woman tells her. I don't know how to help her; catch her eye, and look away. I am given a very short hospital gown and led now into a small medical examination room. Another of my companions is just leaving the room and smiles at me wanly. I climb up on the table. I assume that the examination per-

formed is to check for venereal disease. The woman in the
white smock grins at me, and then at her assistant, who grins
back. No, this too is a search for concealed dope or dangerous
weapons.

I hear myself laugh weakly. Can they frisk us any further
now? As a matter of fact, if their search is really for dope, they
have neglected to look in my ears, or up my nose, or between
my toes. They wouldn't be able to admit it to themselves, but
their search of course is for something else, and is efficient:
their search is for our pride. And I think with a sinking heart:
again and again, it must be, they find it and take it.

Sometimes, all of a sudden, one of them will give it back.
People are everywhere, happily, unpredictable. I am told to
dress again before going to my cell; but I'm not allowed to
wear my tights (because I might hang myself with them?) or
my fleece-lined English snowboots (these are labelled "mascu-
line attire," forbidden). A young Negro guard tells me to find
some shoes for myself in an open locker she points out. I stare
at the heap of old shoes and tell her wearily: "It's hopeless.
Most of these have heels and I can't wear heels. Also, my feet
are very big." She looks at me and smiles. She says, "If you
thought anything was hopeless, you wouldn't have been sitting
down on that sidewalk this morning!" I smile at her, astonished, and feel my spirits return. I tell her, "Thank you. You're
right. I'll find a pair." Before I can, she kneels, herself, and
fishes out some floppy slippers that will do.

But more often the guards are caught up altogether in the
crude rite of exorcism. I remember the ride to jail in Macon,
Georgia, this past November. We are peace and freedom
walkers this time. A number of us who will go to jail again in
Albany have been arrested for the crime of handing out
leaflets.

The guard who drives the paddy wagon begins to chatter
like an excited boy to the second guard, as soon as we're
locked in, seated in back on the length-wise metal benches
against the sides of the cab. He suddenly lurches the car forward, then, with a gnashing of gears, backward; forward
again, swerving the wheel. Knocked against the metal walls,
we link arms quickly, brace our feet, not to be tumbled to the

floor. Later we'll meet prisoners who are black and blue from such falls. "Something seems to be the matter with the gear shift!" he shouts, delighting in the pretense. There are railroad tracks to be crossed; he manages some good jolts here by zigzagging; then takes the car on two wheels round a curve. "Yes, something seems to be the matter with this car!" As the drive ends, and he jerks us again in the prison yard, forward, backward, forward, backward, forward, we put out our hands instinctively to touch one another: you are still there. But the exulting excitement in the driver's voice betrays his opposite conviction: We can't be people any more. He's shaken that out of us.

Now it is Albany, Georgia. This is the city where the police chief, Laurie Pritchett, likes to boast that he has defeated Martin Luther King nonviolently. When we are arrested for walking peacefully down the sidewalk with our signs, and in protest we sit down, conspicuous respect is shown for our persons: we are carried to the paddy wagon on stretchers. But the familiar instinct persists, for all this show. Ralph has been dumped into the wagon gently enough, and I have, and Kit and Tony and Michele. They are bringing John-a-thin. One cop looks at another. Suddenly they tip the stretcher up, the wrong way round, standing John-a-thin on his head.

Magic: Shake it out of them—the fact that they are people. Or tip it out of them. Or frisk them of it. And put them away. Has the relation with them been a difficult one? Now they don't exist.

Our cage in Albany is seven by seven by seven. Three bolted steel walls, a steel ceiling, a cement floor. For bunks, four metal shelves slung by chains—two on one wall, double-decker, two on the wall opposite. Thin, filthy mattresses. No sheets, no blankets, but very recently muslin mattress covers have been added. The chief expects publicity perhaps. Against the third wall, a tiny wash basin. Cold water. Next it, a toilet without a lid.

The mattress of the lower bunk rests against the toilet. The upper bunk is so close above the lower that one can only sit up on the lower bunk with a curved spine. The floor space

allows one to pace one short step—if the number of inhabitants allows it. We are six at the moment, but we'll be more.
Other cells are more crowded. It's not by stretching out that
the prisoner here will recover himself.

The fourth wall is made of bars and a thick barred door,
centered in it. In the corridor outside, guards and plainclothes-
men come and go, day or night. If one is sleeping, a sudden
knock at the bars: "Hey!" Or a little tug at the hair of the
sleeper's head: "What's this one?" No corner of privacy in
which to gather oneself together again.

The dirty windows in the corridor look out upon an alley
and a brick wall. (They are very dirty. A prisoner long ago has
flung a plate of spaghetti against one of them. Shrivelled tatters
of it still hang there. On the window next it a shrunken
condom hangs.) A little weak sunlight filters through to us at
certain hours, but there is no real day.

And no real night. Our only other lighting is a naked bulb
hanging in the corridor out of reach, and this burns round the
clock.

Not enough space. No real time.

From the cage behind us, round the corridor, a man calls to his
wife in the cage next to us: "Are you still there, Vickie?" She
grunts for answer. He calls to her: "I'm still here!"

Laboriously scratched in the metallic gray with which our
walls and ceiling have been painted, are name after name.
RUFUS WAS HERE—was "still here." THE MELTON
BROTERS (sic) WAS HERE. BOB WIMBERLY. JACKIE
TURLEY. "SUPER" NORMON. Was here, was still here.
HAWK—to remind himself—has uttered his name seven
times, has flown from wall to wall to ceiling to wall.

The cops read the names with irritation. It's cheating for
the prisoners to assert in this way that they do exist. "We
hardly get it painted fresh when it's covered over again."
FREEDOM! LULAMAE. The names appear where they
oughtn't, as cries might issue from under the earth.

We have scratched our names, too: QUEBEC-WASH-
INGTON-GUANTANAMO WALK FOR PEACE AND

FREEDOM. EDIE, YVONNE, KIT, MICHELE, ERICA, BARBARA. Later, CANDY and MARY will appear.

George calls to Vickie again: "Vickie!" Silence. "Vickie!" Silence. "Vickie!" "Yeah." "Do you love me?" Very low, very tired: "No. You're no good."

I remember suddenly the first prison cell I ever entered—twenty-six years ago. I entered that day out of curiosity an abandoned New England small town jail, attached to the old courthouse friends and I were turning into a summer theatre. The few cells were like low caves, windowless; the walls whitewashed rock. In one, I noticed on the uneven plaster of the ceiling, scrawled in candle smoke—or cigarette smoke—the declaration I AM A JOLLY GOOD FELLOW. I tried, that day, imagining myself the prisoner—tried and failed. But the words entered my imagination, and they have recurred to me over the years. Today I think of them again.

Hard work, in here, to feel like a jolly good fellow; and so pride almost requires a man to feel he is the very opposite.

From one cell to another an old man calls to a pair of teen-aged boys, just arrived. We've heard a detective talking with them, and they're in for breaking into a store. "Who are you?" the old man calls. His voice is slurred with drink.

"I know who I am!" one of the youths shouts.

"I'll show you who you ain't," the old man teases.

"You want me to come over there and whip your ass?" one of them demands.

"I bet you're tough," says the old man.

"You're goddam right."

"You think you're bad, don't you?"

"BAD, BAD!" asserts the boy.

A little later, "What are you in for?" the old man calls.

There is a pause.

"MURDER!" one of them suddenly shouts.

"What are your names?"

One of them starts to answer and the other cuts in: "The Sizemores," he decides. (Later we'll find that name scratched on the wall of their cell—dated months earlier.) "We're the Sizemores. Ed and my brother Dan and my brother

Richard. He's not here. Ed is. I mean I am. And Dan. Don't
you know the Sizemores? The Sizemores, man—the meanest
motherfuckers in town!" He elaborates upon the theme.

The old man is full of words, half incoherent. Somebody
yells at him, "Shut up, Pop, shut up!" The two boys take it up:
"Shut up, Pop!" He begins to beat against the bars.

"Only baboons beat on the bars," one of them yells, "and
queers. He's a queer, ain't he?"

And now they launch into an endless obscene tirade
against him. Pop returns the compliments. The voices rise in
hysterical crescendo. "Talk to my ass a while, my head hurts."

Both sides tire; there is a lull. I hear the two boys tossing
on their mattresses. One of them groans to himself, "Oh God,
oh God."

Then it begins again. "I'm the motherfucking superior of
you!" the old man suddenly insists; "I'm here because I want to
be!" He begins to beat again upon the bars. They taunt him,
"Keep a beatin', keep a beatin', beat on, beat on!" The voices
swell again, in flood.

Silence. They have tired again. I doze a little; wake. They
are calling again. My companions are awake, too. We stare at
one another. The voices are quieter now, and contain a different note.

The old man is asking, "Did you mean those names you
called me?"

"I did at the time," one of the boys replies.

"How about now?"

A pause. "Give me some reason not to and I'll withdraw
them."

"You're a no-good sonofabitch," Pop relapses.

Silence.

And then we hear the young man call out again in a voice
suddenly as frail as a child's: "You want to be friends? Heh—
you want to be friends?"

"I'd rather be friends than enemies," the old man mumbles
—then abruptly declares, "I'm friends with everybody."

Another night: We hear the familiar scuffling, cursing, the
slam of the metal door. A drunken officer from the nearby Air
Base has been brought in. "Don't put me in here with that

goddam drunk!" he commands; "Get me out of here! Cop
come here! Open this door, open this door!" A fellow prisoner
makes a comment. The officer yells, "Shut that goddam sonofabitch up, or he's dead!" His voice shifts to a growl: "I'm going
to kick the everloving shit out of you." He screams. "Open the
door!" then suddenly, "Leave it locked, you sonofabitches!
Shut up, you're dead." He begins to sob. "Anybody who moves
is dead!"

His voice mounts in hysteria.

Somebody calls, "I know you're tough-assed but take it
easy." The officer breaks into quavering song, to the tune of
BYE BYE BLACKBIRD:

"You can kiss my ass, ya ya!

"You can kiss my ass, la la."

Somebody calls to him, "How long have you been in service?"

"Thirteen everloving goddam years," he groans.

"What are you in—I mean, besides jail? The goddam Air
Force?"

"The Peace Corps," he growls; "Shut up! You're dead!
Open the door, open the door!" he resumes. Then very very
quietly: "Open the door!" Then in a yell.

And then suddenly, almost eerily—we stare at one another
again—there issues out of the midst of all this clamor that
other voice we've heard, frail, child-like: "Heh friend, heh
friend," the officer calls—"You think they'll let us out of here
tomorrow?"

It is another night: Scuffling of feet again, the clanging to
of the steel door. Curses. Groans. More curses. A fellow prisoner calls out, "You're a bad ass, aren't you?" "Yes, I'm a bad
ass," the new man confirms loudly. The familiar exchange of
obscenities begins. The voices mount in the familiar rhythm.
But in the midst of it—we have learned now to expect it—the
voice alters, he calls: "Say—we're friends now, OK?"

We hear the heavy steel doors of the cages clang open; we
hear them clang to, as the cops lock the prisoners in, or let
them out. These arrivals and departures mark the time for us
now—a time which stretches, contracts, no longer tidily di-

vided as it was outside jail. I am always surprised, when I glance at my watch, to learn the hour it is. The rhythm of night, day has been broken, as the light burns round the clock; and round the clock, too, the cops come and go,—the prisoners yell at them and at one another—so that we sleep, when we do, simply in those stretches, whatever the clock says, when the yelling subsides enough to allow it. Mealtimes no longer subdivide a day; we have broken this rhythm ourselves, for my companions are fasting, and I take only a part of one of the two meals the jail provides—a meal that's brought not at the beginning or the middle or the end of the day but at four in the afternoon. We count the separate days as they pass, but as we haven't been tried yet and sentenced, we can't yet count: one day less to serve. Time has its own peculiar quality in here, and—marked as it is by these clamorous arrivals and departures—it takes on a quality more peculiar still as we begin to hear prisoners who have been released being brought back into the cells again. Time, it seems, runs nowhere. We are in Hell.

I remember my first experience of this, in another jail—Birmingham's city jail, May 1963. This was my first imprisonment of any duration—six days. I had been in jail in New York less than twenty-four hours. My crime in Birmingham was walking half a block, a sign round my neck: ALL MEN ARE BROTHERS. I had taken part in one of the Negro demonstrations. The sentence was six months, but the case was appealed, and after six days we were all bailed out. I was separated of course from my companions, put on the top floor of the jail; they were below.

A large airy room, in this case. A cage, still, in fact, but room to pace. (My friends below have less room—very much less of everything.) And we are even let out of the room at certain times—herded downstairs at meal times (three times a day here), very occasionally called down for visits. The guard or more often the matron—comes to the door and yells for one of us or all. And sometimes she yells a very particular phrase, calls the name of the prisoner and then adds ALL THE WAY! This means that the prisoner is being released. Festive phrase! The prisoner hurries to gather up her few belongings, she straightens out her skirt, pats quickly at her hair, grinning, shouts a quick goodbye. I remember Ruth leaving, I remember Flo. I remember—

It is the middle of the night. There is a sudden racket on the stairs; the heavy door is swung open, and I sit up on my top bunk to see who will come in. I have been asleep and for the first moment I feel that I am having a senseless dream. She is wearing a different dress, but that is Ruth who stands there. Her dress is soiled, she's barefoot, one of her eyes is swollen, and she is cursing, her face contorted. "You know what that bitch of a matron did? She slapped me! She slapped me!"

It is two nights later. Racket on the stairs again. The door swings open; and Flo staggers in again. She gives me a funny little sideways smile as she passes—sly and despairing. She wanders distracted for a few minutes in the long aisle between the double-decker bunks, then sinks down on the bunk below me. I fall asleep again, then wake to the sound of splashing water. Flo is squatting in the aisle, her skirts lifted. She suddenly passes out and falls forward, sprawled in the puddle she's made. A skylight is set in the floor at that spot—of thick greenish glass—and the feeble greenish light that glows from it outlines her there, helpless, her red curls unravelled, her dress twisted, her frilled petticoat showing.

Now in the Albany jail we hear derisive shouts, welcoming back a man who's been released three days before. He begins at once to curse at someone: "If your brains were made of cotton, there wouldn't be enough to make Kotex for a red-eyed beetle!"

The cop who's brought him in, on his way out, strolls back past our cell, hitching his pants. The look on his face asserts: A job well done; our city is safer now. He slaps his hand against his pistol holster, as if to reassure himself: Yes, there is power in me; I am a member of the force.

No wonder you touch yourself for reassurance.

I think of the heavy doors shutting, the heavy doors opening. First the rite of casting them out of existence. It is time they serve, not eternity, so then the rite of returning them to society. ALL THE WAY! ALL THE WAY! A cry in a dream. Punishment can almost convince a man that he doesn't exist; it cannot make him feel: now I am one of you. If society was embarrassed by them before, will it be less embarrassed by them now?

Part II

We are not let out of our cage, day or night. There is no mess hall in this jail; my one meal is shoved to me in a tin plate along the floor under the door's lowest bar. (Usually: baloney, which I leave; grits; black-eyed peas; a slightly bitter diced vegetable which I suppose is turnips.) Our toilet is there in the cell. (If a guard comes by while one of us is sitting on it, we hold up a coat for a screen.) There is no prison yard. We get our only exercise climbing up and down from the top bunks. (And Erica, with determination, once a day, stands in the narrow space between the bunks and touches her toes with her hands, brings up her knees to her chin a few times.) Here we are. We sit on our bunks or we lie on our bunks.

We sit and listen to the life about us in the jail. We can see from our cage only the corridor outside and, through the row of dirty windows, the alley, the brick wall. But to our ears the prison lies open—except for one distant room, "the hole"—all on one floor. Acoustics play strange tricks and it's hard to locate exactly from where it is the voices come; but we can shout back and forth to the men in our group—even to Ray and Ronnie and Tyrone, in a segregated cell because they're Negroes. We don't shout very often, because it takes a lot of energy. But Ray, several times a day, sings out to us: "Oh-oh free-dom! Oh-oh free-dom!" Sometimes we join in, sometimes we just let his single voice roll down the corridors, round the various corners, into all the cells.

Now and then the other prisoners call to us. Most often they call to Yvonne. Something in her voice intrigues them.

"Eevon!"

"What?"

"Do you have any cigarettes?"

"No—I'm sorry."

"Alright."

When Candy arrives, they call as often to her—intrigued by her name, of course, and by her youth: she is only seventeen.

"Candy, you there? You alright, baby?"

"Yes, I'm fine. Thank you."

"Alright."

But mostly they call back and forth to one another—teasing, cursing, or appealing. Or they talk or groan to themselves.

We talk among ourselves, too, but for long stretches we sit in silence, listening. I look at my friends and see their faces marked by a kind of awe. I recognise it. I remember suddenly the night in which I left jail after my first brief imprisonment in New York—bailed out, to my surprise, in the middle of the night. I remember walking away, up Greenwich Avenue, turning and turning to look back at the high gloomy building there—my feet, in spite of me, dragging, drawn to retrace my steps and at least touch the walls of the prison; turning to touch it with my eyes, and wondering, as I lingered, at the strength of my feeling that I was walking away from something of which I was deeply a part.

We sit and listen to the cries, the groans, the curses. Who hasn't at some time uttered that groan, uttered essentially that curse—of one estranged from others and from his own groped-for life? Those who have thrown us in here wanted to dispose of us. But instead of throwing us out of society as they would have liked, they have admitted us, by their act, into its inmost room. Here are men and women at their weakest; here, too, society confesses itself at a loss. These are people with whom it has been unable to cope, whom it has been unable to sustain.

A cop unlocks the heavy door of our cell and pushes in with us a pretty curly-haired young woman who's been arrested for drunkenness. She presses her body against the bars, as he retreats, shrieking after him. She pulls off one of her pretty white cowgirl boots and begins to bang at the bars with it in a helpless tantrum. The paper drinking cups we've lined up there spill to the floor and roll. Our underclothes which we've washed and hung there to dry are scattered too. A button goes flying off her boot into the corridor. We try to calm her, ask her questions about herself. She quiets down for a moment

but then begins to rage again: "I'll kill them all, kill them all!"
She takes a bobbie pin from her hair and reaching around the
door, begins frantically to try to pick its lock. We point out that
it's hopeless, laugh at her gently, and she finally begins to
laugh too, her tantrum dissolving—though she picks away for
a little while still. Leaning against one of the bunks, then, she
tells us about herself: "I was married at fourteen. . . . Seven
miserable years with him. . . . I'm nothing but a whore, I
suppose. . . . I called my mother the other day; she sounded
just like my enemy"; turning her eyes on us, lost, shining: "I
never had any kind of life."

In the cell next to us for a while is a young travelling
salesman, member of a fly-by-night company that's been doing
something illegal in town. After he has told us with good
humor of how, if our peace walk came through his town and
"started a ruckus," he'd just as soon shoot us "as anyone"—"A
kid I won't shoot, but if it's a grownup I don't care if it's a man
or a woman"—he goes on to describe his manner of life to us a
little, to tell us of the good times he and the others in his
company have, as they move in a group from one motel to
another—"We don't know till we jump where we go." "We
have a ball—lying in bed and ordering chicken dinners, and
watching television, each with a girl on call too of course."
"Saturday night the boss doles out our money. . . . We shower
up and go to the honky-tonk. . . . Everybody gets drunk." The
recitation of his joys is almost as sad as the recitation of the
young woman's sorrows; he is so hectically eager to have us
believe in them.

One night two cops come to unlock our door and steer
into the cell a drunken weeping woman, huge as a sow—with
pendulous belly, pendulous chins. Tears run from the corners
of her eyes and black rivulets of snuff from the corners of her
mouth. She stands blindly in the small space between the
bunks, staring at us, confused; then sinks—like a mountain
sinking into the sea—onto a lower bunk we've quickly cleared.
We take off her shoes for her. She reaches out her hand suddenly toward me and I take it and she begins to tell us about
herself. "I am so old. . . . My husband . . . doesn't love me . . .
my grandchildren . . . ashamed of me. . . . I'd like to be pretty

like all of you. . . . I am so old." We ask her how old she is.
Fifty. We tell her that isn't old. One of us asks, why doesn't she
see a doctor if it bothers her to be fat. She's been to see a
doctor. "He laughed at me." Have we anything to eat? Have
we any snuff?

In the distance a Negro woman begins to cry: "Oh my
baby! Let me go home to my baby! Oh help!"

The fat woman grips my hand more tightly. What are we
in for? We tell her about our walk. "You didn't walk with
niggers, did you?" she asks, frightened. "They have more than
whites do, you know it—better schools, better everything. I
have a cook, she's a nigger, and she says she wouldn't want
things different." Her eyes implore us. Suddenly she falls
asleep.

She wakes, turning in bed, groaning. "Have you really
walked all this way?" And then—in a voice that's almost a
whisper, "Girls, I want to ask you something—Did you ever do
anything you were so ashamed of you didn't know what to
do?" Yvonne tells her, "No, I believe you do things because
you can't help it." She whispers to us, "Do you think it's very
wrong to go with a young boy? My husband . . . doesn't love
me . . . One day . . . I just couldn't stand it any more. . . The
boy was only twenty-one . . . I got him to drive into the
country . . . We went into the back room of a church." She
ends, her voice flat, "He couldn't do anything." The tears begin
to run from her eyes again.

We stare at each other, helpless; and I stare again at all
the names scratched on these walls: BOBBY. LINDA. JIMMY.
DAVID. RUFUS. Over the toilet, someone has scratched an
arrow and THIS WAY OUT. High up in the corner of the wall
next which the woman lies, in letters slanting down, someone
has scratched: FOR GOD SO LOVED THE WORLD . . .

I remember suddenly a woman in the Macon jail—Evelyn
—in and out constantly for drinking. A handsome restless
woman, she moves to and fro about the room (in Macon's jail
there is space in which to move), conversing with herself when
not with us, to keep up her spirits; making a kind of bitter fun
of herself and of her plight. A plane passes close overhead and
we all stop what we're doing to listen to it. Evelyn raises her

arms—marked with dark bruises where the cops have been rough with her—and cries out: "Mr. pilot! Mr. pilot! Here I am! Help me! Take me away!" The plane passes on, high overhead, the humming of its motor growing fainter. "Mr. pilot!" she cries. "Oh come back, come back, don't leave me! Come back and get me, Mr. pilot!" She throws herself upon her cot—"Mr. pilot! Mr. pilot!"—half laughing, half weeping loudly—"Oh don't abandon me!" We laugh too, we almost weep too. Her comic cry is the cry of almost all in here, and a cry everybody knows, the cry in uttering which Jesus took on the flesh of every person born: "My God, my God, why hast thou forsaken me?" I remember again the first hours I ever spent in jail—in the New York Women's House of Detention. We have been questioned, fingerprinted, photographed, and searched one two three four five times. The elevator doors open and we step out into the ward to which we've been assigned. The doors open and the scene explodes upon us— explodes within us. The clamor of bedlam bursts in our ears: wild giggles, shrieks of rage, distracted pratings. The motions of bedlam meet our eyes. It is the hour just after dinner; the women have not yet been locked in two's in their cramped cells for the night. They wander in the halls like lost spirits, some of them dejected, heads hanging, others running here and there, others clinging together, amorous—timid about this, some of them, some of them eager to be noticed. They roll their eyes in our direction to see who we are. "Where did they pick *them* up? Look, look." And there also bursts upon us the strong smell of the place—disinfectant, bad cooking, sweat, urine, and something more than this: that special distillation of the flesh of those who are miserable, the smell, simply, of human desperation.

We have missed the dinner hour but are given a hasty meal by ourselves in the mess hall, while a prisoner sloshes a mop about the place. On each tin plate a very sticky mass of macaroni and a large turd which we decide is a fish ball. The stuff is hard to swallow; we dump most of it into the garbage pail which stands in the hall. Then it's time for all to be locked in their cells. I'm given a cell with one of my fellow pacifists. Two cots, side by side, a toilet (an empty bottle floats in it), a tiny basin with cold water and no stopper. During the day the one cot can be pushed under the other; when they're side by side, no floor space remains. We talk a little, then try to settle down. This jail provides sheets but they are the size of crib sheets, don't stretch the length of the mattresses. I feel in spite of myself that I share the bed with prisoner after prisoner who has slept here before me, sweated on this mattress, wept on it, exhaled her despair, been sick, been incontinent. I have undressed and put on the knee-length prison nightgown allotted me, but I decide now to put back on my underclothes and my skirt. And I try to curl up so that no part of me touches the mattress itself. And as my flesh shrinks from the touch of certain things here, my spirit shrinks from contact with the life about me. The prisoners are calling to one another from their row of cells. Much of the language is slang and unfamiliar, but the cries sound to me lewd and abandoned. I think with despair: See to what a hardly human condition the human being can be reduced. In a delirium of depression, I begin to laugh. My companion has turned her face to the wall. A guard yells at the women to stop their racket—there's supposed to be no talking after a certain hour. The place hushes for a moment. Then some giggling begins. Suddenly there is a shriek: "What's this in my goddam bed? Matron, turn on the light, turn on the light!" "It's probably Mickey the mouse," someone calls; "Old Mickey never fails." There is more giggling, and a great deal of commotion in that cell. Then another hush.

Then suddenly from the cell across from me a woman imitates the plaintive rather delicate miowwing of a cat. A pause. MOO! MOO!—sad and low. And from another dark cell, staccato: OINK OINK! A trembling BAA! BAA! echoes the length of the corridor. And then a rooster's voice bursts the air in prolonged fireworks: COCK A DOODLE DOODLE DOODLE DOODLE DOODLE DOO!

My depression is scattered. I feel all at once light of heart, and no longer set apart in spirit from these others, able to feel for them only pity and distaste.

Someone calls, "Goodnight, Joan," and someone, "Goodnight, Lola."

"Goodnight, Doris!"

"Goodnight, Cookie!"

"Goodnight, Toots!"

My cell mate is sitting bolt upright, smiling, and I guess from her look that her feelings now are something like mine. She's a young college girl, very bright and very grave with heavy glasses, a somewhat peaked look. We nod at each other mutely, and she lies down again in bed.

I sit there, leaning my head against the wall, listening. From the small window over the toilet, sounds of traffic far below enter our cell—very clear. Down the corridor I hear the small sounds of prisoners turning in bed, or stirring, sighing. I sit there a long time, a peculiar joy rising in me, my sense of distance from all the others here more and more dissolving, a sense of kinship with them waking in me more and more. I reach out and grasp one of the bars of the cage with my hand. I have only to remember that gesture—. I feel a queer stirring in me and it is as though my heart first bursts the bars that are my ribs and then bursts the bars of this cell, and then travels with great lightness and freedom down the corridor and into each stinking cell, acknowledging: Yes, we are all of us one flesh. This motion of my heart seems, in fact, so very physical that when I hear my companion suddenly turn in her bed, I decide abruptly: this disturbance in the air may frighten her. I call it back into its cage, and sit trembling.

I hear a little sound from her. Is she weeping? I whisper, "Are you alright?"

She whispers, "Oh yes, oh yes! You?"

I whisper, "Yes."

We lie now in our cage in Albany, Georgia. Candy and Mary have been arrested, too, and are with us. There are eight of us, and four bunks. We've asked for two extra mattresses and been given them, and they're on the floor. Three people lie there, closely side by side, legs under one bunk, heads half under the other. The third person has her coat over her head, because she lies right next the toilet. I lie alone on a lower bunk tonight; it's my turn to stretch out. From the bunk above me, Edie's thin foot dangles in the air; and in the crack between that bunk and the wall, Erica's square hand is visible. I'm not always as sure which limb belongs to whom.

We lie and listen to the cries, the groans, the curses. We are all of us wakeful tonight, but heavy-headed too. No window has been opened for a long time and the air is thick. A cop has just taken a bottle of corn liquor off someone he's brought in and poured the stuff out in the corridor. The fumes of this spread, too. The man who's been brought in is screaming, "Oh get me out of here, get me out of here!" After Jesus, dying on the Cross, cried out that he felt abandoned, the rocky foundations of Hell are supposed to have been tumbled out of place; and before he ascended into Heaven he went down into Hell, to gather all those spirits who wanted to be gathered.

I think: Let the foundations of every jail that exists be tumbled out of place. Let these Hells be harrowed; let them be emptied. I think of all the men and women cast, for a time, into this damnation, and marked by it. I think of their troublesome return to society. I think of the senseless attempt to build Heaven more securely by creating Hell. The one region can never be shut off from the other. I remember Debs' statement: "While there is a criminal element, I am of it; while there is a soul in prison, I am not free"—not a sentimental statement but a simple statement of fact. I think: The only way to build "the beloved community" is to seek again and again not how to cast out but how to gather, is to attempt to imitate Jesus' action. I remember Evelyn again, whom we met in Macon's jail. "We need more company," she'd said at one point: "I'm going to ride the broom." A battered broom stood leaning against the wall in a corner and she straddled it and trotted energetically back and forth the length of the room. This was supposed to be a kind of magic to bring more company in. I think: Yes, ride the broom, ride the broom! Ride it until you've ridden *all* in who are outside! For if any live in Hell, then all do. "We are members one of another." Let them all know this place. When they know it, let them cry out. Then let the walls fall!

Gene Hoffman

Is the Problem Really Sex?

We Westerners are a peculiar people. We are a society of untouchables. We confuse the need to be touched, held, cherished, with sex.

We Westerners are a backward people. We expect our children to find out everything they need to know about making love by experimenting with each other in the back seats of cars, from reading novels by authors who got their instruction the same way, and from sterile courses in high school in which "sex" is never linked with "joy," but only "procreation."

The furtive, frightened approach to sex in our society comes from the lack of rich, sensuous relationship with one another. None of us is ashamed or reluctant to speak of his delight in holding a baby or small child; that is encouraged, respected and respectable. We suspect the person who cannot enjoy the experience, who is somehow "unnatural." But the half-grown child or the adult must avoid the reassuring touch and warm embrace; to be touched is for them somehow a matter for shame. Our Puritan traditions have taught us to fear the contact of flesh; the incest taboos are so ingrained, we are even afraid of enjoying the embraces of our children or our parents, let alone our relatives and friends. We hope idiotically that falling in love with or marrying "the right person" will solve the need for physical cherishing. We have forgotten that the "laying on of hands" is one of our ancient healing devices and has its being in psychological and physical reality.

Our notion of physical relationships is too narrow and too limited. We have been described as the "genitally-oriented society." If we think of physical relationships as solely related to or always leading toward genital gratification—we lose many rightful satisfactions and become truncated, warped, and sick.

In the nineteen years since the birth of my first child, I have learned much about physical needs. Skin contact with a baby is as important as nourishing food. It took me about three children to learn that because I could not breast-feed them, I needed to compensate by taking baths with them, letting them sleep with us on fearsome nights, and increasing the rocking, cradling and holding. Discovering one is touchable is as basic as eyes to see and ears to hear. It is fundamental to the growth of outgoing love and acceptance.

Touch is a vitally important part of our whole attitude toward life. The people I am drawn to as healthy are warm, sensuous, embracing, unafraid. But how can we be warmly sensuous only in certain restricted areas of our lives and then abruptly cut it off in all others? Where do we stop the need for skin contact, the embrace, the warm pressure of the hand? What rigidity overtakes us, why the distance between us and those we cherish when we move toward physical contact?

Only in the theatre have I found release from antiseptic social relations. There are free, sometimes promiscuous, physical relationships. Theatre people, sometimes hypocritically, are always crying "Darling" and embracing one another. It is always a relief for me to re-enter that environment after spending time in the sensuously sterile community of peace-makers, race-relationists, scholars, or even "normal" people.

I do not want physical contact with everyone. No one does. There is chemistry that produces revulsion. We should act in harmony with our chemistry. But if we were freer to express spontaneously a physical response, we'd be relieved of a lot of problems we lump under the heading of sex. Warmth, comfort, nurture: do we ever, any of us, outgrow the longing for them? Are we ever, any of us, embraced enough? I don't think so. At least, there's never been enough for me.

And how many of us seek, or have sought sexual experience, not from a valid need for it, but out of a valid hunger for acceptance, approval, some tangible demonstration of our own worth and value because this was the only socially recognized way to do so?

We have begun to understand the language of faces, but do we know and approve the language of touch? What words have ever comforted as much as being held lovingly in a moment of sorrow or joy? I have sometimes wished that I were blind so I might trace with my fingers the lineaments of a loved one's body or face. I hope we are approaching an age where no one will need wish he were blind, for all will be free to speak with the voice of touch.

The problem of initiation seems to flow from the first. Curiously, in our sex-ridden culture, references to it are either avoided, secret, fearful, guilty, or crude, joking, shamefaced. We are open with one another about our delights in food, work, art, books. We are closed in conversations about sex. We are told that this restraint is good. "Sex is too intimate, too private, too sacred to be described in words."

But I don't believe an honest, free, searching conversation can strip the mystery from sex, can make it commonplace and debased as does our present hypocritical attitude. It is the mystery that must be maintained, not ignorance. A first step toward initiation for our children would be to approve of healthy, flourishing sexuality in ourselves and in them.

Reflect upon the "rites of passage" we offer our children in their transition from childhood to young adults: we lend our teen-agers the car, give them the choice of their dates, hope they are "trustworthy," and call it freedom.

I read somewhat wistfully of the practices of such cultures as the Kikuyus (in *Facing Mount Kenya* by Jomo Kenyatta) where the transition into physical maturity is enthusiastically prepared from birth, is encouraged and approved, even to the provision of a symbolic ritual demonstration of the sexual act for new-made adults. The entire community participates in this moment with the young people, celebrating their change of estate. Aldous Huxley proposed initiation rites in his book *Island*. These were encouraged by the entire community and received the same approval as do our graduations, confirmations, and weddings. Even the French custom of providing the young man with an experienced woman to teach him the art of sex seems to me better than our no-custom, no-provisions. By acting as though there is no problem and nothing to be done, we create enormous problems of ignorance, more than can ever be undone. We abandon our young people to explore the delicately balanced realms of sex unguided, uninstructed, and, worst of all, unapproved.

I covet for my children the freedom I have gained (and further freedom yet). I covet for them rich, satisfying sensuous experience, joyous delight, and the deep spiritual and psychological meanings possible to sex. I wish they were psychologically healthy enough not to treat sex casually or to confuse it with the longing to be accepted and approved. I hope they will not use others for their own needs and gratifications, not use sex as a substitute for understanding and facing honestly some painful part of themselves, not throw away its integrity (for pain, anguish and destruction follow). I wish they understood their own motivations enough not to need to misuse sex. But when they do misuse it and it hurts, I hope they are able to examine what has happened without blame, self-hatred or despair.

There should be poetry for them in sex; they may have an earlier opportunity than I to discriminate between Dante's Siren (who was invested with her lover's need for an image of perfection), and out-giving love, with a true perception of the one they love. I hope they cherish the divine fire of sex, for only then will it bring them the cherishing it only can provide.

Paul Goodman

From John Dewey to A. S. Neill

One really gets impatient, if not outraged, at the remarks about Progressive Education made by the Rickovers and Max Raffertys. Historically, indeed, the intent of Progressive Education was exactly the opposite of what the critics say; it was the correct solution that Rickover, at least, ought to be asking for, but doesn't know enough to ask for. Progressive Education developed in this country in the intellectual, moral, and social crisis of the development of industrialism after the Civil War. It was the first thoroughgoing modern analysis of the crucial modern problem of every advanced country in the world: how to cope with high industrialism and scientific technology, which are strange to people; how to live in the new cities; how to have a free society in such conditions; how to make the high industrial system good for something, rather than a machine running for its own sake.

The thought of John Dewey was part of a similar tendency in architecture, the functionalism of Louis Sullivan and Frank Lloyd Wright, that was trying to invent an urbanism and an esthetic suited to machine mass-production and yet human; and it went with the engineering orientation of the economic and moral theory of Veblen and others, objecting to money values and the false classicism that had become a leisure-class ornament. These thinkers wanted to train, teach (accustom is perhaps the best word) the new generation to the actualities of industrial and technical life, working practically with the machinery, learning by doing. People could then be at home in the modern world, and possibly become free.

There was a political and economic side to it. Dewey, at least, was distressed by both the robber-baron plutocracy and the bossed mass-democracy. He put his faith in industrial democracy, overestimating the labor union—he did not foresee their bureaucratization. (As a pragmatist, he must have expected that the skilled would demand a say in management and production, and not be content with merely bargaining on wages and conditions!) But at least the school was to be a training in self-rule, democracy and community. And these two ideas, practical learning of the machinery and democratic community, in an atmosphere of free animal expression and freedom to fantasize, instead of the parson's morality and the schoolmaster's ruler, constituted the whole of Progressive Education. With spontaneous interest (including animal desire), rigorously controlled by the hard pragmatism of doing and making the doing work, the young democratic community would best learn the modern world and would also have the will, cooperatively, to change it. It was a theory of continual scientific experiment and nonviolent social revolution.

As was inevitable, our society being what it is, this theory was entirely perverted when it began to be applied, either in private schools or in the public system. Because of the outcry of the conservatives, it began to be toned down. A program of practical training and community democracy, whose purpose was to live scientifically and change society, was changed into a psychology of "belonging" combined with "socially useful" subjects and "citizenship." Driver-training was the type of the "useful." (Dewey would by now, I hope, have been teaching how to curtail the number of cars!) Social dancing was the type of the "belonging." The Americans had no intention of politically changing, nor of broadening the scientific base and taking technological control and expertness out of the hands of the top-managers and their technicians. Democratic community became astoundingly interpreted as conformity, instead of being the matrix of experiment.

At present, suddenly, there is a great cry for scientific and technical training. By strict lessons and draconian grading (plus bribes) we are supposed to find the scientifically gifted, an elite group. Dr. Conant says that the "academically talented" are 15% and these, largely selected by national tests, are supposed to be at home in the modern technical world and be the creative spirits in it. The bother is that the teachers of

science who know what they are talking about—e.g. the consensus reported in Professor Bruner's *The Process of Education*
—ask for a kind of training that looks very like Deweyan
Progressive Education. They counsel practical learning by
doing, avoiding testing and grading, encouraging spontaneous
experiment and guesswork. There is no point, they say, in
learning the "answers," for very soon there will be different
answers. What must be taught are the underlying ideas of
scientific thought as part of the substance of the youngster's
life, fantasy, and experience. My guess is that when Professor
Bruner and his associates explore a little further, they will find
that democratic community is also an essential, because it is
impossible to do creative work of any kind when the goals are
pre-determined by outsiders and cannot be criticized and altered by the minds that have to do the work. Indeed, they will
end up right where John Dewey and others began!

In the past three or four years there has been a significant
revival of Progressive Education in this country, taking a peculiar form. It has been modeling itself on Summerhill, A. S.
Neill's school in England. In most ways the Summerhill idea is
not unlike old-line Progressive Education—it stresses animal
freedom, learning by doing, and *very* democratic community
processes (one person one vote, enfranchising small children!).
But it also emphasizes an issue that to Dewey did not seem
important, the freedom to choose to go to class or stay away
altogether. A child at Summerhill can just hang around; he'll
go to class when he damned well feels like it—and many coming from other schools don't damned well feel like it for eight
or nine months. After a while—since their friends go—they
give it a try.

It is significant, in my opinion, that it is just *this* development in Progressive Education that is catching on a little bit.
The significance is simple. Our entire school system, like our
over-organized economy, politics, and standard of living, is
largely a trap; it is *not* designed for the maximum growth and
future practical utility of the children into a changing world,
that they too will hopefully improve, but is a kind of inept
social engineering to mold, and weed out, for short-range extrinsic needs. And even when it is more benevolent, it is in the

bureaucratic death-grip—from the universities and the boards of education down—of a uniformity of conception and method that cannot possibly suit the multitude of dispositions and conditions. Yet a hundred per cent of the children are compelled or cajoled to remain, for 12 years (!) in one kind of box. If we are going to have real universal education, that educates, probably we have to start by getting rid of compulsory education!

In my opinion, the future—if we survive the Cold War and have a future, which is touch and go—will be more leisurely anyway; and the leisure—if it is not to be complete inanity—will include much more community and civic culture; there will be more employment in human services and less in hardware gadgets; there will be more citizenly initiative and less regimentation; and there will be decentralization of control and administration in many spheres. For these purposes, the top-down dictated national plans and educational methods that are now the fad are quite irrelevant. And on the contrary, it is precisely the society of free choice and lively interpersonal involvement of Summerhill that is practical.

So just as with Dewey, the new wing of Progressive Education is again a good index of what the real social situation is. Let us hope that this time around Progressive Education will not allow itself to be perverted by the pressures of a society which needs it but is afraid of it and will seek to abuse it.

Lewis Mumford

The Forces of Life

No matter how confidently we may boast about our triumphs in science and technics, our best minds feel, covertly if not openly, more than a little anxiety about them. Though we have succeeded brilliantly in the transformation of matter, far beyond the wildest dreams of the ancient alchemists, who would pretend that we have had any equivalent success in the transformation of man? Or rather, we are succeeding fabulously, provided only that we accept the machine as the final goal and sole beneficiary of the transformations. During the last few centuries, men have become more standardized, more regimented, more dependent upon the machine's supervision and care of their whole life; while machines have become more intelligent, more independent, more self-governing, in a word more lifelike and more ominously human. But if man and the machine are merely exchanging roles, who will be the gainer? Certainly not man.

I believe that unless man restores his own confidence in the forces of life, unless he loves himself more than he loves the machine, the papers for his abdication, perhaps for his annihilation, have been signed. The hidden resources that may save him are not to be found in either science or technology, considered apart from man's more central needs: they lie in the nature of man himself, in all his organic complexity, his cultural variety, his historic creativeness and his purposefulness, his still unfathomed potentialities for further development and self-transformation.

Now our present machine-conditioned culture, with its machine centered personalities, has had only a short historic span. It was conceived in the seventeenth century by Bacon and Campanella, intellectually brought to birth by Galileo,

Newton and Descartes, warmed and nourished by generations
of able inventors and engineers, rigorously molded and disciplined by a succession of strenuous industrialists; and it has
been eulogized, indeed adored and worshipped, for the last
century, alike by utopian idealists and hard-headed business
men. Today this culture is still generally acclaimed, as the
ultimate hope of man, both by the totalitarians who call themselves Communists and the totalitarians who call themselves
free enterprisers. But this seemingly wholesale triumph of
the machine does not stand up under critical examination. The
glossy perfection of this new world is matched only by the
inner disintegration, indeed, the outright demoralization, that
has often attended its highest performances—and now threatens completely to nullify them.

Automated Boredom

The most staring example of this breach between our exquisitely rational scientific means, and our irrational and dehumanized ends lies in our present colossal plans for the total
extermination of whole enemy populations in a nuclear war
that would be quite as fatal to the victor as to the victim. In
busy experimental preparation for such a war, the leaders of
Soviet Russia and the United States are now cumulatively pol-
luting the atmosphere, poisoning the world's food supply with
strontium 90 and recklessly threatening both our genetic in-
heritance and our ecological balance. But if you have difficulty
in grasping the irrational nature of these plans, to say nothing
of the infantile moral depravity they exhibit, let me choose a
simpler and a less controversial illustration. Consider the
bright idea engineers are already seriously playing with: the
notion of taking the control of the private motor car out of
the hands of the driver, so that he will become a mere pas-
senger in a remote controlled vehicle. If you take technical
progress as an end in itself, and believe that the "going is the
goal," this seems a natural, and indeed inevitable next step in
automation. But look at the human consequences. The driving
of a car has been one of the last refuges of personal responsibility, of the do-it-yourself principle, in our machine-oriented
economy. At the wheel of his car the most downtrodden con-

formist still has a slight sense of release; he may capriciously choose his destination, alter his speed, explore a side road, or loiter in a woody glen for a picnic lunch. One by one, in the interest of safety or maximum speed, these freedoms are being taken away. The final triumph of automation would do away with all the subsidiary purposes of travel by private vehicle: nothing would change, neither the man nor the occupation nor the scenery. Obviously, the mechanical results have already been more efficiently achieved in a railroad train, while the same boredom could be arrived at more cheaply by the simple non-technical device of staying at home.

Automation is not Automatic

We should not take these tendencies for granted, as if they were immune to any human direction or control. Nothing could be more false than the notion that this automatism is itself automatic. We must realize that Western man, for the last four centuries, has been living in a sort of exploding universe of scientific knowledge and technical invention, and that he himself, originally and now, is responsible for that explosion. Seemingly, however, the process itself has gotten out of hand. The separate members of this galaxy, the individual departments of science and technology, are increasing rapidly in size and moving further and further apart, both from each other and still more from the central nucleus that once held them together: the human self. As a result, we have more knowledge than we can put together in a coherent pattern or intelligently assimilate, we have more nuclear energy than we can yet use safely, and more goods—at least in the United States—than we have learned to distribute equitably or consume wisely. Instead of building up a firm center in the human self, capable of evaluation, selection, and purposeful organization, we have systematically belittled and ignored this central function of man; and we have thereby lost the essential criteria, to say nothing of the self-confidence, that are needed for directing our technical development or directing it into the channels of wider human content and purpose.

The fact is that those who have brought about this explosion have, in their own minds, given to the mechanical transformation of man an absoluteness, an authority and finality, that none of man's earlier transformations show: neither that early transformation from the roaming paleolithic hunter into the neolithic farmer in his settled village, nor that from civilized man, with his law and order, his private property, his slavery and war into the moralized man of the prophetic religions, attempting to widen the role of fellowship, of love, of conscious moral control. And we deceive ourselves if we believe that this technological civilization, this so-called atomic age, is purely the product of external circumstances and forces, independent of the human will. Centuries before flight or instantaneous communication or automatic energy became possible, the fantasies of angelic messengers, speeding through space, and all powerful gods, commanding lightning and moving mountains, swarmed in man's unconscious mind. Our mechanical projects, in other words, had subjective reality in man's dreams and art, long before they had even a glimmer of objective realization elsewhere. That world is in fact a wish-fulfillment, attached partly to a perfectly normal desire for security, symbolized and structured in repetitive acts and stimulated by somewhat paranoid delusions of grandeur and desires for domination over Nature and other men. In any event, the self out of which our machine-conditioned culture sprang was in no sense an extension or projection of the whole man. And so, like all the other transformations of man, it has brought forth and expressed only a small part of man's potentialities.

"Man Conforms"

Yet the belief in the machine as man's ultimate master, if not his Deity, has become a common one today. More than twenty-five years ago, it was summed up in classic form in an official guidebook to the Century of Progress Exhibition in Chicago. I have preserved those three precious sentences over the years because they seem nothing less than the ultimate credo of the machine age, its alpha and omega. Here they are: "Science finds. Industry applies. Man conforms." On those terms, man's historic self transformations are over: his autonomy, his creativity, his freedom, are at an end: only those parts of his nature that can be profitably turned to the account of science or industry may remain. This sense of compulsive conformity to external processes and pressures is widely written over our chief activities today; little more than a veil of residual traditions left over from earlier transformations of man keeps us from realizing how deeply this conception of man's purely passive role, the role of conformity and adjustment, has eaten into our whole life.

As things are going now, man has largely substituted the perfection of machines for his own continued self-development and self-renewal, even though the perfection of machines can have little meaning in a world destitute of other human values and purposes. But there is an ultimate limit to this acceptance and conformity, a limit suggested almost a century ago by the Brothers de Goncourt, in their famous journal, dated 1869. These writers had heard of Berthelot's prediction that "a hundred years hence, thanks to physics and chemical science, men would know of what the atom was constituted and would be able at will to moderate, extinguish, or light up the sun, as if it were a gas lamp." They went on to say that Claude Bernard had "apparently declared that in a hundred years of physiological science man would be so completely the master of organic law that he would create life in competition with God." "To all this," the de Goncourts concluded, "we raised no objection. But we have the feeling that when this time comes in science, God with his white beard will come down to earth, swinging a bunch of keys, and will say to humanity, the way they say at five o'clock at the Salon: Closing time, gentlemen!"

Closing time indeed! There are many points visible now at which the doors might be locked and the lights turned out. An outbreak of nuclear and bacterial genocide, on a world wide scale, would only be the most obvious of them. But this is not the sole path that might lead, within a fairly short period, to the end of historic man. We might also produce a kind of totalitarian society, already partly visible, run by fragmentary men, wholly dedicated to the expansion of the empire of the machine: men conditioned to live in a constricted world, heavily populated but increasingly denuded of organic variety, themselves unloving and unlovable, hostile to every impulse that could not be controlled and profitably regimented.

Under-dimensioned Beings

The design of these under-dimensioned beings, I regret to say, has long passed the drawing-board stage: they are already coming off the production line, in large numbers, packaged in cellophane and duly labeled, price tag and all, with degrees in science, engineering, architecture, warfare, medicine and administration. Many of them are equipped, let us admit it, with exquisitely trained intelligences and an almost unlimited amount of technical expertness; but they have only a dim, vestigial sense of any human purposes and goals except those that derive from the instruments they use. Their "know-how" does not embrace "what for." If called upon to make a response outside the narrow domain they have mastered, they feel pitifully insecure; and they are equally unsure of themselves, even within that domain, if called upon to react to a challenge as a whole human being. If such creatures have any interest in the nature of man, it is only for the Procrustean purpose of rebuilding or reconditioning human beings so that they may conform more closely to the machine's requirements, as we are now trying to fit human physiology to supersonic speeds. Under the guidance of such leaders modern society might, in a not too distant future, incorporate in permanent form a rigid set of limitations, comparable to those buit into insect societies, like the ants, sixty million years ago—limitations that are still unchanged. That would close the door to further human developments; and in a relatively short time of course even technology would suffer.

Now I do not propose to leave you with such an air-conditioned nightmare. Man has still to live with himself, and our contemporaries show many signs that they do not wholly admire this finished mechanical image or relish this new prospect. Possibly the appalling manifestations of hatred, senseless violence, and random destructiveness we increasingly witness in the very centers of civilization are blind instinctual compensations for the feeling of human impotence and personal nullity that our machine conditioned culture has fostered. Did not Dostoevsky, in his *Letters from the Underworld,* warn us long ago that man might turn his back on the stuffy mechanical progress of the nineteenth century and recover his freedom, if

no other way opened, by resorting to crime? But more constructive responses have happily been gathering force, though
they are not yet so conspicuous, perhaps, as the neurotic and
criminal reactions. The do-it-yourself movement in America is
doubtless such a response, even though, in comic contradiction
to its promise, one of its chief incentives seems to be the sale of
a new line of machines. In that characteristic over-emphasis on
equipment, it resembles still another bid for autonomy: our
growing addiction to sport. Still, this emphasis on play is significant, for play in all its forms constitutes one of the great realms
of human freedom and creativity, as engineers themselves
should well know, since many audacious technical devices, the
motion picture, the helicopter, the telephone, had their origins
in children's toys. Perhaps an even more important reassertion
of human dignity and inititative—don't think I am jesting—is
the spontaneous rise in the birth-rate; for making love and
having children are two activities that have no mechanical
counterparts: they are still definitely human.

Ethics in Capsule Form

In the long run, we must all realize that we cannot offset the
costive effects of our depersonalized ideology by attempting at
intervals to supply, in capsule form, as if they were vitamins, a
sufficient dosage of art, philosophy, literature, religion, ethics
and history to overcome radical deficiencies in our daily diet.
That sort of empiric medication may do for the weekly pages
of *Life,* but it does not meet the demands of life itself. In
every situation the whole man must be accessible and ready to
take command, capable of meeting life in all its organic complexity—cosmic, biological, sexual, ethical, esthetic, at every
moment from birth to death. Unless we fortify and widen the
province of the human personality, we cannot prudently trust
those who now exercise their admirable specialized competence. What is perhaps no less important, unless we build up
the central nucleus in the human self, in all its dimensions,
with all its potentialities, we shall overlook the richest resource
that technology can draw on, if it is to develop into a true
polytechnics, capable of meeting every human need on man's
own terms, rather than in terms of the machine's narrow re-

quirements. For lack of such human terms of reference, much of the work done during the last generation in the fields of engineering I am most familiar with—housing, urbanism and highway engineering—will have to be done over again, once the human functions and human values come back into the picture. A society in which fractional scientists talk only to fractional scientists about their fractional interpretations of a fragmented world; in which engineers understand only the problems of other engineers, in which, in short, each specialist sits like a nervous woodchuck, within a few feet of his inviolable burrow and ducks down into it as soon as he hears a strange footstep or sights a human shape—such a society has one fatal defect: it is flatly out of touch with reality. Real life must be lived simultaneously on many interesting and interpenetrating levels; and only those who, as autonomous persons, are capable of moving freely from one level to another, who are acquainted with the ways of love as well as the ways of power, can measure up to the greatest demand of life—that of man's continued development and self-transformation. That job cannot be delegated to a machine.

The terms of the next transformation are already set, since each fresh transformation tends to fill out the places that were left empty in an earlier stage; indeed, the neglected elements become the nucleus for the new growth. Yet as with every previous transformation of man, the next one will continue the main line of human development, by widening the field of human intercourse and association, in cultural as well as economic interchange, and will utilize functions and aptitudes that earlier stages left out of cultivation. Above all, the next transformation will seek to overcome the enclosures and frustrations experienced through the very perfection of our machine-conditioned culture. If current society has overstressed the acquisition of unlimited knowledge and unlimited power, the next stage will accept norms and limits, as essential manifestations of life, and it will concentrate upon the art of love, so that man may do greater justice to his own nature, and be able, through self-understanding, to overcome the unloving omniscience of current science and the unloving omnipotence of current technology. In order to control the machine for his own varied purposes, man must now cultivate his own special capacities as controller and creator. No sporadic revolts will accomplish this. What is needed is a common purpose, as large and over-riding as that which has, since the seventeenth century, drawn forth the energies of the scientist, the inventor, the capitalist, the engineer, and the bureaucrat—and for a while enlisted the hopeful support of all men.

The Center Is Man

What is that new purpose? Nothing less than the next transformation of man. This will call, I believe, for the creation of a unified though highly diverse world culture, which will enable men and women to be at home, as full-fledged citizens, in every part of the planet, in a generous, loving relation of give-and-take with all other cultures; likewise at home with every part of their own selves in all their historic layers and thus capable of drawing into the service of their common purpose energies that, if allowed to expand by themselves, as technics now does, would be disruptive and dangerous. At this point man himself must come back into the center of the stage, no longer content with his present job in the wings as mere property man, stage hand and electrician; he must take on, rather, the role of actor-dramatist, commanding every part of the performance, scenery, costume, dialogue, action, supporting cast, in order to make possible the new drama of One World Man, drawing for the first time upon all the physical and human resources of the planet. That able French anthropologist, Teilhard de Chardin, called this coming epoch the period of planetization. For myself, I would prefer to call it the period of human polarization: an era in which all the fractional parts of man, divided by culture, by race and region and nationality, by all manner of vocational specialization and segregation, will be brought back, greatly expanded and enriched, to the central nucleus, the human self where they originated.

Not the least part of our culture to benefit by this transformation will be the domain of engineering itself: for modern technics will at last cast off the burden of its random expansion in the direction of pecuniary profit and power. All the truly great achievements of the passing age—instantaneous communication, swift transportation, atomic and solar energy in end-less quantities, automatic machinery to perform servile or burdensome work, to mention only those concerned with phys-ical processes—will at last be attached to higher human goals, more worthy of the intelligence that brought them forth. For the first time in history the entire population of the planet will have access to the full human heritage, the near and the far, the past and the possible, the animal and the divine. Here is a creative potentiality that is almost without limit, provided that the arts of love keep pace with the arts of power, and man loves himself and all other living creatures more than he loves the machine on which he has all too intently concentrated.

Within the terms laid down by nature and history, the future remains ours to make. But only on one provision: that we take up again man's two great age-old tasks: the task of self exploration, which has enlarged every dimension of nature and the cosmos, and the task of self-transformation, which has re-vealed the unfathomable and inexhaustible richness of life it-self.

V

The New Beginning

Pierre Henri Delattre

Walking Across China

If you get on a plane
And stop at all the capitals of the world,
The world seems mighty small,
But have you ever tried
Walking across China?

Salamon de la Selva

The Last Illusion

The bullet that kills me
will be a bullet with a soul.

The soul of this bullet would be like a rose
    if flowers could sing
Or the perfume of a topaz
    if gems had fragrance
Or the skin of song
    if it were possible
For our hands to touch naked music.

If it strikes me in the head
it will say: "I am just trying to find out
            How deep your thoughts are."

If it enters my heart
it will say:
    "I just want to show you how much I love you."

Translated from the Spanish by Lillian Lowenfels

William Stafford

Amulet

I held a quiet stone
that took the dog barking
absorbed the hornet
and shadowed every sound.

They snatched the quiet stone
and said, "You are too calm."
(I watched them, small.)
"We order you: care more."

I tried to answer them
and said (but was my voice
from care too low?),
"That stone you took was love."

William Stafford

Encounter

In the bright wind from the fields today
my troubled steps encountered spring
where that farm family on the weedy hill
sold out and left everything.

It is part of my burden to know they are gone,
when I walk past on the public road;
often in storms they may have looked down
and pitied me, there in the cold.

A history of this year that considered that farm
would know many failures, part of them mine;
they couldn't make a go, they were lonely here.
I walk onward through the warm spring wind.

William Stafford

On Being Invited to a Testimonial Dinner

We are trained and quiet intellectuals
who learn all mazes very well
and in the dusk we live in go
around the room and part way up the walls.

If there is a way around, we know;
if there is no way, then our heads know.
Blundering types who push we can forgive,
being sure that such and such makes a so-and-so.

But no man—forceful or not—can live
with credit in our minds at all till we've
checked what he is against all his pretences,
and no forceful man commands our love.

Now, the power in thought lives by surprise.
A heart may feel beforehand; it decides
whatever way it wishes; but a head
may change in the midst of kings, to stay wise.

There was once in the jungle a feast where great men fed.
The cobra—sought to hold on his still head
the ark of dignity for all the kings, whereby
with his assurance their great worth was held—

Returned regrets: "I can't accept," was his reply,
"for my head lives by freedom, low or high,
and though my heart acts tame in the midst of kings
my head may twitch for itself, and those kings die."

George Dennison

Two Short Poems

I

I sprayed the ants that invaded my kitchen
—now here they are, some hours dead,
in the pattern of their highway under the sink,
so rational and ruined, like a city blasted,
whose fragments show where they fed
and dwelt and labored.

II

The little boy insane
has drawn this prehistoric scene:
gray sky horizonless
in front of which two upright bugs
are holding hands
looking at the distant, long-haired sun.

Richard Mayes

An Education

A bitter boy, once,
        fighting with an algebra problem,
out of pure frustration
        jammed the pencil point
hard into his hand
        and wept, and watched
with almost lewd desire
        the blood and tears get mixed
over the obdurate
        printed words:
the man travelling over
        the different routes
at different times,
        at different rates,
and after all this,
        how far has he gone?
Now he's doing
        his Ph. D.
and wanders in beery pools
        in bloody bars
with that same sorrow
        of years ago
slipping surely away
        from his left hand,
and that love
        slipping away from his right.

Richard Mayes

A List of Desires Frustrated

A list of desires frustrated
by fear in me, or by real and great
present power outside, little difference
it really makes: to sleep on the beach
on any one of the three great shores
where I was brought up or I go to,
to have unfurtive sex outdoors
with neither the policeman's flashlight
nor crouching in the narrow car seat
I had when I was young; to choose
what I was going to do or study
daily, instead of being subtly
and unsubtly groomed for the chemical
industry (it might have been,
why not? had I choosing freedom);
to speak facts to the authorities
my parents, teachers, then my bosses,
instead of the obsequious grin
fronting the black-festering spite:
covering all this, the simple truths
making my face red for shame,
or what I tried to make it appear,
a kind of grinning coyness-niceness . . .

These things cut me twice as much
as I lie in this sunlight and sand
and watch the yet-young fingers
of my yet-young hand
slowly gnarl before my eyes,
with the unripened now,
and judging by so far,
all that unripening to come.

Richard Mayes

Proctoring the Bio Exam

The warnings before it were so intense
that when someone dropped a ruler, the crack of it
hung fearfully among the bent heads,
like that sternness I too once heard;
and I had a wild impulse to run screaming
at the nearest boy, "You're cheating, I saw!"
and thereupon to hear a whole crescendo
of shrieks and laughs and schizy gibberish,
tho occurring in my own ringing brain alone,
for they know I will not play that adult's role.

Yet—my formal teacher's function here
is to go and sit among the lively lads
so they can't talk to each other.

(It slowly dies away, I guess, this shrieking desire.)

And when I walk away from the spying points,
and when I turn and see
the faked furrows in those faking foreheads,
or guilty glance-and-turn-away, I know
these animals' biology is not functioning right,

and I too explode with relief
when that bell rattles our teeth,
and I bolt away with the rest.

Richard Mayes

Description of a Photograph
(in the *Daily News*, November 3, 1960)

Most beautiful, most stupendous, most terrifying
    and most powerful
the massed motorcycles around the President's and
    Vice-President's car,
the crash hats and the poise of policemen's heads
    define authority;
and the perfectly uniform symmetry of the windshields
    of the Harley Davidsons
and the squat massiveness of the bullet-proof black
    Cadillac convertible
are our power, our envy, our impregnable protection,
    our incorporated joy;
oblivious of the confetti, of the Christlike gestures
    of the dignitaries,
walk the Security Men, the personal defenders, their looks
    are deadly serious;
we feel they work unobtrusively, efficiently, behind
    the mobbing worshippers,
we give up sarcasm and disrespect, oh we join
    forces with them all,
they will take us in, we can be one of their
    numbers, we can have
their magnificent acclaim, each of us a piece
    in the great mosaic,
the President a central piece, the Vice-President
    no less shining there too,
our hearts can sink away from this obdurate
    complicatedness and fear

sink away toward their powerful massed symmetry,
  away from this terrible
rebellious loneliness, it does not really matter
  for whom we vote,
but that our choice will be surrounded with this might
  of all our industry,
that we can be in that surging sea of hands,
  twenty tons of confetti
we eagerly throw then, eagerly, for the neat handsome
  military bearing
of the motorcyclists, for the impeccable American wariness
  of the Security Men,
for the accepting-acclamation-gestures of the Christlike
  grand dignitaries,
eagerly in lost joy we throw confetti then, at last
  our throats in wild praise.

Paul Goodman

Commencement, 1962

The insulted poor will riot in my city
without community. The air is poisoned
by crazy sovereigns. America
and Europe shamelessly have counterfeited
this ring and book. Thwarted in serving
I grow deluded about my significance
but am in fact confused like an abandoned
hut in the woods with dusty windows
and the town far away, if there is any.
Nevertheless hear the tumultuous spirit
restless in the foliage turning white
that will destroy God knows how much of the world
before retreating he whispers Good-bye
my frightened darling, thank you. He is whining
and sobbing; he will whistle through his teeth
and howl, and the big branches crack and sag
withering. And I remember Shelley's
"Make me thy lyre, even as the forest is;"
Something is breathing me despite myself.
My speech is frantic, I was too nearsighted
to see the expression on Costikyan's
face when I shouted at him to resign,
and when I called on passers in the street
help! help! they stood only staring at
each other with impersonal alarm.
I am misthrown, not meant to be an agent
but the historian of the excellent.

Diane di Prima

Memories of Childhood

1

So I said to him Hey mister what're you doing with that H bomb how come you waving it around like that? You gonna drop it on that building? Hey mister how come you're taller than that there building, is it a Noptical Delusionment?

And he sez to me Go home boy, don't bother me. I'm telling you you make me nervous. Go home or I might get nervous and drop this thing.

So I went home.

2

So my mother was in the kitchen and I ran in and I said to her Hey ma there's a big tall man outside boy is he really big and tall he's taller than our house and he's got this bomb in his hand. I think he's gonna drop this H bomb on our house. Hey Ma I don' wan' him to drop it on our house.

So my mother went to the window and I went with her and I saw his legs standing there and I said There you see ma that's his legs standing there you see him? And she said What are you talking about boy there's nothing out there but the tree.

3

So I waited till my father came home and by then it was dark. And I said Pa I wanna show you something. And he said All right my boy what is it and put his briefcase down on the table.

And I said Pa did you notice anything funny when you came in the house tonight and he said Yes you didn't put your bike away and I said No Pa that's not what I mean.

So I took him to the window and I said Pa do you see a man standing out there, a big tall man I can just see his two legs, huh pa?

And he said I do seem to see something out there, yes my boy I do.

And I said Good I'm glad you see it Pa cause that man's standing there holding a bomb over our house, an H bomb I think Pa and I want you to make him go away.

And he said Now wait a minute boy I think that's just the outline of the tree yes that's what it is it's getting dark out and it had me fooled for a minute but there's no such thing as an H bomb you know son and there's no man out there.

4

So we had supper and after supper I went to my grandfather's room to talk to him and I said Grandpa what happens if an H bomb falls? And he said A what sonny?

And I said An H bomb grandpa you know like an atomic bomb only bigger I think what happens if it falls? And he said It'll never happen sonny.

And I said Why not grandpa huh why not? Don't you believe in H bombs huh? Don't you think there's such a thing?

And he said I believe in god sonny and god will never let it happen now go play.

5

So I went out to play and I got Dick and he said to me Hey you know there's a big tall man by the house and he's holding this bomb and my mother says he's not there.

I said You too the same thing with me what are we going to do.

We have to get it away from him Dick said before something happens.

So we went up to the roof and we took the clothesline and made lassos. And when Dick climbed the chimney and he yelled Hi-yo silver but he couldn't get it and then I tried and I couldn't get it and ma started yelling for me to go to bed.

Then Dick took out his pocket flashlight and he shone it on the face of the Big Tall Man and the man was sleeping. He's sleeping Dick said to me Do you think he'll drop it while he's asleep and I said I don't know.

And then Dick's father came and walloped him good for not being in bed and I went home and they smacked me and I kept thinking he might drop it in his sleep especially if he had bad dreams and then I went to bed.

Lawrence Lipton

I Was a Poet for the F.B.I.

Murder, suicide, mayhem. Wow! The stories I could tell. See my agent. Even before God was insulted at Yale I was at the U of I picking up spondees and trochees in the Co-op and counting the condoms in the boneyard on Monday morning.

I was Ed Hoover's man at YMCA College collecting free verse in the ladies' room and once, disguised as Oscar Wilde, in the men's toilet. Cash McCall is my co-pilot.

At the Green Mask, in the very shadow of the Tribune Tower —may I speak freely? the beard of Henry Wadsworth Longfellow was burned in ritual orgy, hair by hair.

In Chicago I joined the Escalator Movement under the name of Gertrude Stein and nobody suspected anything. From a poet named Rexroth I learned about six different kinds of sex, all of them subversive.

In dives on Rush Street we lay on divans in mixed company and talked about modern art, waited on by naked African pygmies. We sat on the floor and read Edna St. Vincent Millay, aloud. I could name names and places.

On orders from Ezra Pound I infiltrated the Saturday Evening Post *and planted excerpts from Edgar A. Guest. One night I broke into the* Saturday Review *and lopped off Literature from the masthead. Nobody noticed it.*

Four times I escaped from behind curtains—iron, bamboo, dimity and shower, and once I barely made it by way of a bedroom fire escape clad only in pajama tops. Danger is my business.

I found an atheist in a foxhole and reported him to General MacArthur. Twice I was shot down in missions over Union Square, Waldorf Cafeteria, Camp Nitgedieget and the League of American Penwomen. Arthur Godfrey is my co-pilot.

I joined the Brownian Movement before it split with the Fourth Dimensheviks. Big Jim Oppenheimer was its Party boss. I would tell you about my affair with Tillie Zilch but that's still classified.

I was there when they dubbed the Communist Manifesto into the movie of Charley's Aunt, *and nipped the conspiracy to smuggle quotations from Karl Marx into the popcorn bags. Now they're plotting to foul up the rhymes in the singing commercials.*

Ten grand buys my tale of horror at the Cotton Club when Louis Armstrong sang Eli Eli *on secret orders from the Elders of Zion, and the borschtcapades in the Holland Tunnel with Mickey Katz on Walpurgisnacht. Commander Whitehead is my co-pilot.*

For an extra grand I'll tell all I know about free verse, free love, free lunch, free wheeling and free pop at barbecues of the American Academy of Arts and Letters, a Dadaist front controlled by Tristan Tzara and Ogden Nash.

Now, back in the free world, with my unexpurgated copy of Anne Morrow Lindbergh's The Unicorn *and the complete files of the Soviet Ministry of Culture I am Poet in Residence at* Time, Life *and* Fortune. *Zsa Zsa Gabor is my co-pilot.*

Stuart Z. Perkoff

If Everything Returns . . .

if everything returns to one, what does one return to?
                                                        -zen ko-un

    the face in the mirror of
    the human face
    looks out on my face.   *the eyes.*

    the hands in the mirror of
    the human hands
    reach out for my hands.   *the touch.*

    the pain in the mirror of
    the human pain
    strikes out to my pain.   *the love.*

the people
present, the particular
circumstances of his being
there, then

the works, the sermons
the falling three times
under the cross

all these things
naked nailed
flesh by bone by blood by thigh
by heart by tongue by shattered eye
to the wood

a man, naked, screaming, hanging there, only
not
screaming.

did what he knew only
he cd.
    he stayed
there

it hurt, it really
hurt, his hands
hurt & his feet
his whole flesh was real
pain

& he was thirsty.

        the salt in the mirror of
        the human eye
        burns at my eye.   *the face.*

        the wounds in the mirror of
        the human hand
        bleed from my hand.   *the touch.*

        the nails in the mirror of
        the human love
        tear thru my love.   *the pain.*

Gary Snyder

Oil

soft rainsqualls on the swells
south of the Bonins, late at night. light
from the empty mess-hall
throws back bulky shadows
of winch and fair-lead
over the slanting fantail where I stand.

but for men on watch in the engine-room,
the man at the wheel, the lookout in the bow,
the crew sleeps. in cots on deck
or narrow iron bunks down drumming
passageways below.

the ship burns with a furnace heart
steam veins and copper nerves
quivers and slightly twists and always goes—
easy roll of the hull and deep
vibration of the turbine underfoot

bearing what all these
crazed, hooked nations need:
steel plates and
long injections of pure oil.

Dachine Rainer

The Scent of Nicotiana

Its fragrance twines against the already archaic summer night
As we lean upon summer's porch debating Truth
        as Chekov might
The complaining moon contributes its sullen beauty.
        Man? Man. Who is he?

    The discussion proceeds langorously
    We whisper so the shadows cannot hear.

When I am overcome, and all my troubled thoughts
By nicotiana breathing its imperious fragrance
        on the night
Lighting that ghostly miniature moon to blow and warm our
    chilling species
        asserting thus by beauty

    The discussion proceeds langorously:
    Thus and thus by beauty, love, persistency

With heavy patience our bombarded world continues tempo-
    rarily
Thrusting aside prophetic reverberations in its future
        of cold slaughter
And imminent doom—offering man. Man himself. His art, his
    senses—
        sight, scent, touch, form—

    His bloom. His cultivation.
    We whisper so the shadows cannot hear.

*So, on the Moon shrouded, log chinked wall the entwining
     scarlet runner*
*The wild air heavy with troubled roses, my face uncertain
     against your solacing knee*
          languidly we lie
*Your hand in benediction through my tumbled hair. Flori-
bunda, honeysuckle*

> *These massed white flowers may be our bier.*
>   *Man. So this man. But who are we?*
> *We whisper so the shadows cannot hear.*

Our bodies tarry, urge a happier recline,
You bestow love freely as rain, arms and blossoms entwine
          as they would not in the noon sun.
Nicotiana! overcomes madness on my brow.
          Man? Man. He is you.

> *The discussion proceeds langorously:*
> *These massed white flowers may be our bier.*

Dachine Rainer

At the End of the World

Our faces reflect a moonstruck futility
And the not unalarming certainty
            of the earth's decline
The fragrance grows heavier, the massed runners climb.
        Man. What will become of him?

    We whisper so the shadows cannot hear:
    Before summer's end, the end of man.

Rescued from his diabolical plan for our extinction
Only by our senses, by the distinction of love's allegiance
            to life—anywhere
Plant and animal, our own and every other, urged by this
    flower.

    These massed white flowers may be our bier.
    We whisper so the shadows cannot hear:
    Before summer's end the end of man.

So, in mordant memory, I am captured before the world's end
By you, a shy, crenelated bell flower, by love—time's most
    complex moment,
        No longer: Man? Who is he?
You! and a singing mass of white faced pervasive annuals.

    Before summer's end, the end of man.
    We whisper so the shadows cannot hear:
    These massed white flowers may be our bier.

Nicotiana on the summer air! Persistent motion in violet space
The immediacy of your existence defies the holocaust!

       Captivated most by defiant you
In the last blazoning minutes of what they used to call reality.

    We whisper so the shadows cannot hear:
    Before summer's end, the end of man.
    These massed white flowers may be our bier.

How imagine his decline? Man will be lost to nicotiana forever
And to all form of love, absenting himself from the earth's
        natural plunder
From the thorn and the everlasting thunder of life.

    These massed white flowers may be our bier.
    (The discussion proceeds langorously)
    We whisper so the shadows cannot hear:
    Before summer's end, the end of man.

Rubin Falk

The Base on Holy Loch

"We may think of this project as an effort to defend the ethics of Christianity against the new paganism of Moscow . . ." *N. Y. Times* editorial.

To Holy Loch,
the Firthe of Clyde,
invisible, beneath the tide,
majestically, the Word doth glide.

To sermonize
the pagan breed,
to sow the good atomic seed,
to demonstrate the Christian creed.

To Holy Loch
His servants seek
to teach them how to turn the cheek,
and the earth shall inherit all the meek.
                                   pax

Paul Goodman

A Man from Georgia

As to this dirty broken man from Georgia
weeping and with a bandaged head, I gave
my pipe to smoke and thirty cents for breakfast,
neighborly words without disdain, but not
a bath nor clothing nor a ticket home
nor useful information—so myself
in need, I get thirty cents of affection:
thus much I have in me to give and get.

I saw him later, washed and not too bad,
but drunk on apple-wine: "Hey, I know you,
you're the good guy," he said, "the first New Yorker
ever gave me a nickel. Thanks a lot, sir,
and have a drink." I drank it without grace,
to not offend. I am even more confused
about my role and the nature of things
and what is the meaning of our actions.

And yet I know that life is simple; hard
but simple; that it is not complicated
and hard, but very simple and very hard.
I don't think any one would say, to live
is easy; though to some, I can imagine
living which is to me horribly hard
is just that easy, but they wouldn't say so,
they wouldn't say anything.

Bitterly he told me how three niggers
knocked him down and took three dollars of him.
No doubt they did, and no doubt he provoked them.

"I thought," he said, "when I came to New York
I'd be a big shot. Lyin there like that
like a shitty tramp. They left me in the gutter
to die," he wept, "bleedin." I remained
impassive, cheerful, optimistic.

Curtis Zahn

Retrospections of a Man Left of Center

On many a night pump organs
Leaked protestant hymns
While a chairman fingered his nose to suggest singing
The first and last verses
Before we started to stop waiting
For tardy, promised dignitaries
And I, available always
By dialing tollfree numbers
Smelled the tax-deductible franks and beans;
Had memorized some scratched
Patched footage
Of a 1948 Warehouse strike in Ohio
—produced by a professional do-gooder
Provided somebody
Would remember
To bring the projector.

I travelled light those unilluminated years
Burdened only
With a world's problems; moving
Carefully among ants,
Endeavoring to shackle elephants
With legislation
Which got no farther
Than our rented lofts.
I was a letterhead man; a name
Among the few who strode from the crowd.
Starting near the bottom after college,
And NYU,

I worked to the top of the page
And finally
As national chairman
Of the Universal Committee
Moved into the center, heading a petition
To save another Negro boy
From another South.

But;
In a lifetime of selfaddressed envelopes
And collection plates and plate dinners
With 28 peas
The total sound
Of all that money
Was the sound of pennies
Falling into the Grand Canyon
On a stormy afternoon.
Yes, then, men
When they passed the fundboxes the hopeful handfuls
Were on hand, and
Handy with their hands
For the handouts
Of instant coffee, day-old doughnuts,
And handling
Frayed extension cords, signing pledges
And clasping each other in
Undiminished hope; these,
The exhausted troops
Lonesomely bivouaced somewhere between extinction
And the Third Camp. And I as officer
Whispered strategy
From third-floor quarters; a captain
Until the eviction
For five months unpaid rent.

Was it all
Actually
Really worth it? You ask
And I answer with questions; yet
On remembered,

On fewer nights, hot with moon
In some rented park, folk-singers
Exorcised the case
Of mankind's unkindness
To man
With guitars, with banjoes and the
Complaining human falsetto.
And, sometimes, yes.
Admittedly sometimes something
Right and precious was caught
And held there; clutched
Within our fumbling hands
As a new coin from the hardening year.
To this the startled eye, returning asks
What is left
After having been right
By moving to the left
For so long a time?

Millen Brand

Our Friend Papanahoal

In the middle Seventeen Seventies
two manuscripts were written. Noah Pattison,
happening to meet Chief Papanahoal
going from Philadelphia back
to the Indian village of Wekelusing
near Bethlehem, rode along with him.
So much "satisfaction" did he have
from certain conversation with this Chief
that he decided to write it down.
He wrote that Papanahoal was "quiet and easy,"
yet had a becoming "Solidity and Gravity."
"Being ask'd what he thought of War,"
the Indian answered, "It has been told to my Heart,
that Man was not made for that End"
and so "I have ceased from War."
Asked about talk about religion,
Papanahoal mentioned that believers
in one faith contended with those of another:
"These things should not be," he said,
"but whilst one is speaking,
the other should hold down his head
till the first has done, and then speak
without being in a Heat or angry."
He said that he thought he himself
could have "the flesh whipped off me with horse whips"
and "endure it without being angry"
after he had been shown God's goodness.

The second manuscript preserved
is a letter the Agent to Shamokin
to the Indian Trade there wrote
October 16, 1760:
"The old Man," so Papanahoal
is called by this agent in his letter,
"thoght it was unlawful to warr" and
"when they argued very strongly
for a defensive war," saying
"if a man was to come and kill . . .
when it was in their power to prevent it,
they should be accountable for their own deaths,"
the chieftain said to these casuists,
"the White People had a book
which God had order'd to be wrote for them
wherein they were inform'd that God
had made the world and that he had sent
his Son Jesus Christ into the world"
to "shew" them how they should live,
"to which they answered that it was true:
well then said he why did not
Jesus Christ fight when the People
took him to kill him. To this
I do not understand they made him,"
the Agent wrote, "any satisfactory answer.
Then he (that is, Papanahoal)
told them he believ'd the White People
were wery Wicked as they had
so great an Advantage of that Book
and lived so contrary to it."
Some words of an Indian
who lived near Bethlehem.

Barbara Deming

Poem

After my father died, I, one night, in a dream,
Entered the ground in which they had planted him.
I found him, not asleep, but lying at anchor, propped
In a narrow boat, on his elbows, as if rising in bed.
The ribs of the boat were his ribs, old wood,
And his head, toward me, was its figurehead.
A tangle of matted roots, his hair
Had sprouted thickly through the air.
Air, earth, or was it water? All here
Was one dark but transparent matter.
In awe again of parting with him, I dropped
To my knees. Despair of meaning in our lives
Fluttered in me. I groped to touch him. Unreasoning
Hope then thrust my hands
Into the thicket sprung from his brows.
The floating shaggy web embraced me;
I felt my blood race back and forth to me along the vine,
And my breath stop; the sour strong perfume
Of upturned earth choked my lungs;
And in the one harsh stroke
I felt my life renew, and woke.

Paul Goodman

Poem

Loping waltzing marching
quick and happy and proud
—hopping for variety—
we converged on Boston

the bass-drummer beat
and big the brasses blared
but our entry was a rout
as if fleeing in disorder,

"Peace" was the password
that stung from lip to lip
and every man a poet.
The future had no shape.

We met in that crowd
that carried us along,
I shall not forget the light
of recognition in your eyes.

Your name is New Beginning.
I love you, New Beginning.

Contributors

DAVE DELLINGER, an Editor of *Liberation*, is on the executive committees of the Committee for Nonviolent Action (CNVA) and The Peacemakers. He pioneered before World War II in the application of nonviolence to the struggle for civil rights and served three years in Federal prison as a conscientious objector to war. A working printer at Libertarian Press, he is currently on leave of absence writing a book on nonviolence and economic revolution.

A. J. MUSTE, an Editor of *Liberation*, is the subject of a biography by Nat Hentoff, called *Peace Agitator*. A minister of the United Presbyterian Church, he was a founder of the American Civil Liberties Union. Mr. Muste was a Director of the Brookwood Labor College from 1921–33 and was involved in most of the important labor struggles of the 1920's and 1930's. He is Chairman of the Committee for Nonviolent Action (CNVA) and National Secretary of the Fellowship of Reconciliation.

BAYARD RUSTIN is an Editor of *Liberation*. He has served as personal assistant to Martin Luther King, Jr., at intervals since the Montgomery bus boycott (1955–56). He spent three years in Federal prison during World War II as a conscientious objector. He organized the 1963 March on Washington for Jobs and Freedom while on leave as Secretary of the War Resisters League. He has since become a nationally known and respected leader of the civil rights movement.

JAMES BALDWIN's first work was published when he was twelve. His latest work was the Broadway play, *Blues for Mister Charlie.*

ALBERT BIGELOW wrote *The Voyage of the Golden Rule.* In 1963 he spent several months with the Delhi-Peking Friendship March sponsored by the World Peace Brigade. He was Massachusetts Housing Commissioner in 1949–50.

KENNETH E. BOULDING is co-director of the Center for Research on Conflict Resolution and Professor of Economics at the University of Michigan. His many books include *Conflict and Defense, Economic Analysis,* and *The Meaning of the Twentieth Century.*

KAY BOYLE is presently a Fellow at the Radcliffe Institute for Independent Study, preparing a history of Germany. Her most recent novel is *Generation Without Farewell.*

MILLEN BRAND is the author of a novel, *The Outward Room.*

ALBERT CAMUS wrote such noted books as *The Stranger* and *The Rebel* before his sudden death in 1960. He received the 1957 Nobel Prize for Literature.

GORDON S. CHRISTIANSEN is Chairman of the Chemistry Department at Connecticut College for Women. He is a member of the Board of the Connecticut Civil Liberties Union and is on the executive committee of the Committee for Nonviolent Action (CNVA).

SALAMON DE LA SELVA was a well-known Nicaraguan poet who died in 1959.

PIERRE HENRI DELATTRE is a French poet.

LANZO DEL VASTO is a distinguished Catholic layman and founder of the Companions of the Ark, a Gandhian commune located near Bollene, France.

BARBARA DEMING is an Associate Editor of *Liberation.* She has participated in many of the recent peace and civil rights actions. She was a member of the Quebec–Washington–Guantánamo Walk for Peace.

GEORGE DENNISON has published fiction, essays, and poetry in a variety of periodicals. Judson (Church) Poet's Theatre in New York City has produced three of his one-act plays.

LESLIE DEWART teaches philosophy at the University of Toronto. He is the author of *Christianity and Revolution* and *Contraception and Holiness.*

DIANE DI PRIMA edits a poetry magazine, *The Floating Bear*. She has had collections of her poetry published, among them *Dinners and Nightmares*.

RUBIN FALK is a community leader of the New York Council for a Sane Nuclear Policy.

JAMES FARMER is National Director of the Congress of Racial Equality (CORE).

PAUL GOODMAN is a lecturer, teacher, critic, and novelist. His latest book is *Compulsory Mis-Education* and he is preparing a new work, *Ways of Running Things*.

NAT HENTOFF is staff writer for *The New Yorker* and a frequent contributor to *The Village Voice* and *The Reporter*. His latest book is *The New Equality*.

GENE HOFFMAN is producer-narrator of a radio program in Southern California, "Stories Children Love." She also writes the "Food for Thought" column of the Los Angeles *Times*.

MARTIN LUTHER KING, JR. is President of the Southern Christian Leadership Conference. Reverend King was the 1964 recipient of the Nobel Peace Prize.

SIR STEPHEN KING-HALL is a retired Commander of the British Navy. He publishes the *King-Hall Newsletter* in London.

LAWRENCE LIPTON is a writing instructor at the University of California at Los Angeles. He has written several books, including *The Holy Barbarians*, and is working on *The Erotic Revolution*.

BRADFORD LYTTLE is active in nonviolent direct action for peace. A former Secretary of the Committee for Nonviolent Action (CNVA), he served as Coordinator of both the San Francisco to Moscow Walk for Peace (1960–61) and the Quebec–Washington–Guantánamo Walk for Peace (1963–64).

NELSON MANDELA is the leader of the African National Congress in South Africa. He is serving a life sentence for his fight against his government's policy of apartheid.

RICHARD MAYES is a young American poet.

DAVID MCREYNOLDS is an Associate Editor of *Liberation* and Field Secretary of the War Resisters League. His articles appear frequently in *The Village Voice*.

KARL MEYER is active in the Catholic Worker movement and is director of a "house of hospitality," St. Stephen's House, in Chicago.

CHARLES MORGAN, JR. is director of the Southern Regional Office of the American Civil Liberties Union. His experience as an attorney for controversial cases in Alabama are recorded in his book *A Time to Speak*.

LEWIS MUMFORD is a renowned scholar and architectural critic. His recent book, *The City in History*, received great critical acclaim.

JUANITA NELSON works as a speech consultant and "thus manages to continue breaking the tax laws."

JULIUS K. NYERERE is the Prime Minister of the Republic of Tanzania, formed in 1964 by the merger of the Republics of Tanganyika and Zanzibar.

STUART Z. PERKOFF is a young poet from Ocean Beach, California.

JULES RABIN spent six months with the San Francisco to Moscow Peace Walk in the dual role of participant and cameraman.

DACHINE RAINER is a poet, essayist, short-story writer, and the author of a novel, *The Uncomfortable Inn*.

THEODORE ROSZAK has taught history at Stanford University and California State College at Hayward. He is currently serving as Editor of the English weekly, *Peace News*.

BERTRAND RUSSELL is a philosopher, mathematician, historian, biographer, and short-story writer. Lord Russell continues to be active in the peace movement though he has passed his ninetieth birthday.

ARNOLD SACHAR is a student at Queens College, New York City. He contributes frequently to the literary supplement of the Columbia University *Spectator*.

MULFORD SIBLEY is an Associate Editor of *Liberation* and a Professor of Political Science at the University of Minnesota. He is completing a new book, *History of Political Thought*.

DALLAS SMYTHE is Chairman of the Division of Social Sciences, University of Saskatchewan, Regina Campus. Mr. Smythe worked for the United States government from 1937 to 1948, including five years as Chief Economist for the FCC.

GARY SNYDER is an American poet living in Japan.

WILLIAM STAFFORD won the 1963 National Book Award for his collection of poetry, *Traveling Through the Dark.*

ROBERT THEOBALD is an economist who has had several books published, including *Free Men and Free Markets.*

DAVID WIECK has taught philosophy since 1959. He was imprisoned from 1943 to 1946 as a conscientious objector.

ROBERT F. WILLIAMS was a local chairman of the NAACP. He is now in exile in Cuba as a result of charges growing out of his participation in the civil rights struggle in Monroe, North Carolina.

CURTIS ZAHN is the author of a collection of socio-satirical fiction, *American Contemporary.*